THE BOOK OF JOB

The Book of Job

A Contest of Moral Imaginations

Carol A. Newsom

OXFORD
UNIVERSITY PRESS

2003

OXFORD

UNIVERSITY PRESS

Oxford   New York
Auckland   Bangkok   Buenos Aires   Cape Town   Chennai
Dar es Salaam   Delhi   Hong Kong   Istanbul   Karachi   Kolkata
Kuala Lumpur   Madrid   Melbourne   Mexico City   Mumbai   Nairobi
São Paulo   Shanghai   Taipei   Tokyo   Toronto

Copyright © 2003 by Oxford University Press, Inc.

Published by Oxford University Press, Inc.
198 Madison Avenue, New York, New York, 10016

www.oup.com

Oxford is a registered trademark of Oxford University Press

Library of Congress Cataloging-in-Publication Data
Newsom, Carol A. (Carol Ann), 1950-
The book of Job : a contest of moral imaginations / Carol A. Newsom.
p. cm.
Includes bibliographical references and index.
ISBN 0-19-515015-5
1. Bible, O. T. Job—Criticism, interpretation, etc.   I. Title.
BS1415.2 .N48 2002
233'.106—dc21   2002071528

2 4 6 8 9 7 5 3 1

Printed in the United States of America
on acid-free paper

To my parents-in-law,
Mary Ann Perry Matthews and Eual Leldon Matthews,
and to the memory of my parents,
Imogene Peterson Newsom and Donald Lloyd Newsom

Acknowledgments

The idea for this book first took shape in 1991 when I was invited to give the Kittel Lecture at Yale Divinity School. Over the next several years I developed aspects of the topic in the Thompson Lecture at Princeton Theological Seminary (1993), the Thomas Burns Lectureship at the University of Otago in Dunedin, New Zealand (1994), the Craigie Lecture for the Canadian Society of Biblical Studies (1995), and a series of lectures at Stetson University (1995). A Lilly Faculty Fellowship from the Association of Theological Schools in 1994–95 and research leave support from the Candler School of Theology in 1994–95 and 2000 enabled me to continue my work, as well as to prepare a commentary on Job for the *New Interpreter's Bible*. For these invitations and for this support I am deeply grateful.

Portions of the arguments presented here have been published in different form in several journals: "The Moral Sense of Nature: Ethics in the Light of God's Speech to Job," *Princeton Seminary Bulletin* 15 (1994): 9–27; "Bakhtin, the Bible, and Dialogic Truth," *Journal of Religion* 76 (1996): 290–306; "Job and His Friends: A Conflict of Moral Imaginations," *Interpretation* 53 (1999): 239–53; "The Book of Job as Polyphonic Text," *Journal for the Study of the Old Testament* 97 (2002): 87–108; and "Narrative Ethics, Character, and the Prose Tale of Job," pages 136–49 in *Character and Scripture: Moral Formation, Community, and Biblical Interpretation* (edited by William P. Brown). I thank the publishers for their permission to incorporate material from those articles in this volume.

I am also indebted to many people who aided me in various ways. My research assistant Cameron Richardson provided invaluable bibliographic and clerical help. Students Amy Cottrill, Dave Garber, and Dan Mathewson read portions of the manuscript and provided many acute observations. Among faculty colleagues I wish to thank in particular Bill Brown, Ed Greenstein, Jacq Lapsley, and Kathleen O'Connor for their encouragement, support, and advice. Most especially, I wish to thank Jim Crenshaw and David Jobling. I have learned more about the wisdom literature from Jim Crenshaw than from any other scholar. His support for my work has meant more than I can say. David Jobling has been that rarest of all friends and colleagues: someone who will speak the truth. Though this book would have been better had I heeded more of his advice, it owes much to his continual encouragement to me to push my thinking beyond the familiar paths of Joban scholarship.

My greatest debt is to my husband, Rex Matthews. He has truly exhibited the "patience of Job" during the many years that I have worked on this project. In addition to providing moral support, he has been a never failing source of sound judgment as I have pestered him with editorial questions, and of amazing technological expertise as I have sought his help with computer and software problems large and small. He is the sine qua non of this work as of so much else.

Contents

Abbreviations

ABD	*Anchor Bible Dictionary*
ANEP	*The Ancient Near East in Pictures Relating to the Old Testament*
ANET	*Ancient Near Eastern Texts Relating to the Old Testament.* 3d ed.
CTA	*Corpus des tablettes en cunéiformes alphabétiques découvertes à Ras Shamra-Ugarit de 1929 à 1939*
HALOT	*The Hebrew and Aramaic Lexicon of the Old Testament*
KTU	*Die keilalphabetischen Texte aus Ugarit*
NIV	New International Version
NJPS	New Jewish Publication Society Translation of the Tanakh
NPNF²	*Nicene and Post-Nicene Fathers,* Series 2
NRSV	New Revised Standard Version
TUAT	*Texte aus der Umwelt des Alten Testaments*

THE BOOK OF JOB

1

The Book of Job as Polyphonic Text

Every genre has its methods and means of seeing and conceptualizing
reality, which are accessible to it alone.
Pavel Medvedev, *The Formal Method in Literary Scholarship*

Reading the book of Job has never been easy. Not only does its subject matter
touch on some of the most difficult issues of human experience but the form of
the book, the representation of the characters, and the book's overall meaning
have also posed perplexing interpretive problems for readers. Over the centuries, as interpretive communities and their reading strategies have changed, so
have the ways in which the problems are addressed and resolved. The book of
Job lends itself well–perhaps too well–to being read in light of shifting philosophical and hermeneutical assumptions. Its complex and elusive nature allows
interpreters to see mirrored in it perspectives congenial to the tenor of their
own age. This adaptability is truly not to be regretted, for it is what gives the
book its perennial value. The honest critic, however, would recognize as true
Jerome's remark that the book of Job is like an eel, for "if you close your hand
to hold an eel or a little muraena, the more you squeeze it the sooner it escapes."[1] Yet even as interpretive *perspectives* have changed, many of the *features*
of the text seen as problematic and requiring explanation have remained the
same. From Gregory the Great to Maimonides to Aquinas to Calvin to Fohrer,
commentators have pondered over such issues as why God rebukes the friends
but not Elihu, whether Job's words in the dialogue are or are not blasphemous,
what the divine speeches do to resolve the issues raised by the book, and the
significance of the restoration of Job. The answers given by premodern critics
are often different from those one finds in more recent commentaries, but in
many regards the exegetical and interpretive problems perceived by older and
modern critics show significant overlap.

One critical issue, however, is almost entirely the product of the interpretive
assumptions of historical criticism–the problem of the "unity" or "integrity" of
the book. In earlier centuries interpreters puzzled over how the book of Job
should be read and suggested various generic categories to guide readerly expec-

tations. Theodore of Mopsuestia (fourth century C.E.) and Theodore de Beza (sixteenth century C.E.) considered Job to be akin to Greek tragedy. In the seventeenth century Milton suggested that it was like an epic poem. Given the reading strategies of these interpretive communities, however, there was no doubt that the book was a unified utterance. Only with the rise of historical criticism was that assumption challenged.

Although the early practitioners seldom if ever used the term, a heightened sense of *genre* was a significant aspect of historical criticism's new strategies of reading that led to a sense of the disunity of the book of Job. The challenge to the unity of Job was raised first in 1678, when Richard Simon noted the strong stylistic difference between the prose tale and the dialogue and concluded that the prose tale must have been an addition to the poem, comparable to the superscriptions added secondarily to psalms.[2] Simon's insight was essentially a genre distinction. *Genre* is a slippery word and will be examined in more detail later, but in simplest terms the recognition of genre involves a perception that certain texts bear a striking family resemblance to one another. That perception serves to establish some rough and usually implicit assumptions about what to expect from the text in question.

Most subsequent critics did not find Simon's analogizing of the prose tale to psalm superscriptions to be helpful, but many did agree with his perception of the significant difference between the prose and the poetic parts of Job. What biblical studies tends to call literary-critical and traditio-critical arguments were brought forward by later scholars to buttress the impression that two very different sorts of literature were present in the book. Tied to this perception was an assumption commonly but not universally shared: that the different types of literature pointed to different authors. Not all of these arguments were about genre, strictly speaking. Some had to do with perceived contradictions between the two parts of the book. But arguments concerning style, representation, diction, tone, subject matter, and other features commonly used as generic markers were always present. Although scholarship generally reversed Simon's assumption that the prose story was a framework added to a preexisting poem, the basic perception remained that the frame story and the poetic dialogue spoke with such distinct voices that the book was best understood as composed not only of different genres but as the work of more than one author. At the very least it seemed to require an author who reproduced an earlier traditional story of Job as the framework for his own new composition.

Karl Budde, followed shortly by Bernhard Duhm, crystallized the emerging perspective in the late nineteenth century and introduced a genre category into the discussion by arguing that the prose tale was a *Volksbuch*, a preexisting popular story, written or oral, taken up by the Job poet as a framework.[3] Attempts were made to identify traces of such an independent popular tradition concerning Job in other surviving literature.[4] In one form or another the view prevailed that the author/redactor of the book of Job appropriated a relatively fixed traditional story as the framework for his composition.[5]

The significance of comparative literature for understanding the genres, motifs, and intellectual context of the book of Job was given further impetus by the discovery in the late nineteenth century of Mesopotamian texts bearing striking resemblances in form and content to the poetic sections of Job, most notably, *ludlul bēl nēmeqi*, the Babylonian Theodicy, and the "Sumerian Job." Though scholars disagreed over how these texts might be related to Job,[6] their similarity specifically to the poetry of Job sharpened the sense that the two parts of the book, prose tale and poetic dialogue, belonged to different literary, social, and intellectual traditions. Thus, this distinction between prose tale and poetic dialogue became the key to historical criticism's analysis of the book.

Occasional dissenting voices arose, of course, the most notable being Karl Kautzsch and Edouard Dhorme. Dhorme recognized that a critical issue in the debate over unity and single authorship was in fact one of genre and style. Though he granted the differences between the poetry and prose, he rejected the majority opinion that the differences necessitated multiple authorship: "One and the same man can tell a story when necessary and sing when necessary."[7] Historical critics in the Budde/Duhm camp had based their arguments on much more than just features of style, of course. They had catalogued differences of many sorts, bearing on theological perspective, tone, diction, and so forth. Yet Dhorme properly recognized that "it is not only the style but the whole cast of sentiments and ideas which normally change when the voice or the pen abandons one mode to take up another."[8]

The problem with which each side of the debate had to deal, however, was explaining how two such different modes were to be related to one another. In their defense of single authorship and its corollary of a planned composition, Kautzsch and Dhorme diminished the conceptual significance of the prose tale, treating it as not much more than an envelope for the poetry. Kautzsch strenuously denied that the prose tale contains a teaching or doctrine. His approach was resolutely aesthetic. The prose prologue is simply a "dramatic lively narrative of an individual case."[9] The epilogue provides an agreeable ending, placing the reader "once more in a lovely storybook land."[10] Dhorme was even more dismissive, referring to the prologue and epilogue as "accessory narrations. . . . The monument which the author aims at creating is the poem. The Prologue and Epilogue are no more than its entrance and exit."[11] Thus, the cost of preserving unity of authorship is the necessity of taking the prose tale "lightly."

Those who argued for strongly different theological perspectives as well as styles between the prose and poetry, however, also had to give some account of the book as a whole. If they were right about the sharp differences between the two genres that structured the book, what was their relationship to one another? What were the intentions of the poet/redactor who had produced such a curious document? Kautzsch, with considerable exasperation, stated his objections by trying to imagine the poet/redactor of the Budde/Duhm hypothesis.

> The author wished to compose a poem in which the old doctrine of retribution was thoroughly rejected. He finds an old narrative, which "teaches" exactly the opposite—and he has nothing more urgent to do than to copy this old story unchanged (Duhm, p. 1) and to let it go into the world along with his poem! Should we believe this highly talented author capable of such an absurdity—to offer to the public a book which contained within it entirely three different "teachings," of which the third directly contradicted the second and the first had nothing whatsoever to do with the second and third, so that only the reader so inclined might see how he might make sense of this Trilemma? Truly, I believe the author had more redactional skill.[12]

The challenge Kautzsch posed was significant. Any theory of the composition of the book that insisted on strong generic differences between the prose and poetic sections of the book ought to account for why anyone would put these two together in such an apparently clumsy fashion. Despite these difficulties, however, the arguments made by the followers of Budde and Duhm proved largely convincing, and by the mid-twentieth century a set of closely related variations of this position formed the consensus of opinion.[13] Marvin Pope's comment in his classic commentary takes it as self-evident that "the Book of Job in its present form can hardly be regarded as a consistent and unified composition by a single author."[14]

With the confidence and enthusiasm characteristic of a method in its heyday, historical criticism scrutinized the poetic section of the book for more subtle generic and stylistic differences that would provide further evidence for the history of the composition and revision of the book. Opinions differed, but the wisdom poem in chapter 28, Job's closing speech in chapters 29–31, the Elihu speeches in chapters 32–37, and one or both of the speeches from the whirlwind in chapters 38–41 were all identified as possibly secondary. Even the individual sections of the book were analyzed for indications of multiple redactions, an activity that continues unabated in much continental scholarship.

Despite genuine sensitivity to nuances of genre and style in the best historical-critical work, this approach was never able to answer Kautzsch's challenge and give a persuasive account of the final form of the book. It had no theory of the whole, no way to account for the purpose or effect of the juxtaposition of genres and styles. Claus Westermann made what is perhaps the simplest and most appealing suggestion. He noted that biblical writers often put into the mouths of characters songs that do not fit the narrative context and so openly display the fact that "song and story each has a different point of origin."[15] The song is included because it is familiar, and the fact that it does not quite fit is simply not important to the author or reader. Similarly, Westermann suggested, the author of the Job poem affixed the prose story as a frame simply in order to signal to the audience that his poem was not about a newly made-up character but about the Job whom they knew from the traditional story. That the prose tale did not really fit the poem was not a matter of concern. Thus, Westermann solved the problem by shrugging it off. There need be no theory of the whole because the notion of the book as a whole is an anachronism. Whether or not Westermann is correct—and he may well be, historically speaking—his non-solution simply underscores the modern reader's sense of disunity, one described well by Bruce Zuckerman: "Like oil and water, the Prose Frame Story and the Poem naturally tend to disengage from one another despite all efforts to homogenize them. The book of Job therefore appears to be at odds with itself; and however one may attempt to resolve its contradictory picture, the result never seems to be quite successful."[16]

Zuckerman, persuaded by historical-critical arguments that posited multiple authorship and recognizing historical criticism's inherent inability to conceptualize the book *as* a book, undertook to follow the logic of historical-critical analysis to its proper conclusion. Zuckerman took the assumptions of diachronic argument to an ironic but perversely logical outcome and reconstructed the growth of the book as the result of a series of parodies, subversions, and sincere misreadings in which succeeding generations dealt with a growing literary deposit they sometimes did not understand and often feared. Though I do not find Zuckerman's reconstruction persuasive in its details, he did a brilliant job of showing that the logical outcome of the historical-critical method's assumptions about composition has to be matched by a diachronic model for reading. The puzzle posed by the different genres, styles, and perspectives can only be solved by telling the story of its composition. Although Zuckerman suggested that the book can be read as it now exists as something akin to a musical fugue, essentially the meaning of the book is the story of its development.[17]

The limitations of historical criticism are not limited to its inability to conceptualize the final form of the book as a book. Its overstated ambition to recover the actual history of the composition of biblical books has fallen progressively into disrepute, at least in Anglo-American scholarship, as the failure of scholars to achieve consensus concerning the archaeology of particular texts has become increasingly evident. In reaction, recent commentaries, including "chastened" historical-critical ones, as well as more explicitly literary and theological ones, have oriented themselves increasingly to a synchronic, "final-form" reading of the book of Job. These final-form critics claim that the book is best understood as the work of a single author, or at least that it is best read as if it were "the product of a single mind."[18] Echoing some of the arguments of Kautzsch, Dhorme, and others, many of these readings emphasize features that unify the text, in contrast to historical criticism's preoccupation with features that suggest disunity.[19] Although such a concern for unity need not mean that genre is ignored, in fact genre analysis has tended to receive little attention in final-form readings, and much of that is dismissive.[20]

One can see this tendency to minimize genre in what is perhaps the most accomplished of the final-form readings, that of Norman Habel, whose method of interpretation was strongly influenced by the Anglo-American tradition of the New Literary Criticism. Habel acknowledged the presence of numerous small generic forms within the book of Job. The "assumed disjuncture" between prose tale and dialogue, however, is what Habel must reject, since this is what has "bedeviled" those who seek to argue for the underlying unity of the book.[21] One can sense Habel's attempt to minimize the significance of genre in the concessive form he used to approach the topic: "Admittedly the dispute between the sufferer and the friend in the Babylonian Theodicy may have provided a suitable dialogue model for the narrator."[22] But from Habel's perspective, those who have emphasized the generic affinities between the Joban dialogues and the Babylonian Theodicy have erred in failing to see how the author of Job has used the dialogue. His counterinterpretation is that "the artist who created the book of Job has constructed the dialogue *as a feature of the plot* rather than as an independent theological disputation."[23]

The genre of the wisdom dialogue is thus subordinated to the continuous narrative plot, the most important of the techniques that, in Habel's view, give unity to the book of Job. He drew attention also to foreshadowing, thematic progression, verbal allusions, motif repetitions, verbal and dramatic irony, and the legal metaphor, which lend cohesion to the book. The various techniques are understood as evidence of that which ultimately underwrites unity, namely, the presence of the author—the "artist," as Habel strategically called him. The model for Habel's artist/author is the modernist author assumed by New Critical literary theory—a powerful unifying consciousness capable of molding a variety of source materials into a complex, tensive, paradoxical whole.

Setting Habel's work in historical and theoretical context, one can see why genre not only was not but could not be a critical aspect of his analysis, and one can see why it was necessary for Habel to argue against the interpretive significance of genre for the structure of the book as a whole. A focus on genre was characteristic of the type of criticism Habel sought to challenge, a tool of those who worked to disassemble the text. Although genre analysis is certainly not alien to New Critical approaches in general, the multigeneric nature of the book of Job does not lend itself readily to New Criticism's (or Habel's) focus on unity. Therefore, genre does not receive much attention in the final-form reading Habel champions.

Both historical-critical and New Critical literary approaches take for granted modernist notions of text and authorship. What they disagree about is how much stylistic, thematic, and conceptual difference is compatible with the assumption of single authorship. The limits of modernist assumptions about authorship and unity have been challenged recently by postmodern readings of Job, most notably the commentary of Edwin Good, which takes its cue from Roland Barthes, and the programmatic article by David Clines, "Deconstructing the Book of Job," which sketches a Derridean deconstructive reading. These readings posit the "unity" of the text in that they treat the final form of the book, but they are preoccupied with the inherent instabilities of that posited unity. For deconstructive readings, contradictions such as those embodied in the prose conclusion of chapter 42 are of interest not in relation to authorship but in relation to the truth claims of the book. Thus, Clines argues that the poetic and prose parts of the book mutually undermine each other's claims about retribution and how a human being should behave in the face of suffering, depriving both positions of their claim to have "divulged a truth about a transcendental signified that is one and incontrovertible."[24] Similarly, Good treats the contradictions of the book as a disclosure of the illusion of unitary truth and an invitation to the pleasures of indeterminacy, "slipping playfully out from under the walls and fences that the search for Truth has erected around us."[25]

Not surprisingly, neither Good nor Clines devotes much attention to genre. In large part this appears to be because genre analysis is still seen as the tool of historical criticism and its preoccupation with origins. Good deals with genre in connection with the composition of the book in his "Dispensable Introduction." He succinctly states the connection between genre and composition in historical criticism: "How could these different kinds of material have been produced by the same mind?" Rightly, Good finds this assumption that they could not be naive, even though he agrees with many of historical criticism's conclusions about the book's composition.[26] His disinterest in genre, however, is rooted not only in his attempt to free readers from a dismal sort of historical criticism but also in a particular understanding of genre inimical to his own mode of reading. Good pursues a reader-oriented approach, which understands the text as "open" and inviting free play.[27] Something of the same criticism was raised about genre by Jacques Derrida in his essay "The Law of Genre." Reacting against the authoritarian implications of traditional genre theory and against structuralism's attempt to found a science of literature and to establish its laws, Derrida deconstructs the very notion of genre: "As soon as the word 'genre' is sounded, as soon as it is heard, as soon as one attempts to conceive it, a limit is drawn. And when a limit is established, norms and interdictions are not far behind: 'Do,' 'Do not,' says 'genre,' the word 'genre,' the figure, the voice, or the law of genre."[28] Thus, Derrida undertakes the deconstruction of the notion of genre, demonstrating its self-contradictory nature. Although Good does not reflect specifically on genre in his essay "On Reading" and does not invoke Derrida, his rejection of comparisons between Job and other texts[29] suggests that he finds generic classification reductive, betraying a kind of essentialist mentality uncongenial to his reader-oriented approach.

Clines's disinterest in genre is somewhat differently grounded. His deconstructive analysis depends on the contradiction between the truth claims of prose epilogue and those of the poem concerning retribution and suffering. Nevertheless, for good reason genre per se does not play a significant role in his analysis. Clines begins with a formulation of deconstruction taken from Jonathan Culler: "To deconstruct a discourse is to show how it undermines the philosophy it asserts, or the hierarchical oppositions on which it rests."[30] Thus, Clines posits the book of Job as "a discourse," a work that ostensibly intends to present a coherent and unified truth. In this respect Clines's initial assumption is not much different from Habel's. The deconstructive turn, however, is the demonstration that despite its ostensive intentions, the book undermines its own assertions. This sort of deconstructive approach works best with texts possessing a high degree of apparent unity, for it is not simply contradiction but a subtle undermining of what appears as the claim of the text that is the object of deconstructive analysis.

Why Clines does not foreground genre should be evident. As noted earlier, attention to genre has usually been associated with historical-critical attempts to dismantle the book in order to resolve not only stylistic but also ideological tensions between the two component genres. In Clines's opinion that effort is an inappropriate attempt to eliminate discomfort caused by the recognition of an irresolvable contradiction or aporia within the book. Even though the underminings of meaning Clines observes are largely created by the presence of the prose epilogue after the "grand poem,"[31] Clines shifts analysis away from genre and instead reads the book as a series of propositional claims. Read in this fashion, the text does indeed emerge as a "self-deconstructing artifact."[32] Though immensely clever, this type of reading funds its cleverness at a high cost. Meaning is not generated merely through propositions but also through the textures of language, through the invocations of styles and forms of speech that themselves have histories and social resonances.

Each of these approaches—the classic historical-critical model, the literary, and the deconstructive—has its own genius and sees important things. Historical-critical scholarship honed the ability to hear distinctive styles and genres. Unfortunately, given the intellectual climate of the times, these insights were marshaled largely in the service of arguments over authorship and composition. What went relatively undeveloped was an interest in the imaginative capacities of these genres or modes of speech and the rhetorical purposes for which they might be employed. Similarly, the problem of how such a multigenre, multiauthor composition was to be read as a whole never received a compelling answer. As different as they are from each other, both the literary New Critical reading of Job and the deconstructive approach provide powerful models for reading the book as a whole. Nevertheless, whether in the service of an argument for the fundamental unity of the book or an argument for its self-deconstructive nature, both approaches have to minimize or ignore the rich textures of genre and style that historical criticism emphasized.

In what follows I argue for the recuperation of genre as a critical category for understanding the book of Job.[33] Here is a means by which Kautzsch's frustrated and impatient questions can be turned from rhetorical into serious ones to which serious answers can be given. To do this, however, one must have a more robust theory and a more thoroughgoing analysis of genre than historical criticism was prepared to conduct. Yet in order to avoid the "Humpty Dumpty" effect that can come from privileging differences within the book, this revaluation of genre must be closely linked to an alternative understanding of literary unity, authorship, and truth. This understanding is based neither on the modernist assumptions of historical criticism and New Critical literary approaches nor on the assumptions of deconstruction. This approach is based rather on the work of Mikhail Bakhtin, particularly his distinction between monologic and dialogic truth and his conception of the polyphonic text.

Genre

Genre study has endured a bad reputation, not entirely undeserved, as an exercise in mere classification. But, as Alastair Fowler has observed, when properly approached, it is not so much a matter of pigeonholes as of pigeons.[34] Although there are aspects of Fowler's perspective I would not appropriate, his insistence that genre be understood as a form of communication is an important starting point. Genre is a social phenomenon, a set of conventions that mediates both the production and reading of texts.[35] From the reader's perspective, genre is part of the intertextuality that is an aspect of every reading experience. Texts are always read in relation to other texts that serve as points of reference. Patterns of similarity and dissimilarity, that is, the recognition that the text at hand is like these and not those, establish the reader's sense of genre.

The criteria by which one recognizes genre are extremely various, for any feature may become genre-linked. Fowler lists among the possibilities representational aspect (e.g., narrative, dramatic, discursive), external structure, metrical structure, size, scale, subject, values, mood, characteristic occasion, attitude, *mise-en-scène*, character, action of a characteristic structure, rhetorical organization, and the task assigned the reader.[36] Whatever features serve as generic markers, the set of comparable texts evoked by the recognition of genre form a grid through which the present text is read, shaping a "horizon of expectation" for the reader and encouraging the reader to respond in ways consistent with the conventions of the genre.[37]

The functions of genre, viewed from the perspective of the production of a text, are complementary. Genre negotiates the author's communicative relationship with readers but also establishes a dialogic relationship with other texts and genres. To begin with the relationship with the audience, the shared horizon established by the invocation of a generic form allows an author important measures of economy. The intimacy among those who share expectations about an utterance allows certain things to go without saying. An author may use generically grounded audience expectations to create rhetorical effects by minimizing, exaggerating, or thwarting a generic feature. Writing in relation to an established genre also means that the author writes in company and in dialogue. No less than the reader, the author of a generic text engages in a dense intertextual conversation. Genres are not autonomous forms but, as Claudio Guillén observes, part of "a complex of options, alternatives, interrelations."[38] To choose to write in a particular genre is to distinguish the work from other generic possibilities, and yet it is "a difference deliberately made that can become a link."[39]

The reading contract established by invocation and recognition of genre should not be too rigidly understood. Authors often invoke generic models in order to deviate from them, and readers may resist the invitation to read in accord with generic conventions. Moreover, texts do not "belong" to genres so much as participate in them, invoke them, gesture to them, play in and out of them, and in so doing continually change them. Texts may participate in more than one genre, just as they may be marked in an exaggerated or in a deliberately subtle fashion. The point is not simply to identify a genre in which a text participates, but to analyze that participation in terms of the rhetorical strategies of the text.

To speak of genre only in this way, however, is to give too narrow a sense of genre's role in the creation and mediation of meaning. In their arguments against formalist approaches, the Bakhtin circle contended that genres are best understood as modes of perception that conceptualize aspects of reality in distinctive ways. As Pavel Medvedev put it, "Just as a graph is able to deal with the aspects of spatial form inaccessible to artistic painting, and vice versa, the lyric . . . has access to aspects of reality and life which are either inaccessible or accessible in a lesser degree to the novella or drama. . . . Every significant genre is a complex system of means and methods for the conscious control and finalization of reality."[40] Through their capacity to define situations, control perspectives, and give them aesthetic shape, genres are forms of moral imagination. The power a genre possesses to focus one aspect of reality is purchased at a price, however; it cannot see things otherwise. The anecdote, Medvedev says, can grasp "the isolated unity of the chance situation" but not "the unity and inner logic of a whole epoch,"[41] which is the specific genius of the novel. The one form is not closer to reality than the other, nor does it have a more privileged access to truth. The truths and realities they describe, however, are of incommensurate kinds. One could easily overstate the case and suggest a greater rigidity among

genres than actually exists, but the general insight is important. The perceptions, values, and moral imaginations of different texts belong in part to the
genres in which they participate.

Understanding genre as a mode of perception requires a further consideration of the social dimensions of genre. Although some genres may be widely
shared within a culture, others are much more closely linked with specific social classes, cultural subgroups, or occupational or other segments of a society.
As modes of perception, or "form-shaping ideologies," genres articulate values
associated with the social contexts in which they develop. One can easily identify examples from contemporary culture: the academic journal article, gangsta
rap, the romance novel, the evangelical sermon, and so on. Not all genres are
as clearly stamped with the social values of a particular cultural group as these
examples suggest. Moreover, some genres are produced and consumed within
the same community, whereas others may come to be consumed and even produced by persons whose own social horizons are radically different from the
community in which the genre developed originally. In any particular case, the
social analysis may be extremely complex. Nevertheless, it is important at least
to ask whether and how its particular moral imagination may be grounded in
the cultural perspectives and values of a group or segment of society.

From these brief observations it should be evident why a focus on genre can
be fruitful in reading Job. Here is a book that begins its account within the
conventions of one genre only to shift suddenly into an unmistakably different
genre for the middle part of the book and then to conclude with a return to the
first genre. By means of generic markers the reader is invited initially to form
one set of expectations, to respond according to those conventions, and to see
the world from a particular nexus of values and perspectives. Then the reader
is suddenly snatched away from those conventions into a radically different set,
only to be as suddenly snatched back again. In his treatment of genre, Guillén
discusses such phenomena.

> There are authors who fight, so to speak, against the genre they are using by in-
> jecting it with antibodies. Not all genres live peacefully in the center of a single
> work unless the integrity of the whole is called into question—or literature itself as
> tradition and institution. That is precisely what the avant-garde seeks to do. There
> are conventions and traditions that crash and collide with one another. Then the
> genre includes a contragenre within itself.[42]

Guillén's example is Milan Kundera's novel *The Book of Laughter and Forgetting*, which alternates between the genres of narrative fiction and historical-political
essay in such a way that a single narrative voice is impossible to establish for
the book as a whole. That genre is being used provocatively in such cases is
evident. What rhetorical purpose that such play with genre might serve, however, requires considerable exploration.

Before turning to the way in which the use of genre configures the structure and purpose of Job, one must consider the particular problems posed by genre analysis of ancient texts, which often come from literatures that are only partially preserved. A modern reader's sense of the intertextuality that underwrote generic recognition in antiquity is often severely limited. Were the entire written record of an ancient culture preserved, however, a modern reader would still not read the generic cues in the same way as an ancient reader. As Fowler wryly notes, even historically oriented critics always attend to two sets of criteria: the generic state when the text was originally written, and the generic state of the critic's own time, thus demonstrating the "inveterate egocentricity" of the assumption that "our own generic identifications obtain universally."[43] One can see this phenomenon in the way biblical critics often refer to the prose narrative of Job as a "folktale" or "fairy tale," thus implicitly indexing a repertoire of comparative texts from a different era and cultural setting in order to make a generic context for the prose tale. That impulse is not wholly to be regretted. It is part of the way in which texts continue to live in changing cultural contexts and is a legitimate part of comparative literary analysis.[44] A theoretical defense of that state of affairs has been given by Adena Rosmarin, who argues that genre should be understood essentially as a category of the critic with a fundamentally pragmatic function. Genre assignments are not right or wrong in some absolute way but in relation to the questions and purposes of the critic. Thus, she notes that even though Henry Fielding himself identified the genre of *Joseph Andrews* as "comic epic poem in prose," later critics defined its genre quite differently.[45] Even Fowler, who would disagree with much of Rosmarin's argument, notes how the interpretation of a work evolves as the text is read against a changing set of comparison texts, that is, as its generic affiliations are perceived differently.[46] Granting the legitimacy of Fowler's and Rosmarin's claims, if one is interested in the communicative intent of the work as utterance, then the genre conventions of the period of origin of the text are significant, though not exclusively so.

Accepting that it is important to know the repertoire of antecedent or contemporary texts of the same genre, a somewhat different question needs to be asked: Is it possible for texts for which no close parallels are known to communicate a generic context? Can a text communicate to a reader that it is not simply an utterance but an utterance of "that type" if the reader has no access to a comparable repertoire of texts? This question is of some urgency, since some might argue that there are no extant examples of the type of story one finds in the prose tale of Job. Perhaps the question could be put in sharper form by asking if it is possible for an author to create the illusion that a text belongs to a genre, when in fact it does not. These questions can, I think, be answered in the affirmative. For one thing, in the act of reading a text is always and inevitably compared to some larger set of texts. The prose tale of Job may be compared to the larger set of all extant Hebrew narratives. Its very difference from narratives belonging to other genres helps to define a profile of distinctive traits, which may be perceived by the reader as possible generic markers, even if no other narratives of its own type can be identified. This perception of difference is not by itself enough, however, nor does it correspond to what most readers mean when they attach a generic label to the prose tale. What seems to trigger the sense of generic recognition for readers of the prose tale is the highly stylized nature of the text (extensive repetitions, sharp scenic division, exaggerated characterizations, round numbers, simple thematic structure, etc.). By drawing attention to certain traits, texts may signal that they are to be read as an example of a type of text in which just these traits are significant. Such stylization is an internal patterning of the text, but it may create the impression (arguably the illusion) that the whole text is patterned after other such texts, that it is a text of "that type." The more stylized the text, the more likely the impression of its belonging to a generic type functions as an important part of the text's rhetoric.

In point of fact, the case has been made by Hans-Peter Müller that the prose tale of Job can be compared to a body of texts that bear significant family resemblance.[47] His arguments will be taken up in the next chapter. Nevertheless, the limits of analysis with a small sample of texts has to be acknowledged. Although one may respond to a text as an example of a genre even without having an extensive repertoire of other comparable texts, what one cannot do without a significant number of examples is to recognize and appreciate how a particular text may be commenting upon or inflecting the generic repertoire. This limitation affects one's ability to read the book of Job to the extent that one wishes to understand the play of genres paradigmatically. It is difficult to know, for example, how the prose tale engages generic conventions, whether certain details violate implicit norms for "that sort of story." Analogously, because only one clear exemplar of the wisdom dialogue exists (the Babylonian Theodicy), it is too easy to treat it as *the* paradigm and thereby to experience all differences between it and the dialogue in Job as intentional inflections of the generic norm by the author of Job. As much as one would like to know such things, however, the dialogic relationship between this text and others of a similar type is largely out of reach. At the level of the overall structure of the book, however, the limitation is not so significant, since the structure of the book as a whole does not foreground the issue of paradigmatic relationships within a generic type. Rather, the sequence of the book, with its shift from one to another genre and back again, foregrounds the syntagmatic comparison of different genres (the didactic tale and the wisdom dialogue). Particularly if one understands genre in the Bakhtinian sense as a perspective on the world, the "form-shaping ideology" of the prose tale is established in part by how radically it differs from the wisdom dialogue, and vice versa.

Genre and Structure in Job

My argument is not a historical one. We will never know in fact how the book of Job came to be. The various accounts of its composition are valuable not so much as historical reconstructions as suggestions for different ways of reading the book. These accounts are heuristic fictions, invitations to read the book "as if" it had come into being in this or that fashion, with the intents and purposes characteristic of such an origin. For this reason I do not think that final-form literary reading of Job necessarily invalidates historical-critical reading, or that deconstructive reading invalidates literary reading. Similarly, my own proposal is not presented as an attempt to displace its predecessors. Criteria do exist, however, for better and worse readings. A new reading should be judged in part by how well it deals with problems left over by other models, though it will inevitably introduce new ones. It should be rigorously answerable to the text in a nonarbitrary fashion. But if a new reading is to be culturally valuable, it should engage the book by means of emerging reading conventions that are part of the cultural project of the interpreter's present. Thus, historical-critical analysis was valuable in part because it brought to the reading of the Bible the cultural project of the Enlightenment. For the same reason, its practices now seem at least in part problematic. The reading I propose takes its place alongside those of Good and Clines as part of the project of postmodernism, but unlike theirs, it follows a path other than deconstructive criticism.

With these considerations in mind, the heuristic fiction I wish to employ is that a single author wrote the book of Job (except for the Elihu speeches).[48] But he wrote it by juxtaposing and intercutting certain genres and distinctly stylized voices, providing sufficient interconnection among the different parts to establish the sense of the "same" story but leaving the different parts sharply marked and sometimes overtly disjunctive. Such a heuristic fiction concerning the composition of the book accounts both for the disjunctions (the way parts of the text seem willfully to ignore each other or to embody dramatically different styles, values, etc.) and also for the apparent anticipations and foreshadowings that facilitate the reading of the book as one story.

To understand the rhetorical purpose of such a manipulation of genre, it is necessary to supply my hypothetical author with a motive. Let us suppose there was a Judean author, probably from the early Second Temple period, who was aware that in his culture a variety of genres was used to talk about a set of overlapping topics (e.g., the nature of piety, the enigma of inexplicable suffering, the acquisition of wisdom). These genres embodied different perspectives on the world, different aesthetics, different value structures, and so forth. Their differences and commonalities, however, were rarely noted because, as distinct genres, they tended to exist in isolation from one another, closed off not only by the self-contained, "finalized" nature of generic speech itself but also because they tended to be used in different social contexts and perhaps even belonged to different social strata. Would it be possible, my fictive author wondered, to set these different genres in dialogue, so that their different takes on the world would be unavoidably present to a reader? Would it be possible to employ distinct genres in telling a single story so that the story is recognizably *one* story and yet the distinctive generic perspectives of the components remain discrete?

The traditional story of Job the righteous would provide a perfect starting point for such a project. It matters little for the purposes of this heuristic reconstruction whether the traditional story contained the plot device of Job's testing. Indeed, the evidence provided by the reference to Job in Ezekiel suggests that the traditional story known by Ezekiel may well have had a different plot.[49] But an author could take such a figure as Job, renowned for righteousness, and compose a didactic tale in which that character's righteousness was tested and confirmed. In such a didactic story, inexplicable suffering is a plot device designed to allow the hero's character to be foregrounded, but suffering is not a topic of reflection in its own right. What is merely a plot device in the didactic tale, however, is traditionally the focus of attention in the genre of the wisdom dialogue. By devising a mode of composition that allows the wisdom dialogue to interrupt and insert itself into the didactic tale, the radically different moral imaginations of these two genres can be made to engage one another dialogically. This attempt to create a dialogue of genres, in my heuristic reconstruction of the origin of the book of Job, is what accounts for the structure of the book. In Guillén's terms, one may read Job as a genre injected with antibodies, a genre containing a countergenre.

The book of Job consists of more than just the prose tale and the wisdom dialogue, of course. It also includes the wisdom poem of chapter 28 (a recognizable genre), the final speech of Job and God's reply in chapters 29–31, 38–41 (probably not composed according to a generic model),[50] and the speech by Elihu. The wisdom poem and the speeches of Job and God I take to be integral parts of the original design of the book; Elihu's speech I take to be a later addition. Nevertheless all contribute to the fundamentally dialogic nature of the composition, as each genre and voice opens up additional aspects of a complex cultural conversation about the moral nature of reality.

The Dialogue of Genres: The Book of Job as *Bildungsroman*

If we assume the intent to write a work composed in large part by juxtaposing different genres and contrasting voices, the question remains as to the author's perspective. In most books composed by a single author, even books with many characters, the composition is structured so that a single perspective predominates. This privileged perspective may be found in the voice of the narrator or in the character of the hero, perhaps in a minor character who comments upon the action, or even in the way the plot itself renders judgment on characters and their values. Readers may resist or reject it, but that privileged perspective is the one that the book and its implied author encourage the reader to adopt, the voice of "truth" within the narrative world.

The composition of Job in my hypothetical scenario creates a more complex relationship between author and text on the one hand and reader and text on the other, since the "voices" that populate the text are not just character voices but generic voices as well. Nevertheless, the question of the author's perspective is much the same. Is the book so structured that one of the genres or characters represents the privileged perspective? Most readers have assumed this is the case and have read Job with such a model in mind. And most readers, though not all, have identified this privileged position with the voice of God from the whirlwind.

Initially, there is much to commend such an understanding. Not only is it plausible that God, that great authority figure, would represent the perspective of the author, but the structure of the book itself also seems designed to lead the reader through an education of the moral imagination. Even though I finally wish to argue against such an interpretation, it is important to see the extent to which it provides a plausible means of reading the book.

The author introduces Job by means of a didactic narrative, a genre that presents its perspective simply and accessibly, without complex shading. The aesthetic devices of such a narrative (repetition, idealized exaggeration, simple binary character oppositions, strongly evaluative narrator, etc.) create a moral world of clear values and simple truths. But just as the reader is at home in (or bored with) such a narrative and moral world, the author interrupts it, continuing the story with a form of literary and moral conversation that is much more sophisticated (both aesthetically and in terms of the complexity of its moral vision). This new generic voice gives the reader a very different role to play. In contrast to the passive, childlike role assigned the reader in the didactic narrative, here more is required. Aesthetically, the wisdom dialogue is a demanding genre, with a sophisticated poetic style, rare words and archaic verbal forms, complex metaphors and rhetorical devices. Morally, too, the reader is assigned a more sophisticated role. The form of the wisdom dialogue, as we know it from the Babylonian Theodicy and from Job 3–27, has no evaluative narrator to tell the reader what's what, no plot to award victory to one position over another. Instead it simply presents voice against voice, requiring the reader to become much more active in judging the validity of the characters' claims. Although the contending positions of both the friends and Job are well represented, they are not presented as equally persuasive. The energy, passion, and dazzling rhetoric of Job tends to overwhelm the more conventional words of his friends. This is not simply a modern response. Elihu is the earliest reader who realizes that the friends "found no answer" to Job's words (32:3). Undoubtedly, the dialogue works differently for traditionalist and modern, posttraditionalist readers. For the former, who begin with moral perspectives close to those of the friends, the process of recognizing the shortcomings of those perspectives is painful and engaged with great resistance. For the modern critical reader, the identification with Job's defiance takes place more easily, perhaps too easily. In both cases the rhetorical shaping of the speeches nudges the reader toward a more critical stance vis-à-vis the friends and a more sympathetic stance vis-à-vis Job.

The sequencing of the genres encourages the sense that the wisdom dialogue is presented as in some sense a more adequate vehicle for moral reflection. Yet it is represented as finally incapable of adequately comprehending and resolving the moral dilemma of inexplicable suffering. This sense of limitation may be an internal generic feature (cf. the irresolution of the Babylonian Theodicy), but it is dramatized more intensely in Job. Whether by intent or by accident of transmission, the third round of speeches disintegrates, with only a short speech by Bildad and none by Zophar, and with Job's own speeches rife with incongruities. What promised to be a search for truth via the mutual examination of expert sages ends in fragmentation and incoherence. This judgment on the inadequacies of the wisdom dialogue as a means to truth is implicitly endorsed by the introduction of the third major genre, the wisdom poem of chapter 28. Its assertion that human beings cannot search out wisdom undercuts the assumptions upon which the wisdom dialogue is based and prepares the reader for the voice from the whirlwind.

Although it is unlikely that the final speech of Job (chaps. 29–31) and God's reply (chaps. 38–41) are created according to a generic model, they are highly stylized, contrasting forms of speech that construe the world according to radically different centers of value. Each expresses itself according to a different rhetoric, with distinctive patterns of metaphor and trope. The confrontation between their differing moral imaginations is more radical than that between the prose tale and the wisdom dialogue or between Job and his friends. Presented as a self-justification, Job's final speech also makes a claim about the coherency of his moral world and implies a way in which the story might be resolved in consonance with its values. The divine speeches, however, refuse to engage Job on those grounds and even to speak in explicitly moral terms at all. Yet the speeches from the whirlwind, the most dazzling poetic rhetoric of the book, tease the imagination. There is no message in them to be decoded allegorically but rather the sense of a wholly different form of perception which, if embraced, would reorient and reorganize one's entire sense of value and meaning.

Thus, a third mode of response is required of the reader—not submission to the authoritative voice of the prose tale, which seeks confirmation of a truth already known, not the exercise of rational judgment, which discriminates between competing arguments, but the transformation of perception through aesthetic experience. That the divine speeches appear to articulate the privileged perspective in the book is indicated by the fact that Job himself retracts his arguments and confesses to his own changed perception (42:1–6). That the book asks the reader not simply to note what Job has done but to experience personally the sense of changed perception is indicated by the fact that Job is as teasingly elusive about what the content of that changed perception is as he is clear that he no longer holds to his former position. The book will not do this work for the reader, since that would run counter to the moral values implicit in the book's mode of composition.

In this summary of the dynamic structure of the book, I have presented the case for seeing the book as a kind of *Bildungsroman* for the reader's moral imagination. There are, however, problems with this approach. The most obvious is that it has difficulty in accounting for the return of the prose tale. Readers who have intuitively read the book as a progression from less to more adequate moral perspectives often react violently to the return of the prose tale. The entire world of the prose tale's discourse, aesthetic and moral, seems indigestible after the divine speeches. For this mode of reading, the stylistic differences—between the prose and the dialogues, between the friends and Job, between Job and God— have served to educate the reader's sensibilities, to wean the reader from ways of speaking that were familiar but ultimately inadequate. What sense could it possibly make to plunge the reader back into a way of speaking, a way of perceiving the world, that now seems both alien and deficient? For the approach to reading described here, the conclusion of a work should serve to confirm and solidify the book's "message," the perspective for which it has argued. Yet as many commentators from Budde to Clines have noted, the prose conclusion seems morally at odds with the perspective implied in the divine speeches.

Not only at the level of style and moral perspective but even at the most basic narrative level the prose conclusion introduces contradiction. The most famous of these is contained in 42:7, where God says angrily to the friends that they have not "spoken correctly" of God, as has Job. Readers committed to a final-form reading and to unified and coherent meaning have attempted to moderate the contradiction by finding some sense in which the Job of the dialogues can be considered to have spoken "correctly," whereas the friends have not. Such efforts, however, have to overlook the fact that God has just rebuked the way Job speaks, calling him one who "obscures reason" and speaks "words without knowledge" (38:2). The ironic contradictions extend further into the conclusion. Though the friends are rebuked for having spoken what is not correct, a simple check shows that in fact things turn out just as they had predicted. When Job reorients himself toward God and puts the "iniquity" of his arrogant words aside, God turns to him in kindness, removes his misery, and restores him to a life in which he "rests secure" (so Zophar, 11:13–20). Indeed, God makes Job's "latter days" more blessed than his "former days" (cf. Bildad's words in 8:7 with 42:12). And as Eliphaz had predicted, God protects Job through his many trials, so that Job lives to experience prosperity, abundant offspring, and a peaceful death at an advanced age (5:19–27). The prose conclusion, taken on its own terms, offers a narrative of closure, indeed one in which the symbols of closure are exaggeratedly described. Yet when read in the context of the entire book, it prevents closure.

The prose conclusion so egregiously disrupts the model of the text as progressive education of the moral sensibility that it seems necessary to find another model for reading that takes account more adequately of the peculiarity of the book's structure. Both historical-critical interpretations and deconstructive ones can address the phenomenon of contradiction, but neither is particularly adaptable for the investigation of the moral claims of the text, which is at the heart of the inquiry I wish to make. More congenial is the approach explored by Mikhail Bakhtin in his discussion of the nature of dialogic truth and polyphonic texts.

The Dialogue of Genres: The Book of Job as Polyphonic Text

Since Bakhtin's work is not yet well known in biblical studies, I must take some care in laying out the aspects of his thought that bear most directly on the analysis I wish to make.[51] In Bakhtin's account, a polyphonic text has three distinctive aspects: (1) it embodies a dialogic sense of truth; (2) the author's position, although represented in the text, is not privileged; and (3) the polyphonic text ends without finalizing closure.[52]

Bakhtin's distinction between monologic and dialogic senses of truth is fundamental.[53] The monologic conception of truth is relatively easy to grasp, because it is the conception that dominates modern thought, characteristic not only of philosophy but of literature. Three important features characterize the monologic sense of truth. First, monologic truth is essentially propositional, composed of what Bakhtin calls "separate thoughts." The truth of these "separate thoughts" or propositions is referential. They are repeatable by others and just as true (or untrue) when spoken by them. Bakhtin refers to these as "no-man's thoughts."

The second feature of monologic truth is that it seeks unity and thus tends to gravitate toward a system. These may be larger or smaller systems, but in general monologic statements are congenial to being ordered in a systemic way. The third and most important feature of the monologic sense of truth is that in principle it can be comprehended by a single consciousness. No matter how much complexity exists in a proposition or system, a person of sufficient intellectual ability can think it and utter it. Perhaps it would be more apt to say that the proposition or system of monologic thought is structured in such a way that, even if it is actually the product of many minds, it is capable of being spoken by a single voice.

Although the paradigmatic examples of the monologic sense of truth would be philosophical systems, Bakhtin insists that this conception of truth is much more pervasive. Not only is it the sense of truth that undergirds many types of critical activity; it is also the sense of truth embedded in most literature, even the novel. Despite the fact that novels often have many different characters, drawn quite differently and acting as spokespersons for different ideologies, it is finally the author's ideology and perspective that coordinates all the parts of the novel and gives it unity. The governing ideas of such works can be represented as complex and nuanced, but finally monologic statements.

Such monologic conceptions of author, text, and truth have governed both historical-critical study of Job and most literary and theological studies as well. For historical criticism, it was precisely the perception that the book of Job lacked such monologic unity that led to the critical judgment that the prose tale and the Job poem must come from different authors. As the statement of Pope, quoted earlier, insists, the book of Job could not be understood as the product of a single consciousness. In response, the arguments of literary-critical and theological interpreters have been that the book of Job, although containing "dissonance and tension,"[54] can indeed be understood, in the words of Francis Andersen, as the "product of a single mind."[55] For both positions, the assumptions of monologic truth are exhibited in the governing image of the "single mind."

What if a monologic conception of truth is not the only possibility? Bakhtin developed his notions of dialogical truth in order to challenge the dominant conception of truth as systemic and monological. Compared with monologism, it is less easy to describe what Bakhtin means by a dialogic sense of truth, in large part because one is unaccustomed to thinking in such terms. The first and most important characteristic of a dialogic sense of truth is that, in contrast to monologic discourse, it "requires a plurality of consciousnesses . . . [that] in principle cannot be fitted within the bounds of a single consciousness."[56] A dialogic truth exists at the point of intersection of several unmerged voices. The paradigm is that of the conversation. One cannot have a genuine conversation with oneself. At least two unmerged voices are required. If one attempts to "sum up" a conversation, one changes its character, reducing it to a set of monologic propositions. But what distinctively characterizes a conversation is the dynamic way in which different perspectives engage one another, something that cannot be rendered by a single voice.

A second feature of dialogic truth is that, in contrast to the abstract nature of monologic truth, it has an embodied, personal quality. Here, too, the paradigm of the conversation is illustrative. Participants in a conversation are not propositions but the persons who utter them. In contrast to monologic discourse,

Bakhtin says that in a dialogue "the ultimate indivisible unit is not the assertion, but rather the integral point of view, the integral position of a personality."[57] In conversation, statements are not "no-man's thoughts" but "voice-ideas." Who says them is of the utmost importance, because ideas cannot be separated from the perspectives in which they are embodied.

The third characteristic of dialogic truth is that there is no drift toward the systematic. What emerges is not system but "a concrete event made up of organized human orientations and voices."[58] "Event" rather than "system" gives dialogic truth its unity, a dynamic, not a propositional unity. One of the things that drew Bakhtin to Dostoevsky as his privileged example was Dostoevsky's ability to represent the dialogic "image of an idea" in the interaction of his characters. An idea does not live in a person's isolated individual consciousness but only insofar as it enters into dialogical relations with other ideas and with the ideas of others. It may attempt to displace other ideas, seek to enlist them, be qualified by other ideas, develop new possibilities in the encounter with alien ideas. All of an idea's interactions are a part of its identity. The truth about the idea thus cannot be comprehended by a single consciousness. It requires the plurality of consciousnesses that can enter into relationship with it from a variety of noninterchangeable perspectives.

Finally, the fourth aspect of dialogic truth is that it is always open. Bakhtin's inelegant term for this is "unfinalizability." As Bakhtin puts it, "The ultimate word of the world and about the world has not yet been spoken, the world is open and free, everything is still in the future, and will always be in the future."[59]

Texts, of course, are not conversations. Even novels, although they contain staged conversations between characters, are usually not dialogical in Bakhtin's sense. Most literary works, including novels, are monologic in that the voices appearing therein are controlled by the author's perspective. The voices play the role of setting up the monologic truth the work attempts to convey. These voices cannot address the reader directly, since they are approached only through the author's evaluating perspective. Bakhtin, however, believed that it was possible to produce in a literary work something approximating a genuine dialogue, the model of writing he called polyphonic. As suggested earlier, polyphonic writing makes an important change in the position of the author. In a polyphonic text the author gives up the type of control exercised in monologic works and attempts to create several consciousnesses that will be truly independent of the author's and interact with genuine freedom. This is not to say that the author gives up a presence in the work, but that the author's perspective becomes only one among others, without privilege. Plot, as well as authorial position, is also different. Since a polyphonic work attempts to represent the dialogic nature of an idea, its plot is derivative from the idea and shaped by it. Correspondingly, the reader's role also changes. Instead of being asked merely to follow plot and character, the reader is more like a bystander caught up in a quarrel.

The most difficult aesthetic problem for polyphonic writing is the construction of an appropriate ending. For a polyphonic work to end with definitive closure would be utterly inappropriate, since the essence of dialogic truth is its open, unfinalizable character. Even Bakhtin admitted that with the exception of *The Brothers Karamazov*, which presents itself as a fragment, Dostoevsky did not solve this creative problem. Ideally, however, a polyphonic text should end dialogically and openly, inviting the reader "to draw dotted lines to a future, unresolved continuation."[60]

If Job is read in light of Bakhtin's insights, many of the features that "bedeviled" attempts to find a monologic unity in the book appear not as problems at all but as elements of a rhetorical strategy essential for the creation of a polyphonic text. In this polyphonic reading of Job I continue to assume the presence of an author who wished to draw on the genres and cultural voices of his community, one who wished to have positions that tended to seal themselves off from one another be required to engage one another dialogically. But in this reading the author is not setting up the confrontation in such a way that one voice triumphs, for no one voice can speak the whole truth. Rather, the truth about piety, human suffering, the nature of God, and the moral order of the cosmos can be adequately addressed only by a plurality of unmerged consciousnesses engaging one another in open-ended dialogue.

The polyphonic author of Job chooses to begin the book with the didactic prose tale not only because of its narrative form but also because it is an intensely monologic genre. Here is a text possessed of a "ready-made truth," easily stated in propositional terms: "True piety is unconditional, unaffected either by divine blessing or by inexplicable catastrophe." This is the truth of the implied author of the prose tale (not to be confused with the author of the polyphonic work as a whole), the truth that this author wishes readers to endorse. As an essential element of the rhetoric of this monologic tale, the implied author exercises supreme control over the discourse. There are characters who speak contrary views, *haśśāṭān* and Job's wife, but their perspectives are not allowed to address the reader directly as legitimately contending perspectives. They are mere foils for the characters who articulate the truth of the narrative: Job, God, and the narrator.

The polyphonic author's task is to "dialogize" the prose tale, which he does by interrupting its closed narration with the very different genre of the wisdom dialogue. As argued earlier, this new form of discourse embodies a contrasting moral imagination. Although certain genres can be incorporated into a multigeneric work in ways that allow them to "live peacefully in the center of a single work,"[61] the didactic prose tale and the wisdom dialogue are too sharply at odds about the relation of speech to truth for this to be the case. Even while they are both engaged in telling parts of the "same" story in the book of Job, their differences ensure that they remain "unmerged consciousnesses" dialogically engaged.

This wisdom dialogue, as the very label suggests, embodies very different values concerning the way truth is to be apprehended. Bakhtin himself was intrigued by philosophical dialogues of antiquity as generic precursors of the polyphonic novel, although such philosophical dialogues tend not to be fully polyphonic themselves. What such philosophical dialogues do well, however, is to represent "the dialogic nature of truth, and the dialogic nature of human thinking about truth."[62] In contrast to monologic discourse that presents itself as in possession of "ready-made truth," the philosophical dialogue shows how "truth is not born nor is it to be found inside the head of an individual person, it is born *between people* collectively searching for truth."[63] Bakhtin was thinking primarily of Socratic dialogues, which differ in many respects from the highly schematized wisdom dialogues of the Babylonian Theodicy and Job. Nevertheless, even in these works one sees something of this dialogic image of the idea. Job's engagement with the friends leads in unexpected ways to the articulation of ideas that were literally unthinkable at the beginning of the dialogue.

What are the consequences of bringing together the different ideas embodied in the genre perspectives of the didactic tale and the wisdom dialogue and "making them quarrel"? When Bakhtin spoke of the historical emergence of new genres, he observed that "each fundamentally and significantly new genre, once it arrives, exerts influence on the entire circle of old genres: the new genre makes the old ones, so to speak, more conscious; it forces them to better perceive their own possibilities and boundaries, that is, to overcome their own *naiveté*."[64] The technique of juxtaposing genres in the book of Job creates a radically intense form of this cultural confrontation. The possibilities, boundaries, and naiveté of the didactic tale are exposed by the fact of its being interrupted, for its monologic and self-sufficient language is crafted to be largely impervious to heterogeneous accents and alien voices. Just how much is "unspeakable" within its discourse is revealed in Job's harrowing curse in chapter 3. Moreover, the great idea of the didactic tale concerning piety, which seems self-evident within its own monologic discourse, is, in the dialogue, openly rejected by Job and reframed as a quite different religious relationship by the friends.

The act of interrupting has consequences for the wisdom dialogue as well. The classic form of the wisdom dialogue has no framing narrative.[65] In the book of Job, however, the didactic tale speaks first, changing the conditions of speech for the genre of the wisdom dialogue. In interrupting, the genre of the wisdom dialogue must now situate itself in a new discursive context, articulating its own words in the shadow of what has already been said.

The presence of the didactic tale deprives the wisdom dialogue of its universal character. With the didactic tale as frame, the contrasting voices of the dialogue are no longer anonymous voices, as in the Babylonian Theodicy, but persons: Job, Eliphaz, Bildad, Zophar. In the prose tale Job is a subject of narrative, and in the dialogue he becomes a speaking subject. No longer simply a pole in an argument, he becomes a character, one capable of saying surprising things. The passion and daringness of Job in the dialogue are elements that an author might conceivably have developed from within the generic possibilities of the wisdom dialogue alone. But the juxtaposition of the didactic tale, with its static character type of the undeviatingly accepting pious protagonist, and the wisdom dialogue, with its different but nearly equally static character type of the complaining skeptic, produces something that is more than the sum of its parts. It gives the polyphonic book a psychological dimension unattainable in either genre alone. The juxtaposition produces a character who has made a decisive break with a previous worldview and identity. The dialogization of genres that the author creates in Job is in significant measure what makes possible a character who is far more free and far more dangerous than the conventional sufferer in an ordinary wisdom dialogue. Finally, the reader's relation to the characters is changed. Whereas the reader of the independent wisdom dialogue shares with the characters an ignorance of the actual causes of the suffering under discussion, in the polyphonic text of Job the reader knows the unique circumstances of Job's suffering, a knowledge that creates a distance between the reader and the analyses proposed by the characters.

In a reading of the book of Job as polyphonic text, the wisdom poem in chapter 28 plays a role both similar to and different from what it does if the book is understood as a *Bildungsroman* of the moral imagination. As in the earlier analysis, the wisdom poem critiques the limitations of the wisdom dialogue by strategically reframing the concrete conflicts of the dialogue in terms of the metacategories of wisdom and understanding. The problem, as the wisdom poem articulates it, is that the wisdom dialogue as genre overlooks the inherent limitations of human understanding, and so cannot succeed in its search for truth. Far from being merely a setup for the answer from the whirlwind, however, the wisdom poem also takes sides with the prose tale against the dialogue, for in verse 28 it echoes the words of the prose tale when it advises that for human beings "fear of the Lord" and "turning from evil" are the effective equivalents of the transcendent wisdom that remains inaccessible to humans. Since this statement comes after the experience of the exhaustion of the dialogue, it might seem to endorse the monologic mode of the prose tale, as well as being an endorsement of its religious values. Yet things are not quite that simple. Bakhtin observed that agreement as well as disagreement is dialogical.[66] The voice of the wisdom poem is not identical with the voice of the prose tale. Even in agreement, it adds a new perspective, one found as much in its style as in its propositional claims.

Although Job cannot respond directly to the wisdom poem, which exists beyond the frame of the characters, from the reader's perspective Job's speech in chapters 29–31 can be read as a reply, for he presents himself as one who has feared God and turned from evil and who still seeks to have his claims heard and addressed. No consensus exists concerning the genre of Job's final speech, although it is clearly not a disputation addressed to the friends and thus not a continuation of the wisdom dialogue. He embodies in one voice positions that were articulated by different voices in the wisdom dialogue: the assumption of retributive justice as the moral principle of creation and his desire for a legal adjudication of grievances (30:20; 31:35). What Job's final speech does, which is not a part of the ethos of the wisdom dialogue, is to recast the problematic of enigmatic suffering in terms of the social discourse of honor. The more self-reflective and even confessional quality of this speech also creates something of a different character for Job from that developed in the wisdom dialogue.

Despite his ostensive appeal for a dialogic encounter with God (31:35-37), the Job of chapters 29-31 is committed to a view of truth that is monologic. The moral world Job articulates in these chapters is complete and logically self-consistent, as his confident self-presentation in chapter 31 suggests. The values that direct his conduct and shape his identity are also those that structure his image of God. Within this world of values there can be only one truth about Job. Not by accident does Job's final speech contain forensic language, specifically an appeal for a hearing and an opportunity to testify against the writ of his accuser (31:35-37). Although legal proceedings are dialogic in the sense that one party answers another, the function of such speech is to arrive at an incontestable unitary truth. But even as Job calls for the opportunity to present his case, he already has. His speech has the function of testimony, the utterly compelling self-justification he would give in such a forum. What could there be left for God to say, except "you are more in the right than I"? Job's speech is an utterly finalizing account of himself and his world.

The speech of God in chapters 38-41 "dialogizes" Job's monologic perspective by proceeding upon utterly different premises with a set of values and a form of argumentation incommensurate with those presumed by Job. What effect does it have on the place of dialogue within the book as a whole? God's speech plays ironically with the notion of dialogue, explicitly echoing Job's request but at the same time suggesting the absurdity of dialogue with a partner who "obscures reason" and speaks "words without knowledge" (38:2). Similarly, the form of the divine speech mocks dialogue, not only through God's monopolization of speech but also through the extensive use of rhetorical questions. Such a device has the form of a genuine question but is not a true invitation to dialogue. But even though the divine speeches parody the demand for dialogue, might they be understood as a genuinely dialogic response to a speaker so invested in his own strategies of containment that he has, without being aware of it, effectively refused dialogic encounter and so frustrated his own search for truth? This may be so; nevertheless, the voice from the whirlwind does not let itself be interrogated.

In the wisdom dialogue of the Babylonian Theodicy, the gods are spoken about but do not become part of the dialogic process. Here, however, the introduction of this second dialogue (chaps. 29–31; 38:1–42:6) means that God does not remain beyond the frame but becomes a participant, contesting what has been said and offering another construction of reality. But can the polyphonic text, with its commitment to dialogic truth, sustain the divine voice? Or does the attempt to incorporate it repress the very possibility of dialogue? The text of 42:1–6 provides a tense and difficult response to this issue, which is both an aesthetic and a substantive problem. Commitment to the primacy of dialogue appears to be affirmed by the fact that it is Job who must have the last word. The design of the entire, complex book is dependent upon it, for the plot was set in motion by the question of whether Job would curse God to God's face. Until Job has spoken, the question and the plot generated by it remain open.

Although dialogical relation can take shape either in agreement or in disagreement, not every reply is dialogical in Bakhtin's sense of the word. In the course of Job's brief response, the difficult boundaries of the dialogical relationship are brought into view. Job's initial response is not speech at all but a refusal to speak (40:4–5). Couched in polite words, it might be taken for acquiescence, but it is neither agreement or disagreement. God, of course, insists on a reply (40:7). But when Job speaks, his words again foreground the limits of dialogue. Two concepts from Bakhtin bear on the nature of Job's words. The first is the "authoritative" word. In ordinary speech the words one speaks are always partly one's own and partly those of someone else. This phenomenon can buttress one's own speech by invoking the words and phrases associated with someone or some discourse the speaker treats as authoritative. Or it can undercut another position, as in parodic speech. In both cases the speaker's own accents as well as those of the other posited speaker are present and actively engaged in dialogic relationship. But the words of another sometimes appear in one's own speech in a nondialogical way. This is what Bakhtin refers to as the "authoritative word."

> The authoritative word demands that we acknowledge it, that we make it our own; it binds us, quite independent of any power it might have to persuade us internally; we encounter it with its authority already fused to it. . . . It is not a free appropriation and assimilation of the word itself that authoritative discourse seeks to elicit from us; rather, it demands our unconditional allegiance. Therefore authoritative discourse permits no play with the context framing it, no play with its borders, no gradual and flexible transitions, no spontaneously creative stylizing variants on it. It enters our verbal consciousness as a compact and indivisible mass; one must either totally affirm it, or totally reject it.[67]

When God requires Job to reply, Job begins his response with the issues of divine power and authority. He continues, incorporating quotations from the divine speech. Here is no subtle double voicing, no trace of parody. God's quoted words stand out sharply. Citing God's claim that he has "darkened reason without understanding" (38:2; 42:3a), Job acknowledges that he has spoken without insight of things that he "did not understand" (42:3b). Job further quotes God's command to hear and respond (38:3b; 40:7b; 42:4), and in his final utterance Job either retracts his words or abases himself before God (42:6). Thus, Job's words seem utterly undialogical, for they are not even clearly words of assent but simply words that bow the knee before the one "who can do all things."

If this were entirely the case, then the experiment in polyphonic composition would have failed, unable to sustain itself against the authoritative divine word. But Job's words, though they gesture to the limits of dialogue by their performative citation of the authoritative word, are not so entirely undialogical as they appear. Job's final statement, though apparently a word of retraction and self-abasement, contains significant semantic and syntactic ambiguity.[68] Does he say, as the Authorized Version and its descendants have rendered, "Therefore I despise myself and repent in dust and ashes" (i.e., in humiliation)? Or does he say, "Therefore I retract my words and repent of dust and ashes" (i.e., the symbols of mourning)?[69] Or, "Therefore I retract my words and have changed my mind concerning dust and ashes" (i.e., the human condition)?[70] Or even "Therefore I despise and repent of dust and ashes" (i.e., the symbols of religion)?[71] This ambiguity gives Job's words something of the quality Bakhtin describes as words with a "loophole," that is, "the retention for oneself of the possibility of altering the ultimate, final meaning of one's words. . . . This potential other meaning, that is, the loophole left open, accompanies the word like a shadow."[72] Thus, Job's reply, however understood, casts a "sidelong glance" at other possible but not explicitly articulated replies. In this way the conversation remains not only unfinalized but unfinalizable. In his one reference to Job, Bakhtin suggests that he must have understood Job's words in some such fashion, for he observes that "the opposition of the soul to God—whether the opposition be hostile or humble—is conceived in [Job's dialogue] as something irrevocable and eternal."[73]

Ultimately, it is not so much the character Job but the polyphonic author who slyly manages to reassert the continuing claim on truth by voices that were silenced by the authoritative divine voice, or if one prefers, by the forces of compositional and cultural convention. For God's speech to be dialogically engaged one needs a voice that is alien to the poetic dialogue and so escapes being organized by its point of reference. In the book of Job that alien voice is provided by the resumption of the didactic tale. Through the ironic juxtaposing of these two earnest attempts to secure closure (the divine speech and the "happily ever after" ending of the didactic tale), the author ensures that no closure can take place. Indeed, the author of the book of Job plays a trick on both, for it is the resolutely monologic voice of the didactic tale, the voice of the single, ready-made idea, that is forced, quite contrary to its own intrinsic intentions, to revive the contending voices that the divine speech has just quelled. When God in the prose conclusion (42:7) declares that Job has spoken correctly, then the unfinished business of Job's objections comes back into view. And even though God rebukes the friends (42:8–9), the narrative conclusion in 42:10–17 seems a wink of the polyphonic author behind God's back, validating the friends' claims, since the story ends just as they said it would. By means of this ironic and self-contradictory conclusion of unmerged divine and narrative voices, the author has framed the perfect ending for a polyphonic work, simultaneously gesturing in the direction of closure while signaling that the issues are far from settled.

The significant achievement of the book as a whole, however, is to have depicted "the image of an idea" concerning the nature of piety. Although articulated first by the distinctive voice of the prose tale, that idea loses its monologic quality with the eruption of Job's curse and the ensuing dialogue. In that dialogue, rival perspectives concerning piety not only contest one another directly but enlist the aid of associated ideas, disclosing a complex entailment among ideas about human nature, God, violence and justice, the order of the world, the nature of good and evil, and so forth, a network of implications and engagements among ideas one could never have guessed at from the bare monologic statement of chapter 1. Read as a polyphonic work, the purpose of the book is not to advance a particular view: neither that of the prose tale, nor that of the friends, nor that of Job, nor even that of God. Rather, its purpose is to demonstrate that the idea of piety in all its "contradictory complexity" cannot in principle "be fitted within the bounds of a single consciousness." The truth about piety can only be grasped at the point of intersection of unmerged perspectives. The proper response to such a book, as the author of the Elihu speech intuitively grasped, is to inject oneself into the conversation, but with the awareness that the final word can never be spoken.

So one would like to say, in good Bakhtinian fashion. But however much Bakhtin's notions of dialogic truth and polyphony illumine the structure of the book, the play of genres, and the dialogic construction of the image of an idea, Bakhtin's valorization of dialogue cannot explain and indeed threatens to obscure important dimensions of the book. The book of Job thus serves not only to illustrate Bakhtin's concepts but also to reveal their limits, for the book resists being coopted into a simple endorsement of dialogic values as it persistently draws attention to constraints on and failures of dialogue. Bakhtin was consistently reluctant to address the effects of power on dialogic relations, yet as the example of Job's reply to the divine speeches shows, even if read as words with a loophole, the dialogic perspective is preserved in the face of power only by being forced underground. What it cannot say outright it hints at through possible double or triple meanings. More problematic is the inability of such a perspective to address the very speech situation upon which the whole story is founded. The narrative tension set up by the prose tale emerges from an irresistible curiosity to know something that utterly eludes dialogue. For Job simply to be asked if he "fears God freely" would not only raise the possibility that he might lie but also and more significantly that his deepest motivations might not be accessible to his own consciousness and thus would be beyond the limits of the most honest dialogue. The knowledge that is sought by the story can be satisfied only by listening to a type of coerced speech, to words forced out by pain. Nor are Job's suffering-induced words (1:21; 2:10) ever reclaimed for dialogue, for though overheard and commented upon (42:7b), Job himself is not addressed directly (42:8-9), except perhaps in disingenuousness (42:7a).

Although the prose tale itself would choose not to explore the implications of coerced speech, the introduction of the wisdom dialogue shows how such coercion may recoil upon the speech forcer, threatening to undo him.[74] Nowhere else in the Bible is such an unrestrained demolition of the traditional image of God carried out as in Job's speeches, words that once let loose have continued to resonate for millennia. Throughout the wisdom dialogue the conditions that corrupt speech and destroy dialogue are repeatedly examined: excessive power, fear, cupidity, and simple failure of the imagination. In this book, however, God is not the only speech forcer. Job also forces God to speak, and that speech, as unpredictable as Job's own had been, dismantles Job's identity and world. Whether judged to be purely destructive or ultimately redemptive, the dimension of violence in such a speech situation eludes a Bakhtinian analysis. Finally, the Bakhtinian celebration of dialogue has to be confronted by the silences that punctuate the book, the silence of Job in the presence of his friends, in his response to the first divine speech, and in the final narration of his life (2:10, 13; 40:4-5; 42:7-17).[75] These silences gesture to the ultimate limits of dialogue, to the unsayable that shadows speech.

2

The Impregnable Word

Genre and Moral Imagination in the Prose Tale

> As Aristotle observed, [literature] is deep, and conducive to our inquiry about
> how to live, because it does not simply (as history does) record that this or
> that event happened; it searches for patterns of possibility—of choice, and
> circumstance, and the interaction between choice and circumstance—that turn
> up in human lives with such a persistence that they must be regarded as
> our possibilities. And so our interest in literature becomes . . . cognitive: an
> interest in finding out (by seeing and feeling the otherwise perceiving) what
> possibilities (and tragic impossibilities) life offers to us, what hopes and fears
> for ourselves it underwrites or subverts.
>
> Martha Nussbaum, *Love's Knowledge*

In the preceding chapter I argued for reading Job as a polyphonically structured
book. This structure is primarily produced by juxtaposing sharply differing genres
in such a way that they cannot easily be read as articulations of a single voice or
consciousness. Before one can talk about the dialogic sense of truth achieved
by the interaction of these voices, it is necessary to treat them separately, attending to the monologic claims made by each. In this chapter the focus will be on
the prose tale and how it imagines patterns of possibility and impossibility in
the sense in which Nussbaum speaks of them. Perhaps this undertaking seems
a bit foolish. The prose tale has not fared well in modern critical and theological evaluation and is often viewed as a mere setup for the intellectually more
sophisticated and provocative dialogue, and so scarcely worth serious scrutiny.
When it does attract attention, that attention has often been hostile, especially
from theological critics.[1] Biblical scholars usually note its critique of "barter
religion" as worthy, but when the prose tale is appreciated, it is more likely on
the grounds of aesthetic rather than moral values.[2]

The prose tale has been underread, however, because its aesthetic values have
been treated as separable from its moral claims. Those engaged with the study
of ethics have increasingly argued that aesthetic forms lie at the heart of moral
perception.[3] The essential role of narrative in the formation and articulation of
ethical values is perhaps the most familiar claim.[4] Alasdair MacIntyre, for in-

stance, maintains that there is an intrinsic relationship between belief in certain kinds of virtues and the privileging of certain narrative forms.[5] "I can only answer the question 'What am I to do?' if I can answer the prior question 'Of what story or stories do I find myself a part?'"[6] Even more fundamentally, narrative is basic to the way persons constitute experience and identity. Consequently, the sense that things are falling apart, the sense of disintegration Heidegger termed *Angst* is the loss of narrative coherence in a life.[7]

Metaphor, too, is fundamental to moral perception and moral reasoning.[8] All the metaphors that permeate speech—from the taken-for-granted "dead" metaphors, to the embedded but never expressly articulated metaphors, to the innovative poetic metaphors—serve to frame situations, which gives them cognitive and emotive significance. Each metaphor highlights certain aspects of a situation and obscures others, selecting for relevance based on the comparison implicit in the metaphor. Generative metaphors not only have problem-setting functions but because of the systemic nature of metaphorical comparison they also set the directions for problem solving. Metaphors "map" situations so that certain decisions or courses of action appear to be the most proper or logical.[9]

In addition, the conceptual language by which one talks about values, obligations, rights, and so forth—language most persons would take as "literal"—can be seen on closer inspection to be constructed on the basis of deeply embedded metaphors.[10] Though every culture has a stock of such embedded metaphors, this stock will be both diverse and far from coherent. Thus, the potential for moral argument by means of competing metaphors is potentially present in virtually every context.

Narrative structures and metaphors yield fairly easily to analysis. More elusive but equally important are elements of style and diction, for the textures of language are also part of the text's communicative praxis and moral significance.[11] The complexity or simplicity of diction, tonality, the privileging of certain words or syntactical patterns, the use or avoidance of synonyms, and so forth all may be indices of moral commitments of various sorts. In her study of Henry James's *The Ambassadors*,[12] Martha Nussbaum explores the moral significance of various features of style. The "Kantian" character, Mrs. Newsome, typically speaks without making use of proper names, an index of her categorical mode of thought. Contrastingly, Strether, the figure who represents the moral alternative of a life of particularity and perception, is associated with the interrogative and a groping for the right description, often rendered in vivid metaphor. Whether or not James consciously planned these contrasts is not the point. Nussbaum's claim is more sweeping: that every mode of speaking is saturated with moral commitments. "Style itself makes its claims, expresses its own sense of what matters."[13]

Style constructs identity and character, not just for the figures within the text but for the implied author and reader as well. If one thinks of speech in actual social situations, how someone talks tells me who they think they are, who they think I am, and what sort of a relationship exists between us. Subtle and not so subtle differences of class, caste, gender, and other social categories may be exquisitely marked. Whether the relationship is egalitarian or hierarchical, whether it is one of intimacy or distance, what function or purposes the relationship serves, whether a set of common values and knowledge is presupposed, and many other features may be signaled through the textures of speech. Thus, not only character but a particular form of community is constructed through the act of talking. Something analogous occurs in writing. The style in which a text is written–inclusive of everything from diction and syntax to genre–constructs a character for the implied author and projects the character of the one to whom it is addressed. Style establishes what James Boyd White calls "a community of two," a textual community between implied author and reader that has its own norms, ideals, and expectations.[14] Though any particular reader may resist the characterization offered, such resistance is based upon a recognition of what character and relationship is being offered by the implied author. Consequently, one may speak of the ethical and political dimensions entailed not only in a text's claims about the world but also in its claims upon the reader.[15]

To inquire into "the moral imagination of the prose tale" involves reflection on the interrelation between the aesthetic forms of the text–its narrative structure, its metaphors, its style–and the values it endorses as well as those it embodies. Such an inquiry involves both an examination of the world of the text and the relationship provisionally established between text and reader. To pursue this question is to undertake what is currently called "narrative ethics." Not surprisingly, many different approaches share this umbrella concept, not all of which are compatible. The model of narrative ethics most congenial to my work in this chapter is that associated with Wayne Booth and Martha Nussbaum.

Booth more or less reintroduced self-conscious ethical criticism into the study of narrative in 1988 with his wonderfully idiosyncratic book *The Company We Keep: An Ethics of Fiction*. As suggested by the title, Booth's governing trope–an unashamedly old-fashioned one–is that narratives are analogous to friends with whom we keep company. Or, more properly speaking, the implied author of a narrative is the friend, and the story is a friendship offering. The moral framework within which Booth situates his understanding of the effects of narrative is that of the formation of character. Booth's understanding of character and of the human self is that it is not "an atomic unit bumping other atoms"[16] but is dialogically constructed, composed of many internalized and semi-internalized voices (a notion adopted from Bakhtin). From this fluid and mobile understanding of the self it is easy to grasp how character can be formed (or deformed) by keeping company with good or bad friends, whose influences register to some degree in the type of persons we become. We "try out" different ways of being, different characters for ourselves, depending on the company we keep.

The most useful part of Booth's discussion, however, is his analysis of desire in reading and in the formation of character. Narrative interest depends on desire. Except for students forced to read certain texts, narratives can only secure our continuing presence with them by stimulating and offering to satisfy some desire. If we turn the page it is only because we desire more of what we have been offered. Thus, narratives "pattern" our desire and induce us to become "that kind of desirer," at least provisionally and for the duration of the reading experience.[17] Talking about texts as offers to stimulate and satisfy desires, perhaps even desires one did not even know one was capable of having, comes close to a model of reading as seduction. One cannot be naive about the implications of such a metaphor. Some seductions leave one deeply satisfied and fulfilled, whereas others leave one feeling only manipulated and used. One may provisionally surrender to a text, only to discover that one does not want to become the type of person who would desire that sort of satisfaction. Booth's suggested approach to reading poses no threat to "resistant readings," however, for all it asks is that one engage in a reflective way what it might mean to become one who desires what the text offers. After such analysis, resistant reading becomes better informed for having imaginatively entered into what is subsequently rejected.

Although Booth's work has a considerable theoretical and philosophical underpinning, he presents it only incidentally.[18] In contrast, Martha Nussbaum, whose perspective is close to that of Booth, is explicit in locating herself within the Aristotelian tradition of moral philosophy and practical reasoning. In attempting to answer the question "How should one live?" this tradition insists on the incommensurability of values, the priority of particular judgments over universal ones, and the central role of the emotions and of the imagination in rational choice. Thus, it is not surprising that Nussbaum turns to literature as a form of discourse particularly suited to the exploration of ethical choices. Literature, as she says in the quotation that serves as an epigraph for this chapter, "searches for patterns of possibility—of choice, and circumstance, and the interaction between choice and circumstance that turn up in human lives with such a persistence that they must be regarded as our possibilities."[19]

This neohumanist approach has its limits. It deals rather well with the text as a form of moral imagination, but it does so precisely by privileging the cognitive dimension. This is not to say that emotions and aesthetic judgments are given short shrift—far from it. But the entire experience of reading is a means to the end of a rational choice about the type of person one wishes to be, the type of values one wishes to hold, and the nature of the good. The text as a whole functions as something like a proposition: "The world is like this" or "This is how one should live." In this approach something gets left out of what it means to read, and something gets left out of what ethics encompasses. This mode of narrative ethics is not well suited for examining the performative aspect of the text and the ethical issues raised as the text "happens" in the encounter of reading. For this reason it will be useful to contrast a "Boothian" and "Nussbaumian" approach to one that emerges from the perspectives of Adam Zachary Newton. Newton focuses on the act of narrating as a site of ethical inquiry. He develops his approach in conversation with Bakhtin's early work on ethics and aesthetics and with Levinas's ethical philosophy.[20] Its value for the prose tale is that it helps to clarify what is at stake in one of the most common modern debates over the prose tale, that is, whether in a "story like this" it is appropriate or naive to be upset by the test of Job and by the death of his children. Levinas's exploration of the ethical significance of interruption will also provide a means for reflecting on the relationship between the moral world of the prose tale and the interruption of its act of narration that takes place in the structure of the book as a whole.

The Status of the Prose Tale

Before turning to the main work of this chapter, however, there is a preliminary problem to be dealt with, namely, whether or not the prose tale "exists" in a fashion that would make it amenable to investigation apart from the book as a whole. As I argued in the last chapter, the prose tale is a fragment. It has a beginning consisting of two complete episodes (1:1–22; 2:1–10), and a conclusion (42:11–17), but it appears to lack part of its middle, specifically the exchange between Job and his friends, plus God's appearance and words to Job, which would have constituted the third episode (2:11–13; ???; 42:7–10). Many historical critics consider the prose tale to be an actual fragment of an old narrative, although it is also possible to understand it as an artificial fragment, composed by the author of the book in just this fragmentary state. In either case the "missing middle" poses little problem for an investigation of the moral imagination of the tale. As will be discussed below, generically the tale is a didactic narrative. One of the features of such tales is their redundancy. Various narrative, semantic, and other structures reiterate the meaning. Thus, a text "damaged" in the way that the prose tale appears to be will still communicate its meaning effectively.

In fact, such is the clear, schematic structure of the prose tale that, ever since historical critics began to conceive of the prose as the remnant of an independent *Volksbuch*, readers have found it possible on the basis of 42:7–8 to reconstruct schematically what "should" be there but has been displaced, namely, some impious accusations of God by the friends and Job's pious response. Thus, the "missing middle" of the third episode is understood to contain a relationship between Job and his friends that is the reverse of the one actually present in the poetic dialogues. Although there is no way of ever knowing with certainty, in my opinion an independent *Volksbuch* containing such a scene never existed. Even though it is evident what is logically required, the difficulty of making a stylistically satisfying reconstruction of the missing middle suggests that something other than a mere excision of material is involved.[21] More likely, what we have is no more and no less than what the author of the whole book of Job wrote. But the prose tale has been crafted in order to create something analogous to an optical illusion. Just as there are some drawings in which the eye can "see" a line that is not drawn on the page but that is necessary to complete the figure, so readers can perceive the outlines of the missing middle of the prose tale. The illusion created, that what has been displaced is the mirror image of the extant dialogue between Job and his friends, is a part of the overall strategy of the book.

Some historical critics who think the prose tale was an extant story reproduced by the author of the book of Job make a slightly different argument. According to this hypothesis,[22] neither the friends nor a theophany are part of the "actual" prose tale. Rather the first part of the story would have consisted simply of the two tests of Job (1:1–22; 2:1–10). Following the end of the second test, when the narrator says that "in all this Job did not sin with his lips," the story would have continued with the concluding scene in which Job's family comes to console him and his fortunes are restored (42:11–17). The narrative introduction of the friends was made necessary only with the decision to incorporate a dialogue cycle into the prose tale. Thus, 2:11–13 and 42:7–10 are the "hinges" by means of which the dialogue is attached to the prose tale.

One can never know, of course, whether this analysis of an independent prose tale is in fact historically correct. However one understands the prose tale— with or without the friends, as an originally independent story or as an artificial fragment created by the author of the whole book—it is sufficiently intact or mendable to be subject to an inquiry concerning its moral imagination. A more serious issue, however, is raised by the construction of the book as a whole. The book does not present the prose tale on its own but fragments it and juxtaposes it to the poetic materials. This act of juxtaposition will have effects on perception. Just as red surrounded by other colors looks different from red by itself, so the prose tale is perceived differently because of its juxtaposition to the dialogues. Most recent final-form readings have insisted on the importance of reading the prose tale in relation to the dialogues and vice versa. I agree. In contrast to the literary or deconstructive readings, however, which read everything on a single plane of aesthetic or propositional meaning in order to assess the text's (in)coherence, the polyphonic reading I am attempting requires a different, two-stage practice. The first stage is deliberately to prescind from the knowledge of the complex structure of the book in order to elicit with as much care as possible the distinctive moral imaginations of the prose tale and the dialogue independently. Only when that stage has been carried out is one in a position to appreciate more fully how the juxtaposition of these different "moral colors" creates a dialogic whole.

Keeping Company with the Prose Tale: Evocations of Genre

If one wishes to "keep company" with the prose tale of Job in order to perceive the distinctive type of moral imagination it offers, one needs to attend to two things: the genre of the story and the details of the narrative. An inquiry into genre is necessary, since genre is itself a form of perception, a way of configuring an aspect of a human situation (so Medvedev) and often integrally connected with particular conceptions of virtue (so MacIntyre). Because genre is a social convention, recognition of genre facilitates the reader's provisional surrender to the world of the text. That is to say, a particular genre naturalizes certain kinds of actions, plot structures, character types, and values that might provoke different reactions in other types of discourse. Thus, genre is part of the rhetorical strategy of the text, as it attempts to establish its moral claims. Nevertheless, it is not possible to grasp the moral imagination of a particular text simply by analyzing its generic type. One must always keep in mind that stories participate in genres rather than being defined by them. Thus, the means by which one grasps the specific "offer" of a story can only come from a detailed reading.

Virtually every critic recognizes in the highly stylized narrative of the prose tale the marks of a story meant to be experienced as a "type" of tale, but the critical discussion about what type that is has been vexing. For a long time it has been customary to refer to the prose story of Job as a folktale. Such a designation, although instructive in some respects, is also problematic. For one thing, *folktale* is not a genre designation but a broader category that refers to a variety of stories in a culture that contain traditional characters and situations. To speak of *folktale genres* one would need to speak more specifically of trickster tales or hero stories or the like.[23] Although one can identify certain folkloristic character types and motifs in biblical narrative in general (e.g., the younger brother who supplants the elder, the courtier who rises from a lowly state, the impossible question, the grateful dead), it is less clear that the Job of the prose tale is a typical character in that sense, or that his situation is one of those recurring typical situations (i.e., whether the "patient sufferer" is such a folkloristic motif). Job himself is often referred to as a type of the "righteous sufferer" or "emblematic sufferer,"[24] but that designation properly refers to the figure of Job as represented in the poetic sections of the book and the similar figures known from various poetic genres in Mesopotamian literature.[25] It does not provide a parallel to the character of the prose tale.

Ezekiel's reference to Job (Ezek 14:14) might be invoked to argue that Job as exemplary righteous person belongs to folk tradition. Ezekiel groups together the three figures of Noah, Dan'el, and Job on the basis of the power of their righteousness to save "sons and daughters."[26] From the stories as we know them, however, that motif is not the defining character of each. Though Noah's righteousness does save his sons and their wives, that consequence is not high-

lighted by the narrative. The narrative of Dan'el, as known from Ugaritic literature, does concern the father/son relationship, beginning with the problem of
Dan'el's childlessness. It also describes Dan'el's search for the body of his son
Aqhat, killed at the command of the goddess Anat, but the text breaks off before it is clear whether Aqhat is returned from death to Dan'el. In the prose
tale of Job, Job's sons and daughters are in a certain sense killed, not saved,
because of his righteousness. One might, however, link Ezekiel's reference to
the scene of Job's sacrificing on behalf of his children, "in case they have sinned
and cursed God in their hearts" (1:5). Nevertheless, this episode figures in the
text as illustrative of Job's piety, not as a focal issue. One could debate the status of the connection Ezekiel makes. In my opinion it is more likely an ad hoc
grouping of legendary characters for his own specific rhetorical argument, not
the sort of recurrent motif that would warrant an entry in the Stith-Thompson
index. Attempts to locate a Job-type figure in the traditional literatures of other
cultures have not established the existence of a folktale pattern or folk character of which Job is simply the Israelite representative.[27] To be sure, the figure
of Job "the patient sufferer" does eventually enter into folk culture, as the
references of the book of James in the first century and Bishop Theodore of
Mopsuestia in the fourth century make clear.[28] But the question remains whether
that tradition is derived from the canonical book of Job or from an earlier and
independent type of story about Job the patient sufferer. Though they may have
existed, one cannot simply take for granted that there were stories of patient
and righteous sufferers throughout the ancient Near East and that the Job story
is simply one instantiation of that folk character. Thus, it is not clear that the
term "folktale" is in that strict sense applicable to the prose story.

What most people have in mind, however, when they refer to the prose story
of Job in relation to folktales are impressions about the style of the story and
a claim about its social location. The features of style include the story's linguistic simplicity, the naive and anthropomorphic representation of God, the
extensive use of repetition, the nondigressive style, the setting of the story
"long ago and far away," the exaggeration of character and plot, the round
and symbolic numbers, the happy ending, and so forth. These features do
have something in common with the stylistic characteristics of folktales. As Susan
Niditch notes, "One salient trait of traditional literature is patterned repetition.
The repetition takes many forms as symbols, words, syntax, elements of content, structures, and thoughts recur in a profound economy of expression and
density of emphasis."[29] When compared with other Hebrew literature exhibiting folkloristic traits, however, the patterned repetition in Job appears dramatically exaggerated.[30] The Job tale may be alluding to conventions of traditional
storytelling, but the apparent artfulness in its "perfecting" of the trait of repetition (and other features of traditional storytelling) makes it problematic to see
the prose tale simply as an un-self-conscious instance of traditional storytelling.[31]

Those who refer to the prose as a folktale also often intend a claim that unites stylistic with social analysis: a contrast of the naive with the sophisticated, the folk with the learned. They see in the two styles incorporated in the book of Job the voice of the folk played off against the voice of a learned poet. Although unexamined romantic assumptions may be involved in such claims as they appear in commentaries, such a reaction is not simply a modern one. Theodore of Mopsuestia (late fourth–early fifth century C.E.) said as much when he dismissed the canonical book of Job as mere paraded learning, inferior to the oral story popularly told by Jews and others.[32] Since there is evidence that the dialogue participates in a specifically learned scribal genre (see chapter 3), there is some merit in supposing that the contrasting styles within the book invite just the sort of social analysis of style and genre that Theodore made between the canonical book as a whole (dominated by the poetic dialogue) and the popular stories he knew. What both Theodore and many of the early historical critics overlooked, however, was the possibility that a text may invoke naive style without being a naive piece of work. That is the insight of several recent critics who, drawing attention to the prose tale's subtle artistry, have suggested that it be seen as pseudonaive.[33]

While the prose tale of Job does appear to allude to and play with folk traditions and style, what is left unaccounted for is its strong didacticism. In the most sustained study of the genre of the prose tale, Hans-Peter Müller has suggested that it be seen specifically as a didactic tale, a *weisheitliche Lehrerzählung.*[34] Such tales, Müller claims, are character-based stories in which the ethical quality of the main character is critical. The action of the story provides some sort of antagonist for the hero, or at least contrasting figures who represent the opposite of the hero's virtue. Helper figures often appear to assist the hero. Significantly, in this type of story something happens to the hero that appears to be out of joint with the cultural affirmation of the moral values the hero represents. The moral coherency of the world is threatened. Thus, the hero is a suffering hero whose virtue is proved through the way he or she deals with conflict. The declining action serves to confirm the virtue represented by the hero, as virtue and the world order are again realigned. The reward of the hero often concludes the story.

Although Müller constructs his study from an intertextual comparison of a number of stories that have certain of these characteristics (e.g., Joseph, Tobit, Esther, Daniel, Ahiqar, as well as Job), it is evident that the Job tale functions as the template for the genre in his analysis.[35] Müller's study is quite sophisticated, and he is aware of the fluidity of the relation of particular texts to generic forms,[36] yet the prose tale of Job emerges suspiciously like a "pure form" in his analysis. Whereas other narratives fit the generic description more (Tobit, Daniel) or less (Joseph, Esther), only Job fits exactly. It would be a mistake simply to criticize Müller's study as flawed by too great a dependence on the Job tale as normative model. Generic patterns similar to the one he describes do exist cross-culturally.[37] Indeed, the conformity of the Job story to this "ideal type" may say less about some defect in Müller's method than about the rhetoric of the tale itself. As with the comparison to folktale style, so here the Job story appears to exaggerate or "perfect" certain characteristics that are part of the generic repertoire, so that the story becomes a hyperexample of the genre.

There remains, however, a schematic quality that is not illumined by reference either to folktales or to the repertoire of didactic stories Müller invokes. Perhaps by means of these aspects of its style, the Job tale also alludes to another related genre—the type of prophetic example story one finds in the little narrative known as "Nathan's parable" (2 Sam 12:1–14). Although the scale of the two narratives is quite different, stylistic similarities are striking. Both share an affinity for an exaggeratedly simple narrative style, schematic characters arranged in contrasting pairs, verbal repetition, exaggerated action, and even the same syntactical structure for the opening line of the narrative ("a man there was in the land of Uz"; "two men there were in a certain city"). Both attempt to make a serious moral point. In the Talmud, the anonymous authority who argues that Job is not a historical figure but a *mashal* explicitly compares the story of Job with Nathan's parable (b. Baba Batra 16b). Although there is certainly an affinity between the didactic tale and the prophetic example story, the didactic tale serves more generally for entertainment and edification rather than "diagnosis" of a particular situation.

Based on these considerations, I would describe the generic affinities of the Job prose tale as follows. The Job tale appears to be best understood as a type of didactic tale, specifically a story of character and virtue (= Müller's *weisheitliche Lehrerzählung*), which also evokes certain aspects of the prophetic example story and of folktale style.

The Moral Imagination of Didactic Literature

If one locates the prose tale primarily in relation to didactic literature, the question must be raised: What kind of moral perception is privileged by such a type of literature? By what means does it represent its values? Didactic literature has not been a particularly popular narrative form in the modern period, and its popularity with literary critics is considerably less than with the public at large. Consequently, few studies of the features of such narratives exist. One exception to this neglect, however, is Susan Rubin Suleiman's *Authoritarian Fiction: The Ideological Novel as a Literary Genre*. As the subtitle suggests, her focus is on a type of realist novel. She situates her discussion, however, within the broader context of didactic narrative, including parables, fables, and example stories throughout western culture. Thus, many of her observations are pertinent to the value commitments of didactic literature in general.

Perhaps the most obvious thing one can say about didactic narrative is that it is deeply rhetorical. Didactic stories are instruments of persuasion that directly attempt to form their readers by recruiting them to certain beliefs and shaping their attitudes and behaviors. Suleiman suggests that didactic fiction be understood as a type of utopian project, since its authors undertake to change behaviors by telling stories.[38] Even if utopian in this regard, didactic fiction is also realist, in the philosophical if not the literary sense, in that it posits a congruency between the world of the text and the world of the reader. What is true in the text is true about reality. The world often is a confusing place, where it is difficult to perceive truth. In the story, however, truth is made accessible, and the saving knowledge of that truth can be taken back into the world as attitude and action.

While it is common to think of didactic literature as having a socially conservative bent, Suleiman correctly asserts that it is not necessarily either conservative or radical. But whatever social ends a particular didactic story or ideological novel serves, it has a necessarily authoritarian relationship to meaning. Within the world of didactic narrative, truth is neither plural nor elusive nor contestable but is unitary, unambiguous, and absolute. Voices of authority, clearly marked within the text, convey truth to the presumptively compliant reader. Such literature, Sulieman suggests, expresses a characteristic "repressive righteousness."[39] It is repressive in the sense that it attempts to monopolize truth by resisting the possibility of plural reading, of alternatives to its own law. It is righteous in the sense that it deeply believes in the goodness of its values and thus in the propriety of its attempt to establish authority over the reader.[40]

These characteristics make didactic fiction a consummate example of monologic writing. Even if opposing ideologies are represented in the same work, one will be judged correct and the other(s) discredited. Such narratives can also be recognized as examples of what Eco calls "closed texts," in which the model reader's role is carefully inscribed within the text, and narrative devices and discourse are constructed in order to "[pull] the reader along a predetermined path, carefully displaying their effects so as to arouse pity or fear, excitement or depression at the due place and at the right moment."[41] Though such texts may in fact be read according to a quite different set of codes, a large part of the pleasure derived from the formula fiction to which Eco refers is sharing in the conventions that are repeated with little variation in text after text. As Suleiman similarly observes, the conventions of didactic literature assume a compliant reader, never a rebellious or even an indifferent one. Though an actual reader may refuse such a role, Suleiman notes that such a reader "no longer reads the work *as fiction*" but as a failed attempt at manipulation.[42]

As closed texts with a resolutely rhetorical purpose, didactic stories employ a variety of narrative devices to establish their authoritarian relation to truth. Perhaps the most characteristic is the construction of the narrator as a supremely authoritative voice. Typically omniscient, the narrator "'speaks with the voice of Truth' and makes explicit judgments."[43] Often, too, there is a character who serves as the correct interpreter of meaning and whose judgments are authoritative in much the same way as the narrator's. Indeed, didactic fiction tends to be a "talkative" genre in which actions are doubled by interpretive commentary.[44] Borrowing a phrase from Roland Barthes, Suleiman describes the discourse of such literature as one in which "meaning is excessively named."[45]

What Suleiman refers to is more than just the tendency of didactic fiction to state the moral of the story. More significantly, the rhetoric of didactic narrative is based on redundancy. As information theory has shown, redundancy in a message reduces the amount of information transmitted but increases the likelihood of correct reception. Suleiman develops a nearly exhaustive typology of types of redundancy that operate both at the level of story and at the level of narration.[46] Several of these types of redundancy are techniques employed in the prose narrative of Job. For example, the same or similar events may happen to a single character more than once. A single character may manifest the same qualities throughout the story. Several characters may have the same function. Several characters may pronounce the same interpretive commentary or a single character may pronounce the same interpretive commentary more than once. The commentaries of certain characters may be consistently confirmed by events (or consistently disconfirmed). Thus, even if a particular action or event were ambiguous or invited plural reading, the structure of redundancy eliminates ambiguity and adjudicates between alternative readings.

Complementing the technique of redundancy is the tendency of didactic fiction to eliminate superfluous details that are not relevant to the thesis of the work.[47] The presence of such details would both distract from the message and might provide a foothold for readings in opposition to the authority structure of the didactic story. This impulse to eliminate superfluous detail is typically characteristic of shorter didactic fiction and present to a remarkable degree in the prose tale of Job.

Unlike the techniques of privileged interpretive voices and structures of redundancy, which operate in much the same way in virtually all didactic literature, plot may play a variety of roles in relation to the establishment of meaning and the recruitment of the reader. In short instructional fables the plot may simply illustrate how the world works. That the actions and outcome "ring true" in the narrative world of the fable facilitates the transfer of the paradigm to the reader's life world. Similarly, the plots of moral example stories recruit their readers by demonstrating the eventual consequences of certain types of behavior. The coherency of such a "right fit" within the moral world of the story enhances the sense that what is right must in some sense also be true.

The plots of longer, more developed didactic literature naturally function in more complex ways. In the ideological novels she examined, Suleiman noted two plot models. One is the apprenticeship model, in which the main character moves from error to truth; the other is a confrontation model, in which "right" values struggle against "wrong" ones. In the apprenticeship model the reader (who is likely already a true believer) is invited to recapitulate the "process of persuasion."[48] In the confrontation model the reader is expected to desire the triumph of right values over wrong ones, the triumph of the hero over the blocking characters. Even if the reader is not already enlisted by the values of the text, the habit of identification with the apprentice and the hero in such plot structures provides a powerful rhetorical incentive to cooperate with the program of the text.

The characteristics of didactic fiction are so much at odds with critical modern and postmodern tastes that one must reflect on the desires such fictions stimulate and offer to satisfy. Suleiman states the issue succinctly: "It appeals to the need for certainty, stability, and unity that is one of the elements of the human psyche; it affirms absolute truths, absolute values."[49] This description makes it clearer why didactic literature often appeals in times of rapid social change, when an old order is under stress and seeks to reassert the authority of its values in the face of what appears to be a chaotic cultural situation. Such is the basis of the remarkable popularity of such books as William Bennett's *The Book of Virtues* and *The Moral Compass*. Didactic fiction, however, is also a staple of nascent or marginal religious or political movements, whether radical or reactionary. Since such movements are at odds with the dominant culture, the values and truths that provide their identity cannot be taken for granted. Didactic fiction provides a sheltered space of meaning where those values can be experienced as the "self-evident truths" of the fictional world. The novels of the French political Left that Suleiman analyzes would be examples of this sort of didactic fiction, as also, in her opinion, would be the parables of Jesus.

Didactic fiction has a significant place in children's literature for much the same reasons. Moral community is extended intergenerationally through the socialization of children into a shared set of values. Although much of contemporary children's literature is not as overtly didactic as the novels Suleiman investigates, it is still often exemplary literature. The values of sharing, compassion, courage, obeying parents, and so forth are clearly modeled by characters the child is encouraged to imitate. And if the explicit statement of the moral is currently out of fashion, the resolution of the plot leaves no doubt about the moral to be learned and applied. Though books that self-consciously address the moral formation of children through narrative have tended to come from the cultural "soft right,"[50] that is not entirely the case.[51] In actual practice a broad spectrum of values is represented in children's didactic fiction, as the conflict over children's books concerning attitudes toward sexuality and nontraditional families attests.

The instance of children's literature is significant for what it suggests about didactic fiction in general. Suleiman maintains that didactic literature "infantilizes the reader" by serving as the interpreter of the meaning of everything that provides libidinal satisfaction for the reader.[52] The subject position that didactic narratives offer the reader of whatever age is that of a child. What one receives in exchange is the "paternal assurance" provided by the text. This insight helps both to account for the powerful appeal of didactic literature when it is successful, as well as the strong element of hostility toward it. By evoking the parent-child relationship, didactic literature addresses readers' never extinguished desire for security and trust in an older, wiser, benevolent figure who will teach them reliable knowledge of the world. The characteristic narrative simplicity offers the childlike pleasures of easy mastery, the narrative equivalent of "nursery food." The structured response, the predetermined path along which the narrative leads one, involves not just negotiating the narrative per se but includes the moral convergence of the reader with the values of the text. Thus, the pleasures of the text include the pleasure of agreement, of having one's "own" judgment be confirmed by an authoritative voice. Learning the lesson involves the dual satisfaction of pleasing one's "parents" and now of being in possession of what one trusts is reliable knowledge of the world.

Just as the implicit parent-child relationship helps underwrite the appeal of didactic literature, it also is the basis of potential resistance. Children do not wish to remain children always but find ways of rebelling against an authority that seems too controlling of their desire to meet the world on their own terms. So didactic literature provokes hostile responses from those who find in its excessively sheltered world of meaning the threat of perpetual moral immaturity.

The questions posed at the beginning of this section concerned the type of moral perception privileged by didactic literature and the form of its moral imagination. Obviously, in attempting to talk about such a broad range of literature, I will oversimplify many observations. Nevertheless, certain fundamental features do seem clear. First, didactic literature is committed to the perception of truth as unitary and absolute. Thus, it does not value ambiguity in situations or doubt in persons as possibly positive features in a moral landscape. Its commitment to the clear distinction between good and evil, truth and falsehood gives it a tendency toward a binary view of the world. Its heroes will not be tragic ones torn between equally compelling values but those who perceive, or eventually come to see, the one true way.

Second, didactic literature has a high regard for authority figures as the voice of truth. The most important of these is the teller of the tale, who serves as authoritative teacher. Within the story as it is told, other characters may echo this role. Truth is not simply something one figures out on one's own or receives in an epiphanic moment, though such experiences may play a supporting role. Rather, truth is mediated in a personal and hierarchically structured relationship. In the moral imagination of didactic literature, to know the truth is to be joined to a community constituted by that shared meaning. More specifically, the submerged metaphor of parent-child that informs the relationship between text and reader gives the authority of the text an air of self-evident justification and benevolence. Moral maturity within this perspective would consist of receptively internalizing the values of the authorizing voices, not becoming an autonomous and critical moral agent.

Third, principle, not situation, is morally privileged. All those things that Martha Nussbaum finds so ethically significant in the "finely and richly aware" characters of a Henry James novel, whose goodness is utterly irreducible to rules, are decidedly absent from the moral imagination of didactic stories. Here, whether or not the moral of the story is explicitly stated or not, it could be. Truth is propositional, and good and successful conduct is in the broadest sense a matter of knowing and applying the rules, that is, the fundamental principles that are not dependent on context.

Fourth, the moral imagination of didactic literature prizes coherency. Aesthetically, this value is expressed in the predilection for redundancy and the elimination of extraneous detail. It also underwrites the resolutely monologic discourse of didactic fiction. Multiple voices not subject to a central controlling voice would threaten such coherency. Much is invested in simply not seeing what does not fit, hence what Suleiman refers to as the "repressive righteousness" of didactic fiction. Situations (and even the world itself) are represented in a strongly schematic fashion, so that the pattern of meaning is clear and unmistakable.

I fear I have come close to damning didactic literature, and with it the prose tale of Job, in the eyes of my own readers. But such is not my intent. Didactic literature is an important element in moral discourse. Its genius for simplicity, clarity, moral explicitness, and confident assurance enables it to do certain things in the moral formation of individuals and societies that other forms of moral discourse cannot. Didactic literature is capable of presenting powerful and memorable narratives that encapsulate something essential about moral life and the fundamental values that undergird the more complex decisions one must make in real life.

What makes a discussion of didactic literature so fraught with anxiety, however, is that characteristic elements of the moral imagination of didactic literature are embraced by some persons as the template for culture in general. The authoritarian construction of meaning, which may be both useful and enjoyable in a particular parable, fable, exemplum, story, or novel, takes on a troubling significance if it is seen as the privileged form of moral discourse. The factors within modernity and postmodernity that threaten those aspects of the psyche addressed by didactic literature (i.e., the need for unity, stability, and certainty) are well known. Nevertheless, to write large the authoritarian structures of meaning of the didactic story is to pay a very high price for psychic reassurance.

Given this background of contemporary cultural conflict over the relationship of authority and meaning, many modern readers come to the didactic form of the prose tale of Job with considerable ambivalence. This is, in my opinion, one of the reasons so much recent literature on the prose tale attempts to make the case that it is actually a slyly subversive text.[53] Such interpretations make the story "culturally correct" for critical tastes. Many of these readings are highly accomplished and truly answerable to the text, though they accomplish their interpretations by reading against generic conventions or by implicitly arguing that the author himself was subverting the norms of genre. Without wishing to argue that these readings are wrong, I do wish to claim that a rich and good reading of the story, one that reveals it to be surprisingly capable of challenging critical readers, is possible by reading with rather than against its generic conventions. The hermeneutics of hospitality that I extend to the prose tale does not amount to a complete surrender to its claims, however, since I situate those claims within the larger structure of the polyphonic text of the book as a whole.

Moral Imagination in the Didactic Narratives of the Hebrew Bible

In the previous section, I focused attention on those aspects of a certain moral imagination that could be deduced from the generic characteristics of didactic narrative per se. By isolating them one runs the risk of overemphasizing and distorting the significance of those features, since in actual stories broad generic features form only part of the much richer construction of value that the whole of the story provides. Between the abstraction of didactic literature in general and the uniqueness of the particular story, however, lies the middle ground: the repertoire of didactic stories common to a particular discursive community. In this section I wish to return briefly to Müller's grouping of didactic narratives in the Hebrew Bible to see how they share aspects of a common moral imagination. Such an inquiry has to be conducted with a light touch. Many of the stories' assumptions will be common to Israelite religious culture in general. Furthermore, one must remember that genre is not a matter of telling stories "by the numbers." While each of the narratives in Müller's grouping evokes elements of didactic narrative, it also participates in other genres and narrative conventions and uses its invocations of genre to accomplish a variety of rhetorical ends. Nevertheless, one can tease out certain aspects that these stories share and that they use to construct a moral world.

One notable feature of these Hebrew narratives is their focus on character and virtue. Many other ways exist for organizing moral reflection, of course. The rhetoric of Deuteronomy, which combines exhortation and legal prescription in a narrative-historical contexts, explores the question "How should one live?" with a quite different set of resources. But the didactic story of character privileges the events of an individual's life and the exercise of virtue within them as the locus for reflection.

Although the stories have a serious purpose, these narratives of character never forget that they have entertainment value. The stories take place in exotic locales (Nineveh, Babylon, Susa, Egypt, Uz) and make use of local color. Just as the settings are extraordinary, so also are the heroes, who include "the richest man in the East," a vizier of Egypt, the queen of Persia, high ministers of the Babylonian court, and the chief purchasing agent for Sennacherib. But if the characters are exceptional, the virtues they embody are ordinary ones: charity (Tobit), observance of the religious law (Tobit, Daniel and his friends), piety (Tobit, Job, Daniel), kinship virtues of endogamy, family and ethnic solidarity (Tobit, Esther, Joseph, Job), sexual purity (Joseph, Sarah in Tobit; see also Susanna), courage (Esther, Shadrach, Meshach, Abednego), fidelity to God (Shadrach, Meshach, Abed-Nego), humility (Nebuchadnezzar, ultimately), and so forth.[54] By making these glamorous figures the representatives of common virtues, those virtues are strongly recommended. Although he was speaking about the role of character-based example stories in the moral development of children, Bruno Bettelheim noted that the question "Whom do I want to be like?" is more important than the question "Do I want to be good?"[55] The emotional attachment readers can develop toward figures such as Esther, Daniel, Tobit, or Job is instrumental in forming an attachment to the virtues they represent.[56]

The heroes of these stories are not simply characterized by particular virtues in some passive way. Rather, virtues come into focus as active elements of the story in events often presented as moments of decision under trying circumstances (e.g., Tobit's decision to bury the dead, Daniel's decision not to eat the king's food, the three friends' decision not to bow down to the statue of gold, Job's decision to respond to loss with words of piety, Joseph's decision to flee from Potiphar's wife). Virtues are not abstract values but elements of practice, integrated into a person's character through the concrete exercise of that virtue.

Perhaps surprisingly, the *acquisition* of virtue is seldom the focus, despite the fact that the topic is of considerable interest in the didactic genres of wisdom admonition and proverbial saying. In the didactic narrative tradition, however, the hero typically already possesses the qualities of character that will be the focus of the story. The possibility for an interest in character development and moral growth is present in Esther and Joseph, since these characters do appear quite different at the beginning and end of the stories. But the narratives do not develop the process of their transformation with particular attention. What effects the transformation largely happens offstage. Where attention is given to moral development, it is more often in connection with secondary characters. In the Joseph story, how Judah develops a virtuous character is illustrated through

the Tamar episode (Genesis 38), with the results of his mature character subsequently demonstrated in his negotiations with Joseph on behalf of his father (Genesis 43–44). Similarly, the slow and painful moral development of
Nebuchadnezzar in Daniel 1–4 has something of the shape of a *Bildungsroman*.[57]
Judah and Nebuchadnezzar share an important function. They are oppositional
figures whose lack of virtue contributes to the problems of the hero. Their acquisition of virtue is part of the resolution of the conflict.

Notwithstanding these occasional elements of what Suleiman calls the apprenticeship model, the acquisition of virtue is not the major focus of the plot in relation to the main character in Hebrew didactic narratives. The focus is rather on
the testing of virtue. That virtue will be tested in life is the implicit assertion of the
plot of this genre. In some cases circumstances create the moment of decision
(Esther; Daniel), but in others the motif of an intentional test is part of the construction of the narrative (Job 1:9–12; 2:4–6; Tob 12:14). The intentional test as
a narrative device suggests a certain concern about the status of virtue. How does
one know if a person is truly virtuous? Such a test appears explicitly in the Joseph
story, when Joseph tests his brothers' family solidarity. In that situation, of course,
reason existed to doubt their character. Yet the motif of the test of virtue of characters who have given no outward sign of moral weakness (Tobit; cf. Abraham),
suggests a more general concern in the culture with the proof of virtue. The issue
becomes self-consciously thematic in Job. Whether as a result of circumstances or
of an intentional test, virtue increases in moral value as it is exercised in the face
of difficult circumstances. Thus, in these exemplary tales the reader practices by
identification the patterns of proper response and affirms the importance of the
exercise of virtue regardless of consequences.

Despite the dramatizations of such an absolute imperative to act rightly, the
imagination of these tales is neither stoic nor tragic, as one might find in Greek
literature. The moral world of virtue is not in conflict with the values of the
cosmos but is ultimately supported by it. The vision of these tales is comic, as
lovers are united (Tobias and Sarah in Tobit), fortunes are restored (Tobit and
Job), blocking characters are reconciled and integrated (Nebuchadnezzar in
Daniel, the brothers in the Joseph story), and song and celebration occur (Tobit's
song of thanksgiving, Job's naming of his beautiful new daughters, the institu-
tion of the holiday of Purim in Esther).[58] The Hebrew didactic tales are morally
optimistic. Virtue can and does exist. The world is a reliable place after all. The
claim the stories make about virtue is stronger than just an affirmation of the
moral coherency of the world. These happy endings do not just happen, but
are brought about precisely because virtue was exercised in adversity. Thus, virtue is not simply a feature of human character but an active force playing an
important role in the creation and maintenance of a good world.

Implicit in the optimism of these stories is also a claim about moral knowledge.
One can distinguish right from wrong, good from evil, without confusion or

ambiguity. Moral judgments are straightforward and do not require elaborate qualification. Such claims are made by the content but are also supported by the aesthetics of the storytelling style.[59] One might say that the aesthetic correlate of the claim about the accessibility of reliable moral knowledge is linguistic and narrative clarity. These didactic tales create a narrative world that is transparent, coherent, and so well marked that it is virtually impossible to lose one's way. Plots are predictable. There is no chance that Tobit will remain blind or that Tobias will die on his wedding night. (To compose the story in such a fashion would be to create a parody of the didactic tale.) Characters, too, are simply painted and predictable. That Shadrach, Meshach, and Abednego might commit apostasy when faced with the fiery furnace is literally unthinkable within the narrative world of these didactic tales. Just as characters are reliable, so they are without shadows of ambiguous motivation. The complex and morally troubling characters of David, Absalom, and Joab cannot occupy the narrative world of the didactic tale.[60]

If the difference between right and wrong is transparent, that is not the case with the context within which virtue is practiced. Repeatedly in these stories the exercise of virtue is complexly related to a divine intentionality, not known by the actors. Job never learns of his role in the resolution of a quarrel in heaven. Tobit only belatedly learns of his own test and the role of his decision to bury the dead in God's providential working out of a solution to Sarah's distress (Tob 12:11–15). Similarly, Joseph grasps the existence of a hidden divine intentionality behind his misfortune only at the end of the narrative (Gen 50:20). A hint of self-consciousness about this motif may occur in Esther in Mordecai's comment "Who knows? Perhaps you have come to royal dignity for just such a time as this" (Esth 4:14b). Yet the form of the rhetorical question reminds one that even though virtue is an active force which may play a role in the accomplishment of larger purposes, one has to act without knowing that context. In the Daniel stories, the hidden intentionality of God is developed as a central theme, and the interaction between the exercise of virtue and the achievement of divine purpose is strongly marked, as the rigorous fidelity of Daniel and his three friends plays a critical role in the kings' recognition of divine sovereignty.

This chapter began with a quotation from Martha Nussbaum that referred to the capacity of narrative to represent "patterns of possibility—of choice, and circumstance, and the interaction between choice and circumstance—that turn up in human lives with such a persistence that they must be regarded as our possibilities."[61] As this brief overview has suggested, the focal point of such patterns in the Hebrew didactic narratives is the character of the individual enacted in moments of decision. These moments are constructed as starkly binary choices between one action that would embody a virtue and another action that would repudiate it. In the moral vision of these stories, for an action to be truly good, it must be undertaken without regard to circumstances. Moral virtues operate as absolutes. The appeal of such a perspective is easy to grasp. Its radical clarity offers certainty about moral decision making that a contextual approach cannot match. Moreover, within such a moral imagination virtue is a transcendental value. Even if one perishes in the act of choosing the good, something of inestimable importance has been saved, namely, one's identification with the good (Dan 3:16–18). Yet the stories uniformly do not allow the heroes to perish. This is not out of a naive misperception of the world. The violence represented within these stories acknowledges the real power possessed by forces inimical to virtue. But the happy endings function as a narrative metaphor for the ultimate moral coherency of the world. To embrace virtue is to align with something that is in the end more powerful than evil.

The Moral Imagination of the Joban Prose Tale

One can expect the Joban prose tale to exhibit the typical characteristics of didactic literature in general and of the Hebrew didactic tale of character more specifically. The real interest, however, lies not in pointing out those typical features for their own sake but in seeing how this particular text puts those characteristics to work for a specific purpose. Just as the Daniel cycle adapts the genre of the didactic narrative for exploring theological issues made acute by conditions of diaspora, so the author of the prose tale of Job, as I will argue below, adapts the genre of the didactic narrative for purposes of a speculative, almost philosophical investigation that is carried out both in propositional terms and through the aesthetics of the text. The Job tale ambitiously undertakes to expose and resolve a hidden contradiction within the religious ideology of ancient Israel. Thus, even though within the bounds of its own discourse the prose tale is a thoroughly monologic text, it is a part of a larger cultural conversation.

The way a text begins is a crucial element in establishing its "friendship offering" and the desires it will elicit and undertake to satisfy. The text in question may later complicate its offer, but the beginning sets the terms on which the community of two is to be initially constituted. Both Booth and Nussbaum illustrate how distinctive these offers can be by setting side by side the opening lines of a variety of different texts. Consider Booth's set:

> In the beginning was the Word. And the Word was with God. And the Word was God.
>
> > The Gospel According to Saint John

> This is the saddest story I have ever heard. We had known the Ashburnhams for nine seasons of the town of Nauheim with an extreme intimacy—or, rather, with an acquaintanceship as loose and easy and yet as close as a good glove's with your hand. My wife and I . . .
>
> > *The Good Soldier*, Ford Madox Ford

Ours is essentially a tragic age, so we refuse to take it tragically. The cataclysm has happened, we are among the ruins, we start to build up new little habits, to have new little hopes. It is rather hard work: there is now no smooth road into the future: but we go round, or scramble over the obstacles. We've got to live, no matter how many skies have fallen.

Lady Chatterley's Lover, D. H. Lawrence

Driving to the Goodwood races the Duke of Wydeminster thought with satisfaction that his team of horses was the most outstanding that he had ever owned.

Once again, he told himself, he had been proved right, having bought them as foals at a sale held by one of his friends, when the majority of buyers had not considered them worth a second glance.

The Duke however with his expert eye . . .

The Storms of Love 1875, Barbara Cartland

This is an unusual story about the way that I lost my virginity. When I was nineteen . . .

"Nerd Without Nerve," *Penthouse* "Forum"

As Booth summarizes, these stories offer "spiritual salvation (the gospel); a tragic experience (Ford); wisdom about life in our time (Lawrence); true love and horses (Cartland); sexual thrills (*Penthouse*)."[62] If one sets alongside these the opening verses of the book of Job, the offer it makes stands out clearly.

A man there was in the land of Uz; Job was his name. That man was blameless and upright, one who feared God and turned from evil. And there were born to him seven sons and three daughters. And his property included seven thousand sheep and three thousand camels and five hundred yoke of oxen and five hundred she asses and many servants. That man was the greatest of all the people in the east.

The immediate foregrounding of a character and his virtues (cf. Tob 1:3) establishes the offer of a story that attempts to do us good by providing an answer to the question "Whom do I want to be like?" The sequenced description, which moves from good character to large family, great wealth, and high reputation, also suggests that the story intends to recommend and reconfirm the cultural assumption that virtue finds a reward in prosperity. Our desires to do good and to experience good are succinctly elicited by the text.

Booth's question about desires addressed by the text, however, requires a more nuanced reading of these opening verses and their relation to the rest of the story. Although the desire to imitate a model of virtue is assumed by these lines, they also address and seek to satisfy a different sort of desire that can be grasped by moving beyond the content and considering the textures of language in the story. The language of this narrative is simple and accessible. Sentences are uncomplicated, words familiar. Consequently, one might follow Suleiman's suggestion that such language stimulates and offers to satisfy our desire for the psychic security of the child addressed by a kindly parental figure.

As important as the simplicity is the beauty of the language, a beauty that inheres in the balance and symmetry. The short and rhythmic phrases of the first verse beg to be read aloud. What makes them so pleasurable is the patterned repetition: three two-word phrases (*'îš hāyāh bĕ'ereṣ 'ûṣ 'iyyôb šĕmô*), a three-word phrase (*wĕhāyāh hā'îš hahû'*), then again three two-word phrases (*tām wĕyāšār wirē' 'ĕlōhîm wĕsār mĕrā'*). The parallelism that is so much a part of Hebrew verbal aesthetics is emphatically present in the description of Job's virtues in two balanced pairs of parallel terms ("blameless and upright, one who feared God and turned from evil"). Such linguistic textures do not of themselves have meaning, yet they can acquire an iconic significance in context. This significance becomes clearer in the following verses that speak of Job's children and possessions. Although rhythmic parallelism is present here, too, it is the numbers that signify. As often noted, these are not only round numbers but are also grouped to add up to ten and multiples of ten (seven plus three, seven thousand plus three thousand, five hundred plus five hundred). What they suggest is a world in which everything adds up, a world of coherency and wholeness. This, I would argue, is the most fundamental desire the prose tale elicits and offers to satisfy, the desire for a world that can be experienced as supremely coherent, a world of utterly unbreachable wholeness. As the story will go on to show, the experience of such a world is integrally linked to the practice of a certain kind of virtue.

Although Suleiman notes that all didactic narrative addresses the human need for certainty, stability, and unity, these qualities are seldom embodied so densely in the aesthetics of didactic stories as they are in Job. Symmetry, balance, and symbolic wholeness are not merely characteristics of the opening verses but of the entire narrative. They form a permeating trope, the "figure in the carpet." The story itself is structured in four mirroring episodes, arranged in parallel pairs (1:1–5; 1:6–22; 2:1–10; 42:11–17), which make use of extensive patterns of repetition and correspondence. Thus, the idyllic conditions of the opening scene (1:1–5) correspond to those of the closing scene (42:11–17). The celebratory banquet of the sisters and brothers who are Job's children (1:4) corresponds to the consolatory meal of Job's own sisters and brothers (42:11). The two central episodes, which narrate Job's testing, correspond to one another, the first concerning his possessions and family, the second his body. Structurally, each of the testing episodes consists of two scenes, one in heaven and one on earth, the parallels emphasized by extensive verbal repetition in the scenes set in heaven (1:6–8; 2:1–3a).[63] The use of twofold and fourfold structures, already begun with the two sets of paired terms used to describe Job's virtue, are continued with the fourfold destruction of Job's possessions and the four messengers who recount it (1:14–19), as well as by the doubling of Job's possessions and life span at the end of the story (42:12, 16).

Various other aspects of narrative style contribute to the experience of a world where everything is certain, clear, a unity of coherent meaning. Characters are aligned in contrasting pairs of positive and trustworthy characters (God and Job) and negative and untrustworthy ones (*haśśātān* and Job's wife). Once the plot is set in motion, it unfolds predictably. One should not be surprised that disasters as well as blessings are described with symbolic images of completeness (four messenger reports, signifying total destruction, disease that reaches "from the sole of his foot to the top of his head"). The point is not that good things are represented symmetrically and bad things are not. This trait of the text's language is not related allegorically to meaning. Rather, the trait is itself an icon of an aesthetic imagination that orients itself comprehensively to figures of wholeness. Nevertheless, though disaster may be recounted, both the aesthetics of the text and the moral imagination with which it correlates cannot end with disaster but must encompass the reassertion of wholeness in the resolution of the plot and the idyllic conclusion.

What is iconically represented in the syntax, numerical patterns, and other formal features has to be related to the substantive claims the text makes about the relation of character and world. Initially, the story projects a vision of a world in which goodness and flourishing appear to go together unproblematically. Although the term "blessing" is not used in these opening verses (see, however, v. 10), the descriptive sentences concerning Job's virtues and his condition in the world can be read as a narrative rendering of the wisdom psalms' description of the blessings that attend the one who "fears YHWH." "Happy is everyone who fears YHWH, who walks in his ways. The work of your hands you shall eat; happiness and prosperity will be yours. Your wife will be like a fruitful vine within your house, your children like the shoots of an olive around your table. So is the man blessed who fears YHWH" (Ps 128:1–4; see also Psalm 112). As anyone knows who has read the story before, precisely this conjunction will be scrutinized. The ultimate friendship offering of the text will be to define virtue in relation to a value that encompasses but transcends blessing, a value that comes close to what Dorothee Soelle terms "radical acceptance."[64]

Since this is a didactic story, the words and actions of the main character are some of the most important guides to its values. Although Job's character had been briefly described in the opening words of the book, verses 4–5 provide the narrative example that gives content to that general description. In keeping with the hyperbolic style already established in verses 1–3, Job's scrupulous virtue is represented hyperbolically, as he is shown conducting prophylactic sacrifice for his children's possible sin, though there are no indications such a sin has occurred.[65] But the selection of detail in the development of this scene, as one would expect in the economical style of short didactic fiction, is thematically significant. Its importance is underscored by the narrator's quoting of Job's own words, one of only three times in which this happens. Job identifies his concern: "Perhaps my children have sinned and cursed God in their hearts." He does not say, "Perhaps they have stolen property" or "Perhaps they have committed an act of violence." Job singles out the human stance toward God, particularly as expressed in blessing or curse, as the object of paramount concern. As the wisdom tradition makes "fear of YHWH" the beginning of wisdom, so Job implies it is the beginning of virtue. Just as cursing YHWH could open a breach in the wholeness of the world, so Job's actions serve to make whole any breach. Finally, his words foreshadow what will be the focal issue of the story, whether Job himself will curse God openly.

The euphemistic use of "bless" for "curse" in verse 5 and elsewhere in the prose tale is a puzzling feature. Although attested in other Hebrew narratives (1 Kgs 21:13), it is not a universal scribal convention (see Exod 22:27). Since *bērēk* is used both literally and euphemistically in the narrative, the reader must negotiate the contextually proper meaning in each occurrence, heightening its thematic significance.[66] Moreover, the use of euphemism gives the narrator something of the hyperscrupulous character Job displays. Perhaps most important is the performative significance of barring the word "curse" from the diction of the text. Cursing God quite literally has no place in the linguistic or moral world of the prose tale, for its presence would threaten the harmony upon which its vision is based. The possibility of such cursing is raised (1:5, 11; 2:5) only to be defused (1:5) and rejected (1:22; 2:10), but even in this act of exclusion the word itself is already overwritten, its linguistic place occupied by its opposite.

The world described in the first scene of the prose tale is so orderly and stable that one can scarcely imagine its giving rise to the conflict required to sustain a plot. There are no unhappy families, no megalomaniac kings, no jealous rivals to get the story moving. But narrative requires some conflict, and how conflict is represented is thematically crucial. In the prose tale, conflict arises as a conflict of perception between God and *haśśātān* concerning the nature of Job's virtue. As has long been recognized, God and *haśśātān* are not dualistic opposites, nor is *haśśātān* yet the Satan-with-a-capital-S of later Jewish and Christian literature. Rather, *haśśātān* is the heavenly being charged with keeping an eye on the world and spotting disloyalty or falsity.[67] Thus, his function is ostensibly one of the maintenance of its good order, its wholeness. In another more important sense, *haśśātān* embodies a profoundly destabilizing force as the narrative embodiment of a hermeneutics of suspicion. Appropriately, Gordis quotes Goethe's characterization of Satan as "*der Geist der stets verneint*" ("the spirit who always negates").[68] For *haśśātān*, the transparency of meaning, the ostensible coherency at the heart of the moral imagination of the story is an illusion he is prepared to demystify.

Although the conflict is initially represented as a conflict over Job's character, what is at stake is not individual hypocrisy or venality but the very meaningfulness of the concept of piety. *Haśśātān* has uncovered an ideological contradiction in the religious discourse that, when brought to light, threatens to undermine a fundamental category of that discourse. As this proto-Nietzschean figure says in his clever genealogy of piety, "Does Job fear God for nothing? Have you not hedged him about, and all his house, and everything he possesses? You have blessed the work of his hands, so that his livestock have spread out over the land. But stretch out your hand and touch all that he has, and he will surely curse you to your face" (1:10b–11). Fear of God as an absolute value is contradicted by the practice of blessing. What had been represented as the very image of a coherent and meaningful world in verses 1–3 is now argued to be false consciousness. What really underlies the relationship between the divine and the human is more accurately described as a trade relationship. In the second episode, *haśśātān* will make use of a saying apparently drawn from the marketplace ("skin up to [the value of a] skin") to describe the implicit calculations that underlie what appears as piety.[69] This is not to say that either Job or God perceive what they are doing in such terms. On the contrary, religious ideology ensures that they are not conscious of the true motives that organize their relationship. A hermeneutics of suspicion, if persuasive, performs an unmasking by displacing false consciousness with an account that claims to be the real truth. Once exposed, old categories are emptied of meaning, and a world is destroyed. Most hermeneutics of suspicion remain subject to contestation because they lack a means to verify or falsify their claims. But *haśśātān* is more fortunate, since he can propose the conditions under which his claim will be tested.[70]

In this surprisingly philosophical tale, what is at stake is not simply the testing of a virtue but the testing of the conditions that make this virtue possible. In contrast to many other didactic stories, Job is not simply the hero whose character is tried but the vehicle through whom the resolution of the ideological contradiction will be accomplished. As compelling as *haśśātān*'s challenge appears, the conventions of the didactic story ensure that the hero will meet the challenge. The threat will be discharged, and the initial values and the world to which they belong will be restored, made stronger by the successful negotiation of the test. Thus, the interest of the story is not in whether Job will "curse God"— he will not. The interest rather lies in how Job will articulate a form of piety that persuasively resolves the threat of incoherency, to manifest a world in which piety and blessing exist in complementarity, not mutual subversion.

Within the narrative, Job has no knowledge of the issues as they are formulated in heaven. His actions and words will simply address the situation of his devastation as he experiences and understands it. For the program of the prose tale, however, his answer will not only have to express his own grasp of the meaning of inexplicable devastation but must also resolve the apparent contradiction as *haśśātān* has set it up.

The dramatic focus for the first chapter is scene three, in which the audience knows that "all he has" will be destroyed. The scene opens with a detail that both recollects and foreshadows, the comment that "there was a day when his sons and his daughters were eating and drinking wine in the house of their eldest brother" (1:13). On an ordinary day this event would precede Job's sanctification of his children to keep whole their standing before God in case they had "cursed God in their hearts." Yet on this day the reader knows that the issue is whether Job will curse God to his face. Moreover, the joyous celebration of the children foreshadows the climactic loss Job will suffer. Immediately following this scene setting, Job receives the four overlapping reports from the messengers, who announce the sudden devastation of his cattle, asses, sheep, camels, servants, and, finally, children (1:14–19). Job's first response is nonverbal, a series of five actions. The first four are expressions of grief ("Job rose and tore his robe and shaved his head and fell upon the ground," 1:20). But the last action ("and he worshiped") is sufficient to indicate that Job will not curse God. Yet such actions do not of themselves clarify the moral imagination that would unite grief with worship rather than with curse. Attention turns to Job's words, which bear the weight of rendering persuasive a response that is not self-interpreting.

Although apparently simple, Job's words are anything but that, and to grasp the moral imagination they embody, one must attend to various aspects of their rhetoric: formal qualities, embedded metaphors, the semantic framing they provide, the rudimentary narrative they imply, the traces of others' words within his own, and so forth. One may begin with metaphor. "Naked I came from my mother's womb" is at one level simply a literal statement. Its obvious truth and universal applicability are part of what makes it usable for organizing reflection. Contextually, one suspects it is here used metaphorically as well as literally, a judgment confirmed by the second part of the parallel statement, "and naked I will return there." Since one does not literally return to one's mother's womb, the metaphorical quality of the second half of the phrase is evident, as "mother's womb" figures the tomb, Sheol, the earth. That transfer of meaning is facilitated by the use of "there" (šām), a word that may serve as a euphemism for Sheol (Qoh 3:17).[71] More complexly, the metaphorical usage of "mother's womb" in the second part of the statement remetaphorizes the first half of the utterance as well, invoking the common mythic notion of the origin of all humanity from the earth (e.g., Gen 3:19b" ". . . until you return to the ground, for from it you were taken; for dust you are and to dust you shall return"). Through a complex interaction of meaning, a single human being's experience is framed within the common condition of humanity.

Although the metaphorical saying is intelligible on its own terms, within the narrative it is an utterance of response, which frames a situation. Thus, its meaning is not to be understood just through the semantics of the statement itself but also in relation to the preceding narrative. Here attention falls on the word "naked." Again, the literal truth of the assertion that one comes naked from the womb is the anchor that grounds the metaphorical construction of meaning. Implicitly, the saying analogizes both property and human relationships to clothes. They are put on, yet they must be taken off again. However much clothes may feel like a second skin, they are not part of the "naked self." However much one may feel one's identity to be bound up with possessions and relationships, one does not inalienably possess such things. Thus, the word "naked" serves to orient Job to the hard but necessary task of relinquishing what cannot be held. There is also another nuance to the word that requires attention, for "naked" connotes the vulnerability of exposure. Job's words refer himself to images of vulnerability and dependency—the naked bodies of the newly birthed infant and of the powerless corpse. If Job is analogizing possessions and relationships to clothes, the metaphorical statement also names his present experience of loss as like death, for he has been stripped of all that clothes a human life.

There is no obvious or necessary relationship between the events of Job's experience and the metaphorical framework he uses to encompass them. Events do not come already labeled. Only through the active work of the moral imagination are events organized, cast within a prototypical story, framed within metaphor. Kenneth Burke drew attention to what he called "scope" and "circumference" as part of this construction of meaning,[72] and scope plays a crucial role here in Job's moral imagination. When confronted with the devastating events of a particular day, Job's words refer them to a horizon of meaning framed by birth and death. There is no "middle distance," no proximate past and future, no focus on immediate causality, but only the speaker's present sense of devastation referred to the absolute horizons of birth and death. The power of metaphorical speech to construct meaning derives not only from what it highlights but also from what it conceals.

Finally, the narrative structure of the saying should be noted. Although the narrative is rudimentary, in it existence is construed as a story of leaving and returning. This narrative schema is deeply rooted in the human psyche and provides the framework for many traditional stories: for Gilgamesh, for Odysseus, for Jacob. To apply the schema of departure and return to life itself is to give life a unity it does not self-evidently possess. To unite this narrative structure with the emotionally charged image of the mother incorporates death (and the losses likened to it) within a symbolics of security and protection.

By themselves Job's first words articulate his grief but also incorporate his devastating losses within a horizon of meaning both existentially immediate and grounded in claims about the human condition. He has, if one may put it this way, expressed the wisdom of "nonattachment." But those words do not yet explain Job's bringing together gestures of grief with those of worship. To understand that, one must look at Job's second utterance: "YHWH has given and YHWH has taken."

This second statement is formally and grammatically parallel to the first. In both, the verbs are binary opposites (come forth/return; give/take), whereas the noun (YHWH) or predicate complement (naked; mother's womb/there) remains the same. This grammatical parallelism invites one to treat the two statements as part of a paradigmatic set, with the similar terms analogous to one another. The going forth and returning of birth and death are simply one way of describing what can also be expressed as YHWH's giving and taking. Thus, the two verbs, "give" and "take," negotiate the space between the first and final nakedness. One is naked, and YHWH gives those things that clothe life; YHWH takes those things, and one returns naked to death.[73] YHWH is the horizon of experience. That sense of YHWH as ultimate horizon also underwrites the parallel between YHWH and the mother's womb from which one departs and to which one returns. Although the text does not take direct issue with the traditional ancient Near Eastern depiction of death as the land of nothingness, the rhetoric of these sayings implicitly challenges such understandings. In the image of the mother's womb, it is not the abyss but something experienced as protective and loving that frames existence, even in loss, even in death. If it were not so, one could not endure the burden of the gift that cannot be possessed but must inevitably be relinquished. One could not bear to be human. Because Job understands it to be so, he blesses the name of YHWH. Thus, through the work of metaphor and narrative, symmetry and contrast, Job's moral imagination establishes a context within which the connection of grief and doxology is not merely comprehensible but powerful.

Although the second episode can be understood in relation to didactic narrative's characteristic redundancy, it extends the argument of the story to cover elements not encompassed in the first episode. As the metaphor with which Job comprehended his situation in the first episode drew upon imagery of the body's nakedness, and thus highlighted the intimate relationship between body and meaning, so *haśśātān* shifts the locus of the test to Job's body.

In contrast to the first episode, where the messengers simply reported the events of destruction but did not attempt to construct an interpretive framework or suggest a response, in the second episode the words of Job's wife are explicitly directive and gesture toward a moral framework that contrasts with Job's. Her words present on earth the terms of the disagreement framed by God and *haśśātān* in heaven. In 2:3 God had characterized Job's response as holding fast to his integrity (*tummāh*). Job's wife's rhetorical question ("Do you still hold fast to your integrity?" 2:9a) dismisses such a stance as meaningless. Her next words render *haśśātān*'s prediction as an imperative: "Curse God." In contrast to Job's words, hers are not accompanied by any interpretive imagery that would explicate the moral framework within which she concludes that curse rather than doxology is the appropriate response. One is left to assume that it is based on the logic *haśśātān* has suggested. In the monologic context of the didactic prose tale there is no desire to explore such an alternative perspective in any terms that would make it plausible, but only to discredit it. That Job's wife enters the narrative already discredited is evident from her alignment with *haśśātān* and against God.[74] The nihilism of the position she and *haśśātān* embrace is evident from the one word in her speech that is not an implicit quotation of the heavenly voices: "Die." According to the values of the narrative, the perspective shared by *haśśātān* and Job's wife cannot sustain life in the face of catastrophe. Redundantly, Job also discredits her advice by saying that she speaks like one of the *nĕbālôt*, someone whose obtuseness expresses itself as impiety.[75]

But what, if anything, do Job's words in the second episode add to his previous statement? Certain syntactical elements that are similar yet not identical to his previous statements invite one to draw the sentences together for comparison. In the sayings in the first episode, the verbs form contrasting pairs, whereas the other terms are stable. Here the verb ("receive") is the repeated term, whereas the contrast comes with the object, "good" and "trouble." Moreover, the verb "receive" belongs to the same semantic field as the verbs of 1:21b ("give" and "take") and so facilitates reading 2:10b in light of that earlier statement. In those sentences Job dealt with the horizons of existence but not with the particular content of life. Here he supplies that lack. What YHWH gives and humans receive is not simply life but life inevitably characterized by both "good" and "trouble." Such a claim would not be meaningful as a reply to his wife except in the context of Job's earlier statements identifying YHWH as the horizon of all existence. Within such a context, the occurrence of trouble cannot break the stance of radical acceptance modeled by Job.

The phrase "radical acceptance" is one I have taken from Dorothee Soelle, who, ironically, despises the book of Job, especially the prose tale. In my opinion, she misunderstands the prose tale, in part by misjudging its generic affinities. What she terms acceptance bears no trace of masochism, fatalism, or mere submission. It is a stance that recognizes the unavoidability of certain suffering and chooses not to flee from it. Acceptance of suffering is the correlate of acceptance of reality: "It is impossible to remove oneself totally from suffering, unless one removes oneself from life itself, no longer enters into relationships, makes oneself invulnerable. . . . The more strongly we affirm reality, the more we are immersed in [suffering]."[76] Such acceptance is the alternative to nihilistic despair, the condition "of wishing that the world did not exist, of believing that non-being is better than being."[77] That, of course, will be the stance of the Job character who speaks at the opening of the wisdom dialogue in chapter 3. Quoting from Simone Weil, Soelle describes the implications of such a stance: "'To wish that the world did not exist is to wish that I, just as I am, may be everything.' . . . The person is curved in upon himself. . . . He has no future and can no longer love anything. He himself is everything; that is, he is dead."[78] Soelle succinctly describes the alternatives embodied by Job and his wife, as well as the anticipatory challenge the prose tale poses to the opening chapter of the wisdom dialogue in the larger structure of the book.

The second episode of the prose tale as I have read it reinforces rather than undermines the image of Job's unconditional piety. Nothing has changed in Job's stance, and his words are complementary parts of what is essentially a single utterance (1:21; 2:10a). Yet ever since antiquity, subtle differences in Job's replies and the narrator's evaluative comments have attracted notice, and readers have queried whether Job's second response is as unequivocal as his first. In the second statement, although Job refuses to curse God, he does not expressly bless God. Whereas at the conclusion to the first episode the narrator says, "And in all this Job did not sin or charge God with wrong" (1:22), here the narrator comments, "In all this Job did not sin with his lips" (2:10b). In *b. Baba Batra* 15a the observation is made that "Job did not sin with his lips—but in his heart he did." Given the canonical form of the book, the rabbis proved astute readers, for the subtly less explicit affirmation by Job and by the narrator foreshadows the opening curse of the dialogue. In my opinion such foreshadowing is a part of the design of the book as a whole. It provides the narrative mechanism by which a psychological bridge is built between the prose tale and the poetic section. But if one prescinds from the knowledge of the dialogue yet to come, does the conclusion of the second episode undercut the identification of Job as the epitome of pious virtue? There are some grounds for such a conclusion. Even within the narrative context of the prose tale readers might appeal to the previous words of Job who worried that his children might have cursed God "in their hearts" (1:5). Thus the contrast between "heart" and "lips" could be a disturbing discrepancy between expectations established in the first episode and the narrative of the second, though it need not be read so.[79]

Within the conventions of a simple didactic tale, however, such a subversive reading cannot be valid. How the story disambiguates the conclusion of the second episode depends on whether one takes the sequel to be the episode with the three friends or the episode in which Job's brothers and sisters come to console him. If the sequel is the episode with the friends, then the possible change in Job's position would be no more than a tease, a complicit pretense of danger between narrator and audience, as harmless as the physical dangers suffered by the protagonists in countless melodramas. In the episode with the friends, the details of which are almost wholly suppressed in the final form of the book, Job definitively speaks what is right and so receives the approval of God (42:7). Meaning is secure, as everyone really knew all along. Alternatively, if one takes the visit of Job's brothers and sisters as immediately following upon the close of the second episode, then the repetition of the key word "trouble" clarifies the implications of Job's comments. Job's wife's response had read Job's troubles as a sign of alienation, and her proposed action was to respond with a further act of alienation. By contrast, the brothers and sisters seem to act out of the same understanding that Job has articulated. They come to console him "concerning all the trouble that YHWH had brought upon him" (42:11). Rather than seeing the situation as an occasion of and for alienation, they react with solidarity and compassion. Their presence is an emblem of the wholeness available to those whose virtue is grounded in the perspective of radical acceptance that Job articulated. Indeed, their action sketches something of the ethics implied in the stance advocated by the prose tale.

The final scene in which YHWH "blesses" (42:12) the latter days of Job further serves, within the conventions of didactic narrative, as part of the redundancy that disambiguates Job's words. But it does more, since it reintroduces the charged notion of blessing. On one level, now that doubt concerning the possibly corrupting influence of blessing has been dispelled, the condition of blessing that obtained in the beginning can be renewed. But the story leaves inexplicit the relation between blessing and Job's understanding of the divine-human relationship. One might say that what had been presented as contradiction has been recast as paradox: a calculating virtue that sought blessing would have to be repudiated, but a virtue that seeks no blessing finds it. Such an interpretation, though not without merit, takes no account of the content of Job's words. If one begins from Job's words, a less paradoxical meaning emerges. Blessing is a part of the "good" that can and does come from God. But its existence does not negate the possibility of "trouble" that can and does come from God. Though this point will require closer scrutiny in the following paragraphs, I would argue that Job's choice of terminology ("good . . . trouble") is strategically important, because it is more comprehensive than the pairs "blessing . . . curse" or "reward . . . punishment."

So far, this discussion has considered the prose tale largely within its own narrative world. But although a monologic text may not acknowledge its larger discursive context, it is always a part of a broader cultural conversation. I do not mean to suggest that the prose tale is a polemic, occupying one corner in a clearly articulated debate. But any time one talks "about" something, that utterance takes its place in the context of other voices. A topic or theme is, as Menachem Brinker observes, a "semantic point of contact between the individual text and other texts . . . a meeting place of texts of various kinds."[80] Yet it is not just themes that engender an intertextual penumbra. The words in an utterance are always "used" words that bring with them traces of previous usage, even as they are reaccented in a new utterance.[81] Thematically, the prose tale is usually seen as intertextually related to texts that insist on the act-consequence relationship in the moral sphere, texts such as Proverbs 10:24–30 and 11:3–8, which align good and bad fortune with righteousness and wickedness, or with wisdom psalms such as Psalms 112 and 128, which draw a causal connection between "fearing YHWH" and receiving blessing, or with the explicit language of

Deuteronomy 28:1–2: "If you obey YHWH your God . . . all these blessings shall come upon you." Having recognized the problem inherent in such a moral construction, the prose tale presents a means of "otherwise perceiving," an act of moral imagination that offers to "transform the limits of [the culture's] own convictions and commitments,"[82] offering a way in which both virtuous piety and blessing can be affirmed without contradiction. Such a characterization of the cultural work of the prose tale is apt. But it does not tell the whole story.

Less often noted is the friction between the religious vision of the prose tale and that embodied in psalms of lament and thanksgiving. Though it would certainly not count as "cursing," the prose tale could not easily accommodate Job's uttering something like the lament in Psalm 13. While not exactly the wrong words, from the story's perspective they are not the right words. Imagining them in the context of the prose tale exposes their assumptions about the divine-human relationship and the nature of virtuous piety. In contrast to the words of Job, such psalms speak a language of expectation and entitlement, grounded in something like a patron-client social model. As one could not easily put a complaint psalm in Job's mouth in the prose tale, so one could not comfortably put Job's rhetorical question about receiving both good and trouble from God in a complaint psalm. These two discourses of piety are based on different generative metaphors for the divine-human relationship and consequently frame situations of distress differently. Though the prose tale makes use, for narrative purposes, of a highly anthropomorphic representation of God, the piety it commends is based on a view of the divine arguably much less anthropomorphic than that which characterizes the psalmody of personal religion.

Is it possible to locate the type of piety embodied in Job's words within a larger tradition of religious reflection? One may begin with the clearest verbal connections. Job's first utterance in 1:21, the words with which he frames the situation, are words of a proverbial saying, one that is attested in variant forms in Qoheleth 5:14 and Sirach 40:1. Though these other uses of the saying occur in texts later than Job, they suggest that the saying is a traditional one that enjoyed some currency in the literary wisdom tradition. A saying may be adapted for a variety of purposes, but it is worth noting whether it tends to be associated with a particular cluster of topics. Not surprisingly, the distinctive imagery of the mother's womb is connected in each instance with reflection on the nature of the human condition. For Sirach the saying is adapted, along with references to Genesis 2–3, to a comment concerning the burden of work. ("Hard work was created for everyone, and a heavy yoke is laid on the children of Adam, from the day they come forth from their mother's womb until they day they return to the mother of all the living" [Sir 40:1; NRSV]). The use in Qoheleth, however, is more suggestive of the intellectual context of the Joban prose tale. In Qoheleth the saying is part of the argument concerning the futility of the human condition, specifically the inability to secure lasting benefit from purposeful work: "Just as he came forth from his mother's womb, naked he shall return to go as he came, and nothing shall he take from his toil which can go in his hand" (Qoh 5:14). Declaring this inescapable situation to be a "grievous ill" (rā'āh ḥôlāh, 5:15), Qoheleth nevertheless considers what is "good" (ṭôb), namely, to enjoy the eating, drinking, and work that "God gives" (nātan) to a person as his portion (5:17–19). Clustered within the space of a few verses, one finds not only the saying Job cites but also key terminology from his other saying about what God has given and the elements of good and ill in a human life.

The similarities of diction and imagery in Job and Qoheleth do not suggest that one of these texts is directly replying to the other. But they are both working some of the same ground of the problematics of human existence, equipped with some of the same concepts and images available within the discourse of wisdom. To that extent they are part of a long and complex cultural conversation. After all, the similarities between Qoheleth and Siduri's advice in Gilgamesh suggest that the problem of a human existence bounded by death and seeking to experience goodness within those limitations was a perennial one within ancient Near Eastern reflection.

One could draw the comparison between the prose tale and Qoheleth in a slightly different fashion. Both are engaged with the issue of the relation between virtue and reward, yet they frame the problematic differently. The focus for Qoheleth is the unhappy fact that the relation is not a dependable one (Qoh 8:14). Acknowledging that, he explores the implications for the type of existence that *is* possible in light of that recognition. The move is a reluctant one, however, for Qoheleth would prefer a world in which actions produced reliable consequences, virtue was regularly and speedily rewarded, and wickedness punished. Qoheleth is nostalgic for the world as it is perceived in the more conventional sayings in Proverbs. In Proverbs, too, one can find occasional recognition of the contingent quality of existence. But only in Qoheleth does the contingent become a major theme.

For the prose tale, the significance of those realities Qoheleth acknowledges but deplores is quite different. Job's utterances name the things that trouble Qoheleth: the boundedness of existence by death, the inability to possess inalienably, the uncontrollable presence of both good and ill in a life. In the prose tale they become the key to a type of piety unthinkable for Qoheleth. Because Qoheleth cannot break his desire for retributive justice—and yet must acknowledge that it does not exist as a regular, reliable principle—an element of distance, perhaps even of alienation, pervades his piety. For Qoheleth deity is distant, unfathomable, and even arbitrary, though still to be revered as the horizon of existence. But in the prose tale it is precisely because the principle of retribution quite literally has no place in Job's moral imagination (to the chagrin of haśśāṭān) that Job can demonstrate the capacity of the very vulnerability and lack of autonomy characteristic of contingent human existence to provide the basis for a sustaining relationship with deity. Instead of distance or alienation, for the Job of the prose tale an intimacy expresses itself through words of doxology in the midst of grief. Thus, the prose tale takes issue both with the "left" and "right" wings of the wisdom tradition, if one may put it that way, over the significance of the principle of retribution and the nature of contingent human existence in relation to virtuous piety. Both are fixated on the act-consequence relationship in the moral sphere, and that leads to intractable problems. The "right wing" of Proverbs risks the meaningfulness of virtue by insisting on this principle. The "left wing," represented by Qoheleth, by not breaking decisively with the principle, cannot anchor a sustaining piety on the basis of what it sees as the truth about the human condition. Only the prose tale, by making the contingent nature of human existence the primary point of orientation, can both articulate a logic of piety that is unassailable and a form of piety that is unalienated.

Narrative Ethics in a Performative Mode

> The very act of reading, in other words, like prayer or casual looking, permits things to happen.
>
> Adam Zachary Newton, *Narrative Ethics*

The attempt to articulate the moral imagination embodied in the prose story has entailed a particular kind of reading, a self-consciously sympathetic reading, but also one that cooperates with the program inscribed in the generic conventions of didactic narrative. Such a reading orients itself to the "message" communicated propositionally and in aesthetic form by an implied author to a reader. It highlights what Nussbaum called the cognitive interest in literature, the interest in discerning the possibilities and tragic impossibilities life offers. Didactic literature lends itself well to such an approach because its aspiration is to be a proposition in narrative form. Though didactic narrative has a plot, it is as close to a static form of narrative as it is possible to get, since the plot is simply an unfolding of what is already inscribed as truth. It exists as pure illustration.

Or at least it wishes to. But an ineradicable tension exists within didactic narrative for the simple reason that it *is* narrative, and narrative "happens." Narrative has the structure of an event, and there is something irreducibly nonpropositional about events. Drawing on categories from Emanuel Levinas, Adam Zachary Newton identifies these two dimensions of narrative as the "Saying" and the "Said."[83] The "Said" refers to the propositional content, the thematics of a narrative and its moral prescriptiveness. The "Saying" refers to the intersubjective relation established in narrative through its performative aspect. Both make moral claims on readers, but claims of different orders. The prescriptive claims of the Said invite agreement or disagreement with the text's construction of value. The claims of the Saying require more explanation. This mode of reading and the claims that arise from it are based on a tacit analogy, as Newton puts it, "that one faces a text as one might face a person."[84] The encounter with the text is one of immediacy, an immediacy of contact that is prior to meaning.

The analogy has obvious limits. One does not owe to texts or their characters all the same kind of ethical obligations one owes to actual persons. Nor is one related to the world of fictional characters in the same way one is related to the world of persons. Yet the divide between the fictional and the real may not be so sharp as first appears, especially in relation to the issue of narrative and ethics, for narrative is as much a part of the real as of the fictional realm. Moreover, many of the ethical issues raised both by the content and by the performative aspects of the virtual world of narrative are continuous with issues encountered in the world of everyday experience. Common conventions of reading facilitate the analogy. Although one may know a text is fictional, that explicit knowledge becomes tacit in the experience of reading, as one becomes involved in the imaginative "play" of reading.[85] Moreover, the responses to fictional characters and events are also based on the assumption of a mimetic relationship between narrative and the world. The situations that move us in narrative, even nonrealist narrative, are recognizably the kinds of events and situations that occur in the world.[86] Newton's analogy, which is a tacit assumption of much reading practice, thus accounts for important phenomena, such as the emotional reactions readers experience when they read. One may weep for characters, feel joy for them, be angry at them or on their behalf. Behind such emotions stand normative judgments about what is deserved or undeserved, good or bad, worthy or unworthy.[87] To be sure, one cannot intervene in the world of fictional characters, but ethical relations even among actual persons are not all about interventions. Many of our relations with other persons involve listening to their stories, relating their stories to others, and forming evaluative judgments about those narratives. Thus, the analogy Newton claims, "that one faces a text as one might face a person," may be illumining in both directions.

To anyone who has ever taught the book of Job there is nothing esoteric about Newton's distinction between the Saying and the Said and the ways it figures in readers' ethical evaluation of the story. In almost every class there will be those whose reaction to the prose story is visceral, immediate, and horrified. That Job should be subjected to such suffering for no cause, that Job's children should be killed as part of the test of his character, that a new family should be represented as restoration when the first children remain dead—all of this strikes some readers as utterly repugnant. That the narrative asks its readers to approve of it is simply immoral. Yet others in the class will respond impatiently, even dismissively, arguing that such reactions are naive and miss the point that this is *just a story.* They accuse their fellow students of being tone deaf, of failing to understand the conventions of fiction. Usually someone will point out that in

Jesus' parables there are examples of conduct that would be ethically offensive if all the actions and characters in them were understood as models to be imitated. That is to misunderstand the way parables make their point. Similarly, anyone who gets upset about the admittedly outrageous narrative setup in Job is going to miss the real value of the story, the claim it makes about the nature of true piety. Even though students often lack the theoretical background to do second-order reflection on their reactions, their dispute models the two trajectories in contemporary narrative ethics I have associated with Nussbaum and Newton, respectively.

These two ways of encountering the moral claims of a narrative are in many respects incommensurable. In most cases they would not lead to such sharply differing responses as they do in the case of Job, but their difference of perspective cannot simply be harmonized. As one looks through one lens or the other, one simply sees differently.

In the approach championed by Newton, ethical reflection begins with the relation of addressivity established in the act of storytelling. Newton thus stakes out a position even more calculatedly naive than that of Booth. Whereas Booth's model of a story as a "friendship offering" between author and reader draws attention to the status of the story as a thing made and shared between two friends external to the story, Newton's model dissolves the boundaries between story and reader. For Newton it is the narrator, not the author, with whom we have to do. Like the ancient mariner who seizes the wedding guest in Coleridge's poem,[88] the narrator of the prose tale stops us, arrests us in our activity, when we pause and listen to the story of Job. The ethical relations established in this configuration are multiple. In telling the story the narrator assumes a responsibility toward the one whose story is told, for the narrator undertakes to relate the life of another. In the act of storytelling, a burden of responsibility is progressively transferred from narrator to reader, for in submitting to the story, the reader also becomes "answerable."[89] Long before questions of meaning arise, the immediacy of the encounter with the character as well as with the narrator makes a claim upon the reader. Via the work of Levinas, Newton argues that the character whose story is told confronts the reader as a "face." And a face always makes a claim upon another face. Though it is true that a reader cannot intervene in the story, the reader becomes a witness with at least a witness's responsibility.

Newton's account of the dynamics of reading helps explain the ethical discomfort of many "naive" readers of the prose tale, who respond with distress and anger to the mistreatment of Job and his family. It also leads one to note areas of ethical discomfort besides the physical abuse it recounts. The discomfort generated from within the prose tale provides insight into the relation between it and the other parts of the book of Job and thus the significance of the book's dialogic structure. In the story of the prose tale, as discussed above, the focus is on character, and the narrator arrests our attention from the very first words of the story with praise for Job's character. Yet there is room even here for ethical disquiet, for the narrator's relation to Job is one of utter transcendence.[90] The narrator needs Job as example, not as person, needs him as one whose character can be fixed, summed-up, or in Bakhtin's expression, "finalized."

The narrator's claim on the reader is that the reader join in contemplating Job. Thus, Job becomes a spectacle, as the narrator brings Job on stage and positions the reader where she can eavesdrop, overhearing Job's words and watching Job's actions. This status of Job as spectacle is not just a narrative device to get the story started but is intrinsic to the character relations within the story. God's first words concerning Job also cast him as an object of "speculation," for God says to *haśśātān*, "Have you directed your attention to Job?" (1:8a). God's words are words of praise for Job, echoing those of the narrator, but the discomfort some readers experience even at this point can perhaps be illumined by a comment from Bakhtin: "The truth about a man in the mouths of others, not directed to him dialogically and therefore a *second-hand* truth, becomes a *lie* degrading and deadening him, if it touches upon his 'holy of holies,' that is, 'the man in man.' . . . Truth is unjust when it concerns the depths of *someone else's* personality."[91] God's "summing up" of Job, like the narrator's, already includes an element of injustice, for even though what they say is true, it renders him simply as object and as example.

Oddly, it is *haśśātān* who speaks of Job in a way that appears to acknowledge his subjectivity. *Haśśātān* perceives Job as one who may have a complex interiority, levels of motivation that are not so easily identified. *Haśśātān* sees Job as possessing implicit values that Job himself may not even be aware he holds. Despite this ostensibly richer view of Job as complex subject, *haśśātān*'s perception is no less reductive, for with his hermeneutics of suspicion, he claims already to know about Job what Job does not even know about himself. Both God and *haśśātān* seek to narrate Job. They differ only in laying claim to incompatible narratives. They are equally certain they know the truth about him and that they can state it in a single sentence. The violence that will erupt upon Job is already anticipated in the violence done in these attempts to define him.

The violence has another, related source. As noted in the analysis of the didactic aspects of the prose tale, this is a genre with a hyperdeveloped passion for unitary truth. That passion plays out in the performative dimension of the text as a narrative necessity to know. Once doubt has been cast upon Job, that doubt must be resolved. Within such a story, one cannot imagine God, upon hearing *haśśātān*'s counterclaims about the moral character of Job, saying in reply, "Well, I don't think you are right. But I guess we will never know." For this narrative the compelling desire to establish the truth about a person trumps all other values. It permits everything. To the extent that the storyteller succeeds in communicating to the reader the desire for such knowledge, the reader is complicit in the violence against Job. Even the reader who deplores the test of Job but desires the rest of the story is not innocent. The reader who turns the page stands in an ethical relation to Job not so different from God who says, "Very well, he is in your hands" (2:6a).[92]

The Other who is Job is not allowed to remain undisclosed. He must be rendered transparent. Not all seeking of knowledge about another is abusive, of course. There are modes that are just, modes that enact solidarity, modes that are generous, modes that heal or redeem. But in this story the ethical relations governing knowledge of another are deeply perverse. For the truth to be disclosed Job must indeed "speak his own word," but the conditions for truth are not dialogical. Instead, the crucial speech will be coerced speech. This coerced speech differs from torture, where pain is inflicted to elicit a truth someone wishes to withhold. It differs also from the ordeal, where a nonhuman entity "speaks" to disclose a truth the accused cannot be trusted to speak. The forcing of speech in Job has more the structure of a scientific experiment in which the subject is manipulated into a predetermined set of circumstances, disclosing the desired information unwittingly, without knowing the real conditions of his own speech. Thus, ironically, in such experiments deception becomes the essential precondition of truth, and the one whose speech is required is never directly addressed by those who desire to know.

The scenes in which Job speaks have a voyeuristic quality to them. God watches Job, *haśśātān* watches Job, and the reader watches Job. Just as we watched him in an intimate moment of anxiety and piety (1:5), so now we watch him in the intensity of grief and deep physical pain (1:20-21; 2:8-10). The kind of watching to which the story invites and incites is an objectified watching. We are encouraged to watch to see what he will do, what he will say. Such focused, "scientific" watching is the antithesis of the compassionate gaze.

When read with attention to the performative aspects of the narrative and the ethical relations established among the characters, the words Job speaks take on a different resonance than when one is simply asking about the moral imagination they embody. From this perspective one is drawn to the disjunction between the relationship with God as Job assumes it to be and as it has been portrayed in the narrative. Job makes no claims upon God for protection from the contingencies of human existence and even identifies God as the agent who both gives and takes life, who sends both good and trouble. From Job's perspective the relationship is one of utter trust. Yet trust is precisely what is sacrificed to knowledge in the hierarchy of values represented in the events of the prose tale.

The horrific suffering inflicted on Job, culminating in the death of his children and the savaging of his own skin, is the unjustified violence many readers find so disturbing. But those acts are but the ultimate manifestations of a more pervasive ethical dislocation that becomes apparent when one examines the communicative relations within the narrative. Some readers have attempted to find the trace of a guilty conscience in the narrative by pointing to God's remark in 2:3 that *haśśātān* incited God to destroy Job *ḥinnām*, "for no reason," or by observing that the doubling of Job's possessions echoes the law of restitution for stolen property (Exod 22:3, 6, 8). Even if that is so, the narrative does not address the crowning injustice, that Job is not entrusted with the truth about what has happened. Thus, to the end the narrative continues to deprive Job of his subjectivity. He remains the objectified, finalized, utterly narrated example that serves the purposes of the didactic narrator. The reader, who has been the recipient of this act of narration at the expense of Job, may well feel implicated in and contaminated by the abuses it enacts.

I am not arguing that one of these approaches to the moral and ethical dimensions of the prose tale is superior to the other—either the approach that focuses on the moral imagination of the didactic story or the approach that focuses on the performative elements of the narrative. Both are valid and capable of illumining aspects of the tale the other has difficulty in perceiving. Although these two approaches are in no sense contradictory, the different ways in which they focus attention are difficult to hold together. It may be that one must temporarily bracket attending to the performative aspects of the text, the Saying, in order to hear the Said, the particular claim the text makes about the world. To attend only to the ethical issues raised by the performative aspects of the text is to evade the propositional claim. By the same token, to refuse to acknowledge the disturbing issues implicit in the performative aspects of the text is to impoverish the scope of narrative ethics.

Both approaches are important for understanding the structure of the book as a whole, which can be thought of both in terms of a Bakhtinian dialogism and a Levinasian interruption. Attending to the propositional claims of the prose tale and the moral imagination that gives rise to them allows one to hear an important and provocative word about the world. But the monologic form of the didactic genre presents itself as though it were the only word that could be spoken. How can that assumption of superadequacy be challenged, be required to make space for another word? How can it be shown that although the prose tale may speak the truth, it cannot speak the whole truth? There is no way the didactic tale can be written to make it hospitable to voices of dissent and critique, for such hospitality to other perspectives is utterly alien to its genius. It could be challenged by the telling of a rival story, but the author of the book of Job chooses another strategy, breaking into its closed discourse to insert another, alien genre, that of the wisdom dialogue, the language, values, and moral perspectives of which are radically different. By this juxtaposition of genres, ideas and moral imaginations which may have been isolated from one another in the cultural world of ancient Israel are brought together and "forced to quarrel," as Bakhtin puts it.

Levinas's notion of "interruption" adds something not quite perceived by

Bakhtin's dialogism, namely, the ethical imperative of the disruption of discourse. The Said, that is, the thematic, propositional aspect of discourse, is the necessary sedimentation of language. "[In the Said] essence has its hour and its time. Clarity occurs, and thought aims at themes."[93] This is the domain of philosophy, the domain in which the prose tale, too, is at home. Yet this very sedimentation threatens to close off something vital in language, the exposure to the Other that provokes utterance, the impulse of the Saying. Thus, the Said requires but resists interruption. Levinas grasps for a variety of images for the Saying, associating it with the prophetic, with witness, and with the gesture of skepticism. These open up the Said by continual interruption, making it acknowledge that aspect of language which is always saying something else, the possibility posed by the Other who speaks, breaking up the closure of identity and essence. Thus, for Levinas this interruption is where "the ethical," the necessary encounter with the Other, occurs. To return to Job, the fact that the didactic prose tale (the Said par excellence) should be interrupted by the wisdom dialogue—which, as the next chapter will argue, is self-consciously a skeptical genre—suggests that the structure of the book can usefully be understood in light of Levinas's concerns.

Such a tensive relationship between the Saying and the Said is not purely a matter of the juxtaposition of genres, that is, a matter of the external structure of the book, but is already embodied in the prose tale itself. As Levinas maintains, the Saying is always present, even in attenuated form, in every instance of the Said. However much speech attempts to thematize as content the impulse that led to speech, that urgency always remains in some way. Thus, in the prose tale, attending to the performative aspects of the story discloses an urgency already present that motivates and is answered by the structure of the book as a whole. Job in the prose tale is a character who has become an instrument in the disagreement between God and haśśātān, a mere illustration in the thematic discourse of the didactic narrative. By interrupting the story in which Job is narrated in such a diminished fashion, the author of the whole book challenges the adequacy of that narration. By interrupting with a wisdom dialogue, in which characters speak without significant narration, the author gives back to the character Job his subjectivity as an unfinalized presence whose last word is not yet spoken.

3

Critical Curiosity

Genre and Moral Imagination in the Wisdom Dialogue

> In its structure Job's dialogue is internally endless, for the opposition of the
> soul to God—whether the opposition be hostile or humble—is conceived in
> it as something irrevocable and eternal.
>
> Bakhtin, *Problems of Dostoevsky's Poetics*

The end of the preceding chapter showed how attending to the performative
aspects of the narrative creates a tension that cannot be resolved from within
the closure of the didactic tale but is addressed by the interruption of another
way of speaking—that of the dialogue. The dialogue does not simply differ stylistically from the didactic tale but represents a different genre, which means that
it makes present the values and perspectives embodied in that genre and sets
them in conversation with the different values and perspectives of the didactic
tale.

As noted earlier, the perception of genre is a function of the intertextual nature
of all reading, formed as a text is read against a background of other texts that
establish expectations and enable one to recognize salient features.[1] The poetic
part of Job has been read against a variety of texts from the ancient Near East,
resulting in the recognition that various aspects of the poetic section allude to
and play off a number of discrete genres, as well as modes, motifs, and themes
common to several genres. These comparisons have generally not been based
on the assumption of direct contact and literary influence but on the more general assumption of a degree of cultural continuity throughout the ancient Near
East, particularly among Semitic-speaking peoples.

Scholarly attention has focused on five texts from Mesopotamia and Ugarit:
(1) the Sumerian text A Man and His God, (2) *Ludlul bēl nēmeqi*, (3) a Dialogue
between a Man and His God (AO 4462), (4) an Akkadian text from Ugarit
designated RS 25.450, and (5) the Babylonian Theodicy. Despite thematic similarities, these texts are generically disparate. In his study of cuneiform parallels
to the book of Job, Hans-Peter Müller distinguishes between texts that appeal
to the deity for relief of suffering and those that take up the problems of world
order and the nature of reality.[2] Correctly, he judges that of these texts, only

one, the Babylonian Theodicy, is preoccupied with reflection on world order. The rest are appeals for relief and thanksgiving for relief received. Similarly, when one reads these texts in conjunction with Job 3–27, though connections of a sort can be made in every case, only the Babylonian Theodicy and Job possess the critical clustering of formal and content similarities that suggests that the two belong to a distinctive genre, "the wisdom dialogue."[3] Although the examination of that genre will be the major focus of this chapter, it is important to give some attention to the other texts. They form the broader textual horizon against which both the Babylonian Theodicy and the Joban dialogue are to be read. Moreover, certain features of the speeches in the Joban dialogue are better clarified in relation to motifs in these texts than in relation to the Babylonian Theodicy.

Thanksgiving Prayers and Didactic Reflections

Though the texts that contain an appeal to the deity represent two or three different literary genres, they are all drawn together by their focus on a perennial issue in Mesopotamian thought: the situation of extreme suffering and the proper human response to it. Common to all of these texts is the framing of the issue by means of a character who speaks in his own voice.[4] Under the influence of the book of Job, scholars initially tended to refer to this figure as the "righteous sufferer." But as students of Mesopotamian literature have repeatedly pointed out, such a designation is not apt for the Mesopotamian texts, since one of the fundamental assumptions they make is that human beings inevitably sin against the gods and so suffer the expression of their anger. They are sufferers, yes; but by virtue of being human, they are not righteous. Either Karel van der Toorn's designation, "the emblematic sufferer,"[5] or Gerald Mattingly's "the pious sufferer"[6] is preferable. Given this assumption, the intellectual problem posed by Job, that is, the acute contradiction between righteousness and suffering when seen against the background of a strongly retributivist moral order, scarcely makes its appearance in these texts. One does find in *Ludlul* a bewildered protest that the sufferer has been a model of piety and yet is treated as one who neglects the deity (II.12–32), but the tonality is quite different from Job, and the moral confusion is resolved in ways quite different from Job's desire for a trial.[7] Only the grace of the gods, their anger soothed by the prayers of the sufferer, is effective. In this way the consistent piety modeled by the sufferer serves as a cultural norm that underwrites the religious ideology even as the texts recognize the stresses that might put that ideology in question.

Although debate continues about proper generic descriptions for the Mesopotamian texts, they can appropriately be grouped in two sets. *Ludlul* and RS 25.460, an Akkadian text from Ras Shamra,[8] both appear to be praises to

Marduk in thanksgiving for relief of suffering. The structure of RS 25.460 is not entirely clear. Though forty-six lines are preserved, the initial fifteen or twenty lines and the final ten lines or so are not extant. Where the fragmentary text now begins, the sufferer is describing his misery (lines 1–8). At the conclusion of this section, he refers to his family, which was prepared to conduct death rites for him (lines 9–12). In a variation on the description of misery (lines 13–24), he frames it from the perspective of his present restoration to well-being (e.g., "until the Lord raised up my head").⁹ This literary blending of painful past and happy present provides the transition to the direct first-person praise of Marduk (lines 25–46).

The much better state of preservation of *Ludlul* allows for a clearer under-standing of its organization. In general, its structure is comparable to that of a thanksgiving psalm.¹⁰ Nevertheless, it is no simple prayer but a sophisticated literary composition of between four hundred and five hundred lines, composed in the Cassite period, and the subject of a later philological commentary.¹¹ The content of *Ludlul* is as follows. The sufferer, Shubshi-meshre-Shakkan, begins with an extended hymn of praise to Marduk (I.1–40). Following the hymn the speaker recounts his suffering in an extended lament (I.41–120). The first tab-let concludes with a brief expression of hope that his condition might change, that "in daylight good will come upon me . . . the sun will shine." Such hope proved ill-founded, for the second tablet contains an even more extended ac-count of how his sufferings continued and nothing seemed to lessen the anger of the god. By the end of this tablet, Shubshi-meshre-Shakkan considers him-self to have been near death. For him and for his family, "the day grew dim . . . their sun grew dark" (II.119–20). Although tablet three begins by recounting his suffering, the speaker soon describes the appearance of certain figures whom he saw in a series of dreams (III.9–44). A splendidly dressed young man ap-pears and announces that he has been sent by "the Lady" (perhaps the wife of Marduk), though the content of his message is largely missing. Next appears a priest, sent by the king's representative in Nippur, who performs a purification ritual. The third figure is a woman of almost divine appearance who announces an oracle of assurance. Finally, the exorcist priest Ur-Nindinugga appears and declares, "Marduk has sent me! To Shubshi-meshre-Shakkan I have brought a sw[athe], From his pure hands I have brought a swa[the]" (III.42–49). Shubshi-meshre-Shakkan then recounts how all the demons were driven away and his suffering relieved. The fourth tablet continues with an account of his restoration and with the psalm of thanksgiving he performed at Marduk's temple in Babylon. At each of the gates of Esagila he receives the god's grace, and in gratitude performs lavish thank offerings. The composition concludes with the inhabitants of Babylon singing the praise of Marduk.¹²

Whatever *Ludlul* is, it is not very similar to the book of Job, in whole or in part. There are certain similarities between the graphic descriptions of distress in *Ludlul* and the tradition of Israelite lament psalmody, which also influences Job's description of his suffering. One might note the alienation of friends and family (*Ludlul* I.79–92; cf. Job 19:13–22), or the heaviness of the hand of the deity (*Ludlul* III.1–2; cf. Job 23:1–2). More important than superficial parallels between imagery, however, are the ways of setting and resolving the problem of theodicy in each text, comparisons that do not lend themselves to simple assessment. In *Ludlul*, the key to the poem's understanding of suffering and its solution is encapsulated in its description of the two aspects of the nature of deity: "Marduk, with the power to heal (*bēl nēmeqi*) and the mind to heal (*ilu muštālu*), a god of darkness and wrath, but a god, too, of light and sudden and matching mercy."[13] A similar praise of the two natures of Marduk occurs in RS 25.460 in lines 24–39. This conception of the gods in Mesopotamian religious poetry is not unusual. Prayers of lamentation to Ishtar similarly describe her annihilating wrath as well as her overflowing compassion. Here is both explanation and resolution of suffering. Suffering is the consequence of the fury of a god; relief comes when the god's anger is abated and compassion takes its place. Such conceptions of deity are not entirely at home in Israelite religious thought, but neither are they entirely absent (see, e.g., Psalm 90; Lamentations 3; Job 5:18). As I will attempt to show in a later chapter, something like the two natures of YHWH is a part of Israelite lament tradition. Moreover, this tradition is a significant source of Job's imagery of divine violence. Job, however, will use it in a way unthinkable either to Mesopotamian or to ordinary Israelite piety, for he breaks the customary sequenced duality of violent wrath and loving compassion and instead sets even divine violence under the scrutiny of justice.

The other aspect of *Ludlul* that is suggestive for comparison with Job is contained in an extended reflective passage in which the sufferer describes the apparent contradictoriness of his situation. Though pious and scrupulously observant, he is treated as one who ignores the gods (II.12–32). Here is something at least superficially similar to Job's insistence on his own innocence. But in *Ludlul* the experiential contradiction is resolved through the recognition of a chasm between divine and human rationalities and moral orders that defies understanding. Having described his life of devotion, the sufferer exclaims:

> I wish I knew that these things were pleasing to a god!
> What seems good to one's self could be an offense to a god,
> What in one's own heart seems abominable could be good to one's god!
> Who could learn the reasoning of the gods in heaven?
> Who could grasp the intentions of the gods of the depths?
> Where might human beings have learned the way of a god? (II.33–38)

Thus, an epistemological impasse frustrates even the pious person's attempt to know and do the will of the gods. The consequence is that a person's life is unpredictable and his well-being beyond his control.

He who lived by (his) brawn died in confinement.
Suddenly one is downcast, in a trice full of cheer,
One moment he sings in exaltation,
In a trice he groans like a professional mourner. . . .
I have ponde[red] these things; I have made no sense of them. (II.39-42, 48)

The only possible solution is continued trust in the eventual graciousness of Marduk. Although rhetorical exaggeration characterizes Shubshi-meshre-Shakkan's outburst, his description of the human condition is consistent with the basic Mesopotamian understanding.

In the book of Job the ability of humankind to understand the will of God and the extent to which humans share with God a common moral community are topics very much under debate. Zophar (Job 11:2-12) makes the case concerning the limits of human understanding. Eliphaz and Bildad (4:12-21; 15:14-16; 25:4-6) articulate the ancient Near Eastern sense of the radical distinction between divine and human being and its concomitant implication of generic human unrighteousness. Finally, Job's forensic metaphor, which begins with an engagement of this topos (9:2-4), is ultimately based on a contrasting assumption of common moral standards and the mutual intelligibility of human and divine motivations.

In contrast to the monologic structure of *Ludlul* and RS 25.460, the other two texts in question, the Sumerian Man and His God and the Akkadian Dialogue between a Man and His God (AO 4462) have a narrative and even a dramatic structure. The older of the two is the Sumerian text, which its editor, Samuel Noah Kramer, has argued originates at the end of the third millennium, in the Third Dynasty of Ur.[14] Since the body of the text contains a prayer to the speaker's personal god, a number of scholars have identified the composition as an example of a complaint prayer, penetential prayer, answered complaint, or thanksgiving prayer.[15] What these designations overlook, however, is the narrative and didactic framework of the composition.[16] The piece begins in lines 1-9 with instruction phrased in jussive and imperative clauses:

Let a man utter constantly the exaltedness of his god,
Let the young man praise artlessly the words of his god. . . .
Let his lament soothe the heart of his god,
(For) a man without a god would not obtain food. (lines 1-4)[17]

The text then narrates an example, the case of a good young man who nevertheless experienced acute suffering and turned to his god in prayer (lines 10-25). The young man's model prayer occupies the bulk of the composition (lines 26-116). In his prayer he describes rejection by friends and hostility from enemies. But he cries out to his god and acknowledges his guilt and sin, praying for deliverance. At this point the narrative voice resumes, explaining, "the man—his bitter weeping was heard by his god, / When the lamentation and wailing that filled him had soothed the heart of his god for the young man," then the god restored the young man to well-being (lines 117–29). Continuing to model appropriate behavior, the young man is said to have uttered "constantly the exaltedness of his god," and apparently further lines of that praise are cited to bring the composition to a close (lines 130–40).

Succinctly, this composition sets out the fundamental Mesopotamian belief concerning the causes of suffering and its remedy. Suffering is caused by the anger of a god provoked by a human. Though a person may be good, the nature of the human condition ensures that one will inevitably offend against deity, for "never has a sinless child been born to its mother . . . a sinless *workman* has not existed from of old" (lines 102–3). But though suffering is inevitable, the solution lies in the humble but importunate prayer, which the young man models. The heart of an angry god can be soothed.

The significance of such a composition as part of the horizon against which Job is to be read is similar to that of *Ludlul*. First, it highlights the motifs of complaint prayer that play a significant role in the speeches of Job in the dialogues. Second, it lays out the essential understanding of suffering and its remedy that will form an important part of the friends' highly traditional advice to Job.[18] It does not, however, illumine the structure and literary form of the dialogue.

The Dialogue between a Man and His God (AO 4462) bears a certain resemblance to the Sumerian Man and His God, enough for von Soden to raise the question whether the author knew the Sumerian text.[19] The Dialogue between a Man and His God begins with a narrative introduction. There is, however, disagreement over whether the first line should be translated, "a man weeps for a friend to his god,"[20] or, "a young man was imploring his god as a friend."[21] The philological issue is whether or not *ru-i-iš* can be taken as a comparative. If the former interpretation is correct, then this would be the only Mesopotamian text of appeal to a god in which a friend is dramatized as a character. Though the role of the friend is unlike that of the friend in the Babylonian Theodicy and in Job, his presence would mark an intriguing point of comparison between the appeal and dialogue texts.[22] More likely, however, is the second translation, in which the man appeals to the god as a friend. Thus, the text begins with a narrative introduction describing the sufferer's misery and how he falls upon the ground and begins his appeal to the god (strophe 1, lines 2–9). The narrator briefly introduces and summarizes the sufferer's prayer (strophe 2, lines 10–11), which makes up the body of the text (strophes 2–6, lines 12–38). The prayer, unfortunately, is badly broken. In keeping with the notion that the sufferer addresses the god as a friend is his complaint: "The wrong I did I do not know! Have I [. . .] a vile forbidden act? Brother does not de[sp]ise his brother, Friend is not calumniator of his friend!" (strophe 2, lines 13–15). Thus, if the god were behaving as a friend, he would not be treating the sufferer in such a fashion. Apparently, however, the sufferer does recall speaking improperly of the god in the past (strophe 4, lines 24–27). At the conclusion of the sufferer's prayer, the god begins to restore him (strophe 7, lines 39–47). Most striking, however, is the fact that the god's own words are cited in strophes 8 and 9 (lines 48–67). He announces the restoration of the sufferer but also cautions the sufferer that "you must never, till the end of time, forget [your] god / Your creator, now that you are favored" (strophe 8, lines 56–57).[23]

The composition ends with an imperative appeal to the god, "Level his way, open his path. May the plea of your servant penetrate your heart," and the name of the copyist, Kalbanum (strophe 10, lines 68–70). The significance of these final lines is unclear. They do not fit well as words of the narrator internal to the action of the account, since they come after the god's decisive action. The words appear to be external to the narrative but may point to the use of the appeal as a form of literary persuasion. They would in effect say to the god, "Act now for the sufferer who recites this account (or on whose behalf it is recited) as you did for the sufferer described in this story."

Despite the possible sharpening of the language of complaint, the theology of AO 4462 is completely in keeping with the other Mesopotamian texts of the exemplary sufferer. But the narrative and dramatic elements in its composition do warrant a comparison with Job, most particularly, the direct speech of the deity in response to the sufferer's prayer. Here one does have a dramatizing of the divine change of heart that other texts simply report as having happened. It thus represents a distinctively realized form of the pattern Hartmut Gese suggested for all of these Mesopotamian pious-sufferer texts, "the paradigm of the answered complaint" (*Klageerhörungsparadigma*).[24] From the perspective of the book of Job the question is whether or not the material following the wisdom dialogue, when Job gives his final speech (Job 29–31) and God replies (Job 38:1– 42:6) is an adaptation of the pattern of the answered complaint, and specifically of a tradition in which the words of the deity are explicitly cited. Zuckerman argues that this is the case, that "it would appear that the poet of Job determined to amalgamate two genres together, coupling Dialogue with Appeal—the common denominator in both types being the focus upon a Righteous Sufferer— a figure that is certainly quite appropriate as a model for Job."[25] The cogency of this comparison to the genre of the answered appeal or complaint will be taken up in chapter 9, when the relation of Job 29–31 and 38:1–42:6 is discussed.

To summarize, even though the Mesopotamian texts examined here do not belong to the same genre as Job 3–27, they do contain topoi, motifs, and ideas present in the book of Job, either in "straight" form or as the background against which a parodic or subversive representation is constructed. These features include the figure of the exemplary sufferer, the topoi of the innate sinfulness of humankind and the limits of human understanding, the paradigm of the answered lament, the conventions by which suffering are described, the theologoumena of divine wrath and compassion and of the efficacy of prayer in changing the mood of deity.

The Wisdom Dialogue

Although the wisdom dialogue belongs to a different genre from the various appeal-to-the-deity texts, it is not entirely unrelated. The figure of the exemplary sufferer is also a character in the wisdom dialogue, though his role is no longer that of modeling the normative stance of piety in the face of suffering. Important aspects of the theology of the appeal texts also find expression in the wisdom dialogues, primarily through the voice of the friend(s) of the sufferer. However, as Müller has noted, the purpose of the wisdom dialogue is different. It serves as a vehicle for exploring the existence of a moral order in the cosmos, not as representation of suffering and appeal to the deity.

In a recent article, Karel van der Toorn investigated the characteristic features of the wisdom dialogue, which he prefers to call a "literary dialogue."[26] Van der Toorn establishes a corpus of three primary texts that share a distinctive pattern with respect to form, content, mood, and social context. These are the Egyptian text known as the Dialogue of a Man with His Ba (the *Lebensmüde*), the Babylonian Theodicy, and the poetic section of the book of Job. In addition, two other texts are closely related: the Mesopotamian Dialogue of Pessimism and the Egyptian Complaints of Kha-Kheper-Re-Seneb.

The most distinctive generic markers that serve to sort this group of texts from others that bear more distant comparisons include (1) the form of a freestanding dialogue in which a single question is examined by two or more speakers representing two contrasting perspectives; (2) the topic considered, which is that of the problem of inexplicable suffering or, more broadly, the meaningfulness of life; (3) an exploratory stance, which van der Toorn calls the "interrogative" as opposed to the "affirmative" mood and which Giorgio Buccellati calls the stance of critical inquisitiveness;[27] (4) the use of a sophisticated style and techniques of composition that suggest a setting among the intellectual elites, and probably more specifically among professional "academics." Van der Toorn properly distinguishes the dialogues from the *tensons*, or disputes, which were a popular feature of Mesopotamian literature (e.g., The Ewe and Wheat, The Date Palm and the Tamarisk). Though they belong to another genre (characterized, among other things, by nonhuman characters, the topic of precedence, an explicit judgment in favor of one of the disputants), certain aspects of their style of argument bear comparison with the dialogues, as I note later.

Any attempt to discuss a genre for which there exists only a small sample of texts from three different cultures is fraught with problems. Complicating the matter even further is the fact that in one of these examples, Job, the genre has been incorporated as a component part of a larger and more complex multigeneric work. Although van der Toorn does not state explicitly what part of Job he includes in his comparison, he appears to include Job 29–31 and 38:1–42:6,[28] a judgment I find problematic, since none of the other examples includes a divine theophany. As noted earlier, Zuckerman more carefully distinguishes between that part of Job that is structured according to the wisdom dialogue (chaps. 3–27) and that part which may be formally similar to another genre, the appeal of the sufferer to a god (chaps. 29–31, 38:1–42:6), although he acknowledges that motifs characteristic of the appeal also appear in the dialogue portion of Job.[29] While one must be careful not to reify the notion of genre, Zuckerman's discrimination is apt. That chapters 3–27 constitute the appropriate unit for generic analysis is evident not only from comparison with other texts but also from features internal to Job.[30] The poem in chapter 28 is widely recognized as generically distinct from the dialogue and indeed seems to comment upon it. It appears to serve as a "spacer" between one large component genre (the wisdom dialogue) and the different material that follows in chapters 29–31 and 38:1–42:6. In differentiating in this way I am not suggesting that the parts are autonomous or unconnected but only that one needs to attend to the meaningfulness of a technique of composition that involves the juxtaposition of recognizably distinct genres or modes of speech.

The three texts primarily considered by van der Toorn do not all share the same degree of relationship. By far the most striking similarities exist between the Babylonian Theodicy and Job 3–27. In both a righteous sufferer initiates a dialogue with a friend or friends. Topically, the enigma of unjustified suffering dominates, though it leads to reflection on the elusiveness and moral questionableness of the divine, the existence or nonexistence of a moral order in the cosmos, and the ethical distortions of the social order. The friend(s) urge(s) the sufferer to avail himself of the traditional practices of piety, contrasting the passing nature of misfortune with what is lasting, and arguing that the wicked will eventually receive punishment. Stylistically, both compositions reflect a high degree of literary sophistication, though developed through different techniques. The Babylonian Theodicy is structured according to a complex acrostic, the initial syllables of the lines of each stanza identifying the author of the composition ("I, Saggil-kinam-ubbib, the incantation priest, am adorant of the god and the king"). Each eleven-line stanza consists of couplets with a single isolated line that bears special emphasis.[31] The dialogue in Job is arranged according to three cycles of alternating speeches by Job and his friends, though the third cycle, whether by design or by accident, breaks the pattern. Although there is no acrostic structure,[32] the poetry is exquisite and the diction erudite. Rhetorically, after the initial speech, each speaker tends to begin with an observation on the wisdom (or lack thereof) of the preceding speaker and often makes critical judgments on the cogency of the other party's reasoning. In the Babylonian Theodicy the parties to the dialogue are unfailingly polite, whereas in Job, the opening remarks become increasingly hostile and insulting. In both compositions a proverbial aphorism often serves as a focus around which an argument is developed.[33] A number of the same topics occur in both compositions: the prosperity of the wicked, the sudden demise of the wicked, the ultimate reward of the righteous, the failure of observation to demonstrate divine retribution, the remoteness of divine reason from human understanding, and so forth.

In many ways, of course, the Joban dialogue differs from the Babylonian Theodicy. There is no parallel in the Babylonian Theodicy to Job's sporadic direct address to God. The Joban dialogue incorporates many subgenres and set pieces (e.g., psalmic and hymnic genres, the fate-of-the-wicked poems, wisdom instructions) that are not found in the Babylonian Theodicy. The rhetoric of parody, so prominent in Job's own speeches, has no counterpart in the simple earnestness of the Babylonian Theodicy. Job is also considerably more emotionally intense. The Joban dialogue develops in ways more dynamic and even unexpected than does the Babylonian Theodicy. The forensic metaphor, for example, so important to Job, emerges almost accidentally and introduces a *novum* that could not have been anticipated from the initial stance of the characters.

Although the Babylonian Theodicy was composed sometime between 1400 and 800 B.C.E. and remained quite popular, with many copies extant, including one as late as the Seleucid or Parthian period,[34] it would be a mistake to think in terms of direct contact between the Babylonian Theodicy and Job. Zuckerman is correct that the pattern of similarities and differences between the two does not suggest direct influence but rather knowledge of a common genre.[35] The striking similarities between two such sophisticated works in different languages strongly suggest that the conventions of the genre were well defined and broadly recognized across Mesopotamia and the Levant. In all probability other works representative of this genre once existed but are now lost.[36] How such a genre and the accompanying generic competency spread across cultural boundaries we do not know. In the past, scholars have suggested that the city-states of Late Bronze Age Canaan may have been the conduits. Even though no dialogue texts have been found in the West, Akkadian literary and wisdom texts have been recovered from Ugarit and other Canaanite and Syrian cities.[37] But one might also consider the Mesopotamian Jewish diaspora of the Babylonian and Persian periods as a cultural conduit. The incorporation of Ahikar as text and tradition into Jewish literature, as well as the influence of Nabonidus traditions on Daniel or Enmeduranki traditions on the Enoch literature, suggests a widespread knowledge and adaptation of eastern texts and traditions in Jewish literature of the Persian period, the time when the book of Job is generally assumed to have been written.

For my purposes it does not matter that one cannot trace the path of generic diffusion. The comparison of the texts is sufficient to establish that they do share generic affinity. More problematic is the paucity of extant examples, for it makes it difficult to judge which patterns of similarity between the two texts are truly generic markers and, alternatively, which patterns of dissimilarity are simply common variations in the genre and which are intentional inversions or parodies of normally stable elements of the genre.

As discussed in chapter 1, Medvedev and Bakhtin described genre as a means of grasping or perceiving reality, quite literally a *form of thought*. Genres are samples of the world grasped in a particular way. They are not simply forms, nor simply ideologies, but "form-shaping ideologies." No analysis can adequately translate a genre's claims into propositional language that describes the content of its "take" on the world, for the experience it renders is not wholly conceptual, though such analysis can direct attention to features of genre that might otherwise be overlooked. Similarly, no treatment of form can ignore the truth claims of the genre itself, for its very form is a type of claim about the nature of the world. In thinking about genre in terms of what it does, one may adapt Wayne Booth's observations about the relation of particular texts to desire and ask how certain genres offer to stimulate and satisfy certain kinds of desire, how they offer to remake readers, at least provisionally, into different kinds of desirers. Thus, the issues to be pursued in this section are how this genre of the wisdom dialogue perceives reality, and how it attempts to shape the reader's desire.

Perhaps the most significant aspect of the imagination of the wisdom dialogue is the way in which it grasps reality in a nonnarrative engagement between two opposed experiences of the world that alternate in a measured and regular fashion throughout the entire work. Buccellati frames the issues well.

> The dialog starts out *in medias res*, and it folds at the end upon itself, without extra-dialogic statements. . . . The dramatic dimension of these texts, then, derives . . . from the formal channel chosen for expression. The alternation of different personalities is projected unto a plane all by itself, and its impact is thereby strengthened. There is a tensional factor in any dialog, presupposing as it does commonality and confrontation at one and the same time: and when a dialog is presented in and of itself, without an extrinsic setting, it lends a special resonance to the concept of a dialectical juxtaposition of points of view. It appears, then, that the correlation between wisdom themes and dialogic form is a very meaningful one: the dialog, pure and simple, emphasizes the unfolding of a thought process viewed dynamically in its becoming.[38]

Implicit in Buccellati's observations are the insights that for the wisdom dialogue reality is best apprehended (1) by argument rather than story, (2) at its points of contradiction. Concerning the first point, in contrast to the resources of a narrative imagination that explores reality by means of causally related actions carried out in a fictive world (e.g., Gilgamesh's failed and fulfilled quest), the wisdom dialogue grasps reality by means of observation and argument. All the pieces to the puzzle are already at hand, in experience, observation, tradition. Thus, the critical mind is the privileged instrument for the apprehension of the world. Both in the Babylonian Theodicy and in Job the cogency of argument becomes a highly self-conscious topic. Correspondingly, rational argument is burlesqued in the Dialogue of Pessimism. Even reality's resistance to human understanding ("the mind of the gods is remote," etc.) is turned into something of an achievement for rationality in the Babylonian Theodicy, for in recognizing its limits the critical consciousness of the sage also describes with clarity and insightfulness the nature of the world it inhabits.

The connoisseurship of rhetorical argument in the dialogues sometimes seems almost at odds with the urgency of the topic, though perhaps the contrast is not so peculiar after all. Fowler observes that the values of a genre are not necessarily those of the characters or even the moral world depicted in the text.[39] Though many readers over the centuries have chosen to identify fairly directly with the positions and passions of one or the other side in the dialogue, the genre itself seems rather to value the play of thought in its own right. To cite Buccellati again,

> the dialogic form is then especially apt to reflect the spirit of critical inquisitiveness, which represents . . . a major wisdom theme. Since the search itself is a value, and its very experience an achievement, it stands to reason that the correlative literary embodiment should acquire an autonomous preeminence. The dialog is the outward form of a conceptual clarification obtained through a dialectical alternation.[40]

Reflection on the values implicit in the genre allows one to see what a different character such texts give to the reader from that given by the texts of the didactic tales examined in the preceding chapter. There the simple language, conceptual clarity, and redundant structures of narrative and moral authority all work together to produce an infantilized reader. As the didactic tale construes the relations of authority, implied author and implied reader are situated in a distinctly nonegalitarian relationship. The wisdom dialogue could not be more different. The difficulty of the aesthetic forms and language of the text implies a reader who is erudite and capable of appreciating the subtleties of the text. Moreover, the dialogue, with its skeptical as well as traditionalist voices, assumes an intellectually sophisticated but not necessarily alienated reader.

To proceed to the second point, in the imagination of the wisdom dialogues critical inquisitiveness is best exercised and the world most adequately grasped at the point of contradiction. Rather than concealing or softening contradictions as other forms of discourse may do, the structure of the dialogue highlights them. Indeed, contradiction is the governing trope for the wisdom dialogue, represented formally in the binary structure of the dialogue, represented rhetorically in the argumentative contradictions by each speaker of the other's claims, and represented existentially in the contradictions between expectation and experience on the sufferer's part. It would be overly simplistic, however, to say that in the imagination of the wisdom dialogues reality itself partakes of the structure of contradiction, though that may be the claim of particular texts (e.g., the Dialogue of Pessimism). But neither is contradiction merely a device. In order to assess its significance, however, one must address the difficult question of the purpose and outcome of the dialogues.

One of the most important and yet most perplexing issues pertaining to the moral imagination of the genre is whether the arguments are presented in a progressive manner and whether a resolution is intended or achieved. Buccellati is inclined to speak of a dynamic, even dialectical movement inherent in the dialogues, which would contrast them with the utterly static disputation litera- ture (e.g., The Ewe and the Wheat, The Date Palm and the Tamarisk), which are little more than personified binary contrasts in which one figure attempts to establish its excellence over the other, a relation of precedence taken as a given by the form. In the wisdom dialogue, however, "the central question has no predetermined answer."[41] Nevertheless, Buccellati overstates the case in calling the wisdom dialogues a form of dialectic that anticipates Socratic dialogue. Unlike the Socratic dialectic in which "through a dynamic rendering of a process of mental acquisition, the natural birth of an idea [occurs, and] the reader, or lis- tener, identifies so fully with the process that the resulting conclusion is already internalized in its premises,"[42] there is no such smooth development from con- trasting premises to conclusions in the Near Eastern dialogues.

Van der Toorn, who also wishes to see in the literary dialogues some sort of "attempt to contrast opposite views, in order to arrive at a new perspective," nevertheless observes that "one cannot say that the literary dialogues really lead up to their conclusions."[43] Instead, in the *Lebensmüde*, for example, after re- peating "again and again the same idea in different forms . . . the eventual com- promise comes somewhat as a surprise to the reader."[44] Thus, van der Toorn ends up puzzled over how what "look[s] like a poor outcome"[45] was apparently perceived as convincing. The Mesopotamian exemplars he sees as even less capable of reaching the new perspective he had assumed was the purpose of the dialogues, for in the Babylonian Theodicy, though the two friends agree that the gods created humankind with a tendency to perversity, "the conclusion dodges the real issue. The problem of the theodicy remains unresolved."[46] Similarly, the Dialogue of Pessimism "ends on the conclusion that a final answer is beyond human reach."[47] Gray, somewhat dismissively, declares the "answer" given by the Babylonian Theodicy to be "facile."[48]

Despite many acute observations, the problem with these approaches is, as Denning-Bolle has pointed out, the distorting effect of reading the Near East- ern dialogues through the expectations formed by the more familiar Socratic dialogues, which do lead the reader through a dialectical process of thought to a newly perceived conclusion.[49] Rather than assuming that the Near Eastern texts represent intellectual or aesthetic failures, however, one should reconsider whether a different set of generic expectations governs their composition. Given the frustration of modern critics who look in vain for some clear development and resolution, it appears that a definitive answer or the clear triumph of one perspective over another was probably not the intention of the genre. Zuckerman comes closest to grasping the desires such texts stimulate and satisfy when he speaks of their organization "as essentially reiterative rather than linearly progressive. . . . The pleasure derived by an ancient audience in this form of literary expression may be something akin to what we find in listening to a musical piece of theme and variations . . . , a cyclic progression that ultimately turns back on itself, . . . a kind of counterpoint."[50] The analogy, if pursued too far, would become misleading, but it has the virtue of helping a puzzled modern reader begin to grasp as satisfaction rather than as frustration a very different way of thinking about the nature of argument and its relation to the world. Zuckerman's observations are largely directed to issues of structure and style, but if one agrees with Bakhtin that a genre is a "form-shaping ideology," then such elements are also part of a distinctive intellectual stance.

The position for which I will argue throughout this chapter is that the ancient Near Eastern wisdom dialogues seek neither to demonstrate the triumph of one voice over the other nor to argue their way to a resolution. Even in Job, the traditionalist voice is not a mere setup for the triumph of skepticism. But just as resolution is not achieved by the elimination of one perspective, so there is no transcendence of the opposition in a new consensus. There may be pragmatic compromise, as in the *Lebensmüde* or the Babylonian Theodicy, but no true resolution. This is not to say that there is no development in the ideas advanced. Both in the Babylonian Theodicy and much more dramatically in Job ideas develop by means of the dialogue that could not have been articulated at the beginning of the conversation. Yet at the end, two incommensurable ways of apprehending and engaging the world remain simply juxtaposed, both requiring acknowledgment.

The frustration many scholars express at the lack of a linear progression of argument and a definitive conclusion reveals more about modern preferences for monologic truth and its corresponding forms of expression than it does about these ancient texts. A monologic truth may be expressed in the form of a dialogue, of course. In such cases dialogue is simply a pedagogical instrument designed to teach a "ready-made" truth. Indeed, Bakhtin criticized Plato for progressively reducing the genuinely dialogic elements of the Socratic dialogues in just this way.[51] The question I would raise is whether or not one can see in the ancient Near Eastern wisdom dialogues something akin to what Bakhtin meant by genuine dialogue and the dialogic sense of truth.

In many respects the ancient Near Eastern wisdom dialogues would not conform to Bakhtin's ideal, which includes elements specifically shaped by nineteeth- and twentieth-century European values and conceptions of subjectivity. Nevertheless, if one does not press too far, there are several respects in which Bakhtin's notion of a dialogic sense of truth may enable a better grasp of the distinctive imagination of these ancient wisdom dialogues. Though I have drawn attention to the lack of resolution in the wisdom dialogues, this is neither a necessary nor sufficient condition for identifying them as "dialogic" in Bakhtin's sense. Bakhtin was not opposed to the dialogic development of a consensual position. What he identified as the mark of a true dialogue is that there is no "ready-made truth." Rather, truth "is born *between people* collectively searching."[52] Even when such truth takes the form of an eventual agreement, however, it cannot be summed up as a proposition. Such summing up would violate the distinctiveness of the dialogic character, which exists in the way in which different perspectives engage one another. Thus, the nonresolved character of the wisdom dialogues is suggestive of the fact that something different from monologic discourse is present, but this feature should not by itself be identified with a dialogic mode.

In chapter 1, I summarized the four characteristics of the dialogic conception of truth: (1) that a dialogic sense of truth exists at the point of intersection of a plurality of unmerged voices, (2) that dialogic truth has an embodied, almost personal quality, (3) that the unity of a dialogic sense of truth is the unity of an "event" rather than of a "system," and (4) that dialogic truth is always open, "unfinalizable." Each of these four characteristics can be discerned in the wisdom dialogues.

First, a dialogic sense of truth exists at the point of intersection of a plurality of unmerged voices. The difference between dialogic and monologic representation can be grasped if one compares the wisdom dialogues with the meditations on theodicy one finds in certain psalms, for example, Psalms 37, 49, 73. Psalm 73 is particularly instructive, for there both positions, the skeptical and the traditional, are represented, though within the same consciousness. The speaker represents the skeptical position as one he had previously held but now considers to be in error. Thus, the tension between the two positions is resolved by organizing them into a temporal sequence that can be narrated as a story of the movement from error to truth. The skeptical position can no longer "mean directly," as Bakhtin would put it, because it is perceived only through the lens of another position now deemed superior to it. In contrast, the wisdom dialogue, by representing distinct characters presently engaged with contrasting positions, neither of which is self-evidently the spokesperson for the author's privileged view, allows both positions to address the reader with formally equivalent force. The relation to truth between these two genres is quite different. For the meditation, truth can be spoken by a single voice, and summed up. For the dialogue, truth resists summation, for it is expressed in the way in which the opposed observations shade and shadow one another. The difference between the two modes is the difference between the didactic and the dialogic.

Second, dialogic truth has an embodied, almost personal quality. Bakhtin referred to the characters in dialogic works as "voice-ideas." Their vitality as characters was centered in the way they were grasped by an idea and acted out of that idea. What one has to reckon with when such characters speak is not simply a propositional assertion but an "integral point of view, the integral position of a personality."[53] This observation recalls Buccellati's claim that one of the distinctive features of the cultural tradition of Mesopotamian wisdom was the cultivation of the "introspective voice," what he somewhat anachronistically calls the "lyric 'I.'"[54] Though this phenomenon was not restricted to dialogue texts (the voice in the meditative psalm is also an introspective voice), it was indispensable for their project. What Buccellati calls the "introspective voice" is characterized not only by the stylistic use of the first person pronoun but by the way in which specific human experiences and the emotions to which they give rise are enlisted in the service of constructing arguments about universal reality. Although present in the *Lebensmüde* and in the Babylonian Theodicy, the dialogue in Job represents an extraordinary development of the dialogic possibilities of the embodied perspective. Even though the sufferer's experience is most vividly described, one should not think of the wisdom dialogues as exercises in the hermeneutics of tradition versus experience, as it is sometimes stated. Both positions in the wisdom dialogue are experientially grounded; both are represented as the "integral positions of personalities." What is crucial for the dialogic quality of the encounter is precisely that they are differently positioned, noninterchangeable experiences of the world. This feature is what is given up when dialogue is recast as narrativized meditation.

The third feature of a dialogic sense of truth, the quality of its unity as that of "event" rather than "system," is closely related to the embodied, personal nature of the voice-ideas that constitute the participants in the dialogue. This irreducible perspectival difference resists reduction of the dialogue into a conclusion, however carefully nuanced, that could be articulated by a single consciousness. The "image of an idea" involves not just its articulation by an individual voice but its interaction with other ideas. Thus, the notion that there is a deep structure of justice at the heart of existence must interact with the idea of the arbitrariness or hostility of the divine, be complicated by considerations of temporality, engage the epistemological claims of direct observation and the limits of human reason, and so forth. The identity of the idea about the place of justice in the world is the sum of its interactions within the dialogue and beyond it.

As the preceding sentence already suggests, the fourth feature of a dialogic sense of truth is that it is always open, for the ultimate word cannot be spoken.

As Bakhtin noted, constructing a plausible ending for a dialogic or polyphonic work is difficult, for the temptation, at least in the modern tradition, has been to finalize. What annoys so many modern readers of the wisdom dialogues, I suspect, is the genre's fidelity to the formal implications of a dialogic conception of truth. The ending of the Babylonian Theodicy is particularly apt. There each of the participants, without abandoning his own commitments, nevertheless acknowledges something of the truth or necessity of the other's position. The friend does not retract his view concerning the just nature of what is "lasting" in the structure of reality, yet he acknowledges the surd of an ineradicable and divinely created perversity in human nature. The sufferer does not repudiate the reality of the contradiction between his behavior and his situation, yet entrusts himself to the mercy of the gods and the shepherdship of Shamash, god of justice. Herman Vanstiphout, in speaking of the Sumerian dispute literature, noted that even though those works conclude with a decision in favor of one of the disputants, "it is *also* explicitly mentioned that both parties remain necessary to the world."[55] Although I would not claim a close connection between the two genres, the combination of polarity and complementarity that Vanstiphout sees as characterizing the intellectual perspective of the dispute literature seems also to be reflected in the form-shaping ideology of the dialogues.

The issue of the "ending" of the Joban dialogue is problematic, of course, since the dialogue is juxtaposed to other genres (the wisdom poem of chap. 28, the appeal in chaps. 29–31, etc.) for the formation of a multigeneric work. Yet it is noteworthy that one of the persistent critical problems of the Joban dialogue is the way in which Job's speeches in the third cycle appear to incorporate elements of the friends' speeches, specifically versions of the "fate of the wicked" (24:18–25 and 27:13–23) and hymnic celebration of the power of God (26:5–14), whereas the friends grow increasingly silent (a full speech by Eliphaz in chap. 22, an abbreviated one by Bildad in chap. 25, and none from Zophar). Whatever is going on in the third cycle of Job is more complex than what happens in the Babylonian Theodicy, but to attribute it to scribal error is to evade rather than to acknowledge the issues. In the *Lebensmüde* and in the Babylonian Theodicy the exhaustion of dialogue, reflected in the "compromise" with which the texts conclude, is a reflex of the inexhaustibility of dialogue. Though a thorough examination of the third cycle of Job must wait for a later chapter, it seems likely that the Job poet is playing with the conventions for ending wisdom dialogues. In appropriating elements of the friends' set-pieces, Job is doing a version of what is expected of the sufferer; yet the way in which he makes this appropriation deranges the argument rather than shapes an ending for it. At the same time, and much more ominously, the withdrawal of the friends into silence signals not an appropriate ending but a collapse of dialogue. Together these two antimovements invite the introduction of other genres into the work, namely, the critique of the dialogue voiced by the wisdom poem (chap. 28) and the alternative search for a resolution attempted by the appeal/response (chaps. 29–31, 38:1–42:6).

Although attending to the moral imagination represented by the genre perspective of the wisdom dialogue would be important under any circumstances, the structure of the book of Job, with its juxtaposition of genres of contrasting moral imaginations compels such attention. Together the prose tale and the wisdom dialogue expose each other's assumptions, each other's "take" on the world. Whereas the prose tale's sense of wholeness is unbreakable, the wisdom dialogue is fascinated with unmendable brokenness. The didactic tale controls perspectives and dissident voices. The wisdom dialogue privileges dissidence, as it lets unmediated perspectives speak to and against one another. To borrow van der Toorn's expression, one expresses an affirmative, the other an interrogative mood. Stylistic homeliness contrasts with stylistic urbanity. Whereas the prose tale offers the reader an infantilized position, as authority for making moral judgments is lodged with the narrator, the dialogue not only requires the reader to make independent moral judgments but construes the reader as something of an intellectual, a connoisseur of argument. One offers the image of an utterly finalized character, the other a sufferer who may cease to speak but who has not uttered his final word. To tell the "same" story by means of these two genres is to make palpable what each hides from itself when it is allowed to be the only voice.

Attention to genre and to the moral imagination embedded in the features of genre itself is only the first step. As it was necessary to examine in close detail the construction of meaning in the monologic prose tale, so now it is necessary to attempt to trace in some detail the way in which the wisdom dialogue develops in contrasting fashion two profound but utterly incompatible moral imaginations.

4

"Consolations of God"

The Moral Imagination of the Friends

When someone complains—as do some of those who attempt or commit
suicide—that his or her life is meaningless, he or she is often and perhaps
characteristically complaining that the narrative of their life has become
unintelligible to them, that it lacks any point.

Alasdair MacIntyre, *After Virtue*

Since chapters 3–27 are structured according to the form of a wisdom dialogue,
a genre that displays contrasting positions explicitly, it might seem there is little
to do here other than to summarize the claims of the two positions. Such an
approach would not, however, be apt for the issues I want to pursue. Although
the propositional content of what Job and the friends say is important, I am
more interested in the ways their speech gives clues to differences in perspective
that are as much latent as manifest. What are the tropes that figure not just
their speech but their very perception? What generative metaphors govern and
shape their understanding? By what privileged genres do they grasp reality?
Commentators often observe that Job and his friends actually share a number
of assumptions about God and the world, differing mainly on the issue of Job's
innocence or guilt. Though it is true that they share many things, what separates them is not so much a matter of fact—Job's innocence or guilt—as their
radically different moral imaginations, the rhetorical resources by means of which
they each explore questions of meaning and value.

Part of what I want to attempt is a self-conscious rehabilitation of the friends.
Criticized ever since Elihu, they have fared particularly badly in twentieth-century
readings. Frequently, the friends are interpreted as religiously narrow, mean-
spirited hypocrites. Even when given credit for sincerity and initial compassion,
they are seldom taken seriously as articulating a view of reality that might have
its own claims to truth. Such reactions toward the friends, whether hostile or
merely condescending, seem motivated, at least in part, by a sense that to take
their arguments seriously is somehow to join in a vicious blaming of the victim,
a further act of violence against Job. Such an attitude, though nobly motivated,

diminishes the intellectual challenge of the book. What is lost when the friends are dismissed is the generic force of the wisdom dialogue as a confrontation between two significant but incommensurable perspectives. To a certain extent this problem of balance has been addressed and a measure of dignity restored to the friends through the attempt to situate them within their appropriate cultural context: Israelite exemplars of a venerable ancient Near Eastern moral and religious perspective that finds its first expression in ancient Sumerian literature.[1] Such a historicist approach, though an essential starting point, is not all I am after. I seek a hermeneutical engagement with Job's friends. In this regard the fact that their perspectives seem so much at odds with modern critical tastes may prove an asset. Their strangeness may become a means to the self-estrangement that according to Gerald Bruns is essential to the hermeneutical encounter. He distinguishes the hermeneutical from the historicist reading of a text as follows. In hermeneutical engagement "we encounter the other in its otherness, not as an object in a different time and place but as that which resists the grasp of my knowledge or which requires me to loosen my hold or open my fist. . . . I always experience the refusal of the other to be contained in the conceptual apparatus that I have prepared for it or that my own time and place have prepared for it."[2] In place of the "how facile!" or "how awful!" that constitutes such a common modern response to—or deflection of—the friends, I wish to substitute a stance of curiosity about their refusal to be contained in the moral categories that constitute the resources of my own intellectual circle. What is the nature of their "otherwise perceiving"? Whether or not I find in their perception a grasp of the world that can become in some way my own, to have understood what is at stake in that perception is to know my own commitments differently.

Job's Setting of the Issues

Though this chapter will focus primarily on the perspectives of the friends, they do not set the agenda. In the wisdom dialogue that role belongs to the sufferer, whose outcry elicits the responsive words of the friend(s). Thus, it is important to turn first to Job's first speech in chapter 3.[3]

Though too few exemplars remain to know with certainty what conventions may have governed the opening speech of a wisdom dialogue,[4] one might surmise that the sufferer's first speech has two basic and related functions—to announce the speaker's distress and to do so in a way that invites response. If one may take this as a working hypothesis, it is possible to see how differently the Babylonian Theodicy and the Joban dialogue exploit this generic expectation for different effects. The Babylonian Theodicy begins straightforwardly with an explicit appeal by the sufferer to his friend to be allowed to speak of his distress: "O sage [. . .] come, [let] me speak to you [. . .] let me recount to you" (lines 1–2).[5] In the absence of a narrative framing, which the Babylonian Theodicy does not have, such an opening signals the presence of a listener, a second character who would not otherwise yet be discernible to the reader. The sufferer's words in the Babylonian Theodicy specifically construe the friend as an "addressable other." Thus, the words of the sufferer that follow are already dialogical, since they are framed in relation to another and in expectation of a hearing and a response ("Where is one whose reflective capacity is as great as yours? Who is he whose knowledge could rival yours?" lines 4–5).

In speaking to the friend, the sufferer does not simply convey content but makes himself present to the other through his self-witness. He first gives a general characterization of his grief as *lumnu libbi*, literally, an "evil of the heart." This phrase is difficult to render in English. Though Foster's "heartache" echoes the semantics of the phrase, Lambert's "anguish"[6] may better catch its emotional and cognitive dimensions. Having characterized his state generally, the sufferer relates his anguish to the conditions of his life: Orphaned at an early age, he was abandoned without support. He thus entrusts his story to another.

In Job the narrative frame of the prose tale has already established the presence of the friends. This makes possible in chapter 3 what may be a play both with and against the conventions for beginning a wisdom dialogue. Like the sufferer of the Babylonian Theodicy, Job thematizes his suffering with a summary term, "turmoil" (3:26; *rōgez*), and relates it to the conditions of his birth. Job laments not that he was orphaned but that he was born at all. The absence of any directed address or acknowledgment of the presence of another in Job's opening speech, however, is what casts the dynamics of this wisdom dialogue differently from that of the Babylonian Theodicy. Though the bafflement of suffering does not yield to clarity in the Babylonian Theodicy, that work situates the act of dialogue itself under the sign of compassionate presence. Just as the sufferer began his first speech with the appeal for another to hear, so his final speech asks for the compassionate gaze that acknowledges suffering: "You are kind, my friend; behold my grief. Help me; look on my distress; know it" (trans. Lambert). Thus, the Babylonian Theodicy highlights both dimensions of speech as Levinas characterizes them. The Babylonian Theodicy revels in the capacity of wisdom discourse to highlight the Said, that is, the content of the speeches and their thematization of the world. But it frames that philosophical orientation within the ethical dimension of speech, the Saying, that is, the character of the words as address and the ethical relationship established by such address to another.

Whether this aspect of the Babylonian Theodicy is characteristic of the genre of the wisdom dialogue one cannot know. But comparison of the Babylonian Theodicy with Job sets the absence of explicit addressivity in Job's opening speech in sharp relief. That the encounter with the three friends subsequently takes the form of a dialogue is apparently not part of Job's initial intention but is initiated by Eliphaz, who recognizes that he has not in fact been invited to speak (4:2). The relationship between the parties and the conditions for their speech is thus much more ambivalently constructed than in the Babylonian Theodicy and leaves its mark on the ensuing dialogue in a number of ways: from the critique of failed friendship in chapter 6, to the bitter characterizations of one another's speech that introduce the responses (in contrast to the critical but respectful comments in the Babylonian Theodicy), to the eventual collapse of dialogue altogether.

The problem of the lack of an addressable other is also signaled in the choice and modification of the genre Job uses when he does break his silence—the curse on the day of his birth. Here, too, one is hampered by the small number of extant examples, for only in Jeremiah 20:14-18 is there a comparable instance. These two, however, exhibit precise agreement in the parts of the genre, which are four: (1) the curse on the day (Jer 20:14//Job 3:3a, 4-5); (2) the curse on the messenger who brought news of the birth (Jer 20:15-16//Job 3:3b, 6-9); (3) the reason for the curse (Jer 20:17//Job 3:10); and (4) the concluding lament (Jer 20:28//Job 3:11-23). Many have analyzed the form and debated its intent.[7] Whether intended as a "real" curse or only a rhetorical one, the curse on the day of one's birth has the shape of performative speech. Thus, the words orient themselves ostensibly toward their object rather than toward a listener. Nevertheless, one may ask if, despite their overt form, they are not a form of covert address. Zuckerman insightfully describes Jeremiah's use of the curse as a prayer in extremis, a "lament of last resort," intended "to portray a sufferer's distress in the most nihilistic terms possible for the purpose of attracting God's attention and thus leading to the rescue of the sufferer from affliction."[8] The curse on the day of one's birth serves to signify a distress so pervasive and so deep that it makes direct address in a prayer of supplication impossible.

Such an analysis may adequately describe the pragmatic intent of Jeremiah's curse, but it is less clear that it is apt for Job's words. The imagery of Job's curse, with its evocation of the reversal of creation and its excessive development of the concluding lament into a baroque transvaluation of life and death, suggests that Job's curse on the day of his birth cannot be decoded as a tacit appeal for rescue. Death, the condition for which Job longs, is characterized in Israelite thought as the place where all communicative relations with God—both supplication and praise—are ended (Pss 6:6; 30:10; 88:5-6; Isa 38:18). Only the fact that Job breaks his silence and speaks aloud suggests that the addressivity essential to human existence remains present even in an attenuated way in Job.

What makes the fundamental human capacity to address another so problematic to Job is not simply the magnitude of his suffering but its quality, which he describes in more subtle detail than does the sufferer of the Babylonian Theodicy. Job identifies the characteristic feature of his suffering most explicitly in the exquisite pair of verses that conclude the chapter: "Truly, the dread thing I dreaded has arrived, and what I feared has come upon me. I have no ease, no quiet, no rest; what comes is turmoil" (3:25-26). Job experiences his suffering as turmoil (rōgez). At the level of the book as a whole, Job's words refer to the events of chapters 1-2. Even when read that way, however, his words do not describe the events themselves but the way those events are experientially inscribed on Job's psyche. Job's language consolidates them into a single experience that has the quality of a ghastly encounter (note the verbs "arrive" [ʾātāh] and "come" [bôʾ]). This encounter has a complex temporality. It did not take him utterly by surprise, for he first refers to this experience obliquely, in terms of anticipatory anxiety ("the dread thing that I dreaded . . . what I feared"). In his description Job approaches his naming of this thing by indirection, describing first the condition it displaced, namely, tranquility. Only in the last words of the chapter is it named: "what comes is rōgez." But what does he mean? This noun and its cognate verb and adjective denote a state of agitation. With respect to inanimate objects they describe a physical shaking (2 Sam 22:8; Amos 8:8; Hab 3:7); when used of human or divine beings, they denote intense emotional agitation (2 Sam 19:1; Jer 33:9; Joel 2:1; Ps 99:1).

The strategic placing of the thematic term as the last word of his speech sends one back to the imagery of the curse for clues to the connotations of rōgez. Though Job is not ostensibly talking about himself in the curse (vv. 3-10), in fact his curses rhetorically contaminate the day of his birth with the turmoil of his own experience. Rōgez is to the order of lived experience as chaos is to cosmic order; hence Job's choice of anti-creation imagery ("let it be darkness," 3:4, inverting Gen 1:3), imagery of emotional terror (3:5b), and the unleashing of the chaos monster Leviathan (3:8b). The day of his birth would be subjected to the very suffering he now experiences, because it did not prevent his birth and life (v. 10). But the imagery of the curse and Job's words of lament bear a more complicated relationship to each other than this simple symmetry would suggest.

Strikingly, Job invokes as a curse on the day of his birth some of the conditions he positively wishes for himself as relief and release from the miseries of existence. Consider the ambivalence of "light." In the curse, light is a positive value, and to deprive "day" of it is to do day great harm. Yet Job wishes that he himself, like the stillborn child, had "never seen the light" (3:16b). Similarly, the imagery of sociality is inverted in the two parts of Job's speech. Though less often noted than the light/darkness imagery, extensive imagery of sociality occurs in the curse, especially in the curse on the night of conception. There the night is prevented from "rejoicing with"[9] the days of the year, and from entering into the company of the months (3:6). It is to be a barren night, when no child is conceived, when there is no cry of sexual pleasure (3:7). Just as that night will not be permitted to provide the context for human contact and generative meeting, so its own yearning for its partner will be denied. The pairing of evening and morning, night and day is a fundamental part of the cosmogonic order (Gen 1:5; 8:22). In a subtle personification night is depicted in verse 8 as waiting to gaze upon the eyes (i.e., stars) of dawn. Yet this yearning for the face of night to meet the face of day is denied through the extinguishing of light. In contrast Job sees the fundamental elements of human sociality as instrumental in his suffering. He grieves that his mother's womb received the embrace of his father (3:10a) or that the nurture of a child by its father and mother, the receptivity of lap and breasts (3:12), prevented his immediate death.

The embitterment that turns the goods of light/life and sociality into a source of misery can only be understood in relation to the imagery of the lament. In his ironic praise of death, Job begins to characterize the dislocations he will summarize as *rōgez*. The thematic connection is underscored by the presence of several of the key words that will later appear in the summary verse–verse 26 (quiet [*šāqaṭ*], rest [*nûaḥ*], [cessation of] turmoil [*rōgez*]). These thematic words appear in the first verse of each of the two sections describing the condition of the dead (vv. 13, 17).

The peculiarity of the imagery in verses 11-16 is often remarked, for in imagining how fortunate he would have been to have died at birth and so now be at rest, Job observes that he would then be "with kings and counselors of the earth" (vv. 14-15). The point, of course, is not that death provides a way of improving one's social circle. Rather, the subtle irony is at the expense of the great ones, whose lives were characterized by restless but ultimately futile activity, "(re)building ruins for themselves," "filling their houses with silver" (v. 15). If all supposedly purposive activity is but futile agitation, then the dead infant is more fortunate than the magnates, for the one truly desirable thing, the rest of the grave (cf. vv. 21-22), comes to the stillborn child without the trouble of such a life.

The following section (vv. 17-19) is more explicit in characterizing the turmoil of existence in terms of the agitation/exhaustion that derives from the exercise of power. Though one could take these images as social commentary, when read in light of the end of the chapter, they are a metaphorical representation of the dynamics of turmoil itself. Verses 18 and 19, which pair prisoner and overseer, slave and lord, focus on the one subjected to power and suggest that the agony of existence is lack of autonomy, the condition of being subject to forces one can neither resist nor escape. Only death gives rest. More complex is the first image in verse 17. There, too, the "wicked" and the one "worn out by power" are paralleled. The latter expression is ambiguous, however, since "power" might be either subjective or objective genitive, that is, the image might be of one being worn out by being subjected to power or by wielding power.[10] If the first alternative is taken, the verse is similar to verses 18 and 19. What makes the second possibility intriguing is that in verse 17 the thematically important word *rōgez* is associated with the wicked, here in the sense of the agitation of rage ("there the wicked cease [their] rage"). If one takes the two images in verse 17 as equivalent rather than as contrasting ("there those worn out by [wielding] power rest"), then a different claim is made about the turmoil of existence. It is not intolerable only to the one who lacks autonomy, but even to those who can act on others, for they, too, are exhausted by the rage of their emotions and the attempt to use their power in what is ultimately a futile gesture.

In the last section of his lament (vv. 20–23) Job further develops the notion of subjection to force. Here, however, God, not human lords, is responsible for the deprivation of even minimal autonomy, which makes life a matter of dread and death a matter of rejoicing. What characterizes subjected existence is the inability of the person to plan and carry out purposive action, for such a one is "the man whose way is hidden, whom Eloah has hedged in" (v. 23). What is lost is not simply the capacity to act but the meaningfulness of action. The significance of what Job describes is aptly captured by Philippe Nemo in his book *Job and the Excess of Evil*. He characterizes Job's situation in terms of Heideggerian anxiety (*Angst*).[11] The intentionality of human existence, which expresses itself in projects and relationships and gives to life a sense of coherency, has been shattered for Job. All that remains is turmoil—incessant and emotionally charged events without coherent meaning—from which misery only death can provide relief.

Overview of the Friends' Arguments and Job's Resistance

Although Job, unlike the sufferer in the Babylonian Theodicy, has not addressed his words to his friends as an appeal, Eliphaz takes them as such. Since Job has characterized his suffering in terms of *rōgez*, the turmoil that characterizes his existence, Eliphaz and the other friends respond with the cultural resources available to resist such turmoil. One can categorize most of their responses under three headings. First, the friends resist *rōgez* by attempting to construe Job's experience in terms of narrative structures that integrate and ultimately transcend the present turmoil (esp. chaps. 4–5, 8). Second, they strongly advocate the specific religious practice of prayer, which through its symbolic forms, words, and bodily gestures has the therapeutic capacity to enact a form of order that displaces *rōgez* (chaps. 5, 8, 11, 22). Third, they offer Job iconic narratives (the so-called "fate of the wicked" poems) that combine narrative frameworks with a set of generative metaphors that reassert the moral order of the world and thus deny *rōgez* an ontological status (chaps. 15, 18, 21). In addition to these three responses, they also offer Job an account of theological anthropology, stressing the nothingness of humankind in relation to deity (4:12–20; 15:14–16; 25:4–6).

The genre of the wisdom dialogue requires that Job not be persuaded by the arguments of the friends, and so Job strenuously resists their attempt to recuperate his shattered world. He does this first of all by offering counterimages that suggest the radical nonnarratability of human existence in general and his own in particular. Second, Job rejects the praxis of prayer and its therapeutic solution. He exposes its (to him repugnant) assumptions by juxtaposing prayer with the discourse of justice and legal judgment (chaps. 9, 13, 16, 19, 23, 27). Job's exploration of forensic language is facilitated by his parodic engagement of the theological anthropology of the friends (chap. 9). From these resources Job will eventually construct an alternative narrative. Finally, Job contradicts the iconic narrative about the fate of the wicked with a counternarrative that undercuts its claims (chap. 21). Curiously, and most difficult for interpretation, it is the fate of the wicked topos that Job takes into his own speech in chapters 24 and 27.

In the remainder of this chapter, I wish to explore the three main attempts of the friends to address Job's anguish. In the following chapter Job's resistance to those attempts and his engagement of their theological anthropology will be examined. From these discussions it should be possible to trace the outlines of the conflict in moral imaginations that the wisdom dialogue is designed to display.

Narrative and Meaning

Rōgez has come upon Job. It is a moment frozen in time, starkly isolated, an apparently untranscendable present. The only other time or event to which Job can connect it is the "day of his birth," that moment of coming into being that is the distant precondition for his anguish. All other sense of temporality has been shattered. Job's language has also configured himself as frozen in space, hedged in. He is the one who waits in dread, while "turmoil comes," bringing with it the ceaseless agitation that cannot be shaped into purposeful activity. In responding to Job, Eliphaz recognizes the necessity of restoring to Job a sense of the narratability of his experience. It is through narrative that temporality is constructed and events are related to one another in meaningful patterns. Without the resources of narrative the sense of turmoil, of *Angst*, cannot be resisted. Before turning to the specifics of Eliphaz's attempt to recreate for Job a sense of narrative, it is helpful to review some of the recent discussion of the way narrative is related to human experience and the construction of meaning. Though this excursus into theory may seem a long way around to Eliphaz and his companions, it is essential to understanding a dimension of the friends' response to Job and of their own moral imaginations that cannot be grasped if one looks only at the propositional content of their language.

Excursus on Narrative Theory

Of the many theorists who have explored the workings of narrative, the three most pertinent to this study are David Carr, Mark Turner, and Paul Ricoeur. As a phenomenologist, Carr argues that consciousness organizes experienced time in an essentially narrative fashion. In attending to anything, a sense of the immediate past and an expectation of the immediate future forms a temporal horizon. Thus, events are always experienced as *configurations.* Carr's analogy is that of a melody, which is perceived not as individual notes but as an emerging configuration with an implicit beginning and end, because the configuration, not the individual notes, is the subject of attention.[12] The narrative structure of human action is similar. Intentionality, in even the simplest action, as in hitting a tennis ball, has an intrinsically narrative structure that can be expressed in terms of "beginning, middle, and end," "means and end," "departure and arrival," "departure and return" (i.e., rest to motion to rest), "suspension and resolution," or "problem and solution."[13] Such intentional action thus has the structure of an elementary plot. Finally, "narrative structure . . . is the organizing principle not only of experience and actions but of the self who experiences and acts."[14] Narrative functions to provide the basic coherency that makes it possible for an intentional subject to act and to plan and to experience "the value, purpose, and meaning" essential to such action and to the development of what Dilthey called *Zusammenhang des Lebens.*[15]

Carr's analysis underscores the utterly basic nature of narrative. That recognition in turn helps one appreciate the terrible significance of the failure of narrative. Though in one sense narrative is something that we cannot *not* experience, narrative structure is not unproblematically given. The coherency or hanging-together of experience that narrative enables, though perhaps constituting the ordinary state of things, is vulnerable to dissolution. As Carr observes, everyone has had the experience of losing track of such coherency in the midst of an action.[16] One picks up the phone and suddenly forgets whom one has called. The action is clear enough, but its place in a larger narrative structure has been temporarily lost. Effort is required to restore coherency.

We respond to such minor and temporary losses of narrative coherency in intentional action so automatically that we scarcely notice what we are doing. More serious and disturbing are the circumstances in which the dissolution of coherency is radical and comprehensive, when it is not just a specific project but life itself that no longer seems to hang together. As Carr summarizes, "Life can be regarded as a constant *effort,* even a struggle, to maintain or restore narrative coherence in the face of an ever-threatening, impending chaos at all levels, from the smallest project to the overall 'coherence of life' spoken of by Dilthey."[17] The task is not always and everywhere the same but may take one of two forms. It may be a matter of fitting experience into an already existing and accepted narrative, or it may be the more fundamental project of determining "What *is* the story?"[18]

Theorists such as Alasdair MacIntyre have tended to assume that an adequate repertoire of stories is always socially given and prior to the individual. The individual's task is simply to recognize the story and his role in it. But what does one do when the repertoire of socially available stories no longer seems plausible, when the question "What *is* the story?" is unanswerable in the traditional ways? One knows, however, that new stories with the power to organize experience and offer coherence to selves are in fact created all the time. But what is the mechanism?

One way of thinking about this issue that Carr leaves unexplored is by way of Nelson Goodman's clever comment in *Ways of Worldmaking*. He asks, in essence, "What are worlds made of?" and concludes, "Why other worlds, of course."[19] Similarly, one might say, "What are stories made of? Why other stories, of course." The process is essentially a matter of the combination of metaphoric or metonymic processes with narrative ones. A given narrative framework that governs one component of experience may be applied to another or to the whole of life, thus reorganizing and reinterpreting it. The process may be metonymic (the part standing for the whole) or metaphorical (the transfer of the schemata of one frame to another). Either way a reorganizing or redescription of the reality in question takes place.

This question is at the heart of Mark Turner's project in *The Literary Mind*. Like Carr, Turner speaks of the pathos of the loss of the narrative sense that ordinarily provides the horizon of meaning.

> Focus, viewpoint, role, and character in narrative imagining give us ways of constructing our own meaning, which is to say, ways of understanding who we are, what it means to be us, to have a particular life. The inability to locate one's own focus, viewpoint, role, and character with respect to conventional stories of leading a life is thought to be pathological and deeply distressing. It is a principal reason for recommending psychotherapy to people not obviously insane.[20]

In the same context he alludes to the condition of the lost boys of Neverland in James M. Barrie's *Peter Pan*. They will remain boys and remain lost so long as they do not know stories and so do not know how to inhabit roles and thus to have lives. But Turner is also able to give an account of how narrative imagining creatively organizes and reorganizes various realms of experience.

By narrative, Turner does not mean just the richly developed stories told in myths, dramas, epics, and novels. Equally important in the construction of meaning are the "small stories," narrative structures so deeply embedded in our minds and forms of speech that we often do not notice them. Through the capacity of the mind to engage in narrative imagining and to project one story onto another, experience is organized and explored. This combination of narrative imagining and projection, what he calls "parable," is similar in its operation to the metaphorical process, in which the schema organizing one realm of experience is projected onto another, reorganizing its salient features.[21]

Though his project is in many ways different, Paul Ricoeur's analysis of the relation of narrative and experience complements Turner's. Ricoeur is concerned with how human experience is taken up into narrative, rendered in a structuring process that makes experinece accessible to consciousness in a new way, which in turn permits a new relation to the events and conditions of life. The analogy between his understanding of narrative and of metaphor is close and explicit.[22]

Following Aristotle, Ricoeur argues that one of the chief functions of narrative is its capacity to give knowledge. To establish this claim he must relate the realm of the poetic, including narrative, to the realm of experience. Here Aristotle's concept of mimesis plays the mediating role. For Aristotle mimesis is not a sort of platonic "redoubling of presence,"[23] as the term "imitation" might suggest. *Mimesis praxeos*, "representation of action," is rather a term that bridges both the realm of the poetic and the ethical. As "representation," it opens a space for the imagination, the place of the "as if," but as "representation of *action*" it connects with the realm of human events and possibilities, the domain of ethics.[24] Because it belongs to both domains, *mimesis praxeos* has the power to give knowledge and to establish new possibilities for existence. To show how narrative accomplishes this task, Ricoeur analyzes *mimesis* as having a threefold structure.[25] Though Ricoeur would deny that our experience of action already possesses narrative shape (*pace* Carr), he does insist that the structure of action, its intelligibility or meaningfulness within a given cultural framework, and its temporal nature give the realm of action an affinity for representation in narrative structure. It is, in his terminology, "prenarrative."[26] This is the first level of mimesis.

The second level is that of emplotment, the configuration of events into the structure of a story with beginning, middle, and end. This configuration, Ricoeur argues, does not belong to events in themselves but rather to "the kingdom of the *as if*."[27] Here events are represented as an intelligible whole, and emplotment "extracts a figure from a succession."[28] Yet it is precisely the capacity of mimesis to mediate between the realm of events and the realm of aesthetic figuration that gives it the capacity to provide knowledge. Ricoeur cites L. Golden, a commentator on the *Poetics*: "Through imitation, events are reduced to form and thus, however impure in themselves, the events portrayed are purified—clarified—into intelligibility."[29] But there is a third level of mimesis, that which involves the mediation of the realm of the muthos back to the realm of action via the hearer or reader of the story. The narrative projects a world that intersects, through understanding, the world of the reader. But the world of the reader is the world of real action. The encounter between reader and text is thus the encounter with "a world that I might inhabit and into which I might project my ownmost powers. . . . Making a narrative resignifies the world in its temporal dimension, to the extent that narrating, telling, reciting is to remake action following the poem's invitation."[30] In this way narratives make possible particular ways of being in the world.

This brief account of the relation between narrative, meaning, and human experience attempts to show how basic narrative is to existence itself. Though in some sense narrative is simply a given of experience, the more comprehensive narratives that provide human meaning are always vulnerable to dissolution and require considerable effort to recover, restore, or rewrite. Times of crisis, personal or collective, are often the occasions for the rejection of prior narratives and the embrace or construction of new ones. These issues, as well as other more specific aspects of narrative imagining and its limits, take on concreteness as one examines the dialogue between Job and his friends.

The Friends' Attempt to Restore Narrativity to Job's Experience

Eliphaz's task is to restore to Job a sense of narrative, or more fundamentally, a sense of the narratability of his life, if he is to live beyond his sense of turmoil. His initial words to Job take the form of a metaphor enclosed in a rudimentary story, a narrative in which Job has played a role. "See, you have encouraged many, and weak hands you have supported. Your words raised up the one who was stumbling, and knees that were giving way you strengthened" (4:3–4). The references to weak hands, stumbling, and knees giving way all bear a metaphorical resonance. These are transparent images of the human capacity for directed action: hands that grasp and manipulate objects, knees that move the body forward. Metonymically, these body parts represent the whole person as an intentional being. Thus, Eliphaz's metaphor casts the psychic paralysis of a traumatized individual as a physical weakness of hands and knees. As story, these verses focus on the role of the helper, since that was the role Job played. What Eliphaz is doing, in Turner's words, is enabling Job to perform the basic task of "recognizing a story."[31]

Once a story is recognized, the story space may be explored from many perspectives: focus, viewpoint, character, role, action, setting, goal, and so forth. However much the mind plays with these ways of viewing the story, there is a principle of conservation that allows one to recognize it as still in some sense the "same" story.[32] Having attempted to get Job to recognize a story in which he played a particular role, Eliphaz projects that story onto Job's recent experience, or as Turner would say, makes it a parable of Job's experience. He also asks Job to view himself in a different role, this time not as the helper but as the afflicted (4:5). If Job can make that connection, his sense of turmoil can be contained as he grasps his situation in relation to a story that includes images of purposeful action and supportive relationships. This recognition would not make his pain less, but it would restore to him an essential aspect of his humanity.

The (re)construction of temporality and the relation of events to time are also part of the fundamental work of narrative. Eliphaz began with a story of the past (vv. 3-4); in reconfiguring Job's role he moves to the present ("now," v. 5). Finally, he orients his words to the future: "Is not your piety your reason for confidence, the integrity of your ways the ground of your hope?" (v. 6). By projecting a future that is not random but is causally connected to something in the present, Eliphaz implies that Job's experience possesses what Ricoeur calls "a story in its nascent state."[33] Significantly, Eliphaz has located Job's present moment in the middle of a yet uncompleted story.

Within narrative, time is not a uniform succession of equivalent moments, nor are events of uniform significance. Moments and events acquire meaning in relation to the logic of emplotment. Events and moments that belong to the beginning or middle of the narrative are, necessarily, transcended by the continuation of the plot and integrated into a meaning that emerges with the completion of the narrative. By placing Job's present moment of crisis in the middle of a yet uncompleted story, Eliphaz treats it as something that can be integrated and endowed with meaning, a direct response to Job's experience of it as simply and irreducibly "turmoil."

Eliphaz speaks not of some generic sort of narratability for Job's experience but sketches the shape of his story and the endings that are possible and impossible within it (4:7). He uses narrative imagining, as Turner would say, as a "means of looking into the future, of predicting, of planning and of explaining."[34] Eliphaz's narrative repertoire consists of two paradigmatic stories in which disaster figures. In one, disaster is the beginning, and the ending is a happy one (4:6-7). In the other, disaster is the ending itself (4:8-9). Confident that he knows which kind of character Job is, he projects the plot line to which his story belongs—and disaster will not be the final scene.[35]

Merely to say that Job will not perish is not sufficient. Why this is so can be understood in light of Ricoeur's observations about narrative temporality. Although chronological temporality represented in the causality that links event to event is essential to the construction of a story, there is also a temporal dimension represented in the narrative configuration itself, that is, the way in which the narrative "grasps together" all the incidents and events of the story. The entire narrative is in this sense a single event or moment, "the unity of one temporal whole." It is not sufficient merely to say that Job will not perish, because his not perishing after such disaster must be graspable as a meaningful whole. The poetic act, Ricoeur says, "extracts a figure from a succession." Not only does this make the narrative "followable" in its unfolding, but it also provides an aesthetic logic that makes the ending appear not just appropriate but inevitable.[36]

The trope that encapsulates the plot of Eliphaz's narrative is most clearly expressed in the hymnic praise of God in the second chapter of his speech (5:9-16). Although the hymn is not a narrative genre, its praise of God as one who "does great things" sketches several mini-narratives, all of which have the same structure. God "sets the lowly on high," "shatters the plots of the crafty," "saves the poor . . . from the hand of the powerful," and so forth. As Clines notes, all of these images, including sending rain on the earth, are images of transformation, and more specifically, of reversal of fortune as the result of God's active intervention.[37] Thus, the narrative Eliphaz offers to Job is not just a series of linked events but a configured event, a trope of transformation.

Tropes and narratives alike are forms of perception that achieve their interpretive power as much from what they exclude from vision as from what they include. Eliphaz's schematic narratives in 5:9-16 begin with a situation in need of transformation. How or why the "lowly" came to be lowly is not part of the story; what caused the "mourners" to mourn receives no development. Aristotle says of the beginning of a story that it "is that which is not a necessary consequence of anything else but after which something else exists or happens as a natural result."[38] Yet there are no "natural" beginnings, only those constructed by art, and the beginnings of Eliphaz's stories are carefully chosen. Moreover, his narratives also strategically privilege endings over beginnings. They are thus not stories of explanation, which would move backward in time. Such stories might be told, but they would have a different rhetorical and moral function. The figure of transformation with its privileging of endings is crucial to Eliphaz's purposes, because it configures situations as open rather than closed. It opens up the space of a possible future, one that finds its logic in the agency of God, understood as fundamentally moral. Thus, these are narratives of hope, as verse 16a says explicitly. In this way they develop and clarify the paradigmatic narrative pattern Eliphaz sketched in 4:6-7, 8-9.

Eliphaz follows the narratives of transformation in his hymnic praise of God with two narratives of a different type (5:17-18, 19-26). Like the preceding ones, these narratives involve reversals and privilege the end over the beginning. Here, though God again figures as the principle agent of the action, what Turner would call the narrative's focus is on the human who experiences the transformation, especially in 5:19-26. These narratives also differ from the preceding ones in the degree to which they attend to what Ricoeur calls the "discordant" that is a part of every narrative. Although discordant events are most frequently negative, it is not their negative quality that is of the essence but rather the way in which their presence initially disturbs the sense of coherence. They are events in which "meaninglessness threatens the meaningful."[39] Although, as Ricoeur observes, in life the discordant may overthrow the concordant, it is the task of narrative art to incorporate the discordant within the concordant. This is not to say that every such narrative must have a happy ending, for Ricoeur bases his comments upon Aristotle's analysis of tragic art. The concordance of which they both speak is the resistance narrative offers to meaninglessness, so that, as Ricoeur glosses Aristotle, "'one because of [Gk. *dia*] the other' wins out over 'one after [Gk. *meta*] the other.'"[40] The act of narrating, even if it be a tragic story, is an act of resistance against turmoil.

In the small narrative of 5:17-18, the discordance of pain is incorporated into a concordant narrative that ends in healing (v. 18), the whole grasped together under the figure of *mūsar*, moral formation through discipline or chastisement. One could object to the implications of this small story or to its aptness, but my purpose here is not to critique the substance of Eliphaz's particular narratives but to underscore the extent to which the fundamental operation of narrative is the resource with which he attempts to meet the shattering of Job's world.

More agreeable to modern sensibilities is the final narrative Eliphaz invokes (5:19-26), since it avoids justifying calamity, even as it incorporates the discordance of calamity into a concordant narrative. This schematic narrative tells of a person subjected to repeated dangers and disasters—famine, war, vicious slander, violence, hunger, and ravaging beasts—and yet who escapes death, thanks to the protection of God, and is able to flourish again. This is the tale of the survivor, a narrative type especially popular in the modern world among those attempting to sustain themselves during adversity or to make sense of their lives after calamitous events. Although the survivor's tale often carries a theme of divine protection, as in Eliphaz's account, there need be no attempt to attribute a specific purpose to the suffering, as indeed in these verses Eliphaz does not. The concordance that integrates the discordance is simply the figure of survival itself.

The figure of survival allows the narrative to assign different significance to negative and positive events. They are not of equal weight, for the event of deliverance is portrayed as more interpretively significant than the event of endangerment. Such a story might be open to the discordance of endless repetition, which would itself be a kind of shapelessness of time, with security appearing as only a momentary pause in a sea of endless disasters. For the story to be a story of survival, it requires a definitive ending, which retrospectively conveys to all the episodes a sense of the story as a whole. Eliphaz provides his narrative with just such a "sense of an ending" by concluding the story with images of completion and fulfillment: a "covenant of peace," the siring of abundant offspring, and death in still vigorous old age, described as "like a sheaf of grain in its season" (5:23-26). Here death is not a discordant element but rather the seal of the story that denies to discordance any further role.

Although Eliphaz is the friend who most extensively develops the resources of narrative in response to Job's situation,[41] Bildad's allegorical narrative about the two plants (8:11-19) recapitulates all of Eliphaz's narrative patterns, except the one that configures disaster and recovery as a story of divine chastisement. Textual and grammatical difficulties have led to different understandings of this passage, but Gordis's interpretation of it as a double narrative of contrasting fates is the most persuasive untangling of its problems.[42] Making use of the rich analogical possibilities offered by the metaphorical comparison of people and plants,[43] Bildad contrasts the plant that lacks water (i.e., "those who forget El," "the godless," 8:11–13; cf. 5:3) with the well-watered plant (8:16–19), which represents "the blameless" (8:20), such as Job himself. As in Eliphaz's narrative schemas of the God-fearing and the wicked (4:6–7, 8–9), disaster alternately appears as an intermediate (8:18) or final (8:12) episode in their stories. Reversal, too, governs the plot, as the plant that represents the godless appears to flourish but suddenly withers and dies (8:12), whereas the well-watered plant, which appears to have been uprooted is able to sprout again or from another place (8:19).[44] Here, too, the figure of survival, which Bildad projects as the governing narrative for Job's yet unfinished story (8:21), incorporates discordance into a figure of concordance.

Unlike Eliphaz and Bildad, Zophar's first speech to Job does not make extensive use of narrative. Consequently, I treat his speech in a later section. In this discussion my interest in the narratives embedded in Eliphaz and Bildad's speeches has been less in their particular claims than in the narrative impulse itself. When faced with a devastated friend who describes his experience of the world as "turmoil," Eliphaz and Bildad respond primarily by offering the integrative resources of narrative, specifically narrative patterns that privilege endings, and by doing so open up a space within which Job might live beyond the scene of his catastrophe. Most of the time the activity of construing events in terms of narratives takes place so automatically and effortlessly that one does not recognize it for what it is, namely, an active process of construction that is both collective and individual. When that automatic activity is disrupted, whether by a conflict of narratives, or, as here, by an event that threatens to overwhelm narrative's capacity to make meaning, one becomes aware of the significant role narrative imagining plays in constructing the symbolic worlds within which we live. But one may also become uneasily aware of narrative's status not only as something made but also as something "made-up," aware of the ambiguity of what it means to "tell a story." Job's response to his friends, discussed in the next chapter, will explore narrative's role in the collective deceptions implicit in aspects of religious ideology.

The Practices of Piety: Seeking God

The friends' attempt to respond to Job with the resources of narrative draws on two traditional narrative patterns, one of which describes the hope of the pious and the other the fate of the wicked (4:6–7, 8–9; 8:4, 11–19). Although together these two narrative paradigms make a claim about the moral coherence of the world, they are developed and distributed quite differently within the dialogue. The fate of the wicked narrative pattern dominates the second cycle (chaps. 15,

18, 20; cf. 21), where it is developed in a series of elaborate, vivid poems. By contrast, the theme of the hope of the pious is most prominent in the first cycle (chaps. 4–5, 8, 11), where it is developed largely in connection with the advice to engage in certain practices of piety ("seeking God," that is, prayer and the preparation for prayer). The advice to seek God also appears at a crucial moment in chapter 22. There, following Job's repudiation of the claims made about the miserable fate of the wicked (chap. 21), Eliphaz dramatically declares Job to be one of the wicked and his present suffering to be a consequence of wickedness. But rather than treating the application of that narrative pattern as a sufficient response, Eliphaz follows it with a repetition of the appeal to seek God (22:21–30).

Both the coordination of these two topoi and the asymmetry in the way they are developed suggest that they perform different functions within a common moral framework. The fate of the wicked topos, as I will argue later, mostly functions in relation to the hermeneutical task of disclosing the nature of reality as fundamentally moral, though as Eliphaz's speech shows, it can also be used "diagnostically." The topos of the hope of the pious, as embedded in the concrete practices of piety, serves the therapeutic need of coping with suffering. The flexibility with which this combination can function is striking. During the course of the dialogue the friends' judgment concerning Job's moral state changes dramatically from confidence in his innocence (chap. 5 and probably chap. 8) to an opinion that there must be some sin on his part, even if unconscious (chap. 11), to a belief that his moral arrogance itself is sinful (chap. 15), and finally to a conviction of his deep wickedness (chap. 22). Yet the advice they offer remains consistent: Seek God (chaps. 5, 8, 11, 22). The turmoil that is experienced—whether it arises from inexplicable calamity (chap. 5), from a disharmony with the right clouded by false consciousness (chap. 11), or as punishment consequent on deep moral disorder (chap. 22)—can be addressed by means of the reordering practices of seeking God.

Three things are important for understanding the therapeutic work of this practice of piety: first, its status as a practice; second, the nature of the bodily gestures that belong to its enactment; and third, the imagery by which its purpose and power are conceived. Before looking closely at the particular texts, however, it is again necessary to engage in a brief theoretical discussion.

Excursus on Religious Practices

"Practice" is an elusive term, but it refers generally to patterned human activities that are both structured by and structuring of social reality. Though it includes religious ritual, which is important for the passages in Job to be considered, practice itself is a broader category. Recent study understands it primarily in constructivist terms. Bourdieu describes practice as part of the general project of "every established order . . . to produce (to very different degrees and with very different means) the naturalization of its own arbitrariness."[45] Practices play a vital role in the construction of a particular social reality and the socialization of persons to this reality.

One important aspect of practice is termed "misrecognition." Participants in a practice, such as a religious ritual, engage in their activities with conscious intent, specific purpose, and a sense of the meaningfulness of the activity. Although this self-awareness is of great significance, it does not and cannot understand all that is happening in the practice. As Foucault put it, "People know what they do; they frequently know why they do what they do; but what they don't know is what what they do does."[46] What Foucault is getting at is the way in which, in addition to the conscious intents and meanings, practices also embody all manner of unspoken (indeed inarticulable) assumptions, values, and beliefs. It is in the interaction between the conscious intent of participants and the unconscious assumptions embodied in practices that practices achieve their power to constitute a sense of the real. Catherine Bell poses the issue in terms of what practices of ritualization see and, by seeing, do not see. Such activity "is a way of acting that sees itself as *responding* to a place, event, force, problem, or tradition. It tends to see itself as the natural or appropriate thing to do in the circumstances. Ritualization does not see how it actively creates place, force, event, and tradition, how it redefines or generates the circumstances to which it is responding."[47] In essence, ritual practices implicitly define the environment and the terms of the problematic to which they are in turn the obvious means for acting within that environment and negotiating the problem. There is nothing intentionally manipulative about this process. From the constructivist perspective these conditions are always an integral part of human cultural activity. They are the conditions for the effectiveness but also for the limits of any order of social meaning.

What gives practices their truly distinctive role, however, is the fundamental role of the body. Indeed, the study of practice has led to a reconceptualization of the body, which comes to be understood not so much as a physical instrument for the expression of subjective dispositions, but rather as itself, even at its most physical, a social construction. Social practices organize and structure the body. In doing so, they produce selves who have internalized crucial beliefs and values of the social order. In acting "naturally" persons reproduce the social order through the very actions of their bodies. A clear example would be gender-specific postures and modes of movement, which are quite literally embodiments of cultural values and assumptions. These values and assumptions are further internalized and continually reproduced as men and women go about their daily business, moving, as it seems to them, naturally. As Bourdieu suggests, societies treat the body as a mode of memory. It is what stores in condensed and mnemonic form the basic principles of the culture. Such embodiment is a powerful means of pedagogy, for "nothing seems more ineffable, more incommunicable, more inimitable, and therefore, more precious, than the values given body, *made body*" in this way.[48]

The postures and gestures that are so ingrained as to be beyond consciousness are not the only ones that operate in this manner. More formalized and even overtly communicative postures also can be understood as not merely expressive but also performative and productive. The example commonly given is that of kneeling, which though it may publicly express subordination, also enacts it. Because of the close association of a person's sense of self with his or her body, the act of kneeling also produces a subordinated person.[49] This is not to say that bodily practices are a kind of magic, automatically inducing dispositions and convictions to ensure social control. As Bell argues, participation in ritual practices is a negotiated experience, one that may contain elements of resistance as well as acceptance. Nevertheless, "bowing or singing in unison imperceptibly schools the social body in the pleasures of and schemes for acting in accordance with assumptions that remain far from conscious or articulate."[50] Even as Bell's comment underscores the persuasion implicit in bodily participation, she also rightly identifies the participant as an agent. One who undertakes a ritual practice does so as a way of acting upon his or her environment and so achieving a goal or purpose. A necessarily circular relationship is involved, as the participant simultaneously shapes and is shaped by the environment. The actor's body structures the time and space of its environment by projecting organizing schemes onto it. At the same time, these organizing schemes are reincorporated into the body as the nature of reality.[51]

In part because ritual practices do create an experiential sense of the reality of the world, even as it is constructed in and through such practices, they can become a means of empowering participants. The ritual environment offers the participant knowledge of how the world works. It also offers means of appropriating that order and acting on it, what Burridge calls "the redemptive process," which brings together for the participant both power and truth. As Burridge states it, "The redemptive process [is] indicated by the activities, moral rules, and assumptions about power which, pertinent to the moral order and taken on faith, not only enable a people to perceive the truth of things, but guarantee that they are indeed perceiving the truth of things."[52] That access to a reliable knowledge of power and its functioning makes it possible for persons to act in a way that promises to be effective. In its concrete operation, ritual practice thus organizes and interrelates various symbolic systems that structure reality. These symbolic associations should not be conceived as a static structure, however, but rather form a discursive field within which strategic "shiftings" can take place. In this way a problem or dilemma in a nonritualized situation can be organized and nuanced by the symbolic operations of ritual practices in such a way that empowers the actor in relation to the situation.

The Practice of Prayer

These very brief remarks on the operations of religious practices serve, I hope, to make credible the claim that by urging Job to engage in the practice of prayer, the friends are directing him to an important resource of power that he may appropriate for himself, and by doing so gain some control over his experience of turmoil. What appears in the speeches, of course, is not the performance of a ritual, or even a detailed description of such a performance. Rather, the speeches make a rhetorical appeal to Job that attempts to persuade him to engage in prayer. In some ways this representation may be more informative than simply observing someone at prayer, since in order to be persuasive the friends must use vivid imagery that articulates the purposes and achievements of the practice of prayer as they understand them.

In examining what the friends say in urging Job to engage in the practices of prayer, I want to look first at the imagery in their rhetoric and at the body movements and gestures associated with it. The figure that dominates the friends' advice to Job to "seek God" is what I would call the figure of orientation. Eliphaz introduces the notion of seeking God in 5:8: "But if it were I, I would seek El, and to Elohim I would present my cause." Similarly, Bildad says, "If you seek out El, and from Shaddai you seek favor . . ." (8:5). The verbs *dāraš* and *šāhar* do not have the degree of spatial connotation that the English "seek" does, but they do connote the orientation of attention to an object. Beyond the semantics of the verbs, the way in which Eliphaz and Bildad speak models orientation to God through chiasm, as they place the terms for God at the center of the line. In Hebrew the chiasm is particularly striking, since each case also involves the repetition of the preposition *'el* (*'el-'el wĕ'el-'ĕlōhîm, 'el-'ēl wĕ'el šadday*). The choice of preposition is significant, for *'el* is not the preposition otherwise used with the verb "search out" (*šāhar*; 8:5a) and is relatively uncommon with either "seek" (*dāraš*; 5:8a) or "put" (*śîm*; 5:8b). But the preposition *'el* serves both to echo the divine name *'ēl* and to connote a direction or movement toward.

Zophar graphically develops the figure of orientation in his description of the practice of seeking God (11:13–15). His account includes numerous references to the body, its gestures, and its postures. Some references are metaphorical, others are literal descriptions of the reorientation of the body in prayer. Zophar begins with a reference to the religious practice of concentration that precedes prayer, known as "settling the mind" (*kûn lēb*), or, as often translated, "directing the heart." Although no accounts of this practice exist from Second Temple texts, the Mishnah describes it as follows: "None may stand up to say the Tefillah save in sober mood. The pious men of old used to wait an hour before they said the Tefillah, that they might direct their heart toward God" (*m. Ber.* 5:1; trans. Danby). Thus, the practice apparently involved sitting in concentration. Such a practice does at least two things. First, it serves to mark off ritual from nonritual activity by providing a physical and temporal boundary. Second, it disciplines and reorders the body. Thus, this preliminary activity itself, especially if practiced by one with a turbulent mind, would be a means of displacing anxiety and turmoil. From "directing the heart," Zophar goes on to describe the act of prayer itself.

The physical postures of prayer in the ancient Near East were various,[53] though they often involved standing or kneeling with one or both arms upraised, palms facing outward toward the deity. In similar fashion Zophar describes the orientation to God: "and you spread your palms to him" (11:13b). One should not attempt to "decode" the hand gesture in any singular fashion, however. Various explanations have been given,[54] and it is likely that ancient participants themselves would have given a variety of interpretations if asked for the "meaning" of the gesture. Whatever the connotations of the raised hands and outward facing palms, standing itself is a posture of respect for a social superior, especially standing before a superior who is seated (see Job 29:7–8). Such a tableau is often represented on Mesopotamian cylinder seals when a worshiper appears before a god (*ANEP* pls. 514, 515, 518, 529). Though the deity is not physically present in prayer, the frequent verbal imagery of the enthroned deity surrounded by standing attendants (Isa 6:1–2; Dan 7:9–10; and, metaphorically, Ps 89:15b) suggests that the worshiper standing in prayer enacts such a gesture of respect in a hierarchically organized relationship. The body of the one at prayer thus structures an environment and implicitly assigns roles evocative of relationships of power that can be found in the social as well as the religious sphere. Even the simple act of standing in prayer is a highly condensed index of cultural assumptions, values, identities, and expectations, some of which will be made explicit in the rest of what the friends say.

Zophar's account includes a second set of spatial and body imagery—metaphorical imagery that develops what is involved in the acts of "directing the mind" and "spreading the palms" in prayer. This metaphorical imagery operates with the binary categories of proximity and distance in relation to the religious problem of access to the presence of the deity. Spatial categories are fundamental to such religious language (e.g., priestly regulations concerning sacred spaces, entrance liturgies in the psalms). In the preparatory moral self-examination and reordering that Zophar describes, one is to examine one's hands and one's dwelling (tent and body being metonyms) and to put distance between oneself and any wrongfulness.[55] "If sin is in your hand, remove it [lit., 'make it distant'], and do not allow injustice to live in your tents" (11:14). The distancing of sin is the precondition for coming into the presence of God (see the similar imagery in Isa 1:15–16). Although Zophar does believe Job has sinned against God (Job 11:5–6), one should not see this language simply as a reference to Job's particular sin but rather as a reference to part of the ordinary practices of self-examination conducted by any pious person engaging in preparation for prayer. The advice echoes the assumptions of the entrance liturgies concerning the moral state required for entering the "holy mountain" (see Pss 15; 24:3–6). Similarly, Job takes it as axiomatic that no "godless person" (*ḥānēp*, i.e., no one alienated from God or hypocritical in relation to God) can come before the deity (13:16b).

As Zophar describes it, the result of this practice of self-examination and reordering is to create a space of untroubled intimacy with God, again described in terms of the body and its orientation. The expression Zophar uses is "to lift up the face." Although this idiom has a number of nuances, here it seems to refer to the way in which the orientation of the face up or down in the presence of another signals the nature of the relationship, as when Abner seeks to avoid killing Asahel. For how, Abner asks, "could I lift up my face to your brother Joab?" (2 Sam 2:22; see also Gen 4:6–7). What is it about a neglected sin that prevents the lifting up of one's face to God? Zophar metaphorically designates such sin as a "blemish" (*mûm*). As in English, bodily disfigurement serves as the basis for the metaphorical extension of the term to designate moral disfigurement. But the cultural context for the term *mûm* is resonant, for the presence of such a disfiguring blemish prevents an animal from being presented at the altar for sacrifice or a priest from approaching to offer sacrifice (Lev 21:17; 22:20). Unlike the physical blemish, which cannot be altered, the moral blemish is susceptible to removal by the practices described. Through this metaphor Zophar implicitly likens the approach to God in prayer to the physical proximity to the sacred at a sanctuary.

Zophar's imagery contrasts with a related but ultimately quite distinct image used by Job. In the preceding chapter Job, speaking more or less in forensic terms, complained that God's relentless scrutiny prevented him, even if innocent, from lifting up his head (*nāśā' rō'š*; 10:15b). That Job speaks of the head and Zophar of the face is not accidental. Although the two expressions "to lift the face" and "to lift the head" can occasionally be equivalent (see *HALOT*, 725), they tend to have distinct nuances. Job's image, in the context of his language of guilt and innocence, is a metaphor of dignity. Zophar's image, in the context of his language of prayer and piety, is a metaphor of intimacy. The choice of each phrase is an index of the contrasting moral imaginations articulated by the friends and by Job.

Metaphors of orientation and reorientation are most explicit in Eliphaz's final appeal to Job (22:21–30), following his accusation that Job is one of the wicked (22:2–11). The verb with which Eliphaz begins his appeal to Job (*sākan*) is not well attested, but in its other uses in the hiphil it has connotations of familiarity, the knowledge shared between two parties who know each other intimately (e.g., Num 22:30; Ps 139:3). NJPS appropriately translates "be close to Him." This language of orientation is developed graphically with imagery drawn from wisdom's discourse about teaching. Words of instruction, which function to form a person, are metaphorically construed as an object that can be "taken" and "placed." As in Zophar's speech, the body figures the reorientation, as the act of transfer takes place between the body of God and the body of Job. "Take from his mouth instruction and place his words in your heart" (Job 22:22) In the following line the orientation to God is expressed by the verb *šûb*, "return," but now the imagery of direction toward God is paired with the contrasting imagery of distancing oneself from sin ("remove injustice from your tent," 22:23b). Similarly, the imagery of taking and placing, first used to describe the action of receiving God's instruction, is reused in verses 24–25 in an imaginative scene of placing the false gods of wealth where they belong, that is, in the dust and among the rocks. The line enacts through sophisticated wordplay the transformation of values it advocates. As Edwin Good has observed, a pun occurs between the terms "dust" (*'āpār*) and "gold" (*'ôpîr*), as between "treasure" (*beṣer*) and "among the stones" (*bĕṣûr*). These puns operate chiastically across the two halves of the line: "If you place treasure upon the dust and [gold of] Ophir among the stones of the wadis . . ." (22:24). The metonymic association effected both by the act described and by the wordplay reorients values and allows the actor to perceive God as the true value ("then Shaddai will be your treasure and your precious silver," 22:25).

The imagery thus far sketches an outward movement, from heart to tent to wadi. All this language describes preparatory activities, the moral reordering that enables a reordering of commitments (what is "in your tent") and values (what is true treasure). Only now that desire is reordered ("for then your delight will be in Shaddai," 22:26a) does Eliphaz speak of prayer, using the same image Zophar employs; "and you will lift up your face to Eloah" (22:26b). Corresponding to, but reversing the direction of the initial image of communication, in which Job received the words of God, now Job prays and God listens (22:27a). The positive outcome is referred to in a proleptic fashion, as Eliphaz speaks of Job fulfilling his vows, an action that would take place when what had been requested had occurred. The allusion back to the beginning of the passage is also made via the repetition of the verb *šālam*. In verse 21 Eliphaz urged Job to be "wholehearted" (NJPS; *šĕlām*). The completion of the process of reorientation and restoration is marked by the "fulfilling" (*šillēm*; 27b) of vows.

In the preceding discussion I have focused on the language with which the friends have described the practice of seeking God, but I have said relatively little about how the friends evoke the consequences of the practice, that is, the images that describe the well-being that comes from seeking God. Two things stand out. First is the imagery of reversal of fortune. Second are the allusions to the restoration of Job to his place in the social order. These references illumine the relationship between the work of practice in individual redemption and in the reproduction of the social order and its values.

Since prayers of supplication attempt to change situations, it is natural that one who describes the results will speak of a reversal of fortune. And so, succinctly, Eliphaz moves from the advice to seek God (5:8) to the hymnic description of God's transforming activity (5:9–16). This figure of reversal of fortune is also the fundamental structure of virtually all narrative, according to Ricoeur: "Does not every narrated story finally have to do with reversals of fortune, whether for better or worse?"[56] Bildad's affinity for sharply focused binary contrasts is especially effective in connecting the results of prayer with narrative structure, as he coordinates the temporal language of beginning and ending (*rē'šît . . . 'aḥărît*), so crucial to emplotment, with the language of reversal of fortune ("small . . . very great"; *miṣ'ār . . . yisgeh mĕ'ōd*; 8:7). The act of prayer by one who is "innocent and upright" is what sets in motion the divine activity (8:6a) that ensures the unfolding of the plot. Thus, as both Eliphaz and Bildad indicate, the practice of prayer places the actor within an unfolding narrative, not merely as someone who is *told* a story, but as someone who can effect his own life as a story in progress.

Zophar's description of the results of prayer, though it also looks to a transformation of the external situation, is more oriented to psychological dimensions of the experience. The privileged image is that of security. Although the first word used to describe Job's restoration (*muṣāq*) can be interpreted either as referring to the context ("when in straits," NJPS) or as an image of stability ("cast" [like molten metal]), the theme is set by the phrase "and you will not be afraid" (11:15b). If the image is of Job as firmly established like an object formed from molten metal, it contrasts with the representation of his troubles as "like water that has flowed away" (11:16b). The psychological dimension of this experience is underscored by the striking reference to how memory functions, the paradoxical but apt pairing of forgetting and remembering. As Clines observes, "Pain that has been thoroughly worked through is not totally forgotten—as it might be if it were merely repressed—but is remembered as powerless."[57] The efficacy of the practices of piety lies in this capacity to dispel the paralyzing presence of turmoil and to allow trouble to recede psychologically as well as temporally, so that life may continue. Whereas Job concluded his speech in chapter 10 with images of death characterized by the gloom of deep darkness, so Zophar extravagantly describes the capacity of the practices of piety to reestablish life as brighter than noontime, with even the darkness of life made bright as morning light (11:17).

Zophar concludes with images of secure resting (11:18–19a), a counter to Job's langue of restlessness and incessant vulnerability (7:4–15). These images of security follow naturally from his earlier representation of prayer as a form of coming into the presence of God. One can find many instances of such a connection in the psalms, in which the presence of God is experienced as security for the one who prays (e.g., Pss 16:8; 23:4, 6; 121). Perhaps most apt is the connection drawn by Psalm 15, an entrance liturgy that connects dwelling in the presence of God with moral rectitude, concluding that "the one who does these things will never be moved" (Ps 15:5). Similarly, the activity of moral self-examination and reordering that Zophar recommends as preparatory to coming before God in prayer is integrally related to the experience of security that results from prayer and grounds hope. As with the relation to narrative structure, so here, the practice serves as an experiential "sample" of what it promises.

The descriptions of the results of prayer culminates in social imagery of restoration to social position and power (Job 11:19b–20; 22:28–30). In Zophar's description, "Many will seek your favor" (11:19b; lit., "soften your face"). Eliphaz's more elaborate account depicts Job as one whose utterance is effective ("You decree something and it is established for you"), but also as one instrumental in altering the condition of those in trouble. Two binary contrasts are used: To those "brought low" Job says "be lifted up" (22:29a).[58] The "not innocent" are rescued by the purity of Job's hands (22:30). Job's power is intercessory, for though God acts to "save" and "deliver," that action is in response to Job's word and moral status. The homology between the image of Job constructed in those verses and the image of the God to whom Job is urged to pray is striking. This virtual conflation invites one to consider the ritual of prayer in relation to forms of social power.

Ritual practices are complexly related to power. Since the relationships are largely circular, it is easy to misstate them as though the production of effects ran in one direction only. As socialized beings, persons who engage in rituals and who have ritual mastery have internalized various symbolic schemes, which they project on the environment when they engage in a ritual practice, such as prayer. Thus, they construct a field of action. Yet the field of action does not feel constructed but just the opposite. Both the activity of the body and the complex web of associations within the symbolic repertoire give to the environment so constructed not only a sense of naturalness but also of reality. It is to this reality and the power it embodies that the ritual agent orients herself. As Bell puts it, "Ritualization always aligns one within a series of relationship[s] linked to the ultimate sources of power. This cosmos is experienced as a chain of states or an order of existence that places one securely in a field of action and in alignment with the ultimate goals of all action."[59] Thus it is that the friends urge Job to make use of the resources of power embodied in the ritual of prayer.

The power relations of a ritual system are not just of any sort but are the assumptions about power that belong to a particular social order. Though this social order will be most explicitly described by Job in chapters 29–31, certain of its elements are evident here. Power is personal, hierarchical, and highly relational, embodied above all in the "big man," whether human or divine. It operates not so much automatically as responsively. Like the energy generated by falling water, such power is charged by the hierarchical difference between high and low. Bildad describes its dynamics succinctly. Its operation is initiated by the urgency of need and the direct appeal ("eagerly seek," "supplicate," 8:5) from one who has lost status. Thus, need is part of the dynamics of power (cf. 5:8–16). Yet the response of redemptive power is not automatic, for a judgment must be made, a judgment that reaffirms in some fashion the moral order that this power sustains and is sustained by. Though Bildad speaks of the suppli-cant as "pure and upright," and so deserving, Eliphaz shows how such redemp-tive power may also be available to the "not innocent" by a kind of moral sur-rogacy (22:30). In both cases the effect is to strengthen the norms of the moral order. The exercise of power is described in dynamic, personal terms, as God "rouses himself" (8:6a) or Job declares "be lifted up" (22:29a). The result of power is the rebalancing of what has become imbalanced. What was too high is brought low, what was too low is brought high (5:10–16; 22:29), a distinc-tion between the righteous and the wicked is reestablished (8:20–22; 11:19–20), and the worthy suppliant is restored to his rightful place (8:6b). The as-sumptions about power that enable one to engage in prayer as the evident response to a problematic situation are also reproduced and reaffirmed in the act of prayer. Such is the case whether the one who prays is a member of the social elite, like Job, and so restored to a "God-like" position in the social order, or a lowly person whose redemption restores him to the protection of those more powerful than he.

Although the homology between the redemptive process in the social order and the ritual order is not always as direct and close as it appears in the friends' account, even in more complexly configured relationships, the empowerment that derives from ritual action makes use of the assumptions about power inherent in the hegemonic order. Bell concludes her discussion of ritual and power by quot-ing and reinterpreting Durkheim: "For Durkheim, 'The believer who has com-municated with his god is not merely a man who sees new truths of which the unbeliever is ignorant; he is a man who is *stronger*. He feels within him more force, either to endure the trials of existence, or to conquer them.'" These bene-fits, Bell suggests, are not the illusions and delusions of religious emotion. In praying, the individual appropriates the social schemes of the symbolic order in an act of individual redemption. Such a person may indeed be stronger "because these acts are the very definitions of power, personhood, and the capacity to act."[60] Thus, what Eliphaz, Bildad, and Zophar offer to their friend Job is no illusion, no irrelevant and insensitive advice that overlooks his "true" situation. They offer him not simply solace but access to power, the opportunity to take action to influ-ence his situation. They offer him a way beyond turmoil.

Iconic Narratives: The Fate of the Wicked

Why isn't that enough? Why, if the problem is the restoration of Job, is it not enough for the friends to remind Job of the resources of piety, what Eliphaz calls "the consolations of El" (15:11a), what I have termed the therapeutic practices of directing the mind, moral self-examination, and prayer? Why is everyone, including eventually Job, obsessed with the fate of the wicked? In the second cycle it is the only topic addressed by the friends in the body of their speeches (chaps. 15, 18, 20) and is the topic of Job's final speech (chap. 21). In the speech that opens the third cycle Eliphaz reiterates it and applies it to Job (chap. 22). More perplexingly, it also figures prominently in Job's speeches in the third cycle (chap. 24 and 27). If we do not understand this topic and its significance for the participants in the dialogue, we do not understand the book.

The introduction of this topos plays a critical role in setting up Eliphaz's stunning reversal of his opinion regarding Job's moral condition (chaps. 4–5, 22), but that dramatic function can by itself scarcely be a sufficient reason for the preoccupation with the fate of the wicked. A deeper necessity drives the obsession with the subject. If Job had spoken only of his subjective experience of turmoil, the friends might well have stopped with the offer of therapeutic ritual. But Job's own sense of turmoil is developed at the end of the first cycle, particularly in chapter 12, as a claim about God's governance of the world, that is, a claim about reality itself. The poems about the fate of the wicked are the form in which the friends attempt to respond to this issue. Thus, I do not understand these speeches, as many do, as thinly veiled accusations against Job, nor does he take them as such when he replies in chapter 21. He, too, shows that he understands the argument to be about the nature of the world. How this engagement with a metaphysical issue ultimately leads Eliphaz to accuse Job of dire wickedness (chap. 22) is most important, but it can only be understood after a close examination of the nature and meaning of these poems on their own terms.

The poems on the fate of the wicked in chapters 15, 18, and 20 have several related features that require comment: their vividness, their tight focus, the nature of the warrants that introduce them, and the nature of the rhetoric by which they are developed. Intensely imagistic, these poems create dramatic tableaux of the wicked meeting a violent and desolate end. As with much Hebrew poetry, the style favors cinematic sharp cuts, as frame succeeds frame. In Eliphaz's poem in chapter 15, for instance, the opening image of the wicked writhing in psychic anguish, tormented by fear at sounds that may token sudden destruction (15:20–22), is abruptly succeeded by an image of the wicked wandering abjectly, eyed by vultures as a likely meal (15:23). That image gives way to a graphic metaphor of his anguish, now materialized as an attacking warrior-king, a poetic reversal of his own "playing the hero" against God (15:24–26). With another sharp cut, the succeeding image ironically depicts the plump and well-fed figure dwelling in a ruined and desolate city (15:27–28). A series of metaphorical descriptions brings the poem to a close, piling up images of futility, emptiness, lack of fruition, and barrenness (15:29–35). Although the poems are best understood as didactic instructions, the vivid and dramatic scenes give the poem an almost performative quality. As curses often imitate in language or symbolic action the force of the curse, so these graphic poems virtually enact that to which they refer.

Related to the vividness of the poems is their tight focus. Little attention is paid to describing the activity of wickedness itself. The characters are identified as "godless," but that term simply operates as a synonym for "wicked." Eliphaz depicts the wicked as charging at God (15:25-26), and Zophar portrays them as greedy persons who "crush and abandon the poor" and "seize a house by force" (20:19). But one could scarcely develop from these poems a profile of the actions that qualify someone as wicked or godless. That is taken for granted. Rather, the poems invest their considerable energy on the sharply focused moment of the wicked person's collapse, terror, and destruction.

Rhetoricians commonly observe that topics may be developed by two means: arguments and tropes. As one might surmise, in these poems one finds few if any arguments. Though much biblical poetry is strongly imagistic, one can find examples that combine images and arguments, as in prophetic poetry, which often presents reasoned explanations and explores logical connections (e.g., the "because . . . therefore" construction of judgment oracles). Indeed, in prophetic poetry one can find reasoned arguments about the nature and significance of the wicked, as when Isaiah identifies Assyria as an instrument of God's anger to be destroyed because it arrogantly exceeds its role (Isa 10:5-19). Here, however, no arguments appear, only descriptive images and metaphors. Moreover, although the imagery of each poem has a distinctive profile, all of the images in the poems are repetitive variations on a single figure, the insubstantiality of the wicked. Over and over and over, the images repeat: The wicked cannot secure themselves, the wicked cannot hold on to what they seize, the wicked cannot stand. Why the poems favor tropes over arguments is critical to understanding them and will be explored shortly.

Related to the preference for tropes is the nature of the warrants the friends use to introduce these poems. Eliphaz begins with the warrant that this is ancestral knowledge, what the sages and their fathers declared from a time when no strangers were in the land (15:17-19). Zophar, too, presents his poem as knowledge "from of old," from the time humans were placed upon the earth (20:4). Although Bildad offers no explicit warrant, he is apparently alluding to the claims of his poem when he says to Job, "Shall the earth be forsaken because of you, or the rock removed from its place?" (18:4). Thus, he represents his poem as articulating the foundation upon which all stands. Something very important is at stake here.

Many would agree that the poems about the fate of the wicked articulate what *should be* the case in a moral world, but the friends are making a claim for the *truth* of their narratives (15:17-19; 20:4; cf. 5:27; 8:8-10). In what sense can their claim that these narratives tell a truth about the world be sustained? Or, if one wished to argue against it, what form would such an argument need to take? Whenever I teach the book of Job, I find it almost impossible to get a class to entertain, even as a hypothetical possibility, that these poems might be true. It seems obvious that stories about the fate of the wicked are patently false. After all, the students can all name counterexamples. For myself, I do not know whether I believe the story told by the friends about the fate of the wicked is true. I do, however, think that it is one of the most complex, difficult, and provocative claims made in the book, and that it is not adequately refuted in the way my students initially attempt.

To say this raises the question of the nature of the truth such a narrative claims to tell. Some of my students seem to assume that the friends intend the truth claim to be much the same as in a law of physics, which should hold true for every instance of the phenomenon without exception. If apples from time to time fell upward from a tree instead of down, one would have to question the truth of the law of gravity. In defense of these students' interpretation, the surface rhetoric of the friends' statements often sounds as though there are making just such claims. Eliphaz, for instance, asks rhetorically concerning the complementary case of the fate of the righteous: "Recall, now, who that was innocent ever perished, or where have the upright been cut off?" (4:7). Yet if such statements were intended as universal, exceptionless claims, only a deluded fool could believe them, and whatever the friends may be, they are not fools. Moreover, in reflecting on the persuasiveness of these representations, one must account for the fact that something like their depiction of the moral order of the world remained a fundamental and tenacious belief in the cultures of the ancient Near East for millennia. In some sense their stories "rang true" for many people, though they, too, knew that these were not exceptionless descriptions of events.

To understand the truth claims of these poems it is necessary to consider their distinctive rhetoric. As noted earlier, tropes (i.e., images and metaphors, pictures and vignettes) carry the rhetoric of these poems. There are no reasoned arguments about the purpose of the wicked, as one might find in prophetic poetry or in the Thanksgiving Psalms of the Dead Sea Scrolls (e.g., the wicked as a function of God's historical engagement with Israel or as part of a cosmic drama). Arguments in relation to a topic function within a shared context of meaning. Taking for granted certain assumptions about the moral order of the world, the prophets and apocalyptic poets offer explanations for the apparent flourishing of the wicked, which they articulate through a combination of images and arguments. But where the foundations themselves are in question, arguments have little if any power. Persuasion must depend more strongly on the rhetoric of tropes. It is the difference, as a recent article on rhetoric and hermeneutics put it, between "giving evidence" and "making evident." These activities operate on different levels. Giving evidence, which is the province of arguments, has to do with the level of *beliefs* as they are brought to bear on a problem. Making evident, which is the province of tropes, operates at the more fundamental level of the *grounds* that underlie and provide the basis for beliefs.[61]

In his classic study of persuasion Raphael Demos observed that persuasion with respect to worldviews is not simply a matter of intellectual agreement about specific issues but the realizing of a pattern or whole, a realization that takes place by evocation.

> Often the reasons why so much discussion among individuals is futile is that what one person realizes vividly, the other does not. Evocation is the process by which vividness is conveyed. . . . An argument has much less persuasive force than the vivid evocation of an experience. . . . Far more effective is to state a viewpoint in all its concreteness and in all its significant implications, and then stop; the arguments become relevant only after this stage has been completed.[62]

What is at stake between Job and the friends is making evident the nature of the world, which each attempts to communicate through vivid evocations. This work of disclosure is the work of metaphor, the "seeing as" that produces redescriptions of reality. Thus, the dialogue between the friends and Job becomes a struggle over metaphors and a conflict over stories. The task undertaken by the poems that deal with the fate of the wicked is not the work of empirical description but the work of deep mimesis, the evocation in poetic form of the life of the world.

Narrative and metaphor are closely linked in the poems. The accounts, as narratives concerning a representative figure, have something of the character of an anecdote. But unlike ordinary anecdotes, they are not simply accounts of what happened to a certain person or even a certain type of person. They are articulated largely in terms of metaphors. Thus, the claims made by the poems have to be assessed both in terms of the rhetoric of their metaphors and then in terms of the nature of the persuasion embedded in their distinctive narrative form.

Since it would be redundant to examine the metaphors in all three speeches, Bildad's can serve as the example. As a narrative about a representative figure, "the wicked," many statements in the poem appear to be literal descriptions of destruction. Yet they make use of terms with well-established metaphorical significance, and if those metaphorical associations are pursued, new levels of meaning appear. Read literally, 18:5–6 makes a series of banal statements about the lamp in the tent of the wicked going out. But no one versed in the conventions of Israelite poetry could take the statement literally, for "light" has traditional metaphorical resonances of "life," "vitality," "presence,"and so forth (e.g., Isa 10:17; Amos 5:18; Pss 4:7; 27:1; 36:10; 56:14; 97:11; Prov 16:15). Thus, the metaphorical claim obviously has to do with the fading vitality and death of the wicked. The critical element in Bildad's development of the metaphor, however, is the choice of verbs, for Bildad uses only verbs with a middle sense: The light goes out, does not shine, grows dark, goes out (18:6–7). Flames, of course, may be put out by an agent, but a flame goes out by itself when it has no fuel (Prov 26:20). The metaphorical claim is that the wicked is a self-limiting presence because he has no access to the fuel that would allow him to remain vital, a claim previously made by Bildad in the metaphor of the dry and well-watered plants (8:11–19).

The second cluster of images uses the figure of arrested movement. Analogous to the failing light, so the physical vitality of the wicked dissipates as "the vigor of his step weakens" (contrast Ps 18:37–38; Prov 4:12). For the wicked no step is safe, because the world is baited with a bewildering variety of traps and snares, which they cannot see (18:8–10). As with the imagery of light, which has traditional metaphorical associations, so the figure of the trap or snare is commonly used to express anxiety about hostile or uncontrollable situations (Pss 9:16; 124:7; 140:6; 142:4b; Jer 18:22b; 48:44). Thus, the traps serve not only to connote the objective hostility of the structures of reality toward the wicked but also to suggest the inescapable anxiety of the wicked that Eliphaz described in psychological terms (15:21–24). Bildad's imagery does something else as well. The traps, represented as hidden in the environment through which the wicked attempts to walk, are also metaphorically identified as "his own schemes" (18:7b). Thus, the overlapping images make a more complex claim about the nature of wickedness and its relation to the world than first appears. Bildad is not describing a binary opposition of hostility between forces of good and evil, as one finds in some forms of apocalyptic thought (e.g., 1QS 3–4). Rather, the destruction of evil is self-generated. The construction of the world is such that as the wicked person attempts to manipulate it, his aggression is converted into the means of his own destruction. For Bildad, as for the wisdom tradition from which he speaks, evil has an essentially ironic structure.

The third section of Bildad's imagistic account develops out of the previous one, as the picture of hidden traps shifts into the more dramatic image of personified terrors "scattering his steps," as they pursue him like a pack of hunting predators (18:11). Though "terrors" may be psychological, the term is also conventionally used of the servants of Death (see 18:14),[63] and the ensuing imagery moves in just that direction (18:12–13). What characterizes "calamity," "disaster," and "Death's first born" (= plague) is the ravenous hunger with which they consume the wicked. Although Bildad does not make the connection explicit, the fate of the wicked, as he describes it, is a form of poetic justice, for greed, represented as insatiable hunger, is one of the common ways of characterizing the essence of the wicked. Zophar makes this motif the centerpiece of his own imagery in chapter 20, where the wicked is the consumer par excellence. In Zophar's description, emphasis lies on the futility of the wicked person's attempt to consume, since he cannot keep down what he eats (20:15, 18, 20–22). What had tasted delicious was in reality a bitter emetic and a deadly poison (20:12-14, 16). Bildad's account may also be understood in relation to this complex of imagery, as here the wicked, the greedy consumer, becomes the consumed (18:12-13). If this association is made, then the ironic structure of evil is again in evidence.

The image in verses 14-15 completes the account of the wicked person's demise and provides a transition to the concluding verses. Here personified "Terror" (see v. 11) appears again, now as a soldier who arrests the wicked and arraigns him before "the King" (i.e., death), while fire and sulphur purge any trace of the wicked from his former residence. The claim that "fire lodges in his tent" (18:15a)[64] contrastingly echoes verses 5-6, which described the failure of the flame that provided "light in his tent," an image of security. Fire and sulphur are characteristically associated with destruction (Gen 19:24; Ps 11:6; Ezek 38:22), and sprinkling sulphur rendered a place unfruitful and unfit for habitation (Deut 29:22). In this way verse 15 introduces the imagery of the concluding verses. Rhetorically, they function not so much to characterize the nature of the wicked as to convey the completeness of his extermination. The dominant figure is merismus, which expresses totality by naming paired opposites: root and branch, above and below, field and pasture, light and darkness, kin and place of sojourn, west and east (18:15-19). Thus, through the symbolic action of language is the wicked "driven out of the world" (18:18).

If one focuses on the imagery in the poem and particularly on the metaphors that disclose the ironic structure of evil, Bildad's account presents a moral imagination that is at least worthy of serious consideration. This claim about reality, however unobvious it may appear to modern readers, was one of the most widespread and fundamental beliefs in the ancient Near East, attested in many literary forms, though given its most articulate expression in wisdom literature. Restated in conceptual terms, this belief is that good and evil have a different relation to reality. The resilient, enduring quality of good derives from its participation in the structures of creation itself, whereas evil, no matter how powerful and vital it appears, is actually fragile and subject to disintegration because it has no root in that order of creation (e.g., Psalm 1). This contrast between the enduring and the ephemeral contains no denial of the existence of evil; it betrays no curiosity about its origin. Though wicked individuals may perish, there is no eschatological expectation of the elimination of evil as a whole. Many matters that would be of primary concern in other forms of moral imagination simply fall outside the range of interest of this perspective. What this view claims is significant is simply the qualitative difference between good and evil consequent upon the ontological status of each. What it offers is a way of living resiliently in the world and grounds for confidence in enduring and in opposing even that evil that appears all powerful.

One cannot convince another of the truth of this perception by means of argument, for the issue is fundamentally one of perception itself. Rather, as

Demos says, one can only "evoke" a world, a vivid pattern of a whole. Hence the crucial role of metaphors in Bildad's speech, metaphors that continually reiterate the ironic structure of evil. But Bildad does not rest his persuasion upon the power of metaphor alone. He incorporates the metaphors into a narrative, what I have provisionally called, using Kenneth Burke's phrase, a "representative anecdote." By using such a form, Bildad suggests that what he describes can indeed be seen in the world; yet as my students never tire of pointing out, there are plenty of examples to the contrary. Unquestionably, these narratives cannot function plausibly as lawlike descriptions of what always happens. But in what sense can Bildad and the other friends assert these narratives as true, and why did such narratives apparently have such a tenacious hold on the moral imagination of the wisdom tradition? Pushing beyond the description of them as anecdotal, I want to argue that these narratives function in an iconic fashion, claiming to offer a window onto a fundamental structure of reality.

The persuasive power of an iconic narrative does not derive from a simple empiricism. Although it cannot be wholly disconfirmed by experience and remain plausible, the story remains surprisingly resilient in the face of a mixture of conforming and nonconforming experience. Why would this be? Taking a clue from Alasdair MacIntyre, I want to claim that the power an iconic story possesses to disclose truth, its perceived fit with reality or lack of it, has to be assessed in relation to the particular social formation in which the story is embedded and in which it functions. As with ritual practices, the relation between narrative and social formation is circular. Iconic narratives encode fundamental commitments, social roles, and profiles of virtue that constitute the community. These narratives make meaningful—and therefore possible—certain forms of action. That is, only within the contours of such narratives do certain kinds of action acquire meaning and so become the things one does or refrains from doing. These narratives ring true because they define the horizon of meaningful action within an already given social and moral world.

An example from contemporary American culture may illustrate. Consider popular business literature in which the story is told, over and over, of the individual who turns a creative idea into a flourishing business. This is the iconic narrative of entrepreneurial capitalism. Everyone knows that the large majority of new businesses fail, yet the story does not lose its power. The "truth" of this iconic narrative is not an empirical truth but something like a mythic truth. That story is seen as expressing the nature and essence of an entrepreneurial society with all the static cleared away. Several things make the iconic narrative ring true in spite of an abundance of nonconforming examples. First and most powerful is simply the prior existence of the cultural community itself. The stories of business failures, however numerous, have no explanatory power for the existence of the (undoubtedly real) commercial society. The iconic story does. Thus, the stories of business failure and the stories of the good idea that becomes a successful business actually belong to two different levels of explanation. Though formally they might appear contradictory, functionally they are not. One explains specific cases; the other explains the foundational commitments of the social order.

Second, the various component practices that go into developing and running a business—identifying a need, developing a business plan, raising capital, training workers, arranging a distribution network, advertising, and so forth—are all specific practices belonging to the practical logic of a functioning commercial culture that the entrepreneur experiences as real in different ways every day. Each practice makes sense on its own in terms of its proximate goals. But as a totality, such investments of energy and resources make sense only in the context of the iconic narrative. Thus, the very fact of participation—of practices—encourages belief in the underlying iconic narrative, not as a guarantee of outcomes but as a statement of the underlying structures and their "tendency toward" certain outcomes. The mutual implications of the iconic narrative and the existing social structure form the framework for values, encoding both meanings and motivations. In short, they create a lifeworld.

Like the story of the good idea that becomes a successful business, the stories of the hope of the pious and the fate of the wicked need to be understood as functioning within a specific social and moral world and deriving their power to persuade from that context. The narratives of the fate of the wicked and the hope of the pious do not for the most part describe the particular values of this world so much as they assume them. The stock characters of the pious and the wicked serve as summary terms for those values. One can, however, easily draw a thumbnail sketch of the moral culture to which they refer from other texts: wisdom writings, psalms, prophetic speeches, and so forth. This world is a hierarchical, paternalistic social order based on kinship (real and fictive) and something like a patronage system, within an honor/shame culture with a strong purity system. The ethical values of that society attempt to contain disruptive abuses (e.g., insisting on protection for those at the low end of the hierarchy [the poor], those who had been deprived of male kin [the orphan and the widow], those who fell outside the kinship structures [the stranger]). Since the values of this moral world endorse power differentials within the society, they are also concerned to control abuses of power, both by means of moral formation and social sanction. Thus, behaviors and character traits that are discouraged include greed, violence, arrogance, covetousness, adultery, and deception, whereas those that are encouraged include generosity, self-control, respect for traditional authority, and compassion. The limits of hierarchical difference are also set by an affirmation of a common humanity and belief in one God who made all. This thumbnail sketch is not intended as anything like an adequate account but is offered as an evocation of some of the most familiar features of the social and moral order one encounters in biblical traditions, particularly in psalmic and wisdom materials.

The stories of the hope of the pious and the fate of the wicked, grounded in the transcendent warrant of the divine will, serve as the iconic narratives for the concrete values and institutions of this moral world. An anecdote about the success of the wicked cannot explain the reality of this world of values, which is experienced as such every day. Such things may happen, but they are perceived as anomalies, lacking explanatory power. But the story of the wicked overtaken by calamity, like the story of the restoration of the good person, rings true because it is consonant with the foundational values of the society. Correspondingly, the iconic narratives provide the horizon of meaning for the particular actions and practices that give life its moral texture. Such narratives are not (pace *haśśātān*) primarily to be understood in terms of reward and punishment. Rather, they give meaning to particular actions. What does it mean to protect an orphan or to abuse a stranger? More is at issue than just "what we customarily do and don't do here." The iconic narratives of the fate of the wicked and the hope of the pious are claims that such actions derive their ultimate significance from the nature of reality itself. To do an act of goodness is to root oneself in reality. To commit an act of evil is to cut oneself off.

The connection I have been trying to establish between iconic narratives and the meaningfulness of moral action helps explain the dynamics of what takes place between Job and Eliphaz in chapters 21 and 22, in particular why Eliphaz now accuses Job of being one of the wicked. In chapter 21 when Job describes the happy lot of the wicked, he is not simply mentioning nonconforming examples. But that Job adopts the form of a narrative about the wicked that is the mirror image of the one the friends tell is no accident. Since they are struggling over foundational perceptions, Job cannot simply offer arguments. One cannot refute a story by an argument. One has to tell a different story.[65] And that is what Job is doing. This story is no mere anecdote but is a rival iconic narrative, linked associatively with the vivid personal accounts Job has already given concerning his experience of God's violence and injustice (chaps. 12, 16, 19). Eliphaz recognizes that, in repudiating the iconic story of the fate of the wicked, Job's words are an attack on the reality of the entire moral world. If Job's reading of the world is true, then its underlying reality is *rōgez*, a turmoil that provides no warrant for the construction of a moral society.

In the iconic narratives of the fate of the wicked up to this point, the particular conduct that counts as wickedness has not been specified apart from a fairly general characterization. The energy of the speeches has been directed toward a rhetorical enactment of the irreality of wickedness. Only after Job has attacked the plausibility of that iconic narrative does Eliphaz incorporate references to the concrete acts that make a person wicked, as he accuses Job of exacting pledges from family members, even to the extent of stripping them naked. He alleges that Job has refused water to the thirsty and food to the hungry, sending the widow away empty handed and crushing the hands of the orphan (22:6–11).

Though Eliphaz here explicitly connects these acts with Job's present condition, it is too superficial to understand this speech simply as Eliphaz's blaming the victim. His words are a direct response to what Job has said in chapter 21. Does Eliphaz actually believe Job has done these things? So it appears, if one takes his words at face value. But whatever Job has done or not done in the past, from Eliphaz's perspective Job has committed the moral equivalent of those actions by denying that the moral order has a grounding in transcendent reality. The issue that stands in the tense space between Eliphaz and Job in these chapters is close to that articulated by Ivan in Dostoevsky's *The Brothers Karamazov*: "If there is no God, then everything is permitted." If all is *rōgez*, then the foundation that makes it meaningful to distinguish between the goodness of protecting the orphan and the abhorrence of denying food to the hungry is swept away. What is at stake in the argument over the iconic narratives of the fate of the wicked is Eliphaz's belief that one cannot have a stable and coherent moral society in the absence of a belief that the cosmic order is itself ultimately a moral one.

Summary and Assessment

As I have argued in this chapter, the dominant way in which the friends attempt to respond to the turmoil that constitutes Job's suffering is by means of the workings of narrative. This is scarcely surprising, since narrative is the fundamental resource for the human construction of meaning, exercised through its powers of emplotment and its complex mimetic relationship to lived experience. The moral imagination of the friends is not only narrative in its orientation but also binary in its operations. Thus, the repertoire of paradigmatic stories by which they give the world shape has a strongly contrastive structure: the hope of the pious and the fate of the wicked. But though such narratives may be paired in order to express the coherency of the moral cosmos that they figure (4:6-7, 8-11), for the most part they are developed differently in the dialogue and serve different purposes in the debate with Job.

The cognitive and social work of narrative, however, can be understood only in light of its complex relation to practices and institutions. One sees this most clearly in the way in which Job's friends connect the narrative structure of the hope of the pious to their advice to Job to pray. The persuasiveness of the narrative is enhanced through its connection to a social practice. The engagement of the body, the preparatory disciplines, the orchestration of various sets of interrelated symbols, the configuration of temporality, and the embedded social values all work together to construct a field of action within which the one who prays becomes an agent in his own transformation. The practice can be said to activate the narrative and make it appropriable.

No practice comparable to that of prayers of supplication existed to give a sense of experiential reality to the narrative of the fate of the wicked. Cursing would perhaps have been such a practice (5:3), but although it occurs from time to time in biblical texts and even finds a certain place within the structures of prayer (e.g., Psalm 109), the use of imprecation does not seem to have been a regular and consistent mode of dealing with the presence of the wicked. Moreover, in wisdom dialogues such as Job 3–27 the problem of evil is not simply a matter of personal enemies but acquires a more philosophical dimension. Thus the friends, in attempting to argue with Job, make use of the vivid poems that evoke a sense of the transitory and ephemeral nature of evil and of the wicked who participate in it. Despite the fact that the poems are dominated by concrete and personalized imagery, they articulate a systemic and ultimately nonpersonal understanding of good and evil. Through these poems the friends express the classic wisdom perspective that understands good and evil to be ontologically different.

Hermeneutical engagement of the friends' arguments, in particular the poems that deal with the fate of the wicked, has tended to focus on the ethical implications of their understanding of evil and the response to be made to the violence of the wicked. One might, in an intentionally sympathetic reading, relate their perspective to the values of the broader wisdom tradition. Extrapolating from their description of the wicked, how would the pious person respond to evil and its violence? Presumably by the response of nonviolence. To meet the violence of wickedness with a violence of good would be to fail to understand the nature of reality. The disruptions of wickedness could only be countered by acts that isolate it or by acts of righteousness that build up the good and by a stance of immeasurable patience that waits for the self-destruction of evil. Such is the logic of their position, and one could find numerous pieces of concrete advice in Proverbs, as well as in the broader ancient Near Eastern wisdom tradition, that explicitly call for such a stance.

At the same time, it would be disingenuous not to notice the extensive imagery of violence in the poems, as they describe with relish the demise of the wicked. They are "destined for the sword" (15:22), and "fire consumes the[ir] tents" (15:34). They are "torn from the tent in which they trusted and brought to the king of terrors" (18:14), and "driven out of the world" (18:18). The language of these poems tends to speak of actions while obscuring agents. Violent things ultimately happen to the wicked, but the mechanism is unclear. Yet the imagery of the self-destruction of evil blends seamlessly into the imagery of the expulsion of evil. And, indeed, the underlying ontology supports such a connection, for evil is always being refused, forced out; it literally has no place in creation. When one thinks not in abstract categories or poetic images but in terms of actual persons, the susceptibility of this perspective to dehumanizing the person deemed wicked is evident. Gerald Janzen articulates what is at issue when he compares the imagery of Bildad's poem with his memory of a news-reel from World War II, which, as he says, "showed what outraged Italian mobs did with the lifeless body of their erstwhile Il Duce Mussolini, dragging it through the streets, hanging it heels-up against the wall, then pelting it with stones and spitting at it. In viewing the scene, one was drawn into the moral energy of the action; yet more deeply one felt a pathos of horror that any human being, no matter in what moral state, could be so driven out of the world."[66] This collective participation in the expulsion from existence, this annihilation of the one seen as evil makes René Girard's analysis of violence and scapegoating most applicable to this part of the book of Job.[67]

Even though this danger of dehumanizing the wicked and legitimating un-limited violence against them is intrinsic to such a perspective, one cannot say that the friends themselves fall victim to this possibility in their thought. They declare only one person to be wicked—Job himself, in chapter 22. Although Eliphaz's denunciation of Job's perceived wickedness is unsparing, his conclusion is not that Job be driven out of the world. Rather, he gives to the Job-perceived-as-wicked the same advice he gave to the Job-perceived-as-innocent: Engage in the spiritual practice of prayer. Eliphaz's dramatic bringing together of these two parts of the friends' repertoire invites one to look again at the way the friends understand prayer.

Although the practice of prayer to which the friends refer can be illumined in some respects by the repertoire of prayers of supplication found in Psalms, the friends describe the act of prayer as it is understood from the perspective of the wisdom tradition. From Bildad's strongly binary imagery, to the spatial imagery characteristic of Zophar's language, to the references to mouth and heart, word and teaching in Eliphaz's account of the preparation for prayer, their description of prayer is inflected with wisdom accents. Viewed from this perspective, the great power of prayer is its capacity to reorder the disordered. This is why the friends recommend it repeatedly to Job, whether they envision him as the innocent victim of catastrophe, the unconsciously sinful individual, or the morally reprobate perpetrator of violence. For the wisdom perspective of the friends, the goodness of the world is an expression of its fundamental order-liness. Wickedness and violent evil are disorder. The innocent victim of violence suffers not only from the specific injury but also from disorder, that is, from disorientation and a pervasive loss of trust. The therapeutic program of the friends, especially as articulated by Eliphaz in chapter 5, attempts to heal the disorder by engaging the victim in spiritual exercises that reorient him to the fundamentally trustworthy nature of existence. Zophar in chapter 11 ad-dresses the situation of the person who is internally disordered by sin but lacks the capacity to understand and so lives in false consciousness. Eliphaz in chap-ter 22 addresses the situation of the person who is actively morally disordered and so spreads disorder and violence. As they speak of prayer and the preparation for prayer, they invoke imagery of the reordering of the mind, the body, and the dwelling. Wickedness disorders. Prayer reorders. Thus, it is suitable for the victim of catastrophe. But since wickedness is itself an expression of disorder in the soul of the one who commits it, prayer is necessary for the one who does evil. It is a reordering and in that sense a redemption.

In this analysis I have attempted, in as generous a manner as possible, to tease out the implications of the friends' ethic of care, even while acknowledging the potential dangers of their moral imagination. In doing so, however, I have allowed their construction of the nature of evil to stand unchallenged. Now the adequacy of their assumptions must be assessed. For this inquiry I find particularly helpful the analysis of the friends developed by Philippe Nemo. Nemo also understands the friends' response to Job in terms of the therapeutic, but he situates the therapeutic in terms of the broader category of "technique." Ordinarily, technique is identified with a modern phenomenon, the preoccupation characteristic of secular modernity in its concern to "remedy human frailty and the ills besetting it."[68] From the technologies of production to those of medicine to the techniques of psychoanalysis to city planning and criminology, there is no ill that cannot be fixed or at least managed. Nemo sees in the perspective of the friends a premodern expression of the same sensibility, a kind of moral technology.

Technique has several characteristics. Its focus on the efficacious is made plausible by its claim to knowledge. Perceiving the world as unified, systematic, and above all transparent to knowledge, technique has confidence in the validity and universal applicability of its insights. Other claims to knowledge are held to be defective or inadequate. One thinks, for instance, of the psychoanalyst who "knows" the patient in a way that the patient does not yet know himself and his own story, for the psychoanalyst understands her own knowledge to be grounded in a science. Allowing for the obvious differences between modern and ancient society, Nemo's observation about the sciencelike quality of the knowledge claimed by the friends is apt. Indeed, the orientation to the regularities underlying apparently diverse phenomena is a familiar characteristic of the wisdom tradition's way of knowing. Thus, even though the friends speak in concrete and personal images, their claims are about underlying principles of creation that operate with predictability.

This gives the friends' moral technology a powerful claim to efficacy in the overcoming of turmoil. As Nemo puts it,

> Moral technology claims to have overwhelmed what was most serious in evil. The caesura separating the moment in which the ground of the world is still firm from the moment when it falls away like rotten floorboards is regarded by moral technology as a problem that has been pinpointed, bypassed, erased. The world, almost completely transparent to knowledge, is a degree of order superior to all conceivable disorder. . . . Technique masters and computes emotions, pleasures and pains, and the human existence that feels them. It dominates the whole earth.[69]

What Nemo wishes to critique is not technique per se, but "technique's intention to enclose the world within the horizon of thought."[70] In essence, technique fails in its vision of evil, for it literally cannot perceive radical evil, which would threaten its vision of the world as a unified whole.

This issue, of course, is precisely what is at the heart of the brilliantly conceived wisdom dialogue between Job and the friends. Job repudiates the moral imagination of the friends and its commitment to technique. As Nemo phrases it, what Job discloses is "the excess of evil." By excess he does not mean a level of intensity, for he acknowledges that "technique can often overcome evils that are altogether 'extreme.'"[71] Excess is evil's overflowing of technique's attempt to understand and control. What Job perceives is that evil—the disturbance, the disorder—is actually what is always prior. "For what is the Law but a representation whereby man tries to rectify the crooked effects of the unforeseeable, of madness, of evil's excess? . . . Technique, the human effort to dominate the world, is a response to the human impotence that is always already there."[72] The problem is not that technique is limited. The claim is that technique represents a species of false consciousness. It is the excess of evil, its capacity to "humiliate the Law of the world" that reveals evil's priority.[73] In the friends' perspective the wicked are more or less a fact of nature, subject to certain predictable regularities and therefore manageable. They are, as Nemo describes them, "neutral." But not so the evil that Job describes. For it is not neutral but an "intention," an evil that comes looking for him, an evil that "insists."[74] For Job the excess of evil is God. The moral imagination of the friends simply cannot encompass this aspect of Job's experience. Nor does Job have a ready-made worldview within which to organize his experience. It must rather be worked out in the course of the dialogue. And so it is to Job's speeches that we now turn.

5

Broken in Pieces by Words/Breaking Words in Pieces

Job and the Limits of Language

> The breakage of the verse enacts the breakage of the world.
> Shoshana Felman, "Education and Crisis"

One way to assess the gulf between Job and the friends is to observe their different relationship to the common language they have inherited. The friends have an easy relationship with language and are able to speak with untroubled fluency. The privileged terms of value, the tropes, the modes of reasoning, and above all the traditional genres they use appear in their speech as completely adequate instruments for the expression of experience and for knowledge of the world. A certain self-consciousness about language is evident in their speech, specifically in the ways in which they incorporate traditional speech into their own words. Commentators regularly note the abundance of proverbs, aphorisms, traditional figures, parables, and hymnic fragments that populate the speech of the friends (e.g., from the first cycle, 4:11; 5:2; 5:8-16; 8:11-13; 11:7-9, 12).[1] Even though no other extant text preserves the very words one finds in their speeches, the "trace of a quotation mark" hovers about them. They are meant to be heard both as the words of the speaker and as the words of another, the words of authoritative tradition, cited in agreement and support. This phenomenon is one aspect of what Mikhail Bakhtin calls double voicing.[2] How readily such traditional words are incorporated into the speech of the friends is seen in Eliphaz's use of the hymnic fragment in 5:8-16. The words about "the great and unsearchable things" God does are simultaneously Eliphaz's words and recognizably objectified words that have an intentionality independent of Eliphaz. The sounding together of these two voices in his speech is an indication of the way in which the inherited language of moral and religious discourse is one that Eliphaz can inhabit comfortably.

The relationship is even more striking in Bildad's speech in chapter 8. There he urges Job to "inquire of the former generation . . . for we are as yesterday and know nothing. . . . Will they not teach you, speak to you, and utter words from their understanding?" (8:8-10). That Bildad proceeds to teach

Job by means of the parable of the two plants is not an inconsistency. Though the style of the parable is not as formulaic as that of Eliphaz's hymn, it, too, is the voice of tradition. Bildad's identification with the language of the past is complete. He could not, on his own, say anything of use to Job. But he can be the embodiment of the speech of ancestral generations and its wisdom.

In contrast, one wonders how Job can speak at all. One of the frequent consequences of traumatic experience is an initial loss of language and a more persistent estrangement from language. Both phenomena are represented in the book of Job, the loss of language in the seven days and seven nights of silence that separate the prose tale from the dialogue, and the estrangement from language in Job's speech in the dialogues. It may seem odd to refer to Job's estrangement from language in the dialogues, since the author gives Job some of the most brilliant poetry in the book. But the brilliance of his speech is the brilliance of light refracted through shattered glass of many colors. Job picks his way through a shattered language that he can wield only in fragments. His estranged relationship to inherited language and his challenge to its adequacy to express his experience or give knowledge of the world is most often recognized in his parodies of psalmic and hymnic speech (e.g., 7:17-18; 12:7-9, 13-25).[3] Though parody is an important part of Job's repertoire, it is only one of many ways in which his troubled relation to language is expressed. He pries apart words themselves, setting their different meanings against one another, as he tries to bend them to his expressive purpose (e.g., the word *ṣādaq* in 9:2, discussed later). He fragments and recombines motifs from traditional psalms of supplication, re-presenting them in ways that expose repressed aspects of their meaning (cf., e.g., Job 7:19 and Ps 39:14; Job 10:8-14 and Ps 139:13-16). At other times he closely imitates inherited speech, yet in ways that disclose some hitherto unseen obscenity, shocking it into visibility by violating genre conventions and juxtaposing words and forms from disparate discursive traditions (cf. Job 16:7-18 and Lam 3:1-22).

In her study of trauma and witness Shoshana Felman examines the writing of poet and Holocaust survivor Paul Celan. After the war Celan continued to write in German, for, he said, "only in one's mother tongue can one express one's own truth."[4] Yet Celan's relation to this inherited German was deeply problematic and fraught with struggle, as he sought to "reappropriate the language which . . . marked his own exclusion"[5] through a process of dislocation and remolding of its semantics and its grammar. Of one poem Felman says, it is "not simply about violence but about the relation between violence and language, about the passage of the language through the violence and the passage of the violence through language."[6] These observations about Celan cast light on Job's attempts to speak. Though he does not struggle with language at the level of grammar, Job's attempt to express his own truth about the violence he has experienced similarly requires him to dislocate and remold the words, metaphors, and genres through which traditional language had constructed a world of meaning. Like Celan, in order to talk about violence Job must pass violence through language itself.

Though initially Job's energies are directed toward resisting the inherited language that the friends speak so effortlessly, he gradually begins to imagine new protocols of speech and to reappropriate certain words that had earlier lost their meaning. In his exploratory appropriation of the language of courts and legal action, Job moves toward what appears to be the constitution of an alternative rhetorical world. Unsystematically but persistently Job's exploratory verbal play with legal language begins to articulate the three things necessary for a functioning rhetorical world: a set of actors whose roles and relations are defined; the practices in which they can meaningfully engage; and the topics or values to which the actors must appeal if they are to justify their behavior.[7]

In depicting Job in this process it might appear that the author has grasped the great potential of the wisdom dialogue as a genre. Here the argument would not be between two positions in a single rhetorical world (as in the Babylonian Theodicy) but between two alternative rhetorical worlds. Though something like this begins to happen, the author never allows Job's new moral imagination and the rhetoric in which it finds expression to become fully established. The legal imagery that serves as its generative metaphor repeatedly flares but fades. Far from validating Job's new rhetoric as one that can displace that of the friends, the wisdom dialogue ends in an act of linguistic violence that not only exposes the limits of the wisdom dialogue as a genre but also casts in question the possibility of a unified language in a world of acute contradiction.

Resistance to Narrative

As I argued in the preceding chapter, the role of narrative in the construction of meaning is fundamental to the friends' attempt to respond to Job's sense of turmoil. Given the genre conventions of a wisdom dialogue, Job will resist what the friends have to say. What is radical in Job's response, however, is that he does not simply challenge the particular narratives they propose. Instead, he challenges the very narratability of human existence. One could, of course, refer to the images and self-descriptions Job invokes as little narratives,[8] but their configuration is vastly different from those of Eliphaz and Bildad. Much as the antinovels of Alain Robbe-Grillet contest the assumptions of the novelistic tradition by imitating aspects of its form but utterly refusing its structures of emplotment, so Job's little "narratives" undermine the integrative assumptions of the friends' attempt to narrativize human experience.

Specifically, Job contests their representation of time. Eliphaz and Bildad configure time as open and ample. The future, which is always beckoning, is the space within which new things may happen, events that then confer meaning on what has come before. There is always enough time in their narratives. Indeed, the friends' narratives define the shape of time in relation to the plots necessitated by the tropes embedded in them (e.g., transformation, survival and renewal). Job, however, represents time differently, both qualitatively and quantitatively. One sees this most clearly in the series of metaphors and images that opens chapter 7, which provides a kind of phenomenology of time. The preoccupation with temporality is evident from the number of expressions for time or the experience of it ("the days of a laborer," "his days," 7:1b; "[evening] shade," 7:2a; "he waits," 7:2b; "months . . . nights," 7:3; "how long," "evening," "dawn," 7:4; "my days go swiftly . . . come to an end," 7:6). The protagonists of Job's antinarrative are the members of a forced labor gang, the day laborer, and the slave (7:1–2), who metaphorically represent general human experience. These are persons who have been deprived of agency, but it is not that feature by itself that makes their lives unnarratable. Rather, it is the way this status configures time. Time is not open but is the time of "forced labor" (*ṣābā᾿*), which does not end in the shaping *telos* of narrative emplotment and resolution but simply when the time is up. The only way such time might be incorporated into the temporality of narrative would be if the time of "replacement" (*ḥalipāh*) could be seen as its culmination, a narrative imagining Job will later attempt but reject (see 14:14; cf. Isa 40:2, where it is used in just such fashion). Here, however, "forced labor" qualifies all the time of a human being "upon the earth." This is no narrative of forced labor followed by the freedom of release, but only forced labor terminated by death.

The closed time of human existence is figured slightly differently in the following images. "Like the days of the hired laborer (*śākîr*) are his days" (7:1b). The *śākîr* sold his labor for a set period of time. Lacking resources, he depended for survival on receiving wages day by day (7:2b; Lev 19:13; Deut 24:14). Thus, meaningful time for the *śākîr* has a radically limited horizon. The "narrative" of his life extends no further than the end of each day, in a pattern that does not integrate into some larger structure but merely repeats, day after day. So, too, for the slave, who receives not wages but simply the respite of evening shade (7:2a). Even the vestigal narrative of expectation and fulfillment inscribed in the shape of the *śākîr*'s day is undermined in Job's representation, as he describes the wages themselves as paid in the devalued coin of time ("months of futility . . . nights of misery"). Similarly, the narrow but potentially narrative pattern of desire and satisfaction that qualitatively figured the slave's experience of time during the day is frustrated by the elusiveness of evening rest. Inverting the pattern in which desire lengthens time and satisfaction shortens it, the agitation of a body in misery (7:5) lengthens the night for one who is "sated with restlessness."

Job's concluding image (7:6) is the one that most directly engages Eliphaz's attempt to integrate Job's experience into narrative, for here Job challenges

Eliphaz's privileged word, "hope" (*tiqwāh*). The imagery Job invokes, drawn from the act of weaving, is a common source of metaphors for life. The medieval Jewish scholar Ibn Ezra also invoked it when he said that "man in the world weaves like a weaver, and certainly his days are the thread."[9] Already in the Hebrew Bible, King Hezekiah laments his impending death with the words "Like a weaver I have rolled up my life; he cuts me off from the loom" (Isa 38:12b). In those metaphors the woven fabric is the image of a life, its texture and pattern developing from the succession of days, as the act of rolling up and severing the cloth signifies the end of life in death. Even when invoked in a lament, the image serves as an integrative figure that allows life to be grasped as a whole. This is an image Eliphaz could understand and approve. Job, however, reorganizes the signifiers of the metaphor. Like Ibn Ezra, Job is concerned with how the metaphor figures the temporality of life, its "days." But in Job's image the vehicle of the metaphor is not the cloth but the shuttle, which he invokes as a figure of speed—and sudden cessation. Punning on the word *tiqwāh*, which means both "hope" and "thread," in Job's image the shuttle (i.e., the days of his life) stops abruptly *bĕ'epes tiqwāh*, "at the end of the thread" or, as one might also translate, "without hope." For Eliphaz hope is the shape of time (4:6; 5:16a). For Job the shape of time makes hope absurd.

Job's resistance to Eliphaz's narrative time is based in large measure on their different understanding of the relation of the body to time. For Eliphaz narrative temporality is inscribed in the body's regenerative capacity. It is the time of a weakened body recovering its strength (4:3-4), the time configured by the healing of a wound (5:18), or in Bildad's allegory, the time sketched by a damaged and uprooted plant sprouting again from the dust (8:19). Even "timely" death in old age is transcended by the body's capacity to generate offspring "like the grass of the earth" (5:25-26). These narrative metaphors of healing, sprouting, and seeding are powerful images by which the discordant is made concordant. For that very reason they are subject to the critique that Ricoeur raises as a possible objection to the work narrative performs. Are such configuration of the imagination that impose "narrative consonance . . . on temporal dissonance" a form a treachery, a "violence of interpretation"?[10] Do they "tell a story" in the sense of a lie? Certainly that is what Job alleges, and he bases his objection on their false construction of the body.

For Job the basic truth about the body is found in the image of the wound and in the pain of the wound. A significant number of Job's representations of the body are invasive images: the poisoned arrow that penetrates the body (6:4; cf. 7:20), worms that cloak and feed on broken and oozing skin (7:5), dreams that invade the interiority of psychic space (7:14), images that culminate in the graphic description of penetration and disemboweling in 16:12-14. Only by exploring such images can one grasp the violation of reality Job hears in the friends' attempt to narrativize his experience as a story of expectation, a story both literally

and metaphorically represented as healing. For Job the wounded body is a fundamental image of the limits of narrative time as adequate to human experience.
Narrative time is a time of delay, for it tells of an end that can come only after the
playing out of an indeterminate number of necessary events. But the time of a
body in pain is a time of urgency. Whereas Eliphaz and Bildad privilege the future
as the locus of meaning, for Job the present in all its immediacy is the hermeneutically privileged time. Using images of hunger and taste, Job knows with the
certainty of the body's knowledge that the "hunger" that drives him to cry out is
real (6:5), that the taste in his mouth is not that of his own injustice but the taste
of destruction (6:30).

Even if Job believed in the theoretical truth of Eliphaz's narrative of survival,
it would do him no good. He cannot enter into the time of expectant waiting:
"What is my strength that I should wait; and what is my end that I should be
patient? Is my strength the strength of stones, or is my flesh bronze?" (6:12).
Here is the treachery. Narrative bodies can be made as strong as they need to
be, but real bodies are merely flesh. Thus, Job's own "hope," that word that
figures the narrative future of Eliphaz, is that he might experience the severe
wounding that brings immediate death and thus relief from pain and from time
itself (6:8). By the same token the tropes of transformation favored by Eliphaz
and Bildad are exposed as deceptive. In contrast to the metaphor of the person
as a tough and resilient plant, sprouting again from the dust, Job offers the
metaphor of the person as cloud, an insubstantial object whose transformation
into nothingness is as irreversible as it is sudden (7:9; cf. also 14:7–22, where
the image of the regenerating tree contrasts with the images appropriate to the
human condition, the drained sea and the eroded mountain).

Job uses images of the wounded and invaded body not only to render problematic the chronological time of narrative but also to show the destruction of
the qualitative time of subjectivity, that sense of the present in which a person
is "present to" himself. In Job's religious vocabulary the physical and psychic
pain he experiences is imaged as the incessant, invasive presence of God (7:12–
21). The combination of pain and relentless scrutiny, one of the common features of torture, makes the aggressive other always present and so deprives a
person of the time and space of privacy essential to subjectivity.[11] Characteristically, Job uses the body as the ultimate measure of the minimal unit of a subject's
time, the time to swallow one's spit (7:19), as he uses the bed, the metonymic
image of the body asleep, to measure the minimal space of privacy (7:13–14). The
consequence of the violation of the time and space of subjectivity is the disintegration of the self, again graphically expressed in terms of the body: "my throat would
choose strangling [and I would choose] death rather than my bones" (7:15). Not
by coincidence the terms for "throat" (*nepeš*) and "bones" (*'eṣem*) are terms that in
Hebrew become idiomatic expressions for the self, equivalent to the personal
pronoun "I." The body—bone and breath—is the space of the self.

Job resists the notion that narrative time is inscribed in the body as the time of healing, because it misrepresents what it means to suffer the grievous wound and chronic pain of turmoil. That kind of wounding renders impossible the time necessary for narrative and destroys the subject who should be the protagonist of that story. In resisting Eliphaz and Bildad's attempt to transform his sense of turmoil by means of narrative integration, Job has held onto that experience as his untranscendable horizon. But in responding to Eliphaz, Job has been drawn into language, which, though not yet fully narrative, nevertheless endows his experience with more shape than the expression "turmoil" allows. In the description of his situation as one of persecution, including both hostile scrutiny and wounding touch, lie the seeds of a counternarrative.

Resistance to Prayer

Just as Job resists the friends' attempt to construct a livable future for him by means of the rhetoric of narrative, so he rejects the therapy of prayer. As Job comes to believe, the traditional language of prayer is complicit in the violence done to him, authorizing and even valorizing it. Thus, to expose the violence that has come upon him, Job must again do violence to language. Just as Job resisted the friends' attempt to narrativize his life by reference to the limits of the body, so the body plays an important role in Job's struggle against the language and practices of prayer.

Traditional ancient Israelite prayers of supplication often referred to the body as a site of God's activity—creating (Pss 22:10–11; 139:13–16), examining (Pss 17:3; 26:2; 139:1–5, 23–24), and afflicting (Pss 6:2–4; 32:3–4; 38:2–9; 39:11–12). But within the rhetoric of lament the broken body was most significantly presented to God as an object for compassion and a motive for deliverance (Pss 22:15–20; 102:2–12; 109:21–25). As Job struggles to bear witness to his wound, he uses fragmentary motifs from psalmic prayer (e.g., the forgiveness of sin, 7:21a; 10:13–14; cf. Ps 25:7; the ephemerality of human existence, 7:16, 21; cf. Ps 103:15–17; the request that God look away, 7:19; cf. Ps 39:14), including motifs that involve reference to the body (the forming of the body, 10:8–12; the pressure of divine affliction, 7:14–15; divine scrutiny of the inner being, 7:17–18; 10:4–7).[12] In Job's mouth, however, these motifs of psalmic prayer become disarticulated. No longer are they governed by the form of prayer that establishes their meaning. Consequently, Job is able to inflect these motifs with new and disturbing accents.

Of the motifs of prayer invoked by Job, that of divine scrutiny is perhaps the most significant.[13] In the symbolic anatomy of Israelite thought, divine scrutiny is often represented in terms of the body, the searching of the kidneys and heart (e.g., Pss 7:10; 26:2; cf. 73:21). Though such scrutiny is represented by the psalmist as legitimate and even welcome, Job suggests a close, even inevitable connection between looking and harming (Job 7:12-16, 17-20; 10:4-9, 14-17). The act of looking is indeed ambiguous. Though there are benevolent and protective forms of looking (e.g., "watching over," 10:12), the phenomenology of vision suggests why seeing is so readily linked with aggression. To look *at* is to define an object against a field of vision. The thing seen is thus an objectified presence, separate from the one who looks and separated from everything that surrounds it. Levinas notes the similar structures of seeing and seizing, as "vision moves into grasp" in its apprehension of an object.[14] According to Levinas, such violence is resisted when the expressive face of the Other and the speech of the Other disrupts the reductive gaze, making it ethically answerable and forbidding violence.[15] As Job understands it, however, the assumptions underlying the language of psalmic prayer legitimate an invasive scrutiny that does not seek the answering gaze of the human face. In contrast to Zophar, who will speak of lifting up an unblemished face to God in prayer (11:15), Job insists that he cannot lift up his head (10:15). Instead, linked to Job's descriptions of divine scrutiny are images of himself as an object of vision and violence. He becomes a "target" (7:20) and a hunted lion (10:16), one at whom an enemy "looks daggers" (*ṣārî yilṭōš*, 16:9).

Thus, for Job the divine-human relationship to which prayer refers betrays an unacknowledged but fundamentally sadistic structure. His critique of the violence legitimized by the traditional discourse of prayer reaches its climax in chapter 16. Job's description of divine violence develops in a graphic crescendo, beginning with the depiction of God's anger, personified in the features of the face that express rage: gnashing teeth and eyes that "look daggers" (16:9), moving through images of mob violence (16:10-11), and culminating in a description of Job as target for God's archers, his body repeatedly breached and invaded (16:12-14). However horrific these images, they closely echo those found in a traditional type of lament, that represented by Lamentations 3, which uses as its central motif the figure of graphic divine violence.[16] In Lamentations the extensively described violence (Lam 3:1-20) serves as prelude to a word of hope (3:21), grounded in a conviction of the mercies of God (3:22-24). Submission to such suffering is appropriate (3:25-30), because God only reluctantly administers it as punishment for sin (3:31-39). Consequently, one should engage in self-examination and confession (3:40-42), drawing attention to one's suffering as motive for divine compassion (3:43-48). Job's act of resistance to this religiously sanctioned violence is to violate the form of the lament. At the point where the form invites reflection and confession, Job instead calls upon the earth itself not to cover his blood (Job 16:18).[17] What the rhetoric of lament configured as legitimate punishment, Job, by echoing the story of Abel's blood crying out from the ground (Gen 4:10; cf. also Isa 26:21; Ezek 24:7-8), reconfigures as murder. The ravaged body serves not as the basis for compassionate appeal, as in Lam 3:43-48, but as the basis for accusation. Rather than engaging in self-examination and repentance, as the lament urges, Job envisions a witness who would testify against God concerning the wrong done to Job (Job 16:19-21).

At one level Job simply commits an act of linguistic sabotage, rendering the language of the psalm of lament literally and figuratively unspeakable. More profoundly, Job has succinctly set in dialogic opposition two different rhetorics and two different moral imaginations—one grounded in the discourse of prayer, the other grounded in the discourse of legal and quasi-legal dispute. How this emerging alternative rhetoric reconfigures the actors, practices, and topics in the matters under discussion requires further investigation. Before exploring these issues, there is more that needs to be considered concerning the troubling imagery of divine violence that so permeates Job's speeches.[18] Indeed, the representation of that violence and the emergence of legal rhetoric are closely intertwined.

Alterity and the Dynamics of Divine-Human Violence

One starting place for understanding Job's representation of divine violence is his imitation and reorganization of aspects of the language of psalms of supplication. Yet nothing in the psalms, nothing even in Lamentations 3, matches Job's disturbing account of divine violence: "I was at ease, and he broke me in pieces; he seized me by the neck and shattered me; he set me up as his target; his archers surrounded me. He slashed open my kidneys, without mercy; he poured out my gall on the ground. He breached me, breach upon breach" (16:12-14a). Job describes an annihilating rage that knows no limit or measure and that can seemingly find no satiety even as Job is disemboweled, as the reiterative poetry suggests ("he breached me, breach upon breach"). Something else besides the mere heightening of a lament motif generates this language. To understand its dynamics one must search out, perhaps at a level below the conscious intentionality of speech, the embedded figure that generates the distinctive features of Job's language of divine violence. This inquiry must begin with rhetorical and traditio-historical analysis, but it must go beyond them to questions of the symbolic construction of identity, its role in the structure of ethical relations, and the significance of these issues for Job's perception of the inevitability of violence in the divine-human relationship. To anticipate the conclusion of the argument, Job's perception of the nature of divine violence emerges from his relentless exploration of the implications of human and divine alterity. Reflection on the difference between gods and humans was a perennial topic in the religious reflection of the ancient Near East, where it was invoked for a variety of purposes in many different discourses. Thus, Job engages not just the rhetoric of his friends but also traditions of great antiquity.

Although Job speaks of divine violence from the beginning (3:23; 6:4; 7:20), a critical moment occurs when Job engages a statement by Eliphaz (4:17) in an act of bitterly playful punning (9:2-4). In Eliphaz's account of a vision in the night, a revelatory voice says, "Can a human be righteous [*yiṣdaq*] before God, or a mortal be pure [*yiṭhar*] before his maker?" To appreciate what Job does in his appropriation and transformation of Eliphaz's words, one must examine them closely in Eliphaz's own speech. Eliphaz develops his claim rhetorically by means of an argument from greater to lesser, involving a chain of being (God, angels, mortals). This topic is reiterated by Eliphaz in 15:14-16 and by Bildad in 25:4-6 with certain differences in detail. In chapter 15 Eliphaz pairs the verbs *zāqāh* and *ṣādaq* instead of *ṣādaq* and *ṭāhar*, but more significantly he describes human nature as "abhorrent" (*niṭʿāb*) and "corrupt" (*neʾĕleh*), strongly emotive words, suggesting the almost visceral revulsion Eliphaz imagines God to feel toward human beings. Similarly, in Bildad's version humans are referred to as "worms" and "maggots," terms that evoke disgust. This peculiar topos of God's disgust at the innate corruption of human beings is quite unlike the logic of the rest of their speeches. Virtually everything else the friends say can be integrated into their dominant perspective on the world and the relation of good and evil in it, the ground for their "technique." But this claim seems to be drawn from a wholly different discourse.

The traditio-historical background of the topos will be examined presently, but first I wish to look at the imaginative figure at the heart of Eliphaz and Bildad's words: radical otherness. Though stated in almost syllogistic terms in the comparative representation of (1) God, (2) angels/heavenly bodies, and (3) humans, otherness is also described in phenomenological terms in the slow, detailed account with which Eliphaz introduces his topic. Eliphaz begins with an evocation of elusiveness, the sense of an Other that cannot be seized and held. The "word," he says, "crept up stealthily" (*yĕgunnab*), and his ear could grasp only a *šēmeṣ* of it. Though somewhat obscure, *šēmeṣ* apparently means "a small piece."[19] Thus, the word that confronts Eliphaz is not one he can seize and control but one from which he gathers only fragments.

Rather than turning immediately to the content of the word, as best he can express it, Eliphaz describes the temporal and psychological context of the encounter. It is the time of "deep sleep" (*tardēmāh*) when "thought-filled visions of the night" occur (4:13; so NJPS), what we would recognize as that part of the sleep cycle characterized by dreaming. Though ancient and modern terminologies differ, dreaming is a state in which the boundaries of the self become permeable, as intentions beyond the control of the conscious mind express themselves vividly in the intimate spaces of one's own body. Thus, is it not clear whether the state of dread Eliphaz describes in verse 14 is his first intimation of the apparition or simply a further statement of the psychological context, that is, the familiar anxiety associated with the night, when a person feels the vulnerability of human existence. In this state of mind Eliphaz encounters the uncanny otherness of the apparition. Bodiless, it is a wind or spirit (*rûaḥ*) which, though it has some form (*tĕmûnāh*), is unrecognizable (*wĕlō᾿-᾿akkîr mar᾿ēhû*; 4:16).

Eliphaz's narrative vividly creates the sense of an encounter with something radically other, and radical otherness is also the message the voice communicates. The rhetorical question of verse 17 has received a number of translations that, while grammatically possible, are contextually dubious. It is certainly not a question of being more righteous or pure *than* God. But neither is it a matter of being deemed righteous or pure *before* God, a condition regularly required for appearing in the sanctuary (see Psalms 15, 24). Rather, the rhetorical question, which points to something impossible, addresses the issue of a comparison between the being of God and humans: Can mortals be righteous or pure *in relation to* or *over against* God?[20] That the question is one of comparative ontology is evident in the immediately following development in terms of the great chain of being.

The logic of the argument, however, requires close attention. What supports this claim about the inferiority of human moral nature (v. 17) is simply the human propensity to perish. The physicality of human existence (concretely imaged in terms of the body as a house of clay) and its susceptibility to sudden death (vv. 19–21) are the details brought forward in support. This connection is not made as a rational, logical argument, but follows a familiar symbolic association that can also be traced in the development of the English word "corrupt." Though now used mostly as a moral term, it is etymologically derived from a Latin word meaning "broken in pieces." For the breakable human body to be normalized, its fragility must be read as a sign of some inner flaw. Thus, its mortality is associated with moral corruptness and impurity and contrasted with that which is other—immortal, incorruptible, and holy.

A traditio-historical inquiry reveals the background of some of the ideas in this topos, but it also serves to highlight the distinctive development it undergoes in Eliphaz's and Bildad's speeches. Most commentators rightly turn first to Mesopotamian "exemplary sufferer" texts for expressions of the inevitability and universality of sin.[21] The *locus classicus* of this notion is the proverbial saying cited in line 102 of the Sumerian Man and His God text: "Never has a sinless child been born to its mother. . . . [A] sinless *workman* has not existed from of old."[22] Moral disorder is not something humans have introduced on their own, however, for the order of the world as the gods have created it (the *me*'s in Sumerian thought) includes "falsehood, terror, and strife, as well as truth, justice, and peace."[23] Nevertheless, humans are morally answerable to the gods and are punished by suffering for moral and cultic infractions. Though differences exist between Sumerian thought and later Akkadian beliefs, this paradoxical casting of the human situation also occurs in Akkadian literature. Stanza

26 of the Babylonian Theodicy expresses the conviction that "Enlil, king of the gods, who created teeming mankind, / Majestic Ea, who pinched off their clay, / The queeen who fashioned them, mistress Mami, / Gave twisted words to the human race, / They endowed them in perpetuity with lies and falsehood" (lines 276–80).[24] Even though much injustice and consequent suffering can be traced to the way the gods created human beings, in Akkadian literature, as in Sumerian, humans remain exposed to the anger of the gods, which is provoked by acts of transgression.

In Mesopotamian literature this set of ideas characteristically occurs in prayers for deliverance from suffering, as well as in reflections upon the nature of suffering and its remedies. Recognition of inevitable human sinfulness is not incompatible with claims of piety and moral rectitude, since a distinction is maintained between willful wickedness and the unavoidable human propensity to offend the gods. The sufferer's recognition of the innate limits of human moral capacity is itself a sign of a humble and pious attitude and the grounds for appeal to the mercy of the gods.[25] Humble submission is the only stance imaginable.

This approach does not entirely resolve the intellectual problem, however, since the sufferers cannot account for the intensity of their suffering in relation to the modest nature of their inevitable but unintentional sins, nor can they discern a clear pattern of sin and punishment within the world (see, e.g., *Ludlul* ii.10–32). This cognitive dissonance is addressed, though not resolved, by means of a recognition of the radical otherness of the gods, at least in epistemological terms. "I wish I knew that these things [i.e., acts of piety] would be pleasing to one's god! / What is good for oneself may be offense to one's god, / What in one's own heart seems despicable may be proper to one's god. / Who can know the will of the gods in heaven? / Who can understand the plans of the underworld gods? / Where have humans learned the way of a god?" (*Ludlul* ii, 33–38).[26] The irrationality of the experience can be grasped and even made somewhat subject to human agency by means an understanding of divine psychology, what William Moran has described as the two natures of Marduk. The opening quatrain of *Ludlul* is, he suggests, "the essence of the entire poem: Marduk, with the power to heal (*bēl nēmeki*) and the mind to heal (*ilu muštālu*), a god of darkness and wrath, but a god, too, of light and a sudden and matching mercy."[27] Suffering is thus experienced as the consequence of the anger of the gods, which is an instinctive response to the infractions—intentional or unintentional, conscious or unconscious—of the human. But the divine nature is also deeply compassionate, and the heart of the angry god can be soothed by humble appeal.

Though the connection of the ideas of Eliphaz and Bildad to the Mesopotamian tradition is evident, the closest Israelite parallel to the Mesopotamian nexus of ideas is not the speeches of Eliphaz and Bildad but rather Psalm 90. This psalm of supplication is set within a meditation on the difference between divine and human being (vv. 3–6). Divine anger at human iniquity and hidden sin erupts in a consuming fury (vv. 7–9). Yet human frailty itself, coupled with a deep desire to understand what pleases God, serves as the basis for the appeal to God's mercy (vv. 10–17). Elsewhere in the Psalms, too, the inevitability of human sin (Pss 19:13; 130:3; cf. 1 Kgs 8:46) and human finitude (Pss 78:38–39; 103:6–14) are offered as motivations for divine compassion.

Eliphaz's and Bildad's use of these ideas differs in several respects from their representation in the Mesopotamian emblematic sufferer texts and from their reflex in Israelite psalmody. Although Eliphaz's first use of the topos stands within a longer speech in which he also urges Job to "seek God" (5:8), the topos does not appear to be either a logical or a rhetorical part of the advice to pray, as it is in many of the Mesopotamian and psalmic texts. What Eliphaz and Bildad pronounce has more the character of a self-contained teaching. In this regard it is more comparable to the comments of the friend in stanza 26 of the Babylonian Theodicy, quoted earlier. Eliphaz's and Bildad's formulations also involve a sharper contrast between divine and human natures than one finds in the Mesopotamian compositions. Finally, though the Mesopotamian texts speak of the wrath of the gods, they do not contain anything quite like the language of divine loathing of humankind one finds in the Joban passages.

Can one identify other contributory elements to Eliphaz and Bildad's formulations? Certain vocabulary, for instance, Bildad's use of the terms "worm" and "maggot," also occur in psalmic traditions (Ps 22:7; cf. Isa 41:14). In the psalms, however, the psalmist describes himself as a "worm," as part of the rhetoric of humility and pious appeal. In Isaiah 41:14 ("Fear not, O worm Jacob, O maggot Israel")[28] the divine speech is best understood as a citation of the people's self-description, not a distinct divine perspective. In the speeches of Eliphaz and Bildad, however, the notion of divine disgust at human impurity and depravity becomes an almost philosophical teaching on anthropology, distinct from what one finds in the psalms of supplication and praise.[29]

The radical distinction between the divine and the human is a theme that also appears in priestly theologies of holiness. Some of the vocabulary used here (*nit ʿāb*, "abhorrent," the paralleling of *yiṣdaq* and *yithar*) suggests that such priestly discourse on holiness is invoked in Eliphaz's and Bildad's perception of the divine-human relation.[30] In narrative texts the outbreak of the holy against the profane may take the form of annihilating violence (e.g., Lev 10:1–4; Num 11:31–34; 2 Sam 6:6–8). But though priestly provisions for the protection of the sanctuary against impurity may assume a radical alterity between the divine and the human, priestly traditions do not develop the notion as a generalized teaching in the way that Eliphaz and Bildad do.

Though one may trace elements of traditional discourses in the Joban passages, what Eliphaz and Bildad say cannot be reduced without remainder to any of them. Perhaps it is best described as a sapiential development of an ancient

Near Eastern religious topos, which makes novel use of concepts and imagery derived from both psalmic and purity discourses.

Whatever the cultural sources for the development of the teaching, there remains the question of how it figures in the rhetoric of the dialogue. The friends invoke this notion of radical difference between divine and human natures in the service of theodicy. They wish to naturalize what Job experiences as turmoil, the disintegration of his life and body. How the argument works, rhetorically and psychologically, is best understood in relation to Peter Berger's notion of masochistic theodicy. As Berger observes, every society requires a degree of denial of the individual self in its full subjectivity, a phenomenon that finds expression in both religious and nonreligious forms.[31] In certain contexts this orientation may be developed to an extreme degree as a masochistic attitude, which he describes as "the intoxication of surrender to an other—complete, self-denying, even self-destroying. . . . 'I am nothing—He is everything—and therein lies my ultimate bliss.'"[32] The benefit derived by the individual is precisely the relief from the burden of individual existence, always vulnerable to ambiguity, anguish, loneliness, and meaninglessness. By positing the self as nothing and the object of surrender as absolute reality, the terrors of pain, death, and anomie can be transcended. Though the rhetoric of ecstatic surrender is not a part of the formulation of Eliphaz's and Bildad's statements, the logic of their imagery is close to what Berger describes. At its heart is the necessary radical difference between the divine and the human. By embracing the masochistic perspective of human corruptibility (in both the physical and moral senses), one can locate being and meaning in God, that is, safely beyond the reach of all powers of destruction and meaninglessness.

Job, of course, has no intention of embracing the moral imagination of masochistic theodicy, no matter how powerful its homeopathic solution to the pain of human finitude. But it is no accident that Job singles out this and only this motif from the friends' speeches as a claim with which he agrees (9:2). At the beginning of chapter 9 he says, "Truly, I know that this is so: How could a person be in the right [*yiṣdaq*] with God?" For the most part scholars interpret this comment as an ironic echo, playing on the internal dialogism of *yiṣdaq* ("to be morally righteous," "to be legally innocent") to shift the frame of reference from a religious to a forensic context.[33] While this is a vital part of what is going on, it does not exhaust the matter. Job's appropriation of Eliphaz's words may have its irony, but it is also deeply sincere. Eliphaz has given Job the truth he needs to understand his situation—that the source of the violence to which humans are subject is to be found in the radical difference between the divine and the human.

In the parodic description of a trial with God, which follows upon Job's appropriation of Eliphaz's statement, Job is intrigued not simply with the obvious futility of a trial but also by imagining the nature of the violence such an encounter would evoke. His initial description of the violent power of God is expressed through an imitation of hymnic praise of the divine warrior (9:5-10). Such language is in keeping with the intense but almost impersonal depictions of divine wrath one finds in both priestly and psalmic traditions. As Job begins to describe his imagined encounter with God in a trial, however, the language of violence takes on a different quality, personal and insistent. It is the disturbingly intimate violence of torture: "He crushes me for a hair and multiplies my wounds without cause; he will not let me get my breath, but sates me with bitterness" (9:17-18). This is a violence calculated to destroy the humanity of the one who is subject to it. Resorting to imagery of the body, Job depicts his mouth, the organ of his own speech, as testifying falsely against himself (9:20). Just so a person under torture experiences forced confession as self-betrayal, not recognizing that the torturer's voice has replaced his own.[34] As torture annihilates bodily integrity, so it destroys the subjectivity necessary for selfhood ("I am innocent; I do not know myself; I despise my own life," 9:21).[35] Such violence also destroys the meaningfulness of the categories of innocence and guilt. Elaine Scarry quotes the words of a torturer: "If they are not guilty, beat them until they are."[36] Thus, through his parodic sensibility, Job teases out of Eliphaz's ontology of human and divine being a vision of a world necessarily characterized by violence and moral turmoil (9:22-24).

The vision is even darker than this, for it is not simply anarchy that Job perceives but a divine loathing incensed at the appearance of righteousness or cleanness in the human. In verse 30 Job describes the action of cleaning himself, perhaps an allusion to a legal ritual (cf. Deut 21:1-9), or perhaps simply an expression of the common metaphorical connection between innocence and cleanness (Deut 21:6-7; Pss 26:6; 51:4; 73:13; Isa 1:18).[37] Such an action, which asserts agency, dignity, and innocence, provokes God to reverse these self-assertions (Job 9:31), plunging Job into a pit of filth, thus not only metonymically associating Job with dirt, and so with guilt, but also demonstrating Job's inability to control his own body. When loathing is acted out in violence, it has a way of transferring itself to the self-perception of the object of that loathing. The violated one experiences himself or herself as loathsome. In a terrible image of dissociation, Job goes beyond his previous statement (see v. 21) and personifies his own clothes as the perceiving subject now disgusted with *his* filth.[38] The verb used (*tāʿab*) is the same one Eliphaz later employs to describe God's perception of human beings as "loathsome" (15:16a).

Job casts the violence he has experienced as the expression of God's loathing for human existence. But why does God loathe humanity? In a poetic work such as the Joban dialogue, one is presented with images that often contain an implicit logic that must be teased out. So it is with the imagery of divine violence. For Job, as for Eliphaz and Bildad, the divine loathing is connected with the immense gulf between forms of being. They all locate the issue in what we may call the problem of alterity. One might argue, however, that it is not so much the difference itself but the ambiguity between sameness and difference that is the engine for the incredible loathing they identify. The claims of Eliphaz and Bildad have the form of rhetorical questions that presume the answer, "No, a mortal cannot be righteous or pure as compared with God." But why raise the question? No one thinks it relevant to ask if an ox or a stone can be *ṣedeq*. The difference there is a qualitative one that makes comparison irrelevant. Thus, the very act of asking the question points to a fundamental continuity between the divine and the human. Whether by design or by accident, whether by being made in the image and likeness of God or by having exceeded boundaries and therefore having become "like gods," humans share with deity the capacity to make moral decisions.

The ambiguity of the nature and status of human beings was a topic of some fascination in the ancient Near East, most often explored in the context of creation stories and myths concerning the fixing of the place of humans in the created order (e.g., Genesis 1; 2-3; 6; 9; *Enuma Elish* IV; Atrahasis; Adapa). Though there is no direct connection between the topos Eliphaz and Bildad invoke and these creation accounts, they serve to illumine the larger cultural concern for the problem of same and other in the relation between the divine and the human.

The dynamics of identity as it is negotiated in relations of same and other and the emergence of violence from those dynamics have been topics of considerable interest in recent philosophical, psychological, and sociopolitical thought. While one might object that such frameworks, drawn from human interactions, are not applicable to religious speculation on the relation of the divine and the human, models for religious reflection necessarily draw heavily on those that govern human social relations. Certainly Job's language about God is emphatically though un-self-consciously anthropomorphic. The same symbolic devices used in negotiating human identity and difference may well be at work also in religious language.

Identities are largely established relationally and oppositionally. Such relationships are never absolute and may be constructed and reconstructed around any number of symbolic markers (linguistic, ethnic, religious, sexual, class, etc.). But the drawing of boundaries and the making of distinctions are the essential symbolic operations. Though violence is not necessarily inherent in such relationships, the constructed and therefore fragile nature of identity renders any of these relationships susceptible to the exaggeration of differences and even to violence. Miroslav Volf describes the dynamics well:

> The tendency toward violence is, moreover, reinforced by an inescapable ambiguity of the self. The self is dialogically constructed. The other is already from the outset part of the self. I am who I am in relation to the other. . . . As a result, a tension between the self and the other is built into the very desire for identity: the other over against whom I must assert myself is the same other who must remain part

of myself if I am to be myself. But the other is often not the way I want her to be. . . . And yet I must integrate the other into my own will to be myself. Hence I slip into violence.[39]

When identity is threatened, the necessary other may be redefined in ways that reduce the ambiguity. Various strategies may be employed, depending on the context: assimilation, abandonment, domination, and elimination.[40] Though all aim at relieving the anxiety of alterity, I am interested here in the symbolic strategies that work through excessive differentiation rather than assimilation. In these strategies the need to be self-identical leads to a reconfiguration that distances the other radically, that excludes him from the characteristics or qualities precious to one's own identity. The other may be characterized by words that render him subhuman, morally corrupt, dirty. The effect of these exaggerated distinctions in which all that is good resides with oneself and all that is bad resides with the other is to legitimate violence. It is not just permissible but a good thing to act against what is so vile. The other, even when distanced symbolically in this way, cannot be left alone. Not only is its continued presence necessary definitionally, but it also possesses a curious fascination.[41]

What Job recognizes in Eliphaz's attempt to describe the otherness that distinguishes the divine from the human is a symbolic system that can account—in a way Eliphaz does not intend—for the experience he has of being the object of violence. What underlies Job's discourse in chapter 9 is the sense that for God to be God, it does not suffice for humans to be human, for they are too ambiguously "like gods" in their status as moral beings. Thus the human claim to moral integrity, to being righteous (ṣādaq) or morally pure (ṭāhar, zākāh), must be turned into its opposite, an identity characterized by corruptness, loathsomeness, and iniquitousness. Against such arrogant claims violence is legitimated; against such pretense to cleanness, humans must be cast into the filth that they are.

In Job's imagination, the relation between the human and the divine is even more complex, for God does not simply discover the human but creates the human. Job explores this relation and the perversities to which it is subject in chapter 10. Again, the relations can be illumined by recourse to human psychology. The psychology of creation is inherently ambivalent. That which I make is an object over against me but also in some sense a part of me. I may take pride in it, love it, be pleased with it. But insofar as it is, or as I perceive it to be, defective or inadequate, I may despise it, loathe it. In some way it is my defect or my inability to exercise power that is displayed therein. What may give particular intensity to such revulsion is the presence of self-hatred. The Norwegian sculptor Gustav Vigeland made a deeply disturbing piece that illustrates this aspect of the psychology of creation. In it a powerful looking man stands in a violent rage, hurling away from himself some four or five babies, who are flying through the air and landing at his feet. The sculpture is entitled "Brain Children."

What is already a complex and potentially violent relationship between creator and creation is made even more intense when what is created is not an object but another moral being, for here the relation of competition and displacement also appears. This relation is characteristic not just of that between divine creator and human creature but also what marks the relationship between parent and child and to a lesser extent other social relationships in which nurture and rivalry lie close together.

In chapter 10 Job investigates the paradoxes and perversities to which this relationship is subject. As often noted, Job uses the most exquisite language of craftsmanship to describe the intimacies of divine creation of the human. Twice Job refers to the "hands" and "palms" of God (10:3, 8), which form and shape. The creation of the human is described by analogy to the work of a potter (10:9), the making of cheese (10:10), and the weaving of garments (10:11). But the thing that has been made is destroyed by its creator, the pot crushed back into dust (10:8-9). What generates the destructive impulse is the presence of a flaw. Since the human is made as a moral agent, the flaw sought out is not a physical one but a disfiguring "iniquity" or "sin" (10:6). Job rationally appeals to the very difference between God and humans to protest the unnecessary nature of this inquisition. A human, whose perception and time are limited, might be justified in making such an urgent and relentless scrutiny, but it makes no sense to Job that God should be so obsessed by the possibility of a lurking flaw (10:4-6). Job does not consciously resolve the enigma, but he describes well the psychology of ambivalence in creation, as the acts of intimacy and even love involved in creating can mask a hidden determination to find fault (10:13-14). Job also intuits that the ambivalence toward the thing created does not require an actual flaw. To obtain the cathartic satisfaction of violence against the object of ambivalence a flaw will be imputed, whether or not it actually exists (10:7, 15).

In this account of the way the divine and human are problematically related as "same and other," one would seem to have all that is needed for a relationship of fear, loathing, and violence. Yet Job's phenomenology of divine violence suggests that this is not the entire source. The element not otherwise accounted for is the quality of frustrated obsession Job attributes to God. This is represented by the element of fury I noted above, in which God experiences no satiety even when Job's body is literally turned inside out by violence but in which God continues to attack "breach upon breach" (16:14). What is it that God is seeking and apparently cannot find?

This question brings one to the relation of knowledge and violence. Commentators have long noted how Job speaks of God as engaged in an incessant surveilance, a sort of stalking (7:12, 14, 17-19, 21b; 10:4-7, 14-17; 14:13). To Job it seems inexplicably perplexing. He can account for it neither with respect to the nature of his own being ("Am I the Sea, or the sea monster, that you set a guard over me? 7:12) nor the nature of God's being ("Do you have eyes of flesh? Do you see as humans see . . . that you seek out my iniquity and search for my sin, although you know that I am not guilty?" 10:4–7). Job assumes it is some putative sin for which God searches, alluding perhaps to the psalmic tradition in which God searches the heart and the kidneys. But the dynamics may have less to do with some peculiar search for a sin that would only prove what God already assumes (that humans are not righteous as compared with God) and more to do with the nature of the alterity between God and humans.

To understand this element requires supplementing the earlier discussion of alterity as a problem of "same and different" in relation to a common state of being, with a different view of otherness, which one finds in the work of Emmanuel Levinas. Though Levinas is talking about the human "Other," his analysis is illuminating for Job's religious imagination, with its deeply anthropomorphic, personal language for the God-human relation. The "Other," as Levinas presents it in *Totality and Infinity*, is that which is radically exterior to me, that which is utterly transcendent, that which is not opposite to me but separate from me, infinite, exceeding me. To suggest the Other, Levinas uses the metaphors of "the face" and of "speech" (neither of which is to be taken simply as a physical or social feature—both are metaphors and technical terms). The encounter with the Other makes me aware that the world is not simply my possession or an extension of me, but that I share the world. In that sense the Other puts in question the Same, the self, by revealing its limits, but not in a way that need be seen as threatening.[42] The separateness of the Other is what makes sociality possible, and the encounter with the Other founds the ethical moment of freedom and responsibility. But because this is the ethical moment, a moment of freedom, both violence and nonviolence are possible responses. And it is the special character of violence that may be directed toward the Other, toward the Face, that is of particular relevance in understanding certain passages in Job.

One possible response to the Other is the attempt to reduce its alterity, to absorb it into the Same, either by means of knowledge or power. This is in fact a futile gesture, for the Other is precisely what evades one's knowledge and eludes one's power; yet that futility does not prevent the attempt. The knowledge of which Levinas speaks is a reductive, objectifying knowledge, something like what Bakhtin describes as the impulse to "finalize" another, though Levinas's point is not so much that this is bad as that it is impossible. It fails. Correspondingly, one may attempt to dominate or appropriate the Other through power, as one dominates or appropriates things, yet this too fails, because the Other resists appropriation. It does not resist because it has superior power, for it does not; it resists simply because it is Other. Yet this "resistance of what has no resistance"[43] is what may give rise to a particular quality of violence—the murderous violence that aims only at a Face. As Levinas puts it, "To kill is not to dominate but to annihilate; it is to renounce comprehension absolutely. Murder exercises a power over what escapes power. . . . I can wish to kill only

. . . [that] which exceeds my powers infinitely, and therefore does not oppose them but paralyzes the very power of power. The Other is the sole being I can wish to kill."[44]

Here is the analysis that makes sense of the rage Job describes as directed against him. He perceives God as obsessed with the desire to scrutinize him, examine him, know him—yet somehow is frustrated in the attempt. How could that be? The psalmic tradition, too, describes divine scrutiny. There the examination process, though intrusive, is not generally violent. In the psalms the human soul has a transparency vis-à-vis God. The difference is that for the psalmist the human being is God's creature, but not God's Other. Job, however, represents God's obsessive search for the flaw or fault that belongs to the "theme" of human nature as a search that cannot find a resolution. Through no intentional act of his own, Job remains to some degree opaque to God. Similarly, despite what Job describes as God's rage to annihilate, Job, like some hideously resilient monster from a horror movie, cannot be disposed of. Although one may kill concrete others, one cannot kill otherness, *the* Other. And that is what Job intuitively understands himself to represent—God's Other, in a Levinasian sense.[45]

Levinas's reflection on the Other may also shed light on a feature of Job's speeches that has long puzzled commentators, namely, Job's ability to switch almost instantly from his description of God as pathologically obsessed with doing harm to Job to a description of God as receiving Job nonviolently, listening to Job's case, and responding justly to his arguments. But if one thinks in company with Levinas, this fluctuation between murderous violence and receptivity is completely intelligible. The encounter with the Other is what constitutes the ethical moment in all its terrible freedom. In contrast to the friends, for whom God is an expression of the order of the cosmos, and so reliable and predictable,[46] for Job the structure of the encounter is radically ethical, and so has an element of the unforeseeable—violence or nonviolence.

One should not overstate the extent to which Job's actions and perceptions can be illumined by means of Levinas's insights. What does seem evocative is Job's intense desire to come before God face to face and to speak (9:34–35; 13:18–22; 19:26b-27; 23:3–7). The presence of face and speech Levinas calls "expression," and, as he says, "the event proper to expression consists in bearing witness to oneself, and guaranteeing this witness."[47] Thus, in expression "the being that imposes itself does not limit but promotes my freedom, by arousing my goodness."[48] This is what Job hopes for in the encounter with God ("Would he contend against me with his great strength? No; rather he would attend to me. There an upright person might reason with him," 23:6–7a). Of course, for Levinas, the unenforceable command of the Face is always and only "Thou shalt not kill." Levinas is interested in the structure of the relationship constituted by the face-to-face, the situation of the ethical. But Job is concerned with the normative content of a specific set of ethical principles. It is not merely his face or the fact of his speech he wishes to bring before God, but arguments and reasons and testimony. In imagining such an encounter, Job negotiates the dangerous terrain of alterity by establishing the common ground upon which the divine and the human can meet—the ground of justice. Job's strategy is indeed to reduce the alterity of the divine and the human by stressing the common moral nature of God and human beings.[49] Though he acknowledges and fears the truth in what Eliphaz and Bildad have said about the gulf that separates the divine and the human and the violence that lurks therein, Job is determined to bring into the light what their formulation tacitly assumes but represses, namely, the continuity between God and himself. Job will explore, at least within his own imagination, whether one could not imagine a scenario in which one could be found "in the right" vis à vis God. In so doing, he will begin to construct a new language of address, to challenge established practices of piety in the name of another (as yet imaginary) practice of legal confrontation, and to begin to articulate for himself a narrative construal of his experience quite different from either the narrative embedded in the practices of lament and thanksgiving or in the paradigmatic wisdom narratives of the friends.

The Moral Imagination of Legal Discourse

For a generation or more it has been taken for granted that legal language and an underlying legal metaphor permeates Job's speeches and is key to understanding the book itself.[50] Some have gone so far as to attempt to describe the very genre of the work as a "lawsuit drama." Though he rejects that designation, Norman Habel's own claim that the legal metaphor is "integral to the structure and coherence of the book of Job" is nearly as sweeping.[51] In his translations of key chapters and in the interpretive headings by which he introduces them, Habel also maximizes the legal connotations of the Hebrew text. In chapters 9–10, for instance, Habel's headings are: "On the Futility of Litigation," "Characterization of the Adversary," "Considering the Difficulties of Litigation," "Considering Other Alternatives," "Rehearsal of the Case against God," "The Charges against God," and "Closing Complaint and Plea."[52]

Habel's analysis is rich and insightful, yet his interpretive decision to maximize the presence and shaping influence of legal language obscures a more complex and subtle situation. Though Job on occasion uses unmistakably technical legal expressions, much of the language in question is at home both in legal and more general discourse. Context or the clustering of terms may suggest a legal nuance, but the reader often must make an active judgment whether to hear legal overtones or not. Often, too, legal (or arguably legal) language will appear for a verse or two and then recede from the rhetoric. This is not to minimize the significance of the forensic in Job's speech, but it is to suggest that legal language establishes its presence in a much more subtle and exploratory fashion than Habel suggests.

In the following paragraphs, I wish to begin with a close look at the language and rhetoric of chapter 9, where, it is generally agreed, legal language and the framing of Job's situation by means of a legal metaphor first make their appearance in the dialogue. Drawing on theories of discourse and metaphor, I will trace the reappearance of such language in subsequent chapters. The discourse of law, though it never becomes Job's only discourse, is the means by which he exposes and contests the assumptions of the friends, especially as embodied in their advice concerning petitionary prayer. In the concluding part of my discussion I will examine the contrasting assumptions of these two discourses and show why legal discourse is of such value to Job in negotiating the problem of divine-human alterity.

Chapter 9 begins, as is conventional, with the speaker's reference to his partner's words, though Job alludes less to Bildad's words than to those of Eliphaz, as 9:2b closely echoes 4:17a.[53] Job appears to be saying that he agrees with Eliphaz, though this apparent agreement is only the setup for satire. When and how does a reader know that Job's agreement is disingenuous? There is nothing in verse 2 itself, save perhaps the conventions of the genre of the wisdom dialogue, to suggest Job may not be sincere. The trigger for the reevaluation of Job's words comes in the following verse, which recontextualizes the word *ṣādaq*. As commentators regularly point out, the verb is at home in two different discourses, a general moral-religious discourse and a more technical legal discourse. Though Eliphaz had used the term in its moral-religious sense ("to be righteous"), Job's use of *rîb* and *ʿānāh* in 9:3 indicates that he has strategically "misunderstood" Eliphaz, and that he takes the word in its legal sense ("to be in the right," "to be innocent"). Yet Job presents himself as oblivious to such a misunderstanding. He is simply agreeing with his friend's insight.

Job's strategic misunderstanding facilitates a classic example of what Bakhtin calls the dialogization of discourses. In every culture people speak any number of different social discourses, marked by linguistic, semantic, and stylistic differences. Bakhtin refers to them as different social dialects and even as different languages. Ordinarily, these different dialects exist side by side but do not interact. Each has its social purpose and place, and speakers simply move from one to another as occasion demands. As Bakhtin describes it,

> Thus an illiterate peasant, miles away from any urban center, naively immersed in an unmoving and for him unshakable everyday world, nevertheless lived in several language systems: he prayed to God in one language (Church Slavonic), sang songs in another, spoke to his family in a third and, when he began to dictate petitions to the local authorities through a scribe, he tried speaking yet a fourth language (the official-literate language, "paper" language). All these are *different languages*, even from the point of view of abstract socio-dialectological markers. But these languages

were not dialogically coordinated in the linguistic consciousness of the peasant; he passed from one to the other without thinking, automatically: each was indisputably in its own place, and the place of each was indisputable.[54]

Bakhtin's peasant is not alone in this tendency to compartmentalize. It is the normal state of affairs. But once something occurs to trigger the "critical interanimation of languages," then comes the necessary recognition

> that the ideological systems and approaches to the world that were indissolubly connected with the languages contradicted each other and in no way could live in peace and quiet with one another—then the inviolability and predetermined quality of these languages came to an end, and the necessity of actively choosing one's orientation among them began.[55]

This critical interanimation is what Job achieves through his strategic misunderstanding of Eliphaz's use of ṣādaq. Job's rhetoric acquires its scrutinizing power precisely because he does not effect a clean transition from one discourse to another but leaves both in play.

As Job continues, he describes God as "wise of mind" and "powerful in strength," terms at home in religious praise. Indeed, Job supports his argument about the nature of God by reciting a hymnic fragment praising the power of God (9:5–10), culminating in a line identical to one already used by Eliphaz in his praise of God (9:10; cf. 5:9). Several lines follow in verses 11–13 in which Job evokes familiar language used to praise God's transcendent power and unopposable will. Although some critics have assumed Job is parodying traditional doxologies by presenting God's power as destructive and violent,[56] what Job says is paralleled elsewhere in biblical praise of God. Whenever God appears to fight against enemies, mythic or human, the violent effects of the struggle are felt by the whole cosmos (e.g., Pss 18:8–16; 97:1–5; 114:1–8; Nah 1:1–6; Hab 3:3–13; Ezek 32:7–8). Divine violence is traditionally associated with God as victor over chaos (Psalm 29), defender of Israel against its oppressors (Nah 1:1–6; Hab 3:3–13), and the one who delivers the individual from danger (Psalm 18). All of this is unobjectionable within the language of hymnic praise, which valorizes the surpassing power of God. But when Job concludes this passage with the remark, "How then could I answer him or choose my words with him? Even if I am innocent [ṣādaqtî], I cannot answer" (9:14–15a; cf. 9:20), he allows the discourse of legal relations to scrutinize the ideological assumptions of hymnic praise. Contextualized by "answer" and "choose my words," the key term ṣādaq occurs with its legal connotations to the fore. By this means, the immense alterity between God and humans, which is lifted up by Eliphaz and which is a reassuring feature in the divine warrior hymns, appears as disturbing and morally troubling when reframed in a forensic context. The ideological commitment of legal order is that a trial exists *to determine* which of two parties is in the right and which is guilty. For legal procedure to have any meaning, the outcome must be genuinely open, not preempted by violent power. In Israel's legal institutions the existence of disparity of power so threatened the integrity of legal process that social controls were enacted to contain it (e.g., Exod 23:1–3, 6–9). Yet if what is affirmed of God in Eliphaz's teaching and in these traditions of hymnic praise is true, the possibility of justice between God and a human is put in question.

At this point in the dialogue one should not read too much into Job's intentions regarding the potential of legal discourse as a constructive tool of thought. Here it appears primarily as an instrument of parody, whereby the self-evident rightness of what Eliphaz has said can be disrupted. Such reframing allows Job to cast his own devastation not as something "natural" to the human condition but as a directed aggression that violates his humanity in depriving him of the very possibility of being *ṣedeq*.

Though the emergence of legal language is almost accidental, it points up an important feature of dialogue—that its very structure tends to elicit new insights that the participants could not have anticipated at the beginning and that may take them in unexpected directions.[57] Not every locally strategic play with words is systemically productive, however, and one must ask how it is that Job's use of the double nuance of *ṣādaq* comes to serve as a generative metaphor instead of exhausting itself in parody. Even Job seems initially to discount it as a simple category mistake ("For he is not a person like me that I could answer him, that we could come together for trial," 9:32).

One of the things that makes new ways of thinking possible, however, is the overlapping and unsystematic way in which various discourses are present in any cultural context. What gives Job's parody a potential beyond absurdity is that in certain contexts justice was predicated of God. God was praised as the source of justice in the cosmos (Ps 97:1–2; Isa 33:5), the model of justice whose rule in heaven was to be imitated in the king's rule on earth (Ps 72:1–2), the one who judges nations with equity (Ps 96:10–13), the one who insists on justice as the standard for conduct among his people (Exod 23:2–3, 6–8; Deut 16:18–20; Amos 5:24), defender of the victims of injustice (Prov 22:22–23), the one to whom the unjustly accused cries for vindication (Ps 17:1–2). In narrative traditions it was even possible to challenge God's actions on the basis of their inconsistency with the principle that the judge of all the earth should do what is just (Gen 18:25). What Job eventually does, as he moves beyond parody, is to make use of this extensive conceptualization of divine justice to organize an aspect of experience where it did not traditionally function—the right of a person before God.[58]

Just where and how Job begins to be grasped by the potential of the verbal imagery he had initially introduced as parody is difficult to say. Already in the middle of chapter 9 Job's critique of God's failure to do justice in the world (9:22–24), a norm grounded in the hymnic tradition itself, appears to emerge out of his own vivid sense of having been wronged (9:16–21), a wrong he frames by means of his parodic use of legal language. Thus, he is already beginning to use legal categories as a lens to focus his thoughts. But it is at the end of the chapter, as Job considers the conditions that render an actual trial with God an impossibility ("for he is not a person as I am. . . . There is no arbiter between us," 9:32–33) that he simultaneously envisions the conditions of possibility. Though the syntax is ambiguous, the final two verses are probably to be under- stood as conditional sentences: "If he would turn aside his staff from me, so that fear of him did not terrify me, then I could speak and not be afraid" (9:34– 35a; cf. NRSV). Following this cluster of legal terminology, one can readily hear the opening of chapter 10 as what Job would like to say if such a trial were possible. Here, too, several terms with potential legal nuance cluster together, as Job imagines saying to God, "Do not find me guilty [*'al-taršî 'ēnî*]; let me know why you contend [*tĕrîbēnî*] with me" (10:2).

From this point, legal language becomes a medium of exploration, by which Job can configure and reconfigure his situation, though explicitly legal speech actually occurs rather infrequently. In chapter 13 as Job rebukes his friends (vv. 6–8), he uses a cluster of terms ("argument" [*tôkaḥat*], "legal pleadings" [*ribbôt*], "show partiality" [*nāśā' pānîm*], "argue" [*rîb*]) that suggests legal discourse. Later in the chapter, as Job imagines coming before God, he again chooses language that likens the encounter to a legal trial. The phrase "I have prepared a case" (*'ārakti mišpāṭ*, 13:18) is distinctly a legal expression and gives a forensic nu- ance to the following claim, "I know that I shall be found innocent" (*yāda'tî kî- 'ānî 'eṣdaq*). The words describing the imagined speech with God, though not exclusively technical legal terminology ("contend" [*rîb*]; "answer" [*'ānāh*], "speak" [*dābār*], "reply," [*hēšîb*], 13:22), do occur in legal contexts and are given a legal coloration by the preceding forensic expressions. Brief but important references to a "witness" (*'ēd*) and a "bearer of testimony" (*śāhēd*) in 16:19 and to a "kins- man-redeemer" (*gō'ēl*) in 19:25 keep the legal discourse present. The last devel- oped use in the dialogue occurs in chapter 23, where Job again speaks of "lay- ing out a case" (*'e'erkāh lĕpānāyw mišpāṭ*, v. 4a) and filling his mouth with "arguments" (*tôkāḥôt*, v. 4b). He imagines God's reply to his own arguments (v. 5), reverses his earlier sense that God would "contend in power" (*habbĕrob-kōaḥ yārîb 'immādî*, v. 6a), and ultimately envisions "going free from my judge" (*wa'ăpallĕṭāh lāneṣaḥ miššōpēṭî*, v. 7b).

This brief tracking of the appearance of legal discourse in Job's speeches suffices to demonstrate that, though it may not be as pervasive and as ready formed as Habel's analysis suggests, it has a significant presence. What gives the legal language in Job's speeches such interpretive power is the way it func- tions as generative metaphor. Though Job and the friends use various meta- phors, many of these are surface or local metaphors (e.g., "if my anguish were weighed and my calamity set with it on scales," 6:3; "our days are a shadow upon the earth," 8:9). Such metaphors may be conventional or novel and are often rhetorically powerful, but they do not have a particularly wide scope. They organize only a limited aspect of experience. Generative metaphors, though not different in structure from local ones, are those that emerge at the site of a problem or conflict and serve to reinterpret situations. In his discussion of metaphor in relation to public policy, Donald Schön argues that generative metaphor is not so much about problem solving as problem setting. In conflicted discussions, issues are framed in relation to rival narratives and the metaphors that underlie them.

> Problem settings are mediated, I believe, by the "stories" people tell about troublesome situations—stories in which they describe what is wrong and what needs fixing. When we examine the problem-setting stories by the analysts and practitioners of social policy, it becomes apparent that the framing of problems often depends upon metaphors underlying the stories which generate problem setting and set the direction of problem solving.[59]

Metaphor's cognitive power is both intuitive and analytical. Linked to perception, metaphor creates a kind of "seeing as." The analytical and systemic capacity Schön refers to is what cognitive linguists describe as metaphor's role in "mapping" one domain onto another.[60] Cognitive theorists of metaphor similarly refer to the logical "entailments" of a metaphor that nudge thought along certain paths once a given metaphor is in play.[61] These observations on metaphor and its functions help clarify how the legal language that begins to appear in Job's speech plays such an important role in the conflict with his friends, even though it remains somewhat tentative and exploratory.

The friends had offered Job a familiar language, that of traditional piety, by means of which he could understand his situation, appeal to God, and transform his future. This language was structured according to its own narrative patterns, practices, and embedded metaphors. Legal language offers a different way to tell the story of this troublesome situation. Moreover, the practices associated with this language, most notably the trial and its protocols of speech, offer a functional alternative to the discourse of prayer. Though it remains a possibility of the imagination, not a realized practice, the notion of a trial provides a powerful means by which Job can reconfigure the nature of his situation, including the roles, norms, and values that govern his relationship with God. At the same time, it enables him to expose the problematic assumptions by which the friends have defined his situation. What difference does it make that Job starts to tell his story in legal terms?

Within psalmic piety one could insist on one's innocence and even claim mistreatment by God. That is not the fundamental difference. But the embedded metaphors that shape the ethos of the relationship between deity and petitioner in prayer, and thus configure the moral landscape, are radically different from those that Job begins to construct with his rhetoric of legal witness and testimony. Thorkild Jacobsen has argued that the generative model embedded in ancient Near Eastern prayer is the parent-child relationship.[62] Though explicitly parental imagery plays a minor role in the rhetoric of Israelite prayer, paternalistic social relationships (e.g., shepherd, king, benefactor) strongly influence the roles, expectations, and speech practices of prayer. The embedded model in Israelite prayer of supplication is that of the "social father," the patriarch who had personal and moral responsibility for his household or community and to whom dependents might turn for aid. Though the cultural parallels are not exact, the deity is constructed as something like a *patrone*, and the implicit relationship as one of patronage. The social relationships that form this implicit (and occasionally explicit) model for relations in prayer are deeply personal, emotional, and mutual, but also profoundly asymmetrical. The rhetoric of grievance and appeal they make possible is similarly personal, relational, and emotional, as almost any psalm of complaint will show.

The insertion of legal language into such a context challenges those configurations. The rhetoric of psalmic complaint is intensely emotional, designed to evoke a sense of guilt or compassion or even self-interest. The psalmist represents himself as unfairly neglected (Pss 13:2-3, 22:2-3; 42:10), uses graphic descriptions of suffering to evoke pathos (Pss 31:10-15; 38:2-9), and conjoins the honor and shame of God and the petitioner (Pss 22:7-9; 31:18). An unapologetically transactional quality characterizes the appeal, as praise and an enhanced reputation are offered as inducements for deliverance (Pss 22:20-23; 30:10). The rhetoric of grievance in legal discourse is utterly different. As discussed earlier, Job's descriptions of graphic divine violence in chapter 16 initially allude to the place of such language in prayers of supplication. Whereas in psalms of supplication this imagery establishes both the righteous power of God and the neediness of the faithful yet guilty petitioner, Job disrupts the traditional transaction effected by such language by juxtaposing it to legal discourse, as he seeks to preserve his blood and his cry as testimony to a murder, a charge to be argued by his heavenly witness (16:18-19). The account of violence is reconfigured, not as a plea for compassion but as a cry for justice (see further 19:7, "If I call out, 'Violence!' no one answers; I cry aloud, but there is no justice").

Though emotion plays a role in the rhetoric of legal grievance, the complaint tends to be more depersonalized than in prayer. Legal appeal shifts the ground to an objective set of values both sides take as normative, privileging reasoned argument. "I would set out my case before Him and fill my mouth with arguments. I would learn what answers He had for me and consider what He would say to me. . . . There an upright person could reason with him" (Job 23:4-5, 7a).[63] The gulf between these two discourses is clearly focused by the different resonances of a single word, *'ethannan*, "seek mercy." Speaking within the rhetorical world of prayer, Bildad appropriately urges the "blameless and upright" Job to "seek mercy from Shaddai" (8:5b). But when Job speaks in the rhetoric of legal dispute, that the innocent Job should have to "plead for mercy from my judge" (9:15b) is an outrage to justice. What makes perfect sense in one discourse takes on a completely different significance in another.

This difference in the resonance of *'eṯḥannan* reflects the different role that status hierarchy plays in the patronage model of divine-human relations and the legal model. Legal disputes, though they often occur between persons who are not social equals, require the provisional setting aside of inequality (Exod 23:6-8; Deut 16:18-20). Thus, what is essential in the relationship configured by psalmic prayer, that is, the responsibility and affection of a patron for a dependent (Ps 22:10-12), plays no role in a legal dispute. To the contrary, Job seeks someone who would "arbitrate between a man and God *as between a man and his fellow*" (16:21; trans. NJPS, emphasis added). One can see why the legal model, though introduced in parody, becomes essential in Job's attempt to resist the violence he understands to be implicit in the relationship of radical alterity between the divine and the human. If the relationship can be reframed within the resources available in legal rhetoric, the actual difference between God and humans can be acknowledged but set aside as not appropriate to the context (13:20-21), since legal framing of the situation requires the stipulation of provisional equality in the presence of transcendent norms of justice.

Not only status but also the nature of the character roles themselves are reconfigured. Though the image of God as judge and even as accuser is already part of the discourse of prayer,[64] the trope of a trial allows Job to expand the repertoire of roles to include God as accused (16:18-19) and Job himself as accuser (9:17; 19:7; 27:2) and as the falsely accused (9:20; 10:7; 16:17). The newly available role of witness, however, is what fundamentally configures for Job the relations, practices, and topics of this new rhetorical world.

Within the legal model, Job initially imagines himself as failed witness, silenced by pain and intimidation (9:14-15), or even as an unwilling witness against himself (9:20). As he increasingly enters into the imaginative possibilities offered by this new framing, Job articulates the conditions of possibility for taking on the role of witness, including freedom from intimidation (9:34; 13:20-21). The necessity of giving witness becomes so strong that when he thinks of death as preventing him from bringing his accusation or defending himself, Job's imagination supplies surrogates who will speak for him (the earth, 16:18; a heavenly witness, 16:19; an inscribed text, 19:23-24; a *gōʾēl*, 19:25). Yet that is not enough. Though the text of 19:25-27 is difficult, it is best construed as presenting Job at a moment of crisis. He can imagine his case being presented after his death, but his fervent desire is to "see God while still in my flesh, I myself, not another" (NJPS). Hence his last attempt to envision himself as persuasive witness before God (23:3-7).

The importance of the identity of legal witness can be appreciated by comparing Job with the sufferer in the Babylonian Theodicy. The genre of the wisdom dialogue gives the suffering character a voice by which he may speak about himself to another. In the most general sense of the term it provides a structure for self-witness. Though the Babylonian Theodicy is primarily a contest of ideas, the therapeutic value of self-witness is acknowledged in the way the dialogue begins ("O sage [. . .] come, let me tell you. . . . Where is the wise man of your caliber? . . . Where is the counsellor to whom I can relate my trouble?" lines 1, 5–7) and in the way it ends ("You are kind, my friend; behold my trouble; help me; look on my distress; know it," lines 287–88).[65] Such potentially healing self-witness is truncated in the Joban dialogue with the edgy hostility that develops between the parties. Its place is taken by the distinctively legal witness that emerges from chapter 9 on. A legal trial, as Shoshana Felman remarks, is an institutionalized "crisis of truth" in which "the facts upon which justice must pronounce its verdict are not clear, when historical accuracy is in doubt and when both the truth and its supporting elements of evidence are called into question."[66] In such contexts testimony becomes a performative speech act.[67] To testify is to *do* something. Where there is no mechanism for an actual trial— here Felman thinks in terms of the genocide of the Shoah—then the frame of the trial may be transferred to society as such. Correspondingly, the function of witness ceases to be that of a role in an institutional process and becomes instead an identity to be lived out.

Something analogous seems to happen in the course of the dialogue. In chapters 19 and 23 Job speaks in the tones of a witness against God before the friends and imaginatively in the presence of God (see esp. 19:7, 23–24; 23:4). More telling are the words with which he opens his final speech in chapter 27, when he appears to have given up the possibility of a trial with God. Here he swears an oath, appropriate for one who would give testimony. Yet his oath is itself a form of testimony, for he swears "by God who has taken away my right" (27:2a). The oath binds him not merely for the duration of a trial but for life: "As long as there is breath in me and the spirit of God in my nostrils, my lips will speak no wrong and my tongue utter no deceit" (27:4). Job has become a witness.

If the framework provided by the legal metaphor reconfigures the rhetoric of grievance, the relation between the parties, and even the fundamental models for identity, it also brings to the problem of turmoil a different set of resources than those provided by the practice of prayer. Prayer, as described by the friends, addresses the problem of turmoil in part through its mimetic quality, its ability to create an experience of the order and security to which it refers. The practice of legal dispute is not mimetic but hermeneutical, that is, it privileges explanation as it seeks for the truth of a disputed situation (10:2; 19:23–24; 23:4–7).[68] In the dialogue the context of legal dispute reaccents the very idioms of prayer, giving them a hermeneutical nuance. At one point Job imagines the speech he would make before God in a trial (13:18-23). Yet the words he speaks are those one might find in a psalm: "How many are my iniquities and sins? . . . Why do you hide your face?" (13:23-24). In a psalm of complaint such questions do not seek literal answers but are appeals for transformation of the present situation. As Job recontextualizes them within the accents of legal discourse, however, they *are* requests for an explanation and an accounting. Thus, in the moral imagination of legal argument, knowledge—especially knowledge of motive and intention—acquires a significance it does not have in the context of prayer. Or, more accurately, the one-directional knowledge produced by the divine scrutiny referred to in prayer is displaced in the legal model by a necessity for mutual disclosure (13:22; 23:4-5).

Because of its hermeneutical orientation, the legal model also construes the moral significance of time differently than does the discourse of prayer, even as it accommodates and encourages a different narrativization of experience. In the context of prayer, as the friends' speeches so readily show, the nexus of present and future is the privileged configuration. Whatever has occurred to create the situation that now exists is of lesser concern than the belief that the future is open for transformation. Thus, the narratives they construct are forward looking, and the friends devote the concluding part of their speeches to descriptions of the serene future that the practice of prayer can help bring about (5:19-27; 8:21-22; 11:15-20). The legal model, however, with its hermeneutical bent, privileges the past and present as the morally significant configuration. Truth, not hope, is its primary value. Job's imagination does not engage itself with the possibilities of a future in which well-being and happiness are restored. The endpoint of the narrative structure implicit in the legal model is the decisive moment of judgment, which should and can be *now*. Thus, the narrative construction of argument and of testimony leads to the conclusion of a proper judgment that marks the end of the plot (23:7b, "so I will escape forever from my judge"). This is so whether Job talks about his opponent or himself. (For Job's story about himself see, most fully, chaps. 29-31.) In chapter 10, as aggrieved parties or their representatives have always done, Job constructs a story about his opponent designed to make sense of what all can see is the present situation and to assign responsibility for that situation. Job's words are cast in the form of an imagined speech to God ("I will let my complaint loose, I will speak in the bitterness of my soul. I will say to God: 'Do not hold me guilty'" [10:1a-2a]). In this account he describes actions (God's creation and nurture of him in the past, God's vicious and illegitimate destruction of him in the present, vv. 8a/b; 9-12, 16-17) which, apparently inexplicable in themselves, achieve a horrific intelligibility when the hidden motives are disclosed (God's malicious intent to watch for and punish any sin, vv. 13-15). In this manner "turmoil" is organized, interpreted, and made meaningful, so that, as

Ricoeur says, "one because of the other" triumphs over "one after the other."[69] Telling the story, witnessing to it, is itself an act of resistance to turmoil. If there are sympathetic listeners who themselves can bear witness, it may be enough for survival. In a truly legal context, however, telling the story is not enough. The resolution a legal narrative requires is the resolution of judgment, whether through self-confession by the party who has acted wrongfully or by the judgment of a third party. In either case a hidden truth is brought to light and acknowledged.

Every rhetoric exerts constraints on the types of stories that can be constructed and the way they relate to one another, and legal rhetoric is no exception. Legal stories are quintessentially stories of blame or exculpation. The forensic context pares down the rich variety of ways in which social beings may be described as relating to one another (as God astutely suggests in 40:8b). The stories told in psalms of complaint and thanksgiving may be stories about responsibilities honored or neglected, stories about anger and reconciliation, stories about endangerment and rescue, stories about sickness and healing. Though some of these overlap with stories of blame and exculpation, they cannot be reduced simply to those categories.

The legal imagination is also reductive with respect to stories in one other way. Though the confrontational structure of legal disputation invites the telling of rival stories, the structure of judgment implicit in the legal model assumes that alternative stories cannot both be true to the same degree. Either one will be declared right and the other wrong or some third version will be constructed from the encounter of rival accounts. In either case, truth is assumed to be unitary and self-identical. The hermeneutical task of the judicial process is getting *the* story right. So Solomon discloses which woman was telling the true story of the dead baby (1 Kgs 3:16–28) and Daniel exposes the lies of the elders (Susanna). Though stories such as those about Solomon and Daniel demonstrate the power of judgment to distinguish between the lie and the truth, what goes unexamined is the difficulty of discerning which aspects of human experience are susceptible to the powerful analytical force of legal judgment and which are not.

The friends and Job never make explicit this aspect of the disagreement between their rival practices, but the way their different moral imaginations make room for and exclude certain narrative patterns finally makes their dialogue impossible. One catches a glimpse of this mutual unintelligibility in the way each configures the other's speech in chapters 13 and 15. In chapter 13 Job frames his speech in explicitly legal terms ("pleadings" [*ribbôt*]; cf. also v. 18, "case" [*mišpāṭ*]). Thus introduced, Job's accusations that the friends have spoken "falsely" and "deceitfully" for God (v. 7) is an accusation that they have become false witnesses (cf. Exod 20:16; Deut 19:16–19). The legal overtones are reinforced as Job describes the friends "showing partiality" (lit., "lifting the face") as they argue God's case (v. 8; cf. Exod 23:2–3, 6–8). The friends, of course, do not recognize the legitimacy of such a construal of their speech. They see themselves simply as counseling a friend about the proper religious under-standing of his situation. By the same token they cannot hear Job's words to God as charges and defenses seeking resolution in a court of judgment but only in terms of the categories available within their own moral imagination, that is, as blasphemy (15:2–6).

As Job continues to explore how legal discourse is able to expose the sadistic underpinnings of psalmic language (chaps. 16–17; 19), the friends embark on their series of poems describing the fate of the wicked (chaps. 15; 18; 20). For a time it appears that the parties are less than ever engaged in taking account of each other's speech. (At this point the pattern of introductory insults all but ceases.) Yet in a surprising twist, the poems that deal with the fate of the wicked become the site of the most direct struggle over the limits of language itself.

Justice, the Fate of the Wicked, and Speech at the Limits

Although each of the friends has given a speech on the fate of the wicked dur-ing the second cycle, Job only takes notice of their obsessive preoccupation with this topic in chapter 21, where he engages in an explicit repudiation of their iconic story. This repudiation provokes a crisis, leading Eliphaz explicitly to identify Job as one of the wicked (chap. 22). Yet the oddest thing is that in the third cycle, as the friends cease to speak, it is Job who takes up the topos of the fate of the wicked, not repudiating it, but appearing to speak in much the same terms that the friends have. The presence of these words in Job's mouth seems to many commentators so out of place that they propose that the third cycle of speeches has been disturbed, either through accident or by a pious scribe who wished to mute Job's heterodoxy by giving him some "proper" sentiments. Ac-cording to many versions of this theory, the material in 24:18–25 and 27:12–23 originally formed part of the speeches of Bildad and Zophar.[70] The diffi-culty, however, is that no textual evidence exists to support such a theory. It is simply a desperate gesture in response to an interpretive embarrassment. As scholars have become more reticent about rewriting the text before interpreting it, there has been an increased tendency to interpret these portions of the text as Job's own words. For the most part scholars still tend to treat them as the words of Bildad and Zophar, preemptively or sarcastically spoken by Job,[71] al-though the occasional scholar suggests that these words can be understood as Job's own sentiments, without necessarily implying "a belated conversion to his friends' point of view."[72] There is merit in both approaches. Unquestion-ably, these passages are stamped with the distinctive features of the friends' speech, even though they appear in Job's mouth. The interpretive challenge is to "hear" the tonality and so to understand in what dialogic manner Job engages the speech of the friends as he incorporates it into his own. Given the teasing nature of the text, more than one interpretation is possible.

Job first takes up the topos in chapter 21. Even in his introductory words, Job seems to anticipate the radical effect his utterance will have, for he suggests that the friends will take their "consolation" from what he says (v. 2). In a sense, they do. Job's words allow them to resolve the sense of dissonance that Job's devastated innocence presents. Once they can classify Job as one of the wicked (chap. 22), then what has happened to him is no disturbing anomaly but an expression of the order of the world. When Job commands his friends to "face him" and be struck dumb with horror (21:5), and when he speaks of his own terror "as I think of it" (v. 6), it is unclear whether he is referring to his physical condition or the significance of what he is about to say. But just as he was so physically disfigured that the friends could scarcely recognize him (in the prose tale, 2:12), now he becomes in their view—and even to himself—so morally changed as to evoke a similar sense of nonrecognition and horror.

In the body of his speech, Job describes the wicked with images and metaphors that are the opposite of those in the friends' descriptions. Where the friends described the enfeeblement of the wicked (15:29–34; 18:5–7; 20:6–11), Job speaks of their strength (21:7). In contrast to the extinguished line and devastated household (18:14–15, 19; 20:10, 28), Job notes their secure households and well-established offspring (21:8–9, 11). Their wealth does not dissipate (15:29; 20:10, 15) but multiplies (21:10). Instead of being subject to terrors, violence, and premature death (15:21, 30; 18:13–14; 20:23–25), they enjoy a happy and secure life, culminating in a peaceful death (21:9, 11–13). Each image reverses one claimed by the friends to characterize the wicked. Given the context of the second round of speeches, one is tempted to describe Job's performance as a parody of the topos of the fate of the wicked. In another context verses 8–13 would sound like a description of the felicity of the pious, much as Eliphaz described the hope Job could have for his own future (5:19–26), except that the subject is the wicked. To hear it simply as parodic play with a familiar topos is not quite accurate. It misses part of Job's rhetorical strategy.

Job does not begin his utterance in strict imitation of the friends. They begin with declarative statements, Job with the question "Why?" Job thus sets his speech in relation to another genre, the psalmic complaint, where objections to the prosperity of the wicked were a traditional topic (e.g., Psalms 10; 73). But as with Job's evocation of the lament tradition in chapter 16, so here, too, it is employed as a setup, which depends for its effectiveness upon the expectation of a patterned sequence of ideas that Job disrupts.[73] Conventionally, the complaint against the wicked takes the form of an implicit or internal dialogue. Serving as an ideological safety valve, the complaint allows one to identify that which should not be but is—the well-being of the wicked. But the complaint is actually a strategy of containment, for by convention it reaches a turning point at which confidence in the moral order guaranteed by God's presence and action returns to the speaker (Pss 10:12-17; 73:17-28). Or, as in Psalm 37, the speaker may be a sage who acknowledges the protests of an implicit friend concerning the prosperous wicked (vv. 7-8) and who responds with the full repertoire of traditional arguments.

From verse 7 through verse 15 in chapter 21, Job's speech says nothing that would be out of place in the psalms, and in a conventional psalm verse 16 would serve as the beginning of the psalmist's reply to his own doubts ("Behold, their well-being is not in their own power—far from me is the counsel of the wicked!"). Here is the parody. Job pays homage to the convention of implicit dialogue, but he turns it into a real one. Although the device is not made explicit until verse 27 (the reference to "your thoughts"), the second half of the speech is a series of four objections and replies (v. 16/vv. 17-18; vv. 19/vv. 20-21; v. 22/vv. 23-26; vv. 27-28/vv. 29-33). To the objection that the wicked are not really in control of their own well-being (v. 16a), Job, invoking the imagery of Bildad's and Eliphaz's earlier speeches, asks "how often" the lamp of the wicked is extinguished or calamity befalls them (vv. 17-18). Though any order can admit exceptions and any iconic narrative may accommodate nonconforming examples, Job's insistence on an accounting exposes what iconic narratives repress, that is, that they are the product of highly selective perception. Job rejects the defense of retribution upon the descendants of the wicked (v. 19) with the claim that only in one's own life and in the immediacy of one's own consciousness and body ("know," "eyes see," "drink") can evil be effectively repaid, a possibility cut off at death (vv. 20-21).

The problems that death poses for belief in a retributive order are explored in the final two objections and responses. In reply to the pious claim that God's judgments must be appropriate, since one cannot "teach God understanding" (v. 22), Job, anticipating Qoheleth, uses the universality of death's dust and worms to question whether God can be said to "judge" at all (vv. 23-26). Finally, the last objection is the rhetorical question that supports the claim of the ephemerality of the wicked: "Where is the house of the grandee, the tent where the wicked lived?" (v. 28). By invoking the testimony of "travelers on the road" (vv. 29-30), Job is not simply matching anecdote with anecdote but suggesting the existence of a pattern more basic than that claimed by the iconic narrative of the fate of the wicked, one that is seen in all parts of the world. In imagery evoking Eliphaz's description of the security and blessed death of the righteous (5:23-26), Job describes the wicked spared from calamity on the day of wrath, coming to the grave in peace and with honor (21:31-33). Since the moral imagination of the friends mortgages the present to the future, awaiting the reversal that would reestablish the moral order, the moment of death and the quality of death play an essential role in their argumentation (4:8-9; 5:26; 8:22; 11:20; 18:14, 18; 20:7-9, 11). By following the fate of the wicked through escape from calamity all the way to an honored grave, Job eliminates what was essential to the friends' narrative—a place for envisioning the reversal of fortune. This part of Job's speech in particular could never be said in a complaint psalm, for it breaks through the structures of containment used to neutralize discrepant experience.

The way Job takes up the words of the friends and recontextualizes them by reference to a psalmic complaint genre, which is itself then subverted, is simply one last great example of Job's extraordinary ability to speak by means of double voicing the words of others. Though challenging to follow in detail, it presents no real problems to understanding. That is not the case with the appearance of the "fate of the wicked" language in Job's final two speeches in chapters 23–24 and 26–27. There the skills the reader has honed in learning Job's subversive rhetoric no longer suffice. In those chapters Job speaks a more radical language.

One way to begin to think about these peculiar speeches is in relation to the genre of the wisdom dialogue. What conventions might have governed how a wisdom dialogue ends, and how might the third cycle of the Joban dialogue relate to such conventions? Perhaps it is foolhardy to pose such a question, since we have only one other specimen with which to compare Job. But even if the matter is speculative, the act of raising the question may be heuristically useful. Nothing about either the Babylonian Theodicy or Job suggests that such dialogues were designed to end with consensus.[74] It has long been noted, however, that in the last exchange in the Babylonian Theodicy the sufferer and his friend appear to take up some element of the other's position, the friend observing that the gods are indirectly responsible for a certain moral incoherency in the world and the sufferer acknowledging the importance of trusting in deity for deliverance. It is not as though they had exchanged places and now argue each other's positions. Yet the shift in tone and perspective by the participants allows the dialogue to come to an end without an inappropriate triumphing of one position over the other. Both perspectives retain their claim, yet there is some sense of a relieving of the tension that had sustained the debate.

With Job, the interpretive problem with which one has to deal arises precisely from the presence of his opponents' words in his mouth. Consequently, I wonder whether the author of Job is paying a parodic homage to a generic convention. Job takes the friends' words into his mouth in an excessive, almost literal way (with what sorts of intentions we will have to consider). They, however, far from acknowledging something of his perspective, fall silent. Both perspectives from the dialogue remain present, but rather than being represented in some mutual acknowledgment, they are present together within Job's own speech. Most perplexingly, however, Job's speeches not only remain polemical (24:25; 27:12), but he also uses the friends' arguments as though they were a refutation of what the friends had just said. Though in one sense this kind of mad writing brings closure (the friends are literally left with nothing to say), it does not relieve tension but rather exacerbates it.[75] Whether one wishes to see

in this structuring of the end of the dialogue some play with a generic convention, the nature of Job's relationship to the words of the friends that he incorporates into his own speech is the problem to be addressed.

Those critics who appeal to a theory of textual tampering abandon the interpretive task too quickly. Moreover, they construct an insufficiently complex
character for Job. The same objection could be made about those who see in
these passages simply Job's sarcastic preempting of what the friends could be
expected to say. That Job claims these words as in some way his own is evident
from 24:25 ("If it is not so, who can prove me a liar or set at naught my words?")
and 27:11 ("I will teach you what is in the power of God; I will not conceal
what is with Shaddai"). Interpreters who attempt to retain these words in some
fashion as Job's own speech generally refer to his complex and conflicted belief
concerning God and justice.[76]

The two passages in question do not present identical interpretive problems,
however, so it is better to consider them separately. Taking 24:18-25 first, one
should consider the setting within the speech as a whole. Chapters 23-24 take
up two topics, Job's own seeking for justice before God (chap. 23) and his
understanding of God's judgment (or absence thereof) in relation to the oppression of the poor and the depredations of criminals (chap. 24). In chapter
23 the first part of the chapter (vv. 3-12) is framed by the theme of God's elusiveness. Nevertheless, Job speaks with confidence of his vindication whether
he imagines himself facing God (vv. 4-7) or of God's observing and judging
him from a distance (vv. 10-12). This confidence is undercut as Job reflects on
God's power and autonomy (vv. 13-16), rekindling the dread Job feels. Although
the translation of the last verse is problematic, it can perhaps best be read as a
reclaiming of Job's defiance in the face of God's terror-inducing power: "Yet I
am not silenced by the darkness or by the thick darkness that covers my face"
(v. 17).[77] Such a resolution introduces Job's indictment of God's failure to ex-
ecute judgment in the face of the evident injustices that flourish in the world.[78]
The first part of chapter 24 (vv. 1-17) is the third of Job's indictments of God's
governance of the world. Throughout the dialogues Job has most often spoken
of personal grievances, but in chapters 12 and 21 he argues for the moral anarchy
of the world and God's responsibility for it. This passage differs from the other
two, however, in its rhetoric. In both chapters 12 and 21, Job made his claim
through a parody of a form of pious speech—the hymn to God's greatness in chapter
12 and the wisdom complaint psalm and the fate of the wicked poem in chapter
21. Here he drops parody and speaks directly and passionately of suffering and
God's indifference to it (24:1-12). So far he seems quite in character, as he does
when he turns to depict the criminality of "those who rebel against the light"
(vv. 13-17). Only with verse 18 does the cognitive dissonance begin.

The syntactical and semantic ambiguity of verses 18-25 should not be under-
estimated. Pronoun references are vague, several words might be translated in

various ways, and many verb forms could be taken either as indicative or optative in mood. One could read the passage more or less as a "straight" fate of the wicked poem (so NIV). One could (with some grammatical difficulties that can, however, be overcome) read it as a series of optatives and imperatives, giving the whole a curse-like quality (so NJPS and Hartley; see Andersen). One could also read it as an implicit citation of conventional wisdom (vv. 18–20) to which Job responds in verses 21–23 (so NRSV; cf. chap. 21), though the last word (v. 24) would appear also to belong to conventional wisdom. But to what, then, would Job's final challenge in verse 25 refer? "If it is not so, who will prove me a liar and show my words to be nothing?"

I am less concerned to defend one of these options than to think about the force of the dissonance. One can imagine the friends whispering together in confusion: "That's what *we* said. But he can't mean what it sounds like he's saying. He can't mean what we meant. What does he mean by saying that?" What had been the conflict between two positions in a wisdom dialogue, representing alternative constructions of the world, has now become a conflict located within the speech of a single person, though not, to borrow Bakhtin's terminology, within a single consciousness. Job preserves the recognizably alien form, the words of another, to represent a measure of distance as well as a measure of appropriation. He does not mean the same thing the friends do, even if he speaks just like them. One important approach to understanding Job's utterance is through the insight that many have made about Job's conflicted beliefs. Buber puts it well: "Unlike his friends, Job knows of justice only as a human activity, willed by God, but opposed by His acts. . . . [Job] believes now in justice in spite of believing in God, and he believes in God in spite of believing in justice."[79] Though I think Buber is correct, he frames the question in terms of Job's beliefs. My interest is in how one who has experienced "the rent in the heart of the world" can speak of it.

It is difficult to discuss Job's speech without improperly reducing its disorienting quality. At one level, chapter 24 simply produces with respect to the issue of the moral order of the world the same contradictory belief Job holds about his own claim of right. Job's exploration of the legal metaphor enabled him to envision as a real possibility both God's recognition of the claims of justice and God's violent repudiation of them. Analogously, Job can imagine the working out of justice against evildoers, even as he knows the realities of injustice. It is important to read the chapter in light of its first verse. This verse offers a perspective from which the two parts can be coordinated. Gordis's translation is the most persuasive: "Why, since times of judgment are not hidden from Shaddai, do His friends not see His day (of judgment)?"[80] The line parallels "times" and "day," "Shaddai" and "friends," while contrasting the verbs "not hidden" and "not see." A divine capacity for action, which nothing hinders, is mysteriously not realized. Thus, Job's examples describe first the desperate need for days of judgment, then without transition he speaks in the idiom of the friends to describe the enactment of times of judgment. Yet this is, by stipulation, what Shaddai's friends never see.

To describe the way in which the parts of the speech can be seen to be governed by the first verse, however, is to betray them by substituting logical coordination for a perception and a language that verge on madness. Job might have structured a speech in which he said, in effect: What might be, what could be, what should be is absent. But he chooses not to relate to language through the logical construction of coordinated claims. His language can only be the language of radical dissonance, a mimetic embodiment of the rent in the heart of the world. Job does not simply wish to *say* that life is experienced as contradiction. He forces those who listen to him into a painful cognitive dissonance, a loss of mastery, that is an echo, however faint, of what Job has experienced of the world.

Bildad's attempt to reintroduce the topic of God's power and human nothingness (25:1-6) is preempted by Job. Insulting the quality of Bildad's advice (26:2-4), Job continues his dialogue-ending strategy of taking the friends' words into his own speech (26:5-14). Indeed, the theme of divine power is quite compatible with Job's perspective. After Zophar's nonappearance following chapter 26, Job returns to the topic of justice, both with regard to his personal case and to the moral order in general. Here, even more pointedly than in chapter 24, Job signals the place of contradiction in his experience by means of the oath he swears.[81] An oath is a speech act designed to ensure the efficacy, reliability, or integrity of what is sworn. One therefore swears by that which is powerful and itself utterly reliable. In Israelite oath formulae this is most often YHWH or the "life of YHWH" (1 Sam 19:6; 26:10; 2 Sam 12:5; Jer 4:2). Job swears to his integrity by means of the "Life of God who has taken away my right and . . . embittered my soul." Though the words are ostensibly paradoxical to the point of contradiction, they name what has become Job's most reliable experience.

Notably, this last speech is not directed to God but is a final argument against the friends. Job's insistence upon the truthfulness of his words (Job 27:4) requires that readers take seriously what he will have to say. What immediately follows offers no problem to understanding, as Job defends his integrity against the calumnies of the friends (vv. 5-6). The topos of the fate of the wicked is invoked ironically in Job's wish that his enemy be "like the wicked," whom he characterizes as one whose call for help in time of distress goes unheard by God (vv. 9-10). While this would appear to be Job's experience (9:16; 19:7; 23:8-9), he has characterized this as the condition of the wicked, while unequivocally insisting on his own innocence. Though Job ostensibly says only the most conventional words, his contextualization of them shows that he has constructed an unstable and shifting set of equivalences and oppositions. What should be is the opposite of what is, yet he speaks as though all were as it should be. This queasy inversion continues as Job introduces the second part of his speech as a teaching and scolds the friends for having seen the truth and yet persisting in talking nonsense. But Job's own words are a perfect imitation of their speech. Here, as in chapter 24, one can recast this inversion in terms of its logical claims. What Job says is that he will teach the friends what is "in the power" of God (v. 11). That is to say, God could act as Job describes. Yet as all know, God has acted in just the opposite fashion, giving to the pious Job the fate deserved by the wicked and giving to the wicked the fate deserved by the righteous (chap. 21). Job wishes to expose God's incoherency, by speaking a language of inverted coherency. Yet the claim that the friends speak nonsense is a direct claim. Their nonsense is in insisting that the just distinction between the righteous and the wicked is an experiential reality. Job knows it as a possibility made manifest only in its bizarre inversion. In such a "Wonderland" world, Job speaks the only speech possible—an insanely inverted speech in which everything shadows and gestures to its opposite and in which one naturally swears by one's betrayer.

No wonder the friends have nothing else to say. They speak a language of sanity in a presumptively sane world. Job speaks a language bordering on madness in a world turned upside down. Job's language, however, has the quality of a dare or a provocation. He has mastered one of the possible languages of subversive resistance in a totalitarian world. When the one whose existence contradicts the dominant ideology that he nevertheless speaks, while his body silently witnesses to the truth, he lays out the scandal for all to see.

In the reading of the book of Job I am advocating in this study, I stress the semiautonomy of the various component genres. Just as the prose tale could stand on its own, so might the wisdom dialogue. One could imagine Job's words in chapter 27 as the last words of a composition. Whether the author of the Babylonian Theodicy would be horrified or deeply admiring is difficult to say, but I think he would understand what the Joban dialogue attempts and accomplishes. The Joban dialogue has violated what I take to be the conventions of wisdom dialogues—the clever but evenhanded representation of two contrasting perspectives on the question of the moral order of the world and the place of inexplicable suffering in it. Ironically, it is by having Job appropriate the very language of his opponents, which one might have expected to bring closure, that Job destroys the genteel closure of the wisdom dialogue. Job does indeed pass violence through language and language through violence. "The breakage of the verse enacts the breakage of the world."[82]

6

Dialogics and Allegory

The Wisdom Poem of Job 28

To a hammer, everything looks like a nail.
Anonymous

A good deal of critical ink has been spilled over chapter 28, much of it having to do with the relation of this chapter to the rest of the book. Whose words, whose opinions are these? What is the speaker saying, or trying to do in saying them? The absence of a heading at the beginning of the chapter allows it to be taken as a continuation of Job's speech, and a few commentators have attempted to make sense of it this way,[1] though often without a sense of firm conviction.[2] Most commentators, however, struck by the difference in style, tone, and perspective from what precedes, interpret the poem as distinct from the wisdom dialogue, a sort of poetic interlude that serves to separate the wisdom dialogue from the final dramatic exchange—the speech of Job in chapters 29–31 and God's reply in chapters 38–41.[3] Even if one follows this approach to chapter 28, which I think more fruitful than attempting to read it as Job's words, one has not finished with the question of whose words these are.

Historical-critical approaches framed the question in terms of authorship (who wrote it?) with some arguing that the chapter comes from a later reader who dropped his comments into the text in the form of a wisdom poem.[4] Perdue's remarks are typical: "It would seem best to regard the poem as a later insertion, written and placed into the dialogues to represent the views of a pious sage who objects to the quest to discover wisdom. Understood in this way, the hymn condemns at least implicitly both Job and his friends for attempting the impossible, that is, to come to a knowledge of the wisdom of God."[5] This view often goes with the assumption that the poem effectively preempts the divine speeches. To cite Perdue again, "In its current place, Job 28 anticipates and therefore undercuts the shocking nature of God's negation of human wisdom."[6]

Other scholars refine the notion of chapter 28 as a secondary insertion, distinguishing verses 1–27 and verse 28 as two distinct and sequential additions. In this reading, verses 1–27 constitute the skeptical poem denying human access to wisdom, whereas verse 28 is a sort of literary graffiti, a short reply or counter-statement to the skeptical poem. The final verse thus serves to radically reinterpret the skeptical poem by giving it a pietistic twist.[7]

Given the stylistic and thematic similarities between chapter 28 and the rest of the poetic sections, especially the divine speeches, many critics conclude that the author of the poem is the author of the book as a whole (or at least the author of its poetic sections).[8] Thus, the speaker is "the person telling the story, not one of the characters in the story."[9] The function ascribed to the poem is not too dissimilar from those who see it as a secondary insertion, as it "seems to be the poet's personal reflection on the debate thus far."[10] In this interpretation the author's own views, expressed directly in the poem, are to be distinguished from those of the characters in the dialogue but are essentially the same as those that will be placed in the mouth of God in chapters 38–41. The difference between the wisdom poem and the divine speeches is perceived as more of tone than of substance.[11] Robert Gordis, with a suggestion that somewhat splits the difference between the two alternative theories of authorship, argues that the poem was composed by the author of the Job poem but at an earlier time, that is, written by the author when he was a different person than when he wrote the rest of the book.[12]

In this, as in so many questions of actual authorship, there is no decisive evidence. Consequently, the issues are more helpfully framed not in terms of person but of persona. An approach that draws on Bakhtin's observations on voicing and double voicing in texts is particularly helpful. Whether chapter 28 is considered as part of the Job poet's work or as a secondary addition, it introduces a recognizably new voice, different from either the voice of the prose tale narration or from the characters who speak in the wisdom dialogue. This new voice, however, engages what has come before in a dialogic fashion. This is not to say that it makes no interpretive difference whether one understands the process of composition diachronically or not. If chapter 28 is a later addition, then its stylistic and thematic relationship to the divine speeches may have a different purpose and significance than if one assumes chapter 28 is the author's voice or one of the voices created by a polyphonic author. Although I will argue in chapter 8 of this book that the Elihu speeches are a later addition, I do not see distinct marks of belatedness in this poem. Consequently, I take chapter 28 as one voice among others within the original polyphonic text. It need not be identified as the author's own perspective, however, any more than the voice of the narrator, the voice of Job, or any other might be.

The issue of the relationship between verse 28 and the preceding poem is more difficult. The linguistic anomaly of the divine title *'ădōnāy* instead of *'elōhîm* (cf. v. 23) might suggest a voice different from what precedes. Moreover, the notion that verse 28 serves as a direct reply to verses 1–27 is tempting in an analysis that attends to the polyphonic quality of the text. But the question remains whether verses 1–27 comprise a complete utterance. As Zuckerman has observed, without verse 28 the poem would end in an oddly abrupt manner.[13] Furthermore, as I interpret the poem, the significance of the last verse is not opposed in substance to the content of the body of the poem but is essential to the claim that is made by the poem as a whole.[14] Consequently, I choose to treat it as part of the total utterance of chapter 28.

What interests me about the chapter is the distinctiveness of the voicing the author has given to this utterance. It has its own recognizable "dialect," not in the narrowly linguistic sense but in the metalinguistic sense Bakhtin referred to as heteroglossia. Bakhtin and the other members of his intellectual circle were intrigued by the way in which one can identify any number of different modes of speaking within a society, each of which is shaped by and bears within itself traces of distinct social, educational, historical, and other perspectives.[15] Unfortunately, with ancient texts it is often difficult to identify many of these traces with specificity. Nevertheless, one can observe the ways in which a dialect or characteristic way of speaking discloses a manner of conceptualizing the world that differs from other surrounding voices. The Bakhtin circle's analysis of the inherent interpretive slant of social dialects is very similar to its understanding of genre, for genre, too, is a way of seeing the world. Indeed, the various elements that constitute the profile of a particular dialect (its privileged words, the way it uses common words with a distinctive accentuation, its preference for a certain style) may often include a predilection for a particular genre or genres.

How might these observations pertain to Job 28? In this chapter, one encounters a distinctive genre (the speculative wisdom poem), which is part of a larger world of wisdom literature. Wisdom discourse, a "baggy monster" (as Henry James once described the novel), includes a broad range of other genres, modes of speaking, privileged words, ideological perspectives, values, and so forth. Lacking sharp boundaries, its metalinguistic profile overlaps and bleeds into those of other discourses but remains distinctive enough to be recognizable. The speculative wisdom poem shares with this larger discourse many features and values, but it will also have certain distinctive aspects that give it a particular profile and slant. Though I do wish to claim that the genre qua genre has certain perspectives and commitments, one should be careful not to attribute too much intentionality to a genre per se. The expressive capacity of a particular instance is established both by the way in which generic features are inflected over against other examples of the genre and also by the way it is rhetorically employed within a concrete utterance. What Ben Sira or the redactor of Proverbs does with a speculative wisdom poem will not be the same as what the author of Job does.

With these preliminary remarks in mind, I wish to turn more specifically to the genre of Job 28 and to the persona that the author creates by means of it. The designation "speculative wisdom poem" is perhaps not terribly evocative, but it serves well enough to gesture toward the sense of generic similarity that connects Proverbs 8, Job 28, Sirach 1 and 24, Baruch 3:9–4:4, and perhaps *1 Enoch* 42. Genres are not tight classificatory systems, of course, but patterns of similarities and dissimilarities. One might thus also take note of smaller related compositions, such as Proverbs 3:13–20, as well as those that combine aspects of speculative wisdom poems with royal autobiography, as in Wisdom 7–9. Comparison of all these texts reveals a number of generic markers. Most important is the topic, which concerns the place of wisdom in the cosmos and its relation to God on the one hand and humanity or Israel on the other. Moreover, the term "wisdom" in these poems is used in a way distinct from its use in proverbs and admonitions. Michael Fox characterizes the referent of wisdom in the interludes of Proverbs 1–9 as "the perfect and transcendent universal, of which the infinite instances of human wisdom are imperfect images or realization,"[16] something like a Platonic idea. Obviously, the question of whether or not human wisdom and transcendent wisdom are continuous is very much at issue in Job 28, but the interest in the transcendent dimension of wisdom is itself characteristic of the speculative wisdom poems. That is what "wisdom" means in these texts, as opposed to "skill," "prudence," "erudition," and so forth—meanings that the word may have in other contexts.[17] Fundamental to the genre is the trope of seeking/finding (Prov 3:13; 8:1–4, 32–26; Job 28:12, 20, 23–27; Sir 24:7–8, 19–22; Bar 3:9–4:4 passim; *1 En* 42:1), which can be developed in a variety of ways and may be used to express contrary positions. The generic marker is the issue and the trope, not the particular claim about the elusiveness or accessibility of wisdom. The personification of wisdom as female is a common device (Proverbs 8; Sirach 24; Bar 3:37, if not a Christian interpolation; Wis 9:10; *1 En.* 42:1), which facilitates the representation of the relation of wisdom to other entities. Creation imagery and the syntactical style of creation accounts ("when, when . . . then") are often employed (Prov 8:24–31; Job 28:25–27; Sir 1:4; 24:9, 25–29). Both spatial and temporal tropes are used, especially those that span the cosmos (Prov 8:22–31; Job 28:12–14, 20–22; Sir 1:2–4; 24:3–7; Bar 3:29–31), though imagery of particular historical places and times occurs as well (Sir 24:8–10, 23; Bar 3:22–28; Wisdom 7–9). Rhetorically, the speculative wisdom poem has a didactic quality, in which the speaker is presented as a figure of great knowledge. Personified wisdom may herself speak (Prov 8:4–36; Sir 24:3–22), or the text may speak with the voice of a sage. The poem often has a propositional character, in which a certain claim is established. As didactic literature, the poems attempt to persuade the listener of the value of wisdom. Thus, economic imagery or imagery of precious goods is common (Prov 8:11, 18–19; Job 28: 15–19; Sir 1:17; 24:13–17), as is other imagery of benefits or consequences (Prov 8:35–36; Sir 1:18–20; 24:19–22; Bar 3:14). The implications for human conduct or ethical norms are often mentioned (Prov 8:15–16; Job 28:28; Sir 1:26–27; 24:22). Stylistically, the obvious thing to be said is that these are poems, not prose compositions, and that the poetry is elevated and sophisticated (e.g., using chains of rhetorical questions, anaphora, personification). One could continue, but this list should suffice to establish that, for all their variety, these speculative wisdom poems do form a cross-referring body of texts of sufficient distinctiveness to be recognized by readers as a genre.

Any instance of a genre is dialogically engaged with other texts in many planes of relationship. In this case, two sets of comparison are particularly important: first, other texts of the same genre; second, the immediate context within which the text functions as utterance. Literary genres, taken as modes of conceptualization, can often be understood in relation to cultural issues or problems. Thus, the repertoire of instances of a genre, both those contemporary with one another and those that are part of a historical sequence, may be read as a prolonged conversation. The relatively small sample of speculative wisdom poems means that this kind of question cannot be pursued very far, but it is at least worth posing. The issue overtly named in these poems is the accessibility or inaccessibility of transcendent wisdom to human beings. If one asked what is at stake in such a conversation, the answer would be "many things," some of which we can only guess at. At an existential but somewhat abstract level the conversation may have to do with articulating the sense of how humankind is grounded in the world, whether in a condition of strong and transparent continuity or in discontinuity with its foundations. Thus, the poems address a primary human need, namely, the security that comes from understanding how things work. The conversation recognizes the problematic position of finite creatures who desire to grasp the coherency of a world that transcends them radically.

Such existential issues are never wholly abstract, but occur within specific social, economic, political, and religious conditions. Parochial and perennial concerns intersect. In Proverbs 8, for instance, the pairing of an accessible, personified wisdom with an aggressively seductive counterfigure in Proverbs 7 may suggest that the community saw its values under siege from rival discourses, even if it is difficult to specify concretely what these were.[18] The cultural context is more visibly on display in Ben Sira and Baruch, where the identification of transcendent but accessible wisdom with the Torah addresses both an inner-Jewish issue (how is emerging scripture to be related to older cultural forms?) and a Jewish-Gentile conversation (how are we to represent ourselves in relation to the claims of other nations?) The issue of cultural self-identity and rivalry is particularly apparent in Baruch, where wisdom as Torah is accessible to Israel in explicit contrast to its nonaccessibility to Israel's neighbors and relatives, some of whom enjoyed traditional reputations as centers of wisdom. In *1 Enoch* 42, Wisdom's return to heaven, from which she is presumably accessible only by means of special revelation, serves the interests of those who, like the tradents of Enoch, can make just such claims to revealed knowledge. Thus, the topos plays a new role in the competitive claims among Jewish groups in the Hellenistic period concerning access to the will of God, even as it continues to advance the Jewish claim for recognition in the larger Hellenistic world's interest in wisdom by higher revelation.[19]

Of all of the extant examples of the speculative wisdom poems, however, Job 28 yields the fewest clues as to social or historical issues that may inflect its representation of the genre. Various attempts have been made to locate the book of Job and its constituent parts in particular historical and cultural circumstances,[20] though the attempt is largely frustrated by the nonreferential nature of the text. Zuckerman draws attention to the combination of skeptical voice and pietistic framing that one finds both in Job 28 and in Qoheleth.[21] Though it is possible one might look to the Persian and Hellenistic periods as times in which the vastness of empire and the remoteness of the centers of ultimate power were congenial to the skeptical potential of the speculative wisdom poems, such skepticism about human ability to grasp the "mind of the gods" was a theme with deep roots in Mesopotamian wisdom.[22] Thus, although the question of the "cultural conversation" represented by the instances of the speculative wisdom poem with one another and in dialogue with changing historical circumstances is intriguing to pose, we simply lack sufficient evidence to do more than speculate in the most general of terms.

More fruitful is the way in which chapter 28 is dialogically related to the other genres and voices within Job. Most scholars agree that, even though the poem makes no direct reference to the wisdom dialogue, its presence just after the end of the third cycle makes the poem in some sense a comment on what has gone before. Moreover, in its concluding verse the wisdom poem explicitly alludes to the beginning of the prose tale, in which Job is characterized as "one who fears God and turns from evil." Thus, the poem is engaged, implicitly and explicitly, with the claims of both of the genres that have already presented themselves in the book. Indeed, it appears to be attempting to highlight their dialogic relationship by taking sides with one against the other.

Most critical discussion of the relationship of these parts of the book has tended to engage them at the level of propositional claims. Thus, it is claimed, in the view of the wisdom poem the search for wisdom undertaken by Job and his friends is futile, since no one but God can find wisdom. To the extent that wisdom is available to humans, it is in the form and by the means of piety and moral conduct. Interpreters disagree over whether this conclusion is simply a "return to first naivete" and so to "a simpler, precritical faith yet unchallenged by the crisis of holocaust,"[23] or whether it is a recovery of the "terrain in which one has always lived," now capable of being seen from a perspective of "chastened profundity."[24] As valuable as these discussions are, what gets overlooked is the way in which *what* is under discussion has been subtly changed. Some critics have noted that the term "wisdom" (*ḥokmāh*) is used with a variety of different referents by the various characters, most of which are different from the way *hokmāh* appears in the wisdom poem,[25] or that the "same" notion of hidden wisdom may be used for different purposes by different voices.[26] But the extent to which the issues of the book are reframed and dialogically engaged by the generic perspective of the wisdom poem deserves stronger emphasis. That is to say, the persona that speaks in the wisdom poem is not simply another voice. Because it speaks by means of a particular genre, the take on the world characteristic of that genre serves to "read" what has gone on before in terms of its own shaping perspectives.

The use of distinct genres in the composition of the book of Job, which I have stressed throughout my analysis, helps to bring into focus an issue about the nature of dialogue that is raised but not fully explored in Bakhtin, namely, the role of interpretive reframing in all dialogue. Bakhtin insisted that the participants in dialogue be understood as "voice-ideas," that is, not simply as propositions but as "the integral point of view, the integral position of a personality."[27] "Voice-ideas," though not to be equated with genres, have important similarities with them. Genres, in embodying perspectives on the world, create something of a similar "integral point of view." The polyphony of Dostoevsky's novels is facilitated by the roles various genres play ("legends, folk tales, saints' lives, detective stories, dialogues with ghosts and the devil, family chronicles, and journalistic exposés")[28] as means by which the ideas of characters can be tested and transformed, as they are made to resonate in various genres and as they pick up new accents or meanings from their encounter with various genres. But Bakhtin does not pause to examine *how* ideas become reaccented by different genres. What is missing from his discussion is a reflection on the nature of interpretation itself.

This element can be supplied by means of Gerald Bruns's discussion of interpretation as allegory. Bruns claims that "all interpretation is . . . allegorical."[29] Allegory, of course, has for a long time had a bad reputation, its mechanical representation of specific meanings in terms of other signifiers almost always resulting in a boring text. Even the more philosophically sophisticated forms of allegorical interpretation, from Philo to the medieval Christian allegorists, now claim little more than antiquarian interest. But according to Bruns, the allegorical process is fundamental to the act of interpretation itself. That process is "a conversion of the strange into the familiar, or of the different into the same. Allegory is a mode of translation that rewrites an alien discourse."[30] In the act of understanding, the interpreter establishes a correlation of categories. "Ah, when you say X, I recognize that what you are talking about is what I call Y." Whether or not the interpreter agrees with the specific claims of what is being interpreted, she has at least translated its categories into those she considers worthy of engagement. This stance includes both an element of generosity and an element of refusal. It is generous in its assumption that the speaker or text must be saying something worth hearing, if only one can "properly" translate it into the categories by which truth is established. To complete the quotation from Bruns above, "Allegory is a mode of translation that rewrites an alien discourse in order to make it come out right—according to prevailing norms of what is right."[31] This strongly appropriative process is also a refusal of the deep difference that may be represented by the text or utterance. Though that difference may well assert itself as resistance to allegory (Bruns uses the category of satire for that which resists and teases excessive appropriation), I am concerned at this point only with the allegorical process.[32]

How does this insight affect one's understanding of chapter 28 and its relation to the preceding parts of the book? As a reply to what has gone before, the text of chapter 28 shows that it has already implicitly performed an act of allegorical translation, recasting the issues of the prose tale and the wisdom dialogue in categories and problems congenial to its own metalinguistic culture. From the generic perspective of the speculative wisdom poem, the issue worthy of engagement is the problem of the relation of cosmic wisdom to God and to humankind. Thus, its privileged category is *ḥokmāh*, understood in the specialized sense as the wisdom that transcends individual minds. By framing its reply to the preceding dialogue and narrative in terms of a poem that has as its refrain "Where can Wisdom be found?" chapter 28 makes evident that it has interpreted the preceding issues in terms of its own overriding concern.

The term *ḥokmāh* has made a sporadic appearance in the wisdom dialogue, but mostly in terms of human understanding (4:21; 12:2, 12; 13:5; 15:8), and only rarely in terms of transcendent wisdom (11:6; 12:13). In no sense has it been a primary interpretive category. Occasionally, the issue of the limits of human understanding has been raised (11:5–9; 15:7–8), but not as a self-reflective characterization of the activity upon which the speakers are engaged. It is at least an open question whether the participants in the wisdom dialogue or the narrator of the prose tale would agree that what they have "really" been talking about is the quest for transcendent *ḥokmāh*. But that is how chapter 28 reads them, and that is the interpretive perspective it attempts to persuade the reader of the book of Job to adopt.

One can imagine Job vigorously resisting the claim of the wisdom poem. Granted, he has himself used the trope of seeking (23:3–9). But he has not been engaged on some futile "quest for wisdom"; he has been trying to assert a claim of justice. He has been arguing that the deity has behaved violently toward him in a way that demands an accounting. Yes, he has used language and genres of the wisdom tradition, including references to transcendent wisdom, most clearly in chapter 12. But he has done so only in order to claim that divine perversity rather than *ḥokmāh* is a more apt way of accounting for reality. His satiric allusion to traditional platitudes about transcendent wisdom ("With Him are wisdom and courage; His are counsel and understanding," 12:13) are in essence a disputation of the notion that "God knows the way to it" (28:23).

To allegorize his arguments as themselves a futile quest for wisdom is to obscure what is the disturbing element of his speech. "Rightness" (*ṣĕdāqāh*)–which is the fundamental category for Job–is not to be traced to some archaic, transcendent but pervasive wisdom. On the contrary, "rightness" may or may not be achieved by means of a confrontation framed like a trial at law. The poem's allegorization is an act of accommodation that denatures this difference. It is interpretive violence.

What emerges from this initial attempt to "draw dotted lines" between Job's speeches and the wisdom poem is the significance of the contingent in Job's moral imagination and the alienness of such a notion to the moral imagination of the wisdom poem. One can see this distinction in the radically different rhetorics they employ. Whereas the critical spatial figure for Job is the "face to face" encounter (19:26b–27; 23:3), for the wisdom poem it is the broad, cosmic vista, extending to the realms of Sheol and Abaddon and beyond. Temporality is also configured in sharply different ways. For Job, critical temporality is figured as a decisive moment, when mutual recognition comes as word answers word (13:22; 23:4–5). For the wisdom poem, critical temporality is the *arche* of creation. The tonality of the two voices could not be more different, with Job's words characterized by an urgency that finds its opposite in the serenity of the wisdom poem's tone. For Job, the moral order of the world, its very meaningfulness, exists only as a potentiality; for the wisdom poem, it exists as a deep structure not accessible to the rational consciousness, yet in some way is the essential precondition for meaningfulness in human life.

Without letting go of the insight that the wisdom poem does in some significant sense denature Job's arguments, one might also argue that its act of interpretive translation also illumines important dimensions of Job's speeches. There is something of the nature of a quest in Job's speeches. He is tunneling, overturning obstacles, sinking shafts in the search for something that is not only more precious than gold but beyond all other values. What he seeks, though he may not employ the term *ḥokmāh* for it, is a point of coherency,[33] a vantage point from which God, the world, and his own experience make sense. For Job to be vindicated by God presumes the existence of a set of transcendent values, continuous between God and humankind, that serves as the ground by which the distortions of the world can be put right. In order to assert its own claims, the wisdom poem is attempting to shift the plane of the argument by looking at the assumptions embedded in Job's passionate quest. Whatever Job thinks he is doing, his mistake is in presuming that human rationality can grasp and hold the structures of the world in intelligibility. Such an attempt is, as Qoheleth would put it, *hăbēl hăbālîm*.

The friends might be more ready to agree that *ḥokmāh* and *bînāh* are the appropriate umbrella terms for their intentions, for they are attempting to describe a way of living in the world based on an understanding of its intrinsic structures and dynamics. They would undoubtedly agree that "fear of the Lord" and "turning from evil" are closely related to wisdom. Though they do not use the term "wisdom" to characterize it, the experience of well-being and a coherent world is tied to an active piety: "Is not your fear [of God] your grounds for confidence, your hope the perfection of your way?" (4:6). "If you will seek God and supplicate Shaddai, if you are pure and upright, surely he will rouse himself for you and restore you to your rightful place" (8:5-6; see also 11:13-15; 15:4; 22:21-23). They would also likely find congenial the distinction between God's access to wisdom and human access. That is Zophar's point in chapter 11 when he expresses his wish that "God would speak . . . and tell you the hidden aspects of wisdom" (11:5-6). Zophar develops his point in a beautiful set piece that makes use of two differently framed pairs of rhetorical questions that underscore the limits of human knowledge ("Can you find out? . . . What can you do/know?") and four tropes of measure that sketch the vastness of the cosmos ("higher than heaven . . . deeper than Sheol . . . longer than the earth . . . broader than the sea"). The rhetorical devices are much the same as those used in the wisdom poem of chapter 28 and in the divine speech in chapter 38. Yet as van Oorschot has observed, when the friends invoke the topos of hidden wisdom, they do so instrumentally, using it as a tactic of argument in the dialogue with Job.[34] Indeed, Zophar appears to claim to know the functional content of this wisdom. Since he observes that God has forgiven part of Job's iniquity (11:6c) but that God does judge iniquity (11:10-11), Zophar understands this hidden wisdom to be "essentially a knowledge of God's treatment of persons, an insight into his righteous dealings with (always) sinful creatures."[35] Somewhat less perplexing is Eliphaz's use of the topos. Using a trope of temporality, Eliphaz mockingly asks Job if he were "the first human to be born," "brought forth before the hills," like personified wisdom itself in Proverbs 8. Eliphaz seems to posit the existence of an archaic wisdom, spoken in the "council of Eloah." But that esoteric wisdom is not itself the issue. Eliphaz introduces the topic simply to contest Job's pretentious arrogance, mocking him as one who acted as though he had a superior wisdom, restricted to himself alone (15:8b). In fact, Eliphaz claims, they all have access to the same resources of wisdom (15:9-10). There is no indication that Eliphaz sees this wisdom as in any sense problematically limited or inaccessible.

Where the friends would likely part company with the wisdom poem's perspective is in its apparent rejection of an active intellectual process as the means to reliable wisdom. The friends know where wisdom is to be found and where the place of understanding is, namely, in their own discernment and in resources of tradition: "See, this we have searched out. It is true. Listen, and know it for yourself" (5:27). "Ask now of an earlier generation, and consider the investigations of their ancestors. For we are but of yesterday, and do not understand, since our days are a shadow upon the earth. Will they not teach you, speak to you, and utter words from their understanding" (8:8–10; cf. 15:10). Tradition is itself a form of transcendent wisdom, since it overcomes the finitude of the individual. Thus, even the friends, who would appear to hold positions congenial to that of the wisdom poem, may be seen to be rebuked as naive by the wisdom poem for their confidence in equating either their own discernment or tradition with transcendent wisdom.

Perhaps the dialogic engagement between the wisdom poem and what precedes, however, is better taken not so much as an attempt to interpret and respond to the particular participants as to the genre of the wisdom dialogue itself. One of the issues raised by the presence of different genres in the book of Job is the question of the form of inquiry into moral and cosmological truth. What modes of knowing are appropriate and useful? The placement of the wisdom poem suggests that the poem views the wisdom dialogue as a type of futile and misguided quest for wisdom. But the dialogic relationship between the genres might be more subtle than that. The wisdom dialogue, as a genre, is itself something of an exposé of the limits of the human capacity to know, since it does not end in a single solution or insight into the problem it addresses. Its participants do not finally find wisdom or the place of understanding. In that regard the wisdom poem might be seen as simply drawing a conclusion implicit in the wisdom dialogue as a generic form, thus engaging in a dialogics of agreement. Yet the sensibilities of the two genres are very different. The energy of the dialogue and the pleasure it provides reside in the very clash of ideas, perceptions, and worldviews.[36] "Iron sharpens iron," says the proverb, "so one person sharpens another" (Prov 27:17). The limit on human understanding, the fact that one cannot reach the source of understanding, operates not just as an assumption of the wisdom dialogue genre but as a *facilitating* assumption. Only such limits make possible the endlessness of argument. Such dialogue may stop, but it does not finish. Moreover, as the wisdom dialogue in Job shows, this type of argument can actually create surprise. That Job would take a statement about the difference between divine and human righteousness and from there make a radical exploration of divine violence and create a possible alternative mode of relating to deity is a wholly unforeseen turn of events in the dialogue. But that is what provides a significant measure of its excitement and interest. Even if the direction of Job's thought leads ultimately to a dead end, for the wisdom dialogue there is a value in the exercise itself. One judges that the persona of the wisdom poem does not share the sensibility that takes pleasure in such intellectual adventurism.

For the wisdom poem, the "possession" of wisdom and understanding is the highest value. The governing trope of the poem, which plays on this desire, is the trope of wisdom as object. Its very elusiveness only reinforces the desire to have it. The representation of wisdom as object is created in part by the mining imagery itself. Even though the poem insists that one cannot "mine" wisdom from the most remote places, it constructs wisdom as occupying a place beyond places. The language of the refrain uses spatial imagery: "be found," "place of understanding" (Job 28:12, 20). The speaker declares that wisdom cannot be found "in the land of the living" (28:13b), and those places that lie beyond the land of the living—"the deep" and "the sea"—are personified as reporting that wisdom is not to be found in them (28:14). Yet the very denials, far from questioning whether or not wisdom has a "place," suggest that it does—only an unimaginably remote one. That it exists some*where* is suggested by the description of it as "concealed" from all the living, "hidden" from the birds of the air (28:21). The image of a place beyond place is played with tantalizingly, as "Death and Abaddon" state that they have "heard a report" of it (28:22). The imaginative language of the poem appears to be taking one closer to this place of wisdom, even as it declares that humans cannot find it out. The imagery of remote and concealed object is further reinforced as the poem switches from the human perspective to the divine. Place imagery is explicit as the poem reports that "God understands the way to it," "knows its place." That the issue is one of a hierarchy of power and capacity seems to be suggested by the explanation "for he gazes upon the ends of the earth, he sees what is under all the heavens" (28:24).

But had not the poem previously asserted that wisdom is *not* to be found at the ends of the earth and under the heavens? The tendency is to overlook this discrepancy, but I think it should be insisted upon, because it is just at this point that the trope upon which the poem has been ostensibly based is in fact undercut. In the following verses the activity described is not that of searching but that of creating: "When he gave weight to the wind, and set the waters by measure; when he made a limit for the rain, and a way for the thunderstorm, *then* he saw it, recounted it, understood it, searched it out" (28:25-27). God's mode of knowledge is not that of subject and object but that of one who understands a craft of making.[37] It is not because God sees further than human beings that God sees wisdom, but because God sees differently. Wisdom, after all, is not in some place beyond place but in the wind, waters, rain, and thunderstorms, that is, in all the aspects of creation. But it is not "in" them as an object but in their construction and interrelationship, in their presence and limits ("weight," "measure," "limit," "way") with respect to other aspects of the created world. Thus, one realizes that the poem is in no sense saying that humans have no access to wisdom. They will not find it if they look for it as an object (even an intellectual object) but only if they also know it through a comparable mode of being, a way of acting. The disposition of piety and the moral habit of turning from evil are the way in which one will know wisdom and understanding.[38]

Crucially, this is where the poem speaks by means of double voicing, as it echoes the words and even the style of the prose tale (28:28). Agreement, as Bakhtin observed, is every bit as dialogical as disagreement, for no two utterances are ever the same. That difference, even in agreement, is underscored not just by the slight difference in wording (*yira't 'ădōnāy* instead of *yira't 'elōhîm*) but also by the act of appropriation that takes place. The wisdom poem, in agreeing with the prose tale about the importance of its privileged words of value (fear of God and turning from evil), explicitly translates them, or as Bruns would have it, allegorizes them. Verse 28 appropriates the terms from the prose tale as equivalents of its own terms: "See—the fear of the Lord—that is wisdom; and turning from evil—understanding." The prose tale did not claim to be a story about wisdom and understanding. It was a story that explored a conundrum in religious ideology (can true piety coexist with divine blessing?) and provided a role model for the exercise of disinterested piety. The wisdom poem is claiming, in effect, "Yes, yes, but you are saying more than you know. For what your little didactic tale also does is to provide a brilliant narrative of what it means to know wisdom and to have understanding. They can be embodied, but such embodiment is always done in ignorance of what takes place in the heavens, not by apprehension of the transcendent wisdom of the cosmos." The dialogics of agreement recasts the story from a different perspective. Indeed, as I write this, I realize the extent to which the wisdom poem's interpretation of the prose tale has formed the basis for my own. I think it is right in claiming for the prose tale a significance that it does not claim for itself. The prose tale does disclose a radical way of living that can be interpreted as living from within the coherency of wisdom. Moreover, it serves as an important gloss upon what it means to live in *hokmāh* and *bînāh*. Such a way of living does not entitle one to expect freedom from trouble (contra Prov 3:21–26 and the like). The coherency and meaningfulness of such a life is to be found as much within suffering as within peace. Yet it is just such an interpretive act of "transposing the key" of the prose tale that contributes to an exclusive focus on its thematics and so obscures the disturbing aspects of its performative dimensions, as discussed in chapter 2 earlier. Though it is not interpretive violence, the wisdom poem's allegorization of the prose tale diminishes its complexity as narrative.

The dialogic relationship between chapter 28 and the preceding material is easy enough to engage. But what relation, if any, does the chapter have to what follows, namely, Job's final speech? Does it serve merely as a separation between the discourse of the dialogues and the discourse of the final speech? Although there is no acknowledgment of the poem in Job's words (the wisdom poem does not exist on the level of the narrative but in the metanarrative), one can "trace dotted lines" between the two. The Job of chapters 29–31 takes up the challenge of presenting himself precisely as one who fears God and turns from evil. But we certainly do not have a return to the Job of the prologue, for the Job in these chapters is one who experiences himself as falsely accused and seeks a restoration of the dignity and respect that is his due. What one will encounter in chapters 29–31 is a taking up of some of the themes, issues, and topics addressed by the various preceding genres and speakers, but in a configuration quite different from any of them.

Moreover, I would disagree with those who see in the wisdom poem simply another version in a more meditative mood of what God will say in the divine speeches. To the contrary, the sophisticated and satisfying reintegration that the wisdom poem negotiates between the transcendent wisdom of God and human piety, two spheres of reality that initially appeared to be utterly sundered, will be sharply contested by the divine speeches.

7

A Working Rhetorical World

Job's Self-Witness in Chapters 29–31

> Our subject is rhetoric, if by that is meant the study of the ways in which
> character and community—and motive, value, reason, social structure, every-
> thing, in short, that makes a culture—are defined and made real in per-
> formances of language. . . . The object of rhetoric is justice: the constitution
> of a social world.
>
> James Boyd White, *When Words Lose Their Meaning*

Readers intuitively recognize the difference between chapters 29–31 and Job's
speeches in the wisdom dialogue. This speech is not apparently addressed to
the friends and contains no introductory angry response to their words. Indeed,
it is not clear to whom, if anyone, Job's words are addressed. Moreover, this
speech has an internal development strikingly different from the speeches in
the dialogue. An extensive act of recollection begins the speech (chap. 29), followed by a contrasting account of the misery of Job's present condition (chap.
30). A lengthy series of oaths of self-clearance (chap. 31), which implicitly characterizes the present situation as itself unjust, brings the speech to a dramatic
conclusion. One of the consequences of this altered form of speaking is that
Job engages much more extensively and systematically in acts of self-representation
and the representation of the social and moral world within which he understands himself.

This intuitive sense that chapters 29–31 constitute a different way of speaking is sharpened if one considers Job's relation to language in the dialogues
and here. In the dialogues, Job appears as one for whom the resources of traditional language for framing suffering and rendering it meaningful have utterly
failed. His alienation from received language is reflected in his extensive use of
irony, parody, and other means of subverting traditional speech.[1] His repudiation of the language that the friends still speak so effortlessly is evident not only
in his parodies but also, most paradoxically, in his act of literal appropriation
of their speech in the last cycle (chaps. 24 and 27).[2] That gesture raises to intolerable clarity the failure of the resources of their language to comprehend the
realities of Job's torment and puts an end to the dialogue.

The Job who speaks in chapters 29–31, however, has an utterly different relation to language. Here he invites the reader to what one could call a working rhetorical world. The language Job speaks is one in which he is at home, a language adequate both for his presentation of himself and for the expression of his complaint. As I will argue later, it is also a language with which he can act, one sufficiently flexible and resourceful to provide him with what he needs to envision a resolution to his problem. The tonality of Job's speech is perhaps the best indicator of his changed relation to language in these chapters, for here parody and even irony are completely absent.[3] Moreover, though Job uses traditional images, topoi, and speech genres, there is virtually no double voicing, either by the invocation of traditional voices to bolster authority or by the subversive undercutting of the voices of others. In that regard the Job of chapters 29–31 speaks the simplest, most direct language in the book, simpler even than Job's language in the prose tale, where his own speech articulates itself through the appropriation of traditional sayings (1:21; 2:10). This simplification of voicing creates the sense of a person speaking directly and with sincerity, and so contributes not only to the construction of Job's character but also to the image of a moral world where such speech is at home.

Just as Job's relationship with language is different, so is his relationship to the audience implied by his words. In the dialogue, hostility and mutual incomprehensibility quickly come to characterize the way Job and his friends perceive each other as listeners, and this perception leaves traces on the speech itself. The verbal "sidelong glance," the anticipation of mockery or rebuff, and the struggle for possession and inflection of key terms of value characterize the tense speaker/addressee relations in the dialogue. By contrast, the audience inscribed in Job's way of talking in chapters 29–31 leaves no such traces. Instead, the ease and fluency with which Job speaks projects an audience deemed capable of understanding him, one with whom he shares a language of meaning and value, to whom his claims and complaints would be intelligible, whether or not they are accepted.

A Job who talks like this is as unanticipated, as surprising, as incongruous following the wisdom dialogue as is the Job of chapter 3 following the didactic tale. For the third time in the book the same character is rendered through a different cultural-linguistic mode, each of which bears within its practices a different way of constructing a moral world, a type of character, and a set of values. Unlike the didactic tale, the wisdom dialogue, and even the wisdom poem, however, Job's speech in chapters 29–31 does not appear to be cast as a recognizable genre. Numerous attempts have been made to associate parts or aspects of it with various genres—lament, dialogue-appeal, declaration of innocence, appeal for a trial—but it is generally agreed that the speech as a whole is not composed according to a specific literary model but freely uses and modifies a variety of topoi and forms of speech.[4] Although one has to be cautious in light of our limited knowledge of the repertoire of ancient literature and allow the possibility that Job's speech might have generic affinities we can no longer recognize, I agree with the consensus judgment. For pragmatic purposes, however, one may label the speech to indicate something of its character and function, without intending to suggest a formally recognizable genre. I find it most helpful to characterize Job's speech as a form of testimony. In contrast to Habel,[5] who also uses the term "testimony," I do not mean testimony in the legal sense, for even the oaths Job utters do not seem to be intended as specifically legal speech. But "testimony" can be used more generally to refer to the giving of an account of events, of one's experience, or of oneself. Whatever forms Job's words take in these chapters, they are just such an account.

Before turning to a closer examination of the speech, I wish to say a word about the role of these chapters in the book as I understand them. Commentators reflecting on the content and tonality of this section often observe that here Job seems quite close to the values and views the friends have articulated[6] and that Job speaks in ways at odds with some of his previous utterances (cf. 2:10 and 30:26; 24:1-17 and 30:1-8). Traditional historical critics sometimes resolve this tension by recourse to the hypothesis that a different author composed chapters 29-31.[7] Other historical critics and final-form readers address the problem by attributing a more complex and perhaps morally imperfect character to Job.[8] My approach, which stresses the juxtaposition of different genres and modes of speech in a polyphonic text, sees in each shift a new experiment with the resources of language. In the wisdom dialogue, Job is naturally assigned the skeptical role and the task of exposing the limits of traditional language. But what if one finds a way of reassigning the roles? If there were some other form of speech in which the character Job could operate *within* the framework of traditional language, would it be possible to show that it actually contains resources for articulating his grievance and resolving his dilemma far more creative and compelling than were seen in the experiment with the wisdom dialogue? What if one imagined the kind of speech Job might make before an assembly at the gate (30:28b), a testimony by which he attempted to rehabilitate himself in the eyes of his peers and the community at large, a community that has already drawn provisional conclusions about him from their own interpretation of his ghastly fate.

To read chapters 29-31 in this way, one must examine both the question of the audience for the speech and the rhetoric by which Job attempts to persuade his audience. The matter of the audience to whom he speaks is elusive, but perhaps strategically elusive. Within the frame of the book the only persons physically present appear to be Job's three friends. Yet this speech does not seem to be addressed to them. God, of course, is addressed directly in one brief section (30:20-23), but although God may be intended to "overhear," God is not the explicit addressee of the whole. Nevertheless, as commentators generally recognize, the speech has a public character and so is not best considered a soliloquy.[9] In 30:28b Job says that he rises in the assembly and cries out, though it is not clear if that line refers to his present speech or is a stock image in his complaint. Whether actual or imaginary, the assembly of elders makes a plausible rhetorical setting for Job's speech. My interest, however, is not in the dramatic setting of the speech itself so much as in the rhetorical effect of this projection of the sense of an audience beyond the friends.

This effect may be illuminated by considering Mikhail Bakhtin's discussion of addressivity. Bakhtin makes the commonsense but important observation that every utterance has an addressee. Such an addressee may be present or absent, concrete or vague, aware or not; but the addressee is the logical second party in any speech. There is also, as a constitutive element of the utterance, a third party, whom Bakhtin designates as the "superaddressee." Bakhtin contrasts these two addressees by noting that the second party is one "whose responsive understanding" is *sought*, whereas in the case of the superaddressee, that "absolutely just responsive understanding is *presumed*."[10] It is always possible that one's actual audience will fail to understand or will prove incapable of authentic response. But to be able to speak at all, one has to be able to imagine being understood. The superaddressee represents that possibility. As Morson and Emerson comment on Bakhtin's notion, "The superaddressee embodies a principle of hope."[11] The task of persuasion is to conform the actual audience to the ideal audience or superaddressee. By leaving the question of the second party so vague, chapters 29–31 make the role of the superaddressee more palpable. In the dialogue, Job's words were always projected upon the very concrete, alien horizon of the three friends' consciousness, and the anticipation of their critical response cast a shadow on Job's speech. But in chapters 29–31, and in chapter 31 in particular, Job's words bear no trace of such an anticipated hostile reception. As Job speaks, he projects an audience that shares his values, trusts his word, commiserates with his ill-treatment, and can be persuaded by his self-representation. He speaks to the ideal listener. This orientation is one of the features that gives this section of the book its distinctive character and a measure of its rhetorical power.

The use of this rhetorical stance has novel consequences for the polyphonic book. The projection of the sense of an audience beyond the friends breaks open the closed frame of both the prose tale and the wisdom dialogue. It draws the reader more directly into this palpable but only implicitly identified audience. Undoubtedly, this feature facilitates the insertion of the Elihu speeches in chapters 32–37, for he, like the reader, is cast as a bystander who has been listening attentively to all that has been said (32:1–5). His unsympathetic response to Job's words, both in the wisdom dialogue and in the testimony, underscores Bakhtin's distinction between the "absolutely just responsive understanding" of the superaddressee and the unpredictable response of actual listeners. An examination of Elihu's response is the subject of the next chapter.

At this point, however, I want to begin the rhetorical analysis of chapters 29–31 with a look at Job's self-presentation. Here in chapters 29–31, more than in any other rendering of Job in the book, he is allowed to represent himself in terms of a highly specific social identity. Although calling Job the "richest man in the East" in the prose tale (1:3) has a certain function in terms of the dramatic action, it finally plays little role in the construction of value and character. As befits a didactic tale, the character transcends his particular description and functions as something of a universal or generic human.[12] Similarly, although critics have analyzed various clues that suggest the social location and presuppositions of the wisdom dialogue,[13] the dialogue itself makes little attempt to highlight these elements but rather seems to be unconscious of them. It scarcely tries to describe Job's suffering in terms of his social identity (see only 19:13–22). In this regard chapters 29–31 are radically different, for they articulate Job's testimony precisely by constructing a social portrait. They represent the issues of moral concern in Job's suffering as capable of examination only in relation to a lived social reality.

Although the social world that Job 29–31 describes is readily recognizable to anyone who has read biblical and ancient Near Eastern literature, we lack a commonly accepted term for identifying it. For lack of such, I will call it "village patriarchy." This is the social and moral world grounded in the kinship structures of the *šēbeṭ* or *maṭṭeh* (tribe), the *mišpāḥāh* (clan), and the *bêt 'āb* (father's house). It is patriarchal in that lineage is traced through the male line, and authority resides primarily with older male heads of households.[14] The term "village" is appropriate, since the social structure appears to have developed, at least in Israel, in the prestate period in a decentralized, nonurban context. The fundamental social units of village patriarchy are the household and the lineage. The social structures also inscribe nonkinship based forms of dependency and protection one could describe as patronage.[15] Kinship and patronage structure fundamental social relations, with the male heads of households also providing the basis for social organization at a higher level, for example, coming together as "elders at the gate" where legal transactions, disputes, and other matters of public interest could be resolved (Deut 21:19–20; 22:15; 25:7; Josh 20:4; Isa 29:21; 5:15; Ruth 4). Though this social and moral world comes to be in tension with the forms of social organization that develop during the period of state centralization and postexilic civic reorganization,[16] the functions of the *bêt 'āb* continue to be of fundamental importance. Moreover, the social formation of village patriarchy provides the basic categories for the moral imagination that serves as the horizon of meaning and value for urban as well as rural culture, for important aspects of royal ideology, and for religious conceptions and expression.[17]

The structure of Job's account of himself is provided by a carefully sequenced reference to sets of social relationships. Job begins, as one would expect in a patriarchal moral world, with a description of the domestic sphere, the household. The focal image is that of the tent graced with the blessing of God, embodied in the tableau of the patriarch surrounded by his children (29:2–6; cf. Psalms 127; 128). Next comes the social world of the village and the society of his peers. Here the physical setting is the city gate and plaza, and the social relations are with young men, elders, and nobles (29:7–11). Finally comes the context of the socially marginalized: the poor, the orphan, the dying, the widow, the blind, the lame, the needy, the stranger (29:12–17). What is satisfying about life and gives it moral value is expressed in terms of relations in these three social spheres.

An embedded trope further structures Job's account: the trope of spatial relationship. The role of spatial imagery as a sort of symbolic mapping is already suggested by the sequence of contexts that moves from inside to outside, from domestic tent to public gate. In other ways, too, spatial imagery is quite explicit in the text and fundamentally important to Job's moral imagination. His first image is of God as a lamp fixed over his head, by the light of which he can see to walk (29:3). Thus, the body serves as the central space in relation to which other objects, persons, and values are configured. As in Zophar's speech in chapter 11, imagery of the body is succeeded by that of the tent (29:4), for body and tent are metonymically related. Spatial imagery is even more explicit in the following verse, as Job depicts his children as circled round about him (*sĕbibôtay*; cf. Ps 128:3, where children are imaged as "around [*sābib*] your table").

Similarly, Job's entry into the city gate and plaza causes a reconfiguration of those present: Job sits, young men withdraw, elders rise and stand (29:8). Space is made for Job at the center. Space is made for Job in a metaphorical way as well. When he enters, all others fall silent, their hands covering their mouths (29:9–10). What the spatial imagery illustrates, both at the level of textual image and in the social drama of etiquette to which it refers, is the importance of hierarchy in this moral world. Where one is located and what physical posture one assumes is an enactment of one's place in the social order and of one's relation to the creation of social and moral meaning. Unquestionably, it is desirable to be at the center, to be capable of creating the space of deference, but those who surround also participate in creating and receiving value.

Hierarchy has a complex function in the moral world described by the text. When Job takes his place in the gate, the physical arrangement shows that honor is being paid to Job by his peers. Honor, however, is not some autonomous possession. It has a dynamic, transactional character. When Job speaks and acts, those who stand about assess him. As the text says, "When the ear heard, it acclaimed me, and when the eye saw, it testified for me" (29:11). Job's right to deference is dependent on the confirmation of the community that he does embody and enact its moral norms and values. This transaction reaffirms the shared values and ensures that even the highest-ranking members of society understand themselves as guided by and not superior to its moral norms. In return, Job's ability to articulate and enact the norms is seen as life giving. He chooses this image for himself: "My words dropped [like dew] upon them. They waited for me as for rain, opening their mouths as for the late rain" (29:22b-23).

What is the content of the moral norms Job represents, which bring expressions of approval from his peers? Job names the key words of virtue in 29:14 as "righteousness" (*ṣedeq*) and "just judgment" (*mišpāṭ*). So closely is his identity bound up with them that he describes them as his garments of honor. Terms of virtue may be difficult to define abstractly, but they are given clear content by illustration. The examples Job recounts in 29:12-17 consist entirely of images of intervention on behalf of those on the margins of the social order: deliverer of the poor and the orphan, eyes for the blind, feet for the lame, father to the needy, legal advocate for the stranger, rescuer of the victimized. Just as Job was bound with his peers in a social transaction that exchanged his sustaining words for their deference and approbation, so here, the strongest and the weakest in the social order also participate in an exchange. The powerful one gives his protection and intervention. What the powerful one receives is gratitude, which 29:13 describes as the blessing of the wretched and the song of the widow. This is no insignificant thing. Job's social identity, his very meaning, must be established in terms of his relationship with the poor and powerless. It is not just they who are dependent on him. He is, in a different way, also dependent on them.

The moral world that Job has described in chapter 29 is one in which honor and respect are among the highest goods. In this intensely social world, the silent deference of one's peers, their words of commendation, and the grateful blessings of the poor are the public expressions of that honor. The corresponding horror in such a world is to be mocked, shamed, and held in contempt. These are categories that logically imply each other. A society that rewards with honor punishes with shame and contempt.[18] That is precisely what Job speaks of in chapter 30. It is not his former peers, however, whom Job envisions as his mockers; nor is it the socially dependent whom he had previously assisted. Significantly, Job introduces another category of persons as his mockers, those who are themselves contemptible. Rhetorically, that is a powerful image of abjection: to be held in contempt by the contemptible. Although the primary purpose in depicting Job's mockers as the outcast rabble is to heighten the sense of his degradation, it may serve another function as well. If Job's appeal for judgment on his character in chapter 31 is directed to his peers, as I argue, then it is an element of rhetorical tact that Job represents his humiliating treatment as coming from those who have no real place in the social world, those who are least "like us."

More details of Job's social-moral world come into view as he describes what makes his mockers themselves contemptible: "But now, they laugh at me, those younger than I, whose fathers I would have disdained to put with my sheep dogs" (30:1). This is a most economical statement, for in the course of describing what is distressing about his present situation, Job turns his descriptive comment into a multilayered insult against his detractors and a reassertion of the values he holds as self-evident. His detractors violate the norms that govern relations between youth and age, but equally the norms that govern the hierarchical status of different lineages. Thus, Job expresses his own contempt by insulting the fathers of his young mockers. To take Job's comment as simply an assertion that he would not have hired their fathers as shepherds would be to miss the art of the insult, for Job's language also suggests that those men would not have been fit company for his dogs. When one considers what a strong term of contempt the word "dog" itself is, the insult becomes breathtaking.

Whether Job's following words refer to the sons or to the fathers, these persons are further stigmatized: "Wasted from want and starvation, they flee to a parched land, to the gloom of desolate wasteland. They pluck saltwort and wormwood; the roots of broom are their food" (30:3–4 NJPS).[19] Although characterized by abject poverty, it is not so much the poverty itself as social exclusion that marks them. But why are these wretched of the earth cast out? Are they criminal? Not according to the image of 30:5: "They are driven out from society; people shout at them as at a thief." It is their exclusion from society that causes them to be treated as criminal, not their criminality that leads to their exclusion. The concluding line of the description in 30:8 confirms this perception: "Persons of no name," they are "whipped out of the land."

The introduction of this category of the contemptible person completes the social-spatial map of Job's moral world. Its center is the household with its family circle. The next horizon is the civic society of the city gate and its council of elders and nobles. The margins of this social world are filled by the needy who depend on the benevolence and protection of the nobles and whose very dependence is necessary for defining what it means to be a noble in this society. The symbiotic relationship between these two groups makes it clear that the needy have a place within the protecting borders of the social world. But where on the social-spatial map is the place of the "people without a name"? Here one needs to take careful account of the way in which the description of nature is part of the construction of the social and moral world. Job's description of the "persons of no name" as occupying a desolate wasteland—in wadis and rocky ground, among scrub plants—locates them in the territory that lies outside of the sphere of the cultivated, in the desolate ground symbolically associated with divine punishment, with the chaotic, and even with the demonic (Isa 13:19–22; 34:8–15; Hos 2:3b; Zeph 2:13–15; Ps 107:33–34). They are the repressed and excluded element that defines and secures the boundary of Job's symbolic world.

Not surprisingly, Job thinks of his own radical change of status as a displacement, for his thinking is governed by the logic of his symbolic map. He has now become a "brother to jackals, a companion of ostriches" (30:29), animals traditionally associated with the places of desolation (Isa 13:21–22; 34:13b) and the place of exclusion where Job located the "persons whipped out of the land." Up to this point, although Job has contrasted the "months of old" with his present misery, he has not attended to the dynamics that can apparently so suddenly displace a revered and respected noble from the center of the social world to exclusion beyond its periphery. That social resentment would lurk in such a hierarchical society, one formed through the mechanisms of exclusion and contempt as much as by benevolence and honor, is scarcely surprising. But I am not concerned here to pursue a hermeneutics of suspicion in an attempt to identify the "real" mechanism, whether that be cast as some form of mimetic rivalry à la Girard[20] or a socioeconomic analysis.[21] My concern is with the rhetoric of the symbolic world and how it interprets such dynamics to itself.

As any number of references from the Psalms could attest, sudden misfortune of a calamitous nature could be read as divine abandonment or rejection, and as such, an invitation to rejection by the social community. So, here, Job perceives, and perceives correctly, that when the contemptible spit in his face, they do so as the instrument of the social order. They do so because they assume that God has already dishonored Job, making him vulnerable to their violence. In his first description of his subjection to the abuses of the rabble, Job begins and ends with explicit statements to the effect that God has "humiliated" him (30:11), and taken away his "honor" and "dignity" (30:15).[22] The intervening verses, which describe his suffering as attack by the rabble, exploit the image of a besieged city whose protective walls have been breached, allowing the chaotic rabble to pour in. Job explicitly describes God's treatment of him in terms of dishonor and contempt: "[God] throws me into the muck, and I have come to resemble dirt and ashes" (30:19).

The cultural world inscribed in Job's words not only supplied him with the means to articulate what made life satisfying and the images through which to convey its potential for misery. It also provided him with the culturally sanctioned means by which to seek restoration of his well-being, including his honor and his relationship with God. This mechanism, as the friends in the wisdom dialogue repeatedly pointed out, is the psalm of complaint or supplication. The patterns of relationships, the roles and motives that populate such psalms are strikingly similar to those that Job describes in relation to his social world. The world of psalms of complaint is filled with enemies and foes who insult, shame, and attack the psalmist (Pss 22:17–19; 31:12; 35:11–16; 59:2–8; 70:3–4). The religious relationships of the Psalms are also modeled on the social world and power dynamics that Job describes. Just as Job intervenes on behalf of the vulnerable and "breaks the jaws of the wrongdoer, wresting prey from his teeth"

(Job 29:17), so the psalmist sees in God the one who can overcome the power of the enemies (Pss 3:8; 12:4-6; 28:4). In response for such deliverance, God receives the psalmist's praises (Pss 22:23; 28:7; 35:18; 71:22-24), just as Job receives those of the one who was "perishing." In seeking redress, the psalmist appeals to God, often representing himself as "lowly and needy" (Pss 35:10; 69:30; 70:6; 86:1), just as Job was moved to action on behalf of such persons. In the psalms a further theme is taken up that is not developed explicitly in Job, namely, that the psalmist's honor is in some way tied up with God's, and that if God does not act, God's own honor and that of God's people may be jeopardized (Pss 22:8-9; 69:7-8; 71:10). Thus, the structure of relationships and motivations, the mutual transactions of power and honor, provide an important basis for the religious language of psalms.

The majority of psalms that invoke such language depict God as the protector and express confidence that God will fulfill the responsibilities that inhere in that role (Pss 22:4-6, 10-12; 71:4-6; 140:7-9, 12-13). Yet psalmists can also speak of God's neglect, as they plead for attention and redress (Pss 22:2; 43:2; 77:8-10). Such complaints are implicitly based on and legitimated by the assumed social bond with its asymmetrical but mutual obligations. Though it is rarer, God can be pictured as angry at the psalmist, so that God's own violent rejection of the petitioner is correlated with the psalmist's exposure to the violence of others (Pss 38:2, 12-13; 88:7-9; 143:2-3; cf. 71:10-11). Though this motif is much stronger in communal psalms of complaint, it does occur as a motif of the individual laments and is perhaps most strongly expressed in Jeremiah's complaint in 20:7-13. The psalmist may either admit guilt or protest innocence, but in the end the resolution is sought through a reaffirmation of the patronage relationship[23] and the confidence that social roles and expectations will be fulfilled.

Job briefly invokes the language of complaint psalmody when he says, "I cry out to you, but you do not answer me" (30:20a), words that frequently occur in such psalms (e.g., Pss 22:2-3; 28:1; 88:15). But Job's words do not develop into a psalm of supplication. Why the resources of such prayer are found wanting is not entirely clear. Of course, one could say that at the level of the design of the book, the author wishes to explore something other than the familiar world of complaint psalmody. But at the level of the motivation of the character Job, the question requires a different sort of answer.

First of all, Job's words suggest that he considers God not merely to have neglected or abused him, issues that are regularly taken up in complaint psalms, but to have broken the social bond that underlies the relationship upon which complaint psalmody depends. In verse 21 Job says that God has become "cruel" to him and "persecutes" him. The term 'akzār is particularly resonant, for it is most frequently used to describe those who are not linked by social bonds of obligation to the speaker and who are therefore expected to be cruel (military foes from the far reaches of the earth in Jer 6:23 and 50:42, contrasted with "allies" and "lovers" in Jer 30:14). In wisdom literature the cruel are associated both with dangerous outsiders (Prov 5:9, parallel to *'ăḥērîm*) and with the wicked who are a threat to the social order (Prov 11:17; 12:10). Elsewhere the term is used to suggest an antisocial quality in persons so extreme as to render them no longer human but rather animallike, illustrated by the proverbial venom of snakes (Deut 32:33) or the ostrich's lack of elementary bonds of kinship (Lam 4:3). One cannot approach the *'akzār* as one would one's protector, however neglectful. Secondly, but more importantly, Job has invested so much in his presentation of himself in terms of his nobility and status in the community that it would be difficult, psychologically and rhetorically, for him now to take up the stance of the "poor and needy" (Ps 70:6a), petitioning his divine patron for the restoration of his honor and his reintegration into the community.

To be sure, Job cannot in fact do without a reconciliation with God. But for the reasons stated this reconciliation cannot be negotiated directly by means of a psalm of supplication. What other resources does he have? His persuasion of God must be indirect, an implicit concomitant of his persuasion of his peers. Thus, the way is open for Job to take up the position of the man of honor speaking to other men of honor rather than that of the lowly client of a powerful patron, as inscribed in the psalm of supplication. In the verses immediately following (30:24–26), as Job turns back from second-person address to God to address again his human peers, he subtly shifts them into the position of judging between himself and God. He begins by articulating a general moral principle, one he clearly assumes they take for granted. Verse 24 is, unfortunately, difficult and textually corrupt, but its basic gist is clear enough. Whether one retains the vivid metaphor of the person as a "ruin" (*'iy*, so NJPS) or emends to "the needy" (*'ānî*, so NRSV), the idiom "to send the hand against" clearly describes a hostile act.[24] Thus, the line would read either "one does not strike at a ruin," or "one does not turn his hand against the needy." The second half of the line, too corrupt for translation, does include the terms "cry out" (a word Job had used of himself in v. 20) and "in his utter destruction." It thus seems to be in some sense complementary to the first half of the line. Implicitly, God is guilty of having violated this norm, since he has turned his hand against the defenseless Job. Having stated the principle of conduct, however, Job chooses not to make explicit this connection; nor does he return immediately to his complaint. Instead, he indicates his own embodiment of the proper moral stance: "Did I not weep for the one whose day was hard; did my soul not grieve for the poor?" (30:25). Thus, the issue is not framed as a complaint against God for mistreatment but rather as an issue of who properly embodies the social norms— Job or God. In the final verse of his section, when Job turns back to his own situation, he still does not represent himself as a "ruin" or "needy" person. Rather, he continues his self-representation as an upholder of the moral order and casts the issue in terms of the failure of the reciprocal bonds and transactions that should sustain the social and moral world Job had described in chapters 29–30: "Yet when I looked for good, evil came; and when I waited for light, gloom came" (30:26). Both God and his fellows appear to be included in this oblique accusation.

The concluding verses of chapter 30 resume Job's account of his misery in terms drawn in part from the lament tradition. These words are not, however, addressed to God. Instead, as Job says, "I stand in the assembly and cry out" (30:28b). Yet there, too, his place is insecure and his voice so far unheeded, for he goes on to say, "I have become a brother of jackals, a companion to ostriches," the figures who inhabit the wasteland beyond the bounds of the social order (30:29). In his final speech in chapter 31, Job must achieve his own rehabilitation with this community. To do so he must also persuade his audience that God would make the same judgment that they are asked to make about him, for the whole social order, including its divine member, must affirm him. In this manner, Job undertakes to persuade God as well. Job's speech to the assembly thus creates something of a mirror image of the communicative situation usually assumed for psalms of supplication and thanksgiving in Israelite society. Those psalms were addressed to God, but by being "overheard" by the community, they also played a role in reversing social marginalization. Here Job addresses the assembly but evidently intends for God to overhear and reverse God's apparent rejection of Job.

Now one is in a better position to appreciate what sort of an action with words Job attempts in chapter 31. Job's rhetorical task focuses on the issue of ethos. He must construct his character through his speech. For this purpose the genre of the oath of innocence serves particularly well, since it pledges the well-being and even the life of the speaker as surety for the truth of what is claimed. Following an initial assertion (vv. 1–4), the oaths Job makes are of two forms. The more frequent is the abbreviated form, "If I have done X . . . ," which leaves the consequences unspecified and thus functions as the equivalent of an assertion of innocence: "I have not done X." Job uses this form some ten times. The seriousness of the oath, however, is highlighted by the three instances in which Job uses the complete form: "If I have done X, may Y happen to me." Moreover, the oath's association with legal speech also lends gravity to his utterance. To be sure, although Job uses the form of an oath, his words are not performative in the strict sense. Whereas his rhetoric is forensic in that he is asking for a judgment on himself from his audience, this is not a legal court, nor is the testimony about a legal matter. As is often noted, the virtues Job claims for himself are largely not those susceptible to the reach of law.[25] Even his wish for a hearing in verses 35–37, which invokes the most distinctively legal imagery in the chapter, functions as a rhetorical flourish, not as the invocation of an actual process.[26] Through the use of these speech forms, however, Job constructs a character of utter sincerity, one whose complete self-certainty about his moral status invites affirmation from his audience.

The oath has certain other rhetorical advantages. For one, as Job swears to different kinds of conduct, it allows Job to rehearse with his audience the virtues and values they mutually endorse and so to present himself persuasively as "one of us." Moreover, it is an instrument of great tact. By keeping the focus of the audience upon the judgment to be rendered on his own character, the oath allows Job to negotiate his grievance against God and his community in a way that results in the preservation of the honor of all parties rather than the honoring of one at the expense of the shaming of the other. In modern terms, it allows Job to frame things as a win/win situation rather than a win/lose one. To see how both of these things are rhetorically accomplished, it is necessary to look more closely at the content of the oaths and the portrait of honor they construct.

The speech has been analyzed variously, as commentators have attempted to identify a series of ten, twelve, or fourteen claims.[27] Whatever the merits of these formal analyses, considered topically, there are five groups of oaths, interrupted by Job's wish for a hearing in verses 35-37. The topics covered include sexual ethics and general morality (vv. 1-12), justice and social obligation (vv. 13-23), ultimate allegiance (vv. 24-28), social relations (vv. 29-34), and land ethics (vv. 38-40). The moral world is thus recognizably the same as that described in chapters 29 and 30, with its strong concern for the network of social relationships and the obligations and prohibitions that sustain those relations. As in the preceding account, this is a world structured according to male peer relations (the fathers and husbands whose rights are respected in the code of sexual ethics) and hierarchical relations (the paternalistic obligations one has toward servants, the poor, the orphan, the widow, the stranger, the land and its tenant farmers). Loyalty, up and down and across, is the primary social bond. The majority of the oaths, however, are preoccupied with the problem of the ethics of power in relationships of inequality (see esp. 31:13-23, 31-32, 38-40). Since such inequalities offered many opportunities for self-interested but socially destructive actions, the norms that required one not to use power abusively but protectively were a vital part of the moral fabric of the culture. The competitive pressures of an agonistic, honor-based society also required careful modulation, lest the fear of shame or the pleasure of seeing another's downfall become excessive. Thus, Job represents himself as one both willing to own his transgressions publicly, despite the temptation to concealment, and his own self-control in relation to triumphing in the misfortune of his rivals (31:29-30, 33-34).

Even this brief account makes clear the content of the moral order within which Job stakes his claim to honor. Job's language is calculated to appeal to those who recognize themselves and their values within it. But this summary does not completely illumine the rhetorical strategy by which Job reestablishes himself within his community and his relationship with God. The key to the rhetoric is the way in which Job inscribes and reinscribes God in this moral world. At the same time that Job is constructing his own ethos, he is simultaneously constructing the ethos of God. Again and again, Job warrants his own behavior in relation to the expectations and judgments of God, who is the source and sustainer of this moral world. He acknowledges the propriety of God's bringing ruin and disaster upon wrongdoers (vv. 3, 23) and invokes God as the one with every right and obligation to judge him (vv. 2, 4, 6). He represents God as protector of the rights of the vulnerable, the one who would confront Job for abuses against them (vv. 14-15), and he reaffirms his undivided loyalty to God, untainted by false trust in wealth or enticement by astral worship (vv. 24-28). In Job's construction, God functions in a thoroughly Durkheimian way as the social and moral order writ large.

The resources brought into play by this rhetorical approach can be grasped better if they are compared with those used in Job's speeches in the wisdom dialogue. Job's situation is the same in both contexts. He is caught in the utterly contradictory experience of a man of righteousness and honor who is subject to the physical, material, and social consequences normally associated with the punishment of the wicked. The figure of Job constructed in the wisdom dialogue adopts a rhetorical strategy that highlights these contradictions, swearing to his integrity in the name of the God who has "denied me justice" (27:2). The Job of the testimony adopts a very different rhetorical strategy, one that preemptively overcomes the contradiction by depicting God as utterly at one with the normative social order. In contrast to the depictions of God in other parts of the book, there is virtually no alterity between the divine and the human in this account. The brilliance of this rhetorical stance is that the God Job represents in his oath *could not but* declare Job to be righteous and so confirm his honor. I do not mean to suggest that Job's rhetoric is to be read as anything other than simple sincerity. This is not the Job of the dialogues whose capacity for setting and springing traps was a hallmark of his speech. The persona of Job constructed in chapters 29-31 is deeply sincere and utterly committed to the moral world that has made him. In this world there can be no contradiction in reality, only a wrong to be righted. Job is in possession of a language that knows how to refuse tragedy.

But how is Job's honor to be restored without shaming God? Though in chapter 30 Job had invoked complaint language to express his sense that God was responsible for the violence he suffers, in chapter 31 Job does not turn this complaint into a legal accusation against God, as the Job of the dialogues does (16:18-21; 19:6-7, 23-25).[28] Instead, he puts himself on trial in the rhetorical, though not the strictly legal sense. Job does make it clear that God is the one who has wrongly accused him (vv. 35-37), but the delicacy of the situation is to resolve the false accusation in a way that enhances the honor of both. Just as the model for the relationship with God in the psalm of complaint is to be found in the social relations of the dependent crying out to a social protector, so the relationship Job is exploratively negotiating has also to be found in the social relations he has described.

Ultimately, Job is able to imagine approaching his God proudly and with confidence, ready to give "an account of his steps," even though this means exposing God's wrongful judgment of him, because he has already included within his speech an analogy to this encounter, specifically in his description of his own dealings with his servants: "I never refused justice to my male or female slaves, when they brought a grievance against me, for what should I do when El confronted me or what should I answer him when he made inquiry?" (vv. 13–14). Here is the model that substitutes for the unusable prayer of supplication, yet that operates from within the same basic moral world of social relationships and obligations. What God requires of Job is what Job expects of God. That it would not be a matter of shame is evident in the fact that Job himself uses this example as evidence of his own honorableness. The same dynamics are at work in the narrative account of Tamar and Judah in Genesis 38. When Judah had wrongly accused Tamar of adultery and ordered her death, she showed him the tokens by which he recognized himself as the one who had unknowingly impregnated her. Though Judah had been represented in the story as anything but an honorable man, his public statement, "She is more in the right than I" (Gen 38:26), is an act of honor and is presented as such in the narrative. Indeed, in the context of the larger story, this episode serves as the redemptive moment that marks the transition of Judah's character from one of moral ambivalence to the moral leadership that enables him to resolve Joseph's hesitancy to reconcile with his brothers (Gen 44:18–34).

Job, of course, does not really expect God to appear and declare him "more in the right" than God, as the syntax of verses 35–37 indicates (*mî yittēn*, "O that"). But in important respects God's appearance is not even necessary. By employing the resources of his inherited moral language in a novel way, Job has effectively rehabilitated himself. It is not my claim, nor is there any evidence, that what Job does here in his speech of testimony was actually a social practice. The speech is simply a literary device, a fictive innovation of the author. But one could imagine how such a speech might function in a social context. After such a declaration, Job's peers might well conclude that Job had made the case for his own righteousness, indeed, as one that God himself would recognize, and so put an end to the social ostracism and shaming of Job. Thus, the social dimensions of his calamity would have been overcome in ways comparable to the capacity of religious ritual to reintegrate the suppliant into the community. On the narrative level, one could also imagine Job's speech serving as the mechanism by which the story could find resolution. Even without a theophany, one might imagine a version of the prose conclusion following

Job's speech. The restoration of Job's fortunes would itself serve as a tacit indication of Job's vindication by God, an acceptance of Job's own self-declaration and an acceptance of the divine image and role constructed in Job's speech.

One can easily be drawn under the spell of Job's powerful rhetoric in these chapters. Yet what gives them such power is in part the intense monologic quality of the discourse, which is, if anything, even more strongly marked than that of the prose tale. This imperviousness to other perspectives and possibilities is in part what gives Job his supreme confidence not only about his own self-judgment but also about his ability to persuade others, including God, if they will but give him a hearing. There can be but one truth, and Job is in possession of it. The source of the power of Job's discourse is also the source of its deep flaw—the denial of the possibility of any other perspective except its own. For readers whose own moral worlds are constructed quite differently than Job's, it is easy to point out the dark undersides of the values he so prizes: the misogyny that underlies his sexual ethics and the necessary structural inequalities that fund the paternalistic social system. Not all of the problematic aspects of Job's representation of his moral world require the perspective of great temporal and cultural distance in order to become visible, however. The arrogance with which Job is regularly charged in modern commentaries might also elicit comment from ancient readers, for Israelite tradition was well aware of the ambivalence of pride in an honor-based society and rigorously policed the appearance of excess. Indeed, this is a significant part of Elihu's objection to the self-presentation of Job in both the dialogue and testimony.

From the perspective of the structure of the book as a whole, however, Job's representation of God as the normative social order writ large is the most important of his monologic claims. Job's depiction can find warrant in much of Israelite theological tradition that insists on the fundamental continuity between the moral nature of God and the moral values of its own community (see, e.g., Leviticus 19; Psalm 72). Yet Job "selects and perfects," as Kenneth Burke would say, only one aspect of a much richer repertoire of theological assertions about the complex patterns of continuity and alterity that exist between the divine and the human. Various voices in Israelite tradition also insisted on the radical otherness of God, expressed above all in its strongly aniconic tradition (e.g., Deut 4:15-19) and in the priestly-prophetic reflections on the *kābôd* of God (e.g., Isaiah 6; Ezekiel 1). The tensions and potential conflicts between these two commitments are largely allowed to remain unexamined in Israelite literature, with the notable exception of Job's own speeches in the wisdom dialogue. The dialogic and polyphonic commitments of the book of Job as a whole, however, ensure that monologic perspectives will not be allowed to speak unchallenged. As with the case of the prose tale, the presence of such a powerfully integrative and monologic discourse as Job produces in chapters 29-31 requires a sharp and shocking clash with another radically different discourse based on radically different assumptions about the world. Such will be provided above all by the theophany, which challenges the Durkheimian image of God in Job's testimony with one more evocative of Rudolf Otto. In doing so it creates a dramatic confrontation of incompatible moral worlds and reintroduces the tragic as a possibility. But such a polar confrontation, if it were the design of the book originally, has now been itself disrupted by the presence of Elihu, the reader who understood all too well that a polyphonic book invites its readers to become a part of the dispute itself.

8

The Dissatisfied Reader

Elihu and the Historicity of the Moral Imagination

A book is interrupted discourse catching up with its own breaks. But books
have their fate; they belong to a world they do not include, but recognize by
being written and printed, and by being prefaced and getting themselves
preceded with forewords. They are interrupted, and call for other books and
in the end are interpreted in a saying distinct from the said.

Emmanuel Levinas, *Otherwise Than Being*

We read to usurp.

Harold Bloom, *Agon*

What to do with Elihu? This problem bedevils every interpretation of the book
of Job. Redaction critics who consider his speeches to be secondary additions
have generally reflected their view of his marginal significance by giving the
chapters only cursory treatment, though few have gone so far as J. C. L. Gibson
and actually relegated treatment of Elihu to an appendix![1] As striking as the
brevity of comment is its tone. Although Elihu has had a few defenders (more
so in the nineteenth than in the twentieth century), the majority of critics are
hostile to him, often treating him as an object of ridicule. Why Elihu has attracted such vehement reaction is not entirely clear. Perhaps it is readerly frustration at having the structure of anticipation and fulfillment in Job's final speech
and God's reply interrupted. Thus, Elihu appears as someone who has defaced
a cultural monument with his graffiti and forever destroyed a part of the observer's
satisfaction. But hostile critics also justify their irritation in terms of the self-
presentation of Elihu and the apparent discrepancy between what he promises
and what he delivers. Elihu justifies his intrusion (at length) by criticizing the
failure of the friends to answer Job effectively and promising different and more
effective arguments. When modern critics find little that is new or more persuasive in Elihu's speeches, they treat him to the ridicule he appears to have invited. Finally, there is something of a display of manipulative power in the way
the Elihu speeches have been inserted into the book. Though he invites Job to
reply (33:32–33), the author of the Elihu speeches has no interest whatsoever

in imagining counterarguments.[2] Thus, Job's silences between Elihu's speeches are made to appear as defeated silences. Similarly, the anticipation of the rhetoric of the divine speeches at the close of Elihu's seems to align him opportunistically with the voice of God.

One might think that recent attempts to argue for the originality of the Elihu speeches as part of the primary design of the book, as in the commentaries of Habel and Janzen, would indicate a deeper interest in these chapters. In Habel's reading, for instance, Elihu is a bystander drawn into the quarrel he has overheard, a character who recognizes that the friends have not appreciated and responded to the legal metaphor within which Job has cast his complaint. Since it would be improper for God to answer the arrogant Job in a human court, the task falls to him.[3] Yet these understandings of the book almost necessitate that Elihu be cast as a "self-consuming artefact," a voice that subverts itself and so makes way for the divine speeches.[4] Thus, Elihu is again reduced to an object of disdain, though as one intentionally designed that way by the author rather than one who betrays himself unwittingly.

There is much that is appealing in these negative treatments of Elihu, not the least being the genuine passion with which the critics respond to him. Nevertheless, something worthwhile may get lost in the rush to dispatch Elihu. To be clear, I am certainly not going to argue for a rehabilitation of Elihu as the moral center of the book. No more than most of my modern colleagues do I find his arguments compelling. But I want to drop back from the temptation of making a visceral response to Elihu and to view him with a more dispassionate and deliberately generous curiosity. Whether or not I agree with this character, what does he understand himself to be doing? On what grounds might he perceive his words to be what he says they are—a genuine contribution to and enrichment of the dialogue? Is it possible to delineate the differences between his moral imagination and that of the other characters?

Before proceeding further, I need to make clear my position on the issue of Elihu's status in the composition. Though my own critical framework for reading the book of Job as polyphonic text could accommodate either an analysis of the Elihu speeches as original or as secondary, I remain persuaded by the classic arguments for the secondary nature of the Elihu speeches.[5] These arguments are persuasive on historical-critical grounds, but they also have the benefit of opening up the text to interpretive issues much richer and more nuanced than those available on the assumption that the Elihu speeches are part of the original design. Above all, this perspective introduces a diachronic element into the book, blurring the boundary between text and reception by incorporating within its bounds what Francis Andersen called its own "first commentary."[6] A book that was "fixed," that had become a "Said," now finds itself interrupted by a voice it did not know, one that upsets its symmetry and serves to this day as an irritant. Though we do not know how much time elapsed between the composition of the book of Job and the introduction of the Elihu speeches, there is enough, as I will argue later, to produce a small but discernible gap between the culture of moral argumentation presumed by the main part of the book and that of Elihu.

The relationship between Elihu the character and the author of the Elihu speeches is a teasing one, as is the way this author/character situates himself in relation to the rest of the book. In siding with the traditional historical-critical arguments, my governing assumption is that Elihu is not simply another character; he is a reader of the book of Job, one who literally writes himself into the text. Though commentators have often puzzled over what symbolic significance the names in his extended genealogy might have, it is not impossible that this is simply the real name of an actual reader. After all, Jesus son of Eleazar son of Sirach of Jerusalem writes his own name in his wisdom teaching. However that may be, even if the name is that of the actual author, the Elihu figure is fictionalized into the story. He presents himself as one who has been listening and who now inserts himself into the conversation. Yet even as "Elihu's" status as reader is masked by this fiction, it is simultaneously disclosed by certain ways in which his speeches differ from those of Job and the friends. In the wisdom dialogue, although the participants acknowledge and reply to each other's arguments from time to time, only Elihu actually quotes from the text of the speeches in the dialogue (cf. 33:9–11 with 13:24, 27, and 34:5 with 27:2a). Moreover, even though he cannot make direct reference to the divine speeches that follow, Elihu nevertheless clearly shows an awareness of them and skillfully anticipates aspects of their themes, imagery, and style. Thus, even in becoming a character in the book, the author of the Elihu speeches retains his transcendental position as reader.

In certain ways, Elihu represents the position of all readers, most significantly through his belatedness. The reader always comes to a conversation that has begun without him and yet at which he finds himself present, a conversation that engages him and yet has no place for him. Hence the need to interrupt, if not by such direct means, then by interpretive commentary or criticism. In Elihu's self-introduction, belatedness is indirectly alluded to in two tropes by which the character represents himself and his relationship to the other speakers: his youth and his astonishment that the friends have no more to say, while he himself is like an unvented wineskin.

Reference to Elihu's youth and its relation to his reticence appears first in verse 5 of the prose introduction and becomes the focal point of his first speech (32:6–22). In a provocative argument, Bruce Zuckerman maintains that this motif is not simply a device to explain the belated entry of the character Elihu into the conversation but is a trope by which the Elihu author describes his temporal and cultural relation to the preexisting book: "The Elihu-author makes a prominent point of his protagonist's youth in order to emphasize that his literary work speaks for a later generation, before whom the original Poem of Job already looms as an awesome literary monument."[7] I do not agree with Zuckerman's particular interpretation of the development of the book (the product of various redactions produced by "sincere misunderstanding" of the preceding Joban texts) or with specifics of his interpretation of Elihu. For Zuckerman, Elihu reflects a kind of postexilic survivor's guilt, an interpretation I think is anachronistic and not sufficiently grounded in the details of Elihu's speeches. Nevertheless, I do find Zuckerman insightful in recognizing in the depiction of Elihu not simply an agonistic relationship with a powerful text in the abstract but an agonistic relationship made necessary by changing historical and cultural circumstances. Whether or not we can locate Elihu's context with any specificity remains to be seen, but that he himself experiences a distance from the moral world of the dialogue is evident in the images with which he expresses his anger and frustration, in particular his images concerning speech itself.

The central image Elihu uses to express his bewilderment and consequent anger with the friends is that of the depletion and renewal of speech. The prose introduction begins with the notice that "these three men ceased answering Job" (32:1a) and concludes by saying that "when Elihu saw that there was no answer in the mouth of the three men, he became angry" (32:5). Though they have talked extensively, in Elihu's opinion they have stopped too soon, without saying what is most necessary. Elihu declares that the three are psychically "shattered," unable to answer any further, for "words have left them" as they "stand stopped" with "nothing further to say" (32:15–16). Elihu even seems to puzzle over the design of the book, considering whether to attribute some rhetorical strategy to the perplexing refusal of the friends to say a decisive word. "Do not say, 'We have found the wise course. Let El refute him, not a human'" (32:13). To Elihu such a stance is not only foolish but also unnecessary, for in contrast to the depletion of speech in the friends, he himself is "filled with words" (32:18a). Though his image of himself as an unvented wineskin about to burst with the fermentation of new wine (i.e., words) is often made an object of ridicule by modern commentators, such trivializing does credit neither to Elihu nor to the interpreter.

What Elihu touches on here, without being fully aware of it, is the issue of the exhaustion and renewal of human discourse. How is it that human culture never finishes with what it has to say about perennial issues of existence? There are, to be sure, moments of pause, when it seems that everything that can be said has been said, but those moments do not last. The inexhaustible source of human discourse lies in the fundamentally perspectival nature of claims to truth, what Kenneth Burke calls its "contexts of situation."[8] A stalled conversation is reinvigorated by someone eccentric to the original discourse. In recent years we have become increasingly aware of the invigorating potential of the eccentric speech of persons differentiated by gender, ethnicity, social class, and so forth.

But even if participants were indistinguishable on those grounds, the sheer historicity of human existence would suffice to renew speech.

For Elihu's generation the moral world has tilted, perhaps ever so slightly, on its axis. That tilt, however, is sufficient for moral and religious issues to be configured differently and to require the words that Elihu so urgently wishes to speak. The modern interpretive difficulty is that the axis of our own moral world has tilted considerably more, so that it is hard to measure and appreciate what appear to us extremely subtle differences between Elihu and the Joban dialogue. But if we take Elihu at his word, as I think we should, then we may come to appreciate the fine grain of moral difference as it develops within a certain intellectual tradition in the early to middle Second Temple period.

Critic Harold Bloom helps to put in perspective one other critical factor in the situation of a reader like Elihu. In *Agon: Towards a Theory of Revisionism*, Bloom argues programmatically for what is simply the historicity of interpretation, what he calls the belatedness of all reading. As Bloom describes it, every act of interpretation performs a "swerve," such that even what appear to be the same words are not in fact the same but on their way to different meanings.[9] But the act itself is what intrigues Bloom, who argues that "interpretation is implicitly hierarchical, and cannot proceed without a usurpation of authority."[10] This necessary but culturally uncomfortable usurpation of authority is what Elihu negotiates in chapter 32.

Before turning to see how Elihu performs this usurpation, however, it is important to ask if it is possible to know the specific cultural and historical context within which Elihu's moral imagination is framed. Unfortunately, recent treatments of the date and provenance of the Elihu speeches only underscore how little hard evidence there is. A terminus *ad quem* is provided by the appearance of the Elihu speeches in a manuscript of Job in the Dead Sea Scrolls (4QJob[a], probably first century B.C.E.). Avi Hurvitz's arguments for an exilic or early postexilic date for the linguistic profile of the prose tale provides a terminus *a quo*,[11] if one agrees that the Elihu speeches postdate the book of Job as a whole and not simply the poetic dialogue (as Zuckerman assumes).[12] A more specific date might be argued for the Elihu speeches on the basis of their own linguistic profile, especially the presence of Aramaisms. Although the significance of this evidence has been long debated,[13] it suggests that the Elihu speeches are probably the latest of the wisdom writings in the Hebrew Bible. H.-M. Wahl's recent study attempts to locate Elihu's ideas and assumptions in relation to those of Qoheleth, Ben Sira, and other early Hellenistic literature and leads him to suggest a third century B.C.E. date.[14] Although the points of comparison I will make below differ from those Wahl identifies, I, too, find Ben Sira, along with Daniel 1–6, to be important for clarifying the intellectual location of Elihu's speeches, if not his absolute date. Yet it is essential to remember that ideas and the imaginative patterns that carry them neither change abruptly nor uniformly in a culture. Although I suspect that a late Persian or early Hellenistic date for the Elihu speeches is probably correct, there is no way of knowing for certain. In what follows, the task is to let the Elihu speeches define for themselves the difference between their own moral imagination and that of the dialogues, while seeking for similar genres, topoi, and motifs in the literature of the middle Second Temple period. These comparisons, while suggestive, do not amount to hard evidence for a date or even for the relative dates of the various compositions.

Elihu as Wise Youth (Chapter 32)

Let us begin then with the way in which Elihu struggles to justify his "usurpation of authority." Though Zuckerman is probably correct that the depiction of Elihu as "younger" is a trope that figures the relation between the temporal belatedness of the Elihu author and the authority of an imposing text, the trope has to have cultural currency if it is to work. Elihu draws on several cultural commonplaces, some traditional, some perhaps more recent, in making his case. The deference that youth owes to age and the presumption that age correlates with superior wisdom are both principles already well established in the dialogues (12:12; 15:10; 29:8; 30:1) and indeed in the culture in general (e.g., Sir 32:7–9). Thus, it is the appropriate starting point for Elihu's self-presentation. His remark "I am young in years" is on one level simply a conventional self-deprecating comment, an element of the rhetoric of politeness. Yet it is the sort of description that often occurs in narratives concerning the choice of an exceptional leader, for instance Gideon (Judg 6:15), David (1 Sam 16:11), and Jeremiah (Jer 1:6). In the call schemas it is a conventional reply, yet it serves as a foil for the aptness of the divine choice in defiance of cultural norms. But though there may be a distant echo of such paradigms, they are not the primary basis of Elihu's argument.

The crux of Elihu's justification is contained between the inclusio of two parallel but opposite phrases in 32:6b ("I was afraid to tell you what I know") and 32:10b ("I will tell you what I know; I myself"). Cleverly, Elihu represents his argument as the *internal* argument he had to negotiate in order to convince himself of the legitimacy of his speaking, even though the actual audiences to be persuaded are, on the literary level, the three friends and, on the pragmatic level, the readers of the post-Elihu book. His argumentation takes the form of comparing axiom with axiom. He begins with the shared assumption that wisdom belongs to the aged ("I said, 'Let age speak, and let many years teach wisdom,'" 32:7). But that axiom is countered by another, which also has traditional currency, that the spirit of God gives insight ("But there is a spirit in a person, the breath of Shaddai which grants understanding," 32:8; cf. Gen 41:48; Exod 31:3; Num 11:26–30; 27:18; and particularly Isa 11:2).[15] Armed with this second axiom, Elihu can then argue that it is not age (alone) that is the source of wisdom (32:9). His politely unstated additional premise is that he is one who possesses just such divine spirit. In this way Elihu can move persuasively from his initial stance of deferential silence to the claim to an authority that commands a hearing: "Therefore I said, 'Listen to me; I will tell what I know; I myself'" (32:10).

Elihu's sense of the origin of his wisdom is similar to that of Ben Sira, who also speaks of "the spirit of understanding" that enables the sage to "pour forth words of wisdom of his own" since "the Lord will direct his counsel and knowledge, as he meditates on his mysteries" (Sir 39:6–7; NRSV).[16] Ernst Haag sees Elihu's self-presentation as also similar to that of the inspired scribal sage modeled in the Daniel narratives.[17] Thus, Elihu seems to differentiate himself from tradition by a new sense of a quasi-prophetic understanding of the source of his insight. The notion of the spirit of God as means of special understanding becomes a commonplace in Qumran literature (e.g., 1QH^a IV, 17; VI, 8–13; 1QS V, 20–24). But Elihu's coupling of the claim to insight and his insistence on his youth suggest that he is representing himself according to the cultural image of the youth whose God-given insight permits him to succeed where older and presumably wiser authorities have failed (see Joseph in Genesis 41 or Daniel and his three friends in Dan 1:17–20; 2:10–23). Although the youth of Joseph and Daniel is a feature of the stories, it is not particularly emphasized by explicit contrast with the age of other figures of supposed wisdom. Strikingly, Psalm 119:98–100 does foreground such a contrast. There the speaker attributes to his constant study of God's *miṣwôt*, *ʿēdôt*, and *piqqûdîm* an insight that exceeds that of his teacher and the elders, as well as his opponents. To be sure, this verse is an example of hyperbolic rhetoric. Yet it depends for its meaningfulness upon the image of the exceptional youth of precocious learning and insight. This contrast between youth and age is most sharply drawn in the LXX version of Susanna, as the clever youth Daniel foils the plot of the wicked elders. There the motif of insight given through God's spirit is explicit (the "Lord's angel [following orders] gave an insightful spirit to a young man named Daniel," v. 45).[18] Opinions differ over whether or not the LXX is attempting to make a general polemic against the leadership of an older generation,[19] but in either case the narrative does problematize the assumption of authority and truth that tradition associated with age: "Now don't focus on the fact that these are elders, saying, 'Surely they wouldn't lie'" (v. 51). By contrast, true wisdom and leadership is exercised by the inspired youth, Daniel. That this is not a tangential issue but a significant part of the story's agenda is made clear by the "moral" stated explicitly at the end: "Therefore youths are the beloved of Jacob because of their integrity. . . . For if the youths live reverently, a spirit of understanding and insight will be in them for ever" (v. 62).

My intention is not to suggest a specific line of influence between Elihu and any of these particular passages from the late Persian and Hellenistic periods.

But the presence of several different, apparently unrelated uses of a similar motif suggests that the image of the inspired youth who bests his elders was becoming something of a cultural type in the moral imagination of Judaism at this period and was available to be invoked for a variety of purposes. This image is the one by which Elihu represents himself to the reader of Job.

Elihu's Moral Imagination

If one is willing to give provisional credence to Elihu's claim that his arguments will not be those of the friends, in what way does he frame them differently? What is distinctive about his moral imagination? Critics have often been frustrated by these issues because the inquiry has been cast too narrowly as a quest for propositional differences only and because they have set the standards for novelty very high. Yet what gives distinctiveness to moral argument is not only propositional difference. Differences may also arise from a reframing of what counts as relevant, or a shift in the perspective from which an issue is examined, or a change in the way temporality is represented. There may be shifts in the metaphors or analogies used to construct an argument or a change in the genres by which the argument is carried out. When Elihu's speeches are examined not only for propositional content but also for shifts in metaphor, genre, temporality, and framing, one can begin to see the outlines of a moral imagination that is in significant ways different from that of the friends. This moral imagination is produced by means of Elihu's close reading of and interaction with the existing book of Job, as it is brought into conversation with his own cultural frameworks, which I take to be a product of the late Persian–early Hellenistic period.

In what follows I want to examine and engage two of the common suggestions concerning what constitutes Elihu's distinctive contribution (his appropriation of Job's forensic metaphor and his argument for redemptive suffering) and to suggest two others that have not been remarked (the similarities between his imagery and the construction of time in the protoapocalyptic narratives of Daniel 1–6, and his use of a particular wisdom genre otherwise known only from Sirach). These examples by no means exhaust what could be said about Elihu, but they will suffice to suggest how his moral imagination does indeed differ from that of the other voices in the book.

Elihu and the Forensic Metaphor (Chapters 33 and 35)

Building on the work of Heinz Richter and Sylvia Scholnick, Norman Habel has argued that Elihu, alone among the friends of Job, recognizes and responds to the legal framing of Job's argument, specifically his request for an arbiter or judge, a *môki'aḥ* (9:33; 16:21) or *šōmēaʿ* (31:35): "But no one was forthcoming. Job's friends on earth and his witnesses in heaven (16:19) were now silent. In that void Elihu sees his opportunity to shine. He steps forward as arbiter and attorney for the defense."[20] This is an appealing interpretation, but is it true? Habel's argument depends in large part on the presence in Elihu's addresses, as earlier in Job's, of terminology that can have a legal nuance or even a technical forensic meaning (*mišpāṭ*, *ʿānāh*, *dĕbārîm*, *'ămārîm*, *ṣādaq*, *rāšaʿ*, etc.). Thus, in his translation he intentionally uses English terms that have distinctively legal or forensic connotations, in order to show the extent to which Job's and Elihu's speeches can be heard as filled with legal terminology.

This provocative translation strategy is also obviously problematic. Although the Hebrew words in question may have forensic nuances, they are also quite at home in other discourses, including the discourse of ordinary moral admonition. What Habel's translation obscures is what Bakhtin calls the internal dialogism of the word and the rhetorical uses to which it may be put. In Habel's interpretation, embodied in his translation, the legal metaphor springs fully developed and unmistakable from the mouth of Job from chapter 9 onward. But is something more subtle at work? Each of the words in question bears within it the traces of its many prior uses in various discourses. Which ones may be accentuated in a given instance of speech, however, belongs not to the simple occurrence of the word but to some contextual or rhetorical feature. If a word belongs both to general discourse and to a specialized discourse, something must trigger the nuances of the specialized meanings for them to become a part of the communicative transaction. It may be the clustering of many terms that occur together only in specialized discourse, or it may be the presence of a word distinctive to the specialized discourse, or some other device. Once the connection is made, however, then the further recurrence of such words, even without a special contextualization, allows those specialized nuances to be heard. The internal dialogization of the word and its multiple allegiances to different discourses hovers in the conversation.

In order to make the case that Elihu is specifically recognizing and engaging Job's framing of his situation in forensic terms, it is not enough to note the possible presence of forensic terminology. One must look, too, for the trigger that foregrounds those nuances. At least two such instances exist, though there may be others. First, as Habel points out,[21] the framing of Elihu's first speech in 33:1–11, 31–33 is replete with echoes of Job 13:17–29, a passage in which Job rather explicitly invokes legal terminology and relationships. Also, in 33:13 Elihu specifically alludes to Job's words in 9:2–4, with which he first introduced the legal metaphor. Thus, intertextuality provides the trigger for the foregrounding of the forensic nuances. Second, in 35:2 Elihu again cites Job's words from 9:2 and also, toward the end of the speech, uses explicitly legal terminology: "So why do you say that you do not see him, that the case [*dîn*] is before him and that you are waiting for him?" (35:14). Thus, though I differ with Habel regarding the extent and purpose of forensic nuances in Elihu's speech, his basic insight—that Elihu does recognize and respond to Job's use of forensic terminology and imagery—is unquestionably correct.

Since I take the Elihu material to be a later addition, this feature of the speeches is important to my argument for what it suggests about the author of the Elihu speeches as a reader of the book of Job. In taking up the forensic language, the author of this material shows that he recognizes a new mode of moral and religious discourse in Job's use of legal language to recast the terms of his relationship with God, a mode of discourse he finds deeply troubling. Even though Job eventually retracts his words and declines to speak to God in legal terms (40:3–5; 42:1–6), there is no clear and explicit examination and refutation of Job's legal discourse as a possible model for engaging God and world. This task Elihu takes up, particularly in chapters 33 and 35.

That Elihu recognizes and engages Job's framing of his situation in legal terms is evident from more than just the echoing of terms. Often when Job used the language of a trial with God most explicitly, what preoccupied him was the trial as a mode of communication. Whether Job imagined a fair trial or a travesty of one, the ideal of the trial served the normative function of establishing the way in which two parties might speak, listen, and answer in order to clarify and change a situation (9:3, 14–16, 32; 13:18–22; 23:4–7). In chapters 33 and 35 Elihu's own argument focuses specifically on contesting Job's understanding of how one is to listen and speak to God.

In chapter 33, in contrast to Job's position that God is unjust because he refuses to answer Job's righteous claims (v. 13), Elihu responds with his elaborate description of the ways in which God does speak to human beings: in dreams, through suffering, and even through angelic mediators (vv. 14–30). What Elihu is doing is frame shifting. Identifying the issue in dispute in terms that will allow him adequate rhetorical flexibility (e.g., the willingness of God to speak to mortals), Elihu reframes the context of such divine communication in a way that allows him to recast the moral significance of that divine speech (from an issue of justice toward humans to an issue of mercy toward humans).

In chapter 35 his strategy is somewhat different. This speech has sometimes been disparaged as a mere recapitulation of Eliphaz's speech in chapter 22, but the two are quite different in intention and purpose. Though both use a similar topos (the noneffect on God of human sin or righteousness), the nature of the speeches is quite different. Eliphaz's speech serves as a personal appeal to Job. He uses the topos to ground his conviction that Job's suffering is punishment for wickedness; yet the goal of his speech is to urge Job to pray, to "submit to God and be at peace" (22:21), and so find restoration. Elihu employs the topos in a more rigorously intellectual way, using it to dismantle the cogency of the legal model Job has urged. The fact that Elihu understands his words as a reply to "you and your friends with you" (35:4b) may suggest that he intends this speech as a corrective to Eliphaz as well as a refutation of Job.

Though legal language is often not explicit in this chapter, Elihu does suggest that Job's legal perspective is his starting point, as his quotation of Job suggests: "Do you consider it just that you say, 'I am more in the right than El'?" (35:2). As readers will recall, this phrase was initially used by Eliphaz (4:17) in a general moral sense and later tweaked by Job (9:2) to cause it to disclose its forensic possibilities. As I suggested in the previous chapter, this is the implication of Job's self-presentation in chapters 29–31. The quotation is thus the essence of Job's legal argument. The perspective that undergirds it includes the assumptions that there is right and wrong, innocence and guilt, that an injury is to be made whole, that what is sinful is punishable, and that there is a kind of justice that balances the scales. Elihu alludes to these assumptions by citing another alleged opinion of Job concerning the advantage or lack of such to be obtained by not sinning against God (35:3). Though Job has not said precisely such words, Elihu is not unjustified in seeing the sentiment as entailed in Job's stance.

Having established the assumptional bases of Job's legal argument, Elihu proceeds to dismantle it. The legal argument fails because it makes an unwarranted and incorrect analogy—that the relation of God to human is analogous to the relation of one human to another (cf. vv. 6–7 and 8). But to the contrary, a sin against God is not like a tort against a person, nor is righteousness like a benefit conveyed to a fellow. Because of God's immeasurable transcendence, human sin does not do anything to God, nor does righteousness create a type of transaction that might sustain a claim. These calculations, Elihu argues, pertain only to relations with "a person like yourself" (v. 8).

The following verses do not initially seem to engage Job's legal reasoning, yet they may begin from an allusion to one of Job's speeches in which Job indicts God. Elihu describes unspecified people "crying out" (zāʿaq) and "calling for help" (šûaʿ) because of oppression (v. 9). In 19:7, using almost the same pair of verbs as in Elihu's speech, Job referred to himself as "crying out, 'Violence!'" (ṣāʿa q ḥāmās) without being answered, and calling for help (šûaʿ) yet receiving no justice. Elihu attempts to explain the apparent nonresponse of God by distinguishing between various ways of calling out to God, one of which has the hallmarks of piety, the other of arrogance. As the friends do, Elihu also endorses the language of prayer, though he refers more explicitly than they to the prayers of lament. In Elihu's view the one who cries out in prayer, "Where is God my maker?" can expect a response that the arrogant cannot (vv. 10–13; cf. Jer 2:5–6). It would be difficult to sustain Elihu's distinction if indeed he means that all speech not in the form of prayer is a mark of arrogance (cf. Exod 2:23–25). His target, however, is apparently more specific, for in the next verse he again cites Job's words, this time making explicit that the nature of Job's cry and appeal has been in the framework of a legal case (dîn). What comes out of

Job's mouth (v. 16) is the "empty talk" (*hebel*) that is indeed the equivalent of the "worthless" speech (*šāw'*) of the arrogant (v. 13).

In these two chapters Elihu shows that, unlike the friends, he does recognize the power of Job's legal metaphor to reorganize the moral and religious categories by which divine and human relations are constructed. To confront what he sees as a dangerous new discourse, Elihu focuses on Job's complaints about God not answering when he speaks. In chapters 33 and 35 Elihu reasserts the traditional values of the lament and thanksgiving traditions of prayer as the appropriate mode of organizing relations with God, showing that Job neither knows how to listen to God (chap. 33) nor how to speak to God effectively (chap. 35). Job's legal metaphor is based on a false analogy (35:6–8) and so is intellectually bankrupt (35:14–16).

Given this understanding of the way in which Elihu engages Job's legal discourse, I am inclined to disagree with Habel more generally about the way Elihu relates to the forensic terminology. Elihu's primary self-representation is as a sage, not as a legal mediator. Though in certain cases he does highlight the legal overtones of language Job had also employed, his own use of that speech does not seem to be that of one who takes up the language in order to provide in an ironic or sarcastic fashion what Job claims he wants. His double voicing of the legal language is better heard as a different sort of agon. Elihu is struggling to disqualify the legal overtones as inappropriate to the situation and to reclaim those words for what he considers their proper context, namely, the discourses of piety and traditional moral admonition.

The Process of Repentance as a Moral Focus (Chapter 33)

Almost every critic and commentator regards chapter 33, with its account of redemptive suffering, as presenting Elihu's most significant contribution to the Joban dialogue. Although framed as a counterargument against Job's claim that God does not "speak" to humans, the significance of what Elihu claims goes considerably beyond this issue. I am not particularly concerned to assess the value of his assertions normatively.[22] Rather, my interest lies in locating the distinctive features of Elihu's argument, first, in relation to the way other characters in the book have framed Job's predicament, and second, in relation to similar accounts in late Persian–early Hellenistic literature.

One way to grasp the differences among the moral imaginations of the various speakers in the dialogue is to compare how they frame Job's situation in narrative schemata and, in particular, to note the aspect of time each schema privileges. As discussed earlier, the friends offer Job the narrative schema of the good person who endures suffering, is delivered by God, and enjoys a peaceful and prosperous life after deliverance. They offer several variations of the schema (5:19–26; 8:8–20; 11:13–19), but in each the crucial element of time is to be found in the happy ending. The outcome of the narrative does not so much serve to integrate and give meaning to all that has come before as to enable it to be voided of significance—to be forgotten, or to be remembered without affect, as Zophar suggests (11:16–19). Job's early speeches, by contrast, resist the narrativizing of his situation, stressing the moral significance of the unresolved present, the encompassing "now" of acute pain (6:5, 11–12; 7:11–16). But as Job's imagination becomes engaged with the metaphor of a trial, a certain narrativization develops. Trials are a place for the construction of rival narratives, as in the classic account of Solomon's judgment between the two women who give opposing accounts of the death of one child and the survival of the other (1 Kgs 3:16–28). Similarly, as Job imagines what he would say to God, Job begins to create his account (e.g., 10:2–17; 16:7–17; 19:6–20) even as he invites God to present God's own version of their relationship (e.g., 13:22–24; 23:5). In a judicial context the privileged moment is that instant of clarity in which one story is seen to be true and the other false, as in the case of Tamar, when the presumed account of her conduct is suddenly seen to be false, as she produces Judah's seal and staff. So Job imagines the climactic moment in which he is cleared and released by God (23:7). Thus, judicial time is punctive time, the clarifying moment of decision that puts an end to an alleged state of affairs. For both the friends and for Job the end of the story is what truly matters. That is the moment weighted with significance. In Elihu's account in chapter 33, however, the morally significant dimensions of time are construed differently. For him what matters is not the end in itself but the "process time" of psychological transformation, from suffering to crisis of knowledge to restoration. In contrast to the other narrative models, in Elihu's schema the end does not eclipse what went before. Every element that transpires remains of significance and is integrated into a story that is not merely recognized as a meaningful whole but that must be told to others. Thus, one might say that if the narrative model for the friends is the fairy tale with its happy ending and for Job the courtroom drama with its decisive judgment, for Elihu the narrative model is the *Bildungsroman*.

Although some textual and translation difficulties exist, the basic elements of Elihu's narrative schema are clear. Arguing that God does indeed "speak" to persons, Elihu describes God sending a revelatory dream at night, which terrifies and is intended to serve as a warning to turn away from pride and so prevent the death that would otherwise follow (vv. 14–18). In what is apparently a second act of warning, the person suffers terrible pain, loss of appetite, and wasting of the body, until he comes near to death (vv. 19–21). The role of the angelic mediator is disputed. Does his action take place only in heaven, or does he have a dual role to play, first with the sufferer on earth and then with God in heaven? The phrase *lĕhaggîd lĕʾādām yošrô* (v. 23b) might mean either to "to tell the man what is right for him" or "to declare the man's righteousness." Since the preceding actions of God have had the intention of creating understanding in the mind of the sinner (vv. 16–17), it seems most likely that the angelic mediator here speaks first to the sinner himself. But he also has a role to play with God. Having accomplished his work with the sinner, he must then appeal to God for the sinner's redemption. "And he [the angel] has pity on him [the sinner] and says [to God], 'Redeem him from going down to the pit. I have found a ransom!'" (v. 24). The nature of the ransom is somewhat obscure under either interpretation, but it may be the sinner's repentance itself, expressed in the prayer (v. 26).[23] God's acceptance and the sinner's joyous restoration to the presence of God follow (v. 26). The story is completed as the sinner recounts to the congregation the story of his sin and God's graciousness (vv. 27–28).

The traditional background that forms the basis for Elihu's narrative is the tradition of the lament and thanksgiving psalms, in which a person at the brink of death is brought back to well-being and gives public thanks to God by recounting God's saving deeds. More particularly, one might identify the penitential psalms as an important point of reference. As argued earlier, the three friends, too, insist on the importance of the prayer of lament as a ritual act essential to the restoration of the sufferer (5:8; 8:5; 11:13). Yet one can see the distinctive elements of Elihu's moral imagination most clearly revealed in the way in which he explores precisely what the lament tradition and the friends' use of it passes over: the conditions for and nature of the transformation that occurs. For Elihu this situation presents something of an enigma. What is morally interesting is the problem of human resistance, which presents itself as an entrenched inability to recognize the true nature of the situation of moral peril.

One should realize that the figure of the repenting sinner was not always a stock part of Israelite moral discourse. It appears to become such in the Persian and Hellenistic periods. Very little is ever wholly novel, of course, and one might point to the classic story of David's repentance in response to Nathan's parable as a similar narrative (2 Samuel 12). It also involves God's communication of the knowledge of sin to a sinner by means of a mediator and results in an act of recognition and repentance. Yet the comparison underscores the contrast. In the story of David, the moment of repentance, though dramatic, is not the culminating event of the drama nor the place where interest in David's psychology focuses. That attention is rather focused on God's punishment of David through the illness and death of his child by Bathsheba and on David's unexpected behavior during and after that process. It may be the case, however, that the appropriation of the penitential Psalm 51 for the David story by means of a superscription ("A psalm of David, when Nathan the prophet came to him after he had gone in to Bathsheba") is an attempt during the middle Second Temple period to assimilate the narrative account more closely to the model of the repenting sinner that seemed to exercise an increasing fascination.

The closest analogies to Elihu's account are to be found in narratives concerning Manasseh, Nebuchadnezzar, and Antiochus IV Epiphanes. These are not, of course, parallel to the narrative Elihu constructs in every detail, nor would one expect them to be. But at this time there is a pronounced interest in the figure of the repenting sinner as a moral type. Though the details may be adapted to a variety of contexts and purposes, sufficient "family resemblance" exists among the accounts to suggest that a sort of cultural model has developed. Consider first the outline of the story of Manasseh. God attempts to "speak to Manasseh" (2 Chron 33:10) by means of seers (33:18), yet he refuses to pay attention. In a second stage Yahweh brings the commanders of the armies of Assyria, who "took Manasseh captive in shackles, and bound him in fetters, and brought him to Babylon" (33:11). Only then in his suffering does Manasseh pray and humble himself. God hears his plea and restores him. The consequence is that "Manasseh knew that YHWH was indeed God" (33:13). Though commentators often pass over this story as simply necessary to the Chronicler in order to make sense of Manasseh's long reign, the detail with which it is narrated and its similarity to the account in Job 33 suggests that the process of repentance itself has become a matter of interest, and that it tends to be portrayed in a somewhat formulaic manner.

Variants on this motif are found in 1 Maccabees 6 and 2 Maccabees 9, where the story of the death of Antiochus IV Epiphanes is told. Both versions begin with Antiochus on campaign in the east, when he hears a report of the success of Judah the Maccabee. In 1 Maccabees, Antiochus becomes "sick with disappointment" (1 Macc 6:8). As he realizes he is dying, the king remembers "the wrong I did in Jerusalem," seizing the temple vessels and destroying the inhabitants. Accepting his fate as just, he confesses, "I know this is why these misfortunes have come upon me" (1 Macc 6:13). The more lurid account in 2 Maccabees 9 places the events earlier, before the purification of the temple. Here the news of Judah's victory over Nicanor and Timothy sends Antiochus into an arrogant rage ("I will make Jerusalem a cemetery of Jews," 2 Macc 9:4), provoking God's judgment. The means of judgment is a sudden illness, which causes both pain and the decay of his flesh. On his deathbed Antiochus repents of his arrogance and acknowledges God: "It is right to be subject to God; mortals should not claim equality with him" (2 Macc 9:12). Moreover, he vows to make Jerusalem a free city, to devote lavish gifts and support to the temple, and to become himself a Jew, visiting "every inhabited place to proclaim the power of God" (2 Macc 9:17). Despite these apparently sincere, if extravagant, statements, God does not show mercy on Antiochus, as God did for Manasseh. When Antiochus realizes he will not receive mercy, however, he accepts his judgment (2 Macc 9:18).

It is unlikely that the story of Antiochus in 1–2 Maccabees looks back directly to that of Manasseh. The more direct line of tradition is rather the classic story of the repentance and confession of the Gentile monarch Nebuchadnezzar in Daniel 4. The story of Nebuchadnezzar is also the one most comparable to the narrative model used by Elihu. The similarity between the two accounts was first noted by Duhm, though he did not develop the observation.[24] Other commentators on Daniel have occasionally noted the connection—Plöger[25] in a brief comment and Haag in a more extended discussion. Haag's focus, however, is more on the "self presentation of the sage and his religious-paranetic expression of the conduct of God in judgment and salvation,"[26] not on the moral type of the repentant sinner. Yet Nebuchadnezzar and the person described in Elihu's speech both embody this typical figure. Naturally, each account adapts the model for its own contextual purposes. Even so, the common elements are striking.

In both accounts the moral problem to be addressed is that of "pride" (Job 33:17; Dan 4:3, 27). The pragmatic problem is communication. For both, a terrifying dream is the initial medium by which God attempts to warn the prideful person (Job 33:15-16; Dan 4:2), and in both cases the dream by itself fails to produce the intended results (Job 33:14; Dan 4:26-27). The difficulty the prideful person has in hearing and understanding the divine warning contributes to the drama of the account by prolonging the narrative, but it also helps set up the moral interest in the situation. The requisite knowledge of one's peril is not easily grasped. Both accounts make use of a mediator figure, who attempts to resolve the crisis. In the story of Nebuchadnezzar, Daniel plays this role as he interprets the dream to Nebuchadnezzar, but also as he shows compassion for the king and admonishes him directly concerning his sin and what he should do to atone for it (Dan 4:24). In Elihu's account the mediator is the angelic figure whose role comes later in process. As noted above, the ambiguity of the Hebrew in Job 33:23 has led to debate over whether the angel's role is simply to speak to God on behalf of the person ("declaring him righteous") or whether the angel's role is first to speak to the person ("to declare to him what is right"), that is, serving as an interpreter of the messages of God, and only then to appeal on behalf of the now repentant sinner for deliverance and atonement.[27] Understood in the latter way, Daniel and the angel serve similar functions.

Wherever the mediator is located within the account, the necessity of a second communication, embodied in physical suffering, is presumed. Thus, in Elihu's account the person is subjected to pain, a wasting away of the flesh, and the near approach to death itself (Job 33:19-22). Nebuchadnezzar's affliction is a kind of madness, though one accompanied by physical manifestations (Dan 4:29-30). While his life is not in danger, his suffering brings his humanity to the brink of destruction. This moment of crisis is the point at which the story turns and redemption begins. Here is where Elihu places the angelic mediator, who succeeds in giving understanding to the sufferer and who successfully appeals for his restoration. In Daniel 4 the termination of the crisis is handled through the mechanism of a predetermined period of time ("at the end of the days," 4:31). But the moment of turning is marked physically by a lifting up of the eyes to heaven and the consequent restoration not just of reason but of the understanding that leads to praise of God. Similarly, the person in Elihu's account prays to God and is accepted. Both are restored—Nebuchadnezzar to his sanity and his kingdom (Dan 4:33), the sinner to his righteousness and well-being (Job 33:25, 26). The understanding they have received is not, however, simply a private recognition, but it takes on a public character as Nebuchadnezzar recounts his story in the form of a royal letter and the sinner recounts his story in the form of a traditional psalm of thanksgiving (Job 33:27–28).

The pattern of similarities in the story of the repentance of Manasseh, Nebuchadnezzar, and the person in Elihu's account is not offered to suggest any relations of direct dependence but rather to demonstrate the emergence during the Persian and Hellenistic periods of a particular focus of moral interest embodied in an exemplary character type that had not always been a part of the moral imagination of Israelite religion. This is not to say that repentance itself had not previously been a matter of interest but rather that the process, in its psychological and divine dimensions, had come to engage the imagination in a new way. This is in part what the Elihu author saw as defective in the dialogue between Job and his friends. For all their talk, none of them, not even Eliphaz in Job 5:17–26, had seen what was so obvious to Elihu—that the moral significance in what had happened to Job was to be found in the way in which Job's experience modeled the pattern of the one whom God warns in order to turn him from pride. Job's inability to understand has been like that of Manasseh and Nebuchadnezzar. If Elihu claims a role for himself in relation to Job, it is not so much that of a legal *môkiaḥ* as it is a role like that of Daniel and the angelic mediator of his own account, that is, as one who tries to interpret the "language" of Job's suffering.

Paradigms of Power and the Sovereignty of God (Chapter 34)

Elihu's claims about God's justice in chapter 34 are not substantially different from what the friends have already said. Yet for the question I am pursuing that is not the only relevant thing. What gives the moral imagination its historical and contextual particularity is not simply its propositional content. The texture of moral discourse may shift in many ways, and a change in the rhetoric of argumentation is not necessarily to be dismissed as "mere rhetoric," for it is through the various means of symbolic framing that the understanding of a situation is constituted. One important aspect of cultural rhetoric is the privileging of certain paradigms, so that a class of examples or a discourse located within a specific social realm takes on particular interpretive and persuasive power. These examples or privileged vocabularies serve as templates for clarifying other situations and may even come to be the starting point for organizing an understanding of reality as such. In the modern world, paradigms and vocabularies from the fields of science, psychology, and business have played such a role in supplying templates for moral discourse about aspects of human existence far removed from the original area of the specialized vocabulary. When a paradigm has cultural privilege, an argument stated in its terms will often seem more powerful than one stated in the terms of an outmoded discourse. What I want to examine in Elihu's speech in chapter 34 is the appearance of just such a privileged paradigm, one that I think can be located in the distinctive historical and cultural circumstances of the early Hellenistic period.

Elihu introduces his speech in the mode of a public disputation (34:4). Topically, the speech is concerned with the issue of the justice or wrongdoing of God. As often, Elihu alludes to the words of previous speakers. His opening rhetorical defense of God in verses 10b, 12 ("Far be it from El to do wrong or Shaddai to do injustice. . . . Truly El does not act wickedly or Shaddai pervert justice") recalls a similar opening statement by Bildad in 8:3 ("Shall El pervert justice or Shaddai pervert the right?"). His defense of retributive justice (34:11) also echoes that of Bildad (8:4). Later, his insistence that no "darkness" or "deep darkness" can hide the acts of evildoers evokes the similar imagery used by Eliphaz in 22:13-14.

This speech is not so much a seconding of the arguments of the friends, however, as it is a disputation with Job, who has impugned God's justice. As becomes increasingly evident, it is Job's critique of God's just rulership in chapter 12 that Elihu is particularly concerned to overcome. Even in his opening appeal (34:3), Elihu had appropriated the wisdom saying used previously by Job in 12:11 ("the ear tests words as the palate tastes food"). Also, in representing God's sovereignty in terms of the dependency of all upon God's spirit and breath (34:14-15), he echoes a similar saying by Job in 12:10, though to a rather different effect. The most distinctive point of connection between the two speeches, however, is the reference to various categories of rulers and persons of authority. Job names counselors, judges, kings, priests, the mighty, the trusted, the elders, princes, the strong; Elihu refers to kings, princes, nobles, the mighty, the godless who rule. What is often overlooked is that none of the other participants in the dialogue focuses on the topic of political power.

Though Job and Elihu uniquely share this attention to the realm of the political as a place where God's agency can characteristically be seen, they take their orientation from completely different contexts of moral discourse. Job's language, with its reference to "counsel," "effectiveness," "understanding," "strength," evokes the categories found in sapiential discourse. In Proverbs 8:14-16 these are the qualities that divine wisdom makes available to human rulers for the sake of sound governance. Job parodically claims that these are qualities unquestionably belonging to God (Job 12:13). Then he goes on to show how God undermines rather than supports effective governance on earth (12:17-25).

Elihu takes his cue from a different discourse about God's sovereignty and human political power. In his speech kings, nobles, and the mighty are not positive figures of necessary human governance but negative or at least ambivalent images of corruptible power that must be checked by the intervention of God. God's supreme sovereignty is thus contrasted with the provisional sovereignty of kings and other rulers. The featured elements of the relationship that Elihu describes are as follows: the accusation God brings against the rulers ("scoundrel," "wicked," v. 18); the suddenness of their demise ("in a moment," "before half the night," v. 20); its inexplicability in terms of ordinary human political processes ("not by human hand," v. 20); the continual oversight which allows for the sudden judgment ("without investigation . . . knowing their works," vv. 24-25); the transfer of rulership ("sets others in their place," v. 24); the mysterious and unaccountable timing of God's intervention ("no set time," v. 23; "when he is quiet . . . when he hides his face," v. 29)—aspects that are correlated with the motif of sudden action.[28]

This way of framing the issues is characteristic of the theological problem posed by the existence of Gentile rulers who exercised sovereignty over Israelites. One can find elements of it already in Isaiah of Jerusalem in the prophetic judgment on the "king of Assyria" in Isaiah 10:5-19. It is more clearly developed as a topos in Jewish literature of the Hellenistic period, specifically in Daniel and Sirach. In each case the texts have their own agendas, which are not precisely the same as that of Elihu. What one sees, however, is a flexible topos that has become an important part of the repertoire of moral discourse. The similarities to Daniel 2 and 5 are the most noticeable. There the sovereignties of God and the king exist in a degree of tension. It is God who has given the ruler sovereignty ("who removes kings and sets up kings," Dan 2:21; cf. "he shatters the mighty . . . and sets others in their place," Job 34:24). In Daniel 5 Belshazzar is confronted with the accusation that he is unworthy in his arrogance ("you did not humble your heart even though you knew all this," Dan 5:22-23; cf. "scoundrel," Job 34:18). As a consequence the judgment of death comes to him "that very night" (Dan 5:30; cf. "in a moment, before half the night," Job 34:20). In Nebuchadnezzar's dream the Gentile kingdoms are ultimately struck down by the symbol of God's sovereignty, a rock cut out "by no human hand" (Dan 2:34) just as Elihu sees the death of the mighty rules taking place "by no human hand" (Job 34:20). If the figure of the repentant one in Job 34:31-32 is also to be taken as referring to a ruler, then it brings to mind the model of Nebuchadnezzar, discussed in relation to Job 33. Time and knowledge are also motifs in both contexts. Daniel praises God who "knows what is in darkness" (Dan 2:22), as Elihu asserts that "there is no gloom or deep darkness where evildoers may hide" (Job 34:22). Finally, though the connection is less explicit at the level of verbal connection, the narratives in Daniel deal in part with the problem of the hidden sovereignty of God, whose hiddenness, far from being a cause for complaint, is understood by the wise as a sovereignty that reveals itself in its own time. Elihu, too, speaks to that issue in Job 34:29-30.

The similarities between Elihu's speech and Ben Sira's reflection on kings in Sirach 9:17-10:18 are less extensive but still significant. Ben Sira begins with the traditional wisdom reflection on the relation between the moral caliber of the ruler and that of the people. Yet he, too, includes the reminder that ultimate sovereignty belongs to the Lord, who determines who shall rule (10:4). His comments appear to segue into a discussion of arrogance in general, but his example is drawn from the political arena: "Sovereignty passes from nation to nation on account of injustice, insolence, and greed" (10:8). Many commentators consider Ben Sira's references to be specific allusions to the battles of Raphia in 217 B.C.E. and Panium in 198 B.C.E., by means of which sovereignty over Palestine was transferred from the Ptolemies to the Seleucids.[29] Ben Sira, too, is intrigued by the death of kings as an illustration of the fate of the proud. Verses 10-11 ("A slight illness—the doctor jests; a king today—tomorrow he is dead . . . worms and gnats and maggots"; trans. Skehan) may be an allusion to the sudden and gruesome death of the dissolute Ptolemy IV in 203 B.C.E.[30] The general theme is summed up in the following verses: "The thrones of the arrogant God overturns and enthrones the humble in their stead; The roots of the proud God plucks up, to plant the lowly in their place" (Sir 10:14-15, trans. Skehan; cf. Dan 4:14, 34).

To return to the case of Elihu, even though what he says about the justice of God's reign, considered propositionally, may not be substantively different from the comments of Eliphaz and Bildad, he does speak from a moral imagination shaped differently by a distinct historical and cultural context. Elihu's moral attention, like that of his rough contemporaries, is arrested by the significance of the fate of kings and magnates. The problem of their place in the order of things had become an issue that demanded reflection by Jewish authors of the Hellenistic period. As it was encompassed in their understanding of the sovereignty and judgment of God, so the fate of these rulers became a privileged part of the repertoire of moral argument more generally. Thus, it is not difficult to see how the author of the Elihu speeches sensed an omission in the dialogue between Job and his friends. He was thus able to provide what the friends could not, namely, an argument persuasive to the tenor of his own times that not only contested Job's sarcastic speech about divine governance in chapter 12 but also allowed him to challenge Job's complaint that times (for judgment) are not reserved by Shaddai (Job 24:1) and that the cry of the oppressed goes unheeded (24:12). For what is the mysterious overthrow of the godless ruler, so often seen in the Hellenistic period, if not a divine response to the cry of the afflicted (34:28, 30)?

Reframing Perception: The Sapiential Hymn (Chapters 36–37)

Elihu's final speech is long and complex. The first part (36:1–23), which is argumentative in its structure, serves to summarize the themes and reasoning he has developed in his previous speeches. The latter part (36:24–37:24) provides a segue to the divine speeches, first by means of a hymn of praise that uses extensive nature imagery (36:24–37:13), second by means of a short section imitating the rhetorical questions of the divine speeches (37:14–20), and third by means of a comparison between the awesome splendor of the sun in its shining and the appearance of God in glory (37:21–24). Though I wish to touch on all of these parts, my concern with Elihu's rhetorical sense and the shape of his moral imagination naturally draws me to the hymn, for here Elihu introduces a novel genre at the very end of his entire cycle of speeches. Commentators and translators disagree over where to delimit the beginning and end of the hymn, but I think it best to recognize 36:22–23 and 37:14 as transitional verses that serve to integrate the hymn into what precedes and follows and to take the hymn proper as 36:24–37:13.

The rhetorical purpose, indeed necessity, of the hymn can be understood in light of Elihu's introductory speech in chapter 32. As I noted earlier, when he records his disappointment at the ineffectiveness of the friends' response to Job, he seems to puzzle over the sharp difference between the friends' speeches and those of God. He imagines and rejects a sort of feckless rhetorical strategy on their part ("Do not say, 'We have found the wise course; let El refute him, not a human,'" 32:13). Here is a glaring lack in the argumentation that Elihu knows how to supply. To restate this observation in terms of the author rather than the character, one might say that the author of the Elihu speeches apparently wondered why a form of speech well known to him and of obvious relevance— the sapiential nature hymn—was not used by the author of Job as part of the rhetorical repertoire of the friends.

We can never know, of course. Perhaps the author of the Joban dialogues knew and avoided such a form of speech precisely in order to increase the contrast between the friends' speeches and those of God (though he did not avoid other cosmological descriptions of the divine power and majesty, as in chaps. 25 and 26). But it is also possible that the genre Elihu knows had not yet developed when the dialogues were composed. Genres are, after all, historical phenomena, developing out of antecedent forms and eventually being transformed into other forms of speech. The only other text that bears a distinctively close relationship to Elihu's hymn is Sirach 42:15–43:33. If it were the case that the genre was a relatively new one, then Elihu's consternation at the lack of such a genre in the friends' repertoire of rhetorical resources would be another instance of his belatedness and of the subtle but inexorable shifts that occur in the forms of discourse over time. Since it is not possible to prove the date of origin of this form of speech, however, all one can say is that the Elihu author observes that a rhetorically useful genre, well known to him, has not been employed and that he incorporates it into his own composition.

That the divine speeches are the impetus for Elihu's hymn is evident from what he himself says in 32:13. Could one think of the hymn in 36:24-37:13 as simply a paraphrase or transposition of the divine speeches? Most commentators aptly note a number of similarities between the two compositions. Elihu's focus on themes of nature, specifically meteorological phenomena (rain, clouds, lightning, thunder, cold storm winds, snow, ice) anticipates the meteorological elements of the divine speeches in 38:22-38. There are also stylistic similarities in the vivid descriptive manner employed by each composition. Both have the function of eliciting awe before the divine. Despite these evident similarities Elihu's hymn does not seem to be directly imitative of the divine speeches. Where Elihu does wish to imitate that style, he knows how to do so, as he shows in the section following the hymn proper (37:14-20). There the rhetorical questions concerning Job's inability to know how God works and to do what God is able to do are directly imitative of the divine speech, as is the use of an imperative demand to speak (cf. 37:15-16 with 38:34-35; and 37:19 with 38:4b). Thus, however much Elihu has composed the hymn in awareness of the following chapters, and however much it is positioned to provide a transition to them, the hymn itself is no mere paraphrase of the divine speeches, adapted for a human voice.

To grasp what Elihu is trying to do requires an investigation of the genre itself. Yet a survey of commentaries (including my own) indicates a curious lack of attention to the question of the genre of this part of Elihu's speech and a consequent neglect of its striking similarity to Sirach 42:15-43:33. Typically, commentators analyze the propositional content of the speech, clarifying the imagery, noting parallels to various motifs, and comparing it with the divine speeches. Only Wahl's monograph deals with the question of genre,[31] and even he seems to be satisfied by supplying a label rather than reflecting on what such a genre does and why Elihu would find it so important rhetorically.

As I argued in an earlier part of this book, genres are not just forms of speech but also forms of thought. To invoke a genre is to invoke a way of perceiving the world, a way of arranging values, and a particular stance or set of dispositions. As a way of framing a situation, a genre has a rhetorical and even an ideological force. One must not forget, however, that there are no such things as pure types. Texts invoke or participate in genres, often several at once; they do not belong to them. And with every instantiation of a genre, the performance adds to and thus modifies the generic repertoire, changing the contours of what passes for that genre.

With these thoughts in mind one can begin to reflect on Elihu's speech in light of Wahl's generic characterization. Wahl's designation, *weisheitlicher*

Lehrhymnus,[32] though very general, is apt. The praise song and the hymn are the primary genres in comparison with which he identifies and differentiates Elihu's performance. Like those forms, Elihu's performance announces its relation to the hymnic tradition through its stated purpose, the praise of God. Moreover, it employs characteristic elements of the hymn, including the imperative call to praise (v. 24) and the substantiation of praise in clauses introduced by the particle *kî* (v. 27). Yet anyone who reads Job 36:24–37:13 alongside Exodus 15 or Psalm 33 or 113 recognizes that Elihu is speaking differently. Wahl rightly notes that Elihu's hymn also draws on the traditions of didactic speech, as for example in Proverbs 22:17–29, with its invitation to wisdom, direct advice, and substantiating reasons.[33] Aphorisms, characteristic of the wisdom tradition, punctuate the passage (e.g., Job 36:26). Though elements of both the hymnic and sapiential traditions of discourse are often separately recognizable in Elihu's speech, there are elements that are equally at home in both, such as the attention given to natural phenomena as disclosing the power of God. Sometimes, too, elements of the traditions blend inseparably, as when the hymnic demand to praise God is formulated as a kind of admonition ("Remember, then, to magnify his work, of which people sing," 36:24).

Wahl's analysis primarily takes the form of comparison of the elements combined from various antecedent genres and discourses, though he also briefly compares Eliphaz's hymn in 5:8–16 and the divine speeches in chapters 38–39 as a way of showing how Elihu is "going beyond" what they attempt.[34] Yet it is most unlikely that Elihu is creating something radically new. From the very sophistication of the performance it appears that Elihu is composing according to the sense of an established generic template. As he begins, he "knows how to go on," even as he creates this particular composition for its unique context. One can understand what Elihu is doing much better if one can compare it to another example of the same genre, as well as to note its similarities and differences from neighboring but distinct genres. Although Wahl seems to recognize just such an example of the same genre in Sirach 42:15–43:33, he makes no attempt to compare it with Elihu's composition.

There are evident difficulties and dangers in attempting to develop one's sense of genre competency from a repertoire of only two examples, but even that small a sample can provide some sense of how a genre is put together. My assumption is that both authors are working from an implicit knowledge of how one composes this sort of sapiential hymn. Even though Elihu's composition may well be older than Ben Sira's, it is helpful to examine Ben Sira's first. In part, this order is suggested because it is helpful to look away from Elihu's speech initially in order to come back to it with a sense of what to look for. Also Ben Sira presents the sapiential hymn as an independent composition, clearly marked out though not entirely unrelated to its surroundings, whereas Elihu's hymn is more integrated into a series of strongly rhetorical speeches. Thus, certain aspects of the genre may be clearer in Sirach, though one should guard against the assumption that it somehow represents a "purer" example. Since so little attention has been given to Ben Sira's hymn, this discussion will of necessity be somewhat lengthy.

The Sapiential Hymn in Sirach 42:15–43:33   The hymn in Sirach 42:15–43:33 has a clearly marked beginning and end. The beginning states the author's intention to describe the works of the Lord" (42:15), whereas the end is signaled by Ben Sira's confession that the topic is inexhaustible and by his admonition to his hearers to praise God (43:27–33). The reiteration of the topic of God's transcendent greatness, beyond all possible praise, forms a thematic inclusio (42:17–21; 43:27–33). A concluding reference to God's giving wisdom to the pious ('anšê ḥesed, partially preserved in Ms B) serves to link this poem with the following composition in praise of the ancestors.

Several features of style, structure, content, and purpose stand out as significant for understanding the kind of speech this is. First is the explicitly stated intention: the recital of the "works of the Lord" for the purpose of praise. To recite such a composition is to situate oneself in a disposition of piety. As the concluding verse asserts, it is to just such persons that God gives wisdom. Thus, the recitation of the hymn is both a reflection of and an instrument for the cultivation of a particular character. It does other things as well. The didactic intent of the composition is established by means of the opening first-person speech, in which the speaker offers to tell "what I have seen," a self-presentation evocative of the didactic opening of Psalm 78. The self-conscious act of telling and the inscription of an audience into the poem defines a didactic intent to create a community of those who will share the knowledge and insights of the speaker and thus also his disposition toward God.

The poet, however, exhibits a strategic ambivalence about his task. Though he will praise God by enumerating God's works, he cannot do so with any completeness, for not even the angels are capable of reciting all the wonders of God (42:17). The double claim of the theoretical impossibility of praising adequately but the utter necessity of praising to the utmost of one's ability is recapitulated at the end of the poem (43:27–30). This trope simultaneously develops the character of the speaker and of God. The speaker is sketched as a person whose piety is marked by a modesty about knowledge, even as God's unimaginable transcendence is described by paradoxical reference to its indescribability. The contrast between creator and creatures is further developed as the speaker refers to the scope of God's knowledge. Though creatures, angelic and human, are unable to tell all the wonders of God, by contrast God knows everything, from the far reaches of the abyss to the human heart, both what is past and what belongs to the future (42:18–21). And yet, even though human knowledge is circumscribed, contemplation of the phenomena of nature does provide a true, if incomplete, knowledge of God. In making this claim, Ben Sira already invokes nature as the persuasive analogy: "As the shining sun is clear to all, so the glory of the Lord fills his works" (42:16; trans. Skehan). Moreover, the very wisdom that enables him to perceive and describe the presence of God in the works of creation is itself one of the works of God, who "gives wisdom to the pious." Thus, the epistemological connections are established that make the recitation of such a poem a means of knowing God.

Consequently, the poem can be understood not simply as a display of wisdom but also a form of spiritual discipline that cultivates a sense of the presence of God through the contemplation of God's works. The experiential dimension is suggested by the emotional and sensuous language used to describe both the act and the objects of contemplation. The works of God are "pleasurable" (nḥmd[ym]; 22a), "a jewelled rosette, a sight to behold" (ʿd nyṣwṣ wḥzwt mrʾh; 22b).[35] This sense of beauty and the pleasure derived from contemplation are, however, closely related to the perception of a moral order revealed in nature, a stance characteristic of wisdom's perspective. The orderliness of creation, the complex complementarity it exhibits, and its purposiveness are all a part of what inspires the sense of beauty and delight (42:23–25). Thus, though one should not overemphasize the didactic dimension of Ben Sira's description, Gian Luigi Prato is not wrong to treat this passage in his discussion of theodicy in Sirach.[36] But throughout the poem, especially as it turns to the specific description of the phenomena of creation, the tone is not so much one of instruction as of delighted wonder.

These extended acts of description occupy the central portion of the poem. Perhaps in imitation of the orderliness of creation itself, the poet's description is developed in systematic fashion, moving from heaven to earth to the sea, or from above to below. Cosmological elements (the heavens, sun, moon, rainbow) are followed by meteorological ones (storms with clouds, hail, thunder, and wind; the snow, frost, ice, rain, and dew that settles on the earth). Why the descriptive sequence concludes with the seas is not clear. Perhaps it is the motif of water that leads from the description of the moisture falling upon the earth to the expanses of water in the sea. In his classic article on Job 38, von Rad sees also in Ben Sira an indirect literary reflex of the ancient Near Eastern "scientific lists of cosmic and meteorological phenomena,"[37] most anciently represented in the Egyptian onomastica. Although his view is often cited positively,[38] one should probably be even more circumspect than the already cautious von Rad.[39] There is no doubt that the systematic, sequential lists were used to structure many different types of composition. Though the fondness for structuring lists represents a recognizable schema and perhaps even a characteristic turn of mind, the device is unlikely to have had a single origin.

What is striking in Sirach 42:15–43:33, however, is not the list itself but the way in which it is developed. Psalm 104 makes use of a similar list of created things as an organizing principle, but whereas each is mentioned briefly, what distinguishes Ben Sira's poem is the extended, closely observed, and vivid description of each phenomenon. Thus, one of the distinctive features of this sort of poem is its modeling of a certain quality of attention, one lacking in other list poems such as Psalm 104 and 148 and the Song of the Three Youths (though it does have a partial parallel in the divine speeches of Job 38–39, especially in the account of the animals).

One customarily thinks of the repertoire of imagery in ancient Semitic poetry as consisting of stock images, as opposed to the passion for novelty in modern western poetry. That may be the case also in the sapiential hymn. But even if Ben Sira is drawing from a standard set of images characteristic of this type of poetry, one needs to recognize the values embedded in the repertoire itself. An extravagant and playful imagination is highlighted. Nowhere is this more evident than in the description of the winter storm and its effects. Drawing his tropes from human, animal, plant, and mineral analogies, Ben Sira struggles to express the fascination of the movement of snow, which evokes both the flight of birds in its swirling and the settling of locusts in its clustered fall. The color of frost is evoked by comparing it to salt poured out, but the strange crystalline shapes it forms are likened to blossoms. Ice on ponds is seen as a kind of armor. In an apparent delight in description itself, human playfulness responds with poetic richness to the divine creativity.

The attentiveness of description is equally present in Ben Sira's account of the heat of the sun. Heat itself is experienced by the body in various ways (cf. Elihu's description of hot clothes in Job 37:17), but it is not a visual phenomenon. In describing the sun's heat, however, Ben Sira seeks out visual images that bridge between the appearance of the sun and the effects of its heat. He likens the sun to a cast-metal furnace heated to a glowing heat by bellows. Shifting imagery, he describes hyperbolically the terrible power of the sun's rays as a destructive force that "sets aflame the mountains," the rays imaged as (an animal's?) tongue reaching out "to destroy the inhabited world." Even as Ben Sira piles up visual images, the sun, like the God whose power it reflects, resists his gaze, for as he says, "the eye is burned by its fire." The harshness of the imagery will eventually be tempered, for as Ben Sira moves through his account of meteorological phenomena, he concludes the series with a reference to the rainclouds and dew that relieves the parched mountains and meadows.

For Ben Sira no sharp division exists between the pleasure that comes from describing the thing in itself and in recounting its purposiveness within divine creation, as can be seen in his description of the moon. Inventive visual description occurs here, too, most notably in Ben Sira's likening of the clouds to an army, with the moon as the fire signal that guides them (43:8b). But the account of the moon is organized primarily around the changing of its phases, its capacity to renew itself, and its role in guiding human beings in ordering the seasons of their worship of God (43:6–8, 10).

As these examples suggest, one cannot reduce Ben Sira's descriptions to a kind of rationalistic theodicy. A wide range of emotional tone and a wide range of relation between the natural and the human is sketched through his descriptions: the dangerousness—even hostility—of the sun's heat, the beneficence of the moon, the simple splendor of the rainbow, the theophanic violence of the storm, the marvels of the varieties of frozen water, the restorative power of rain and dew, and the astonishing expanse of the sea and its creatures, Rahab subdued but awesome. This is not an "argument from nature." Rather, the work of the poem is fundamentally its effort to communicate a sense of wonder, an effort in which it succeeds brilliantly.

But what, one may ask, is the significance of wonder and the intentional cultivation of a sense of wonder? What is its role in the inculcation of wisdom? Or, as we might now phrase it, what is the cognitive and moral significance of wonder? Several things might be suggested. First, the very act of prolonged description that serves in Ben Sira's poem as the instrument for the production of wonder is a type of discipline of attention with important effects. This discipline of description requires that the person "bracket" herself, that is, be provisionally absent to herself as she focuses attention on the object to be described. Yet the person is not truly absent. Rather, her presence is concentrated in the act of contemplating and describing. She experiences herself in the emotion of delight or awe that results from the contemplation. Second, and related to this, the experience of wonder produced by such an exercise is fundamentally an experience of something *other*. Even familiar objects, when perceived as objects of wonder, are temporarily estranged, made new and surprising. Third, the kind of attention achieved in a state of wonder differs qualitatively from other forms of apprehension. The gaze of wonder differs from the calculating utilitarian gaze, even as it also differs from the frozen attention of terror. In each of these forms of apprehension the subject-object relationship and the sense of value is different. In the utilitarian gaze, subject and object are clearly distinguished, and the object is evaluated for its goodness or badness in relation to a project of the viewer. In terror the object contemplated is utterly bad, an annihilating Other that radically threatens the viewer's subjectivity. But in wonder the ordinary subject-object dichotomy is disrupted with the bracketing of the self, and what is gazed upon is seen in its essential goodness.

Despite the risk of anachronism, I wish to set Ben Sira's sapiential hymn in relation to the work of a modern philosopher, Erazim Kohák, who is also concerned with the role of nature in the creation of moral understanding. The issues Kohák engages in a post-Enlightenment world are, of course, very different from those of Ben Sira, for he is concerned with the moral estrangement of technological civilization from the natural world. But his goal is the creation of a mode of understanding of the divine, the natural, and the human that is strongly reminiscent of certain perspectives within the Israelite wisdom tradition. Kohák's philosophical background in the phenomenological tradition leads him to a mode of reflection that is also evocative of Ben Sira's hymn in that it also includes minute attention, description, and even observation rendered in detailed drawings of objects and scenes.

> The sense of nature which stands out in the radical brackets of dusk . . . includes also a dimension of value, not merely as utility but as intrinsic, absolute value ingressing in the order of time. The chipmunk peering out of the stone fence is not reducible simply to the role he fulfils in the economy of nature. There is not only utility but also an integrity, a rightness to his presence. When humans encounter that integrity in a trillium or a lady's slipper, they tend to acknowledge it by speaking of beauty, and it is not inappropriate. It is, though, also more—the presence of absolute value, the truth, the goodness, the beauty of being, the miracle that something is though nothing might be. With the encounter with nature in its integrity, there comes also the recognition that its presence is never free of value, acquiring its rightness only contingently in its utility. It is primordially good. The order of nature is also an order of value.[40]

Though this particular quotation from Kohák might suggest that he thinks only in terms of the gentle, appealing side of nature, he, no less than Ben Sira, takes into account those aspects of creation that point to the vulnerability of the human in a world that has a place for the human but is not designed primarily for our benefit: "The order of time is an order of passing and perishing—and celebrating it as the creator of novelty does not alter that fact."[41] Indeed, Kohák is more equipped by tradition and culture than is Ben Sira to explore the place of pain and of grief in the world. Yet it is the reality of pain and grief as much as of beauty that makes the encounter of the natural world in wonder essential. In Kohák's terms such an encounter allows one to grasp not only the order of time but also the order of eternity. It is not that eternity somehow makes up for the pain of temporal existence. Rather, the order of eternity holds both the beauty and the pain in their eternal validity, not as merely something that is swallowed up in the passing of time. This is not so different, I think, from what Ben Sira suggests when he insists that in the contemplation of the beings of creation, so intimately tied to the order of time (the sun at its rising and at noon, the moon in its phases, the snow and ice of the winter season), one may also, though never fully, grasp a sense of the glory of the God who created them; that is, one may grasp the order of eternity.

For both Kohák and Ben Sira such a recognition is of importance because it also provides the basis for the moral law. Kohák reflects that

> the glory of being human is the ability to recognize the pattern of rightness [in creation] and to honor it as a moral law. The horror of being human is the ability to violate that rightness, living out of season. . . . [The] common motif is the law

of respect for the sacredness of being. . . . Ultimately, that is the moral sense of nature, infinitely to be cherished: that there is something. That is the eternal wonder articulated in the rightness and rhythm of time which humans honor in their commandments, the wonder of being."[42]

Ben Sira, of course, does not put it that way, but something like that perception underlies his recognition of the seasonal rightness of the moon's phases and the responsive rightness of the worship humans give as the moon directs them concerning their "sacred seasons and pilgrimage festivals." Even more pointedly, he concludes his hymn with the lines "It is the Lord who has made all things, and to those who fear him he gives wisdom" (43:33). Insight into the order of creation (wisdom) and the embodiment of the moral law and of piety (the fear of God) are mutually implicated.

The sapiential hymn as it is embodied in Sirach 42:15–43:33 is thus not simply an act of praise or simply a teaching but an experiential union of the two, best understood as a type of spiritual practice. By means of a disciplined act of description, set within a framework of praise and gratitude, the one who recites or hears such a poem is led to experience the created world in wonder as a means of the disclosure of God. Though the poem is not a theodicy in any rational sense of the word, it attempts to make available an experience of the goodness of creation and of the God who is known through it.

Elihu's Sapiential Hymn in Job 36:27–37:13   This extended excursion into the poetry of Ben Sira must now be related to the larger purposes of the present discussion—the final speech of Elihu. One must be careful. Although everything that Ben Sira writes is an expression of the potential of the genre, not every invocation of the genre will embody just that set of potential meanings. Ben Sira cannot be "read into" Elihu indiscriminately. Nevertheless, having attended to what Ben Sira does with such a genre, one is in a better position to see the similar and different purposes for which Elihu employs it. That the two of them are employing the same genre can be seen from the number of generic markers the two share.

The traits that establish Job 36:24–37:13 as the same sort of composition as Sirach 42:15–43:33 are of various sorts. Some of the most notable include the representation of the speaker, the characterization of the purpose of the speech, and the content, including its organization and style of presentation. In each composition, the speaker is represented as a sage who addresses an audience with a teaching. In Ben Sira the initial first person speech serves to characterize him as such (Sir 42:15), a representation resumed in the latter part of the poem by admonitions and statements concerning the source of wisdom (43:27–30). Although Elihu does not use first person speech in the same way, the deictic interjections (Job 36:26, 30), admonitions (36:24; 37:14), wisdom pronouncements (36:26), and other such features give him the persona of the sage. Elihu's characterization of God the creator as "teacher" (36:22) in his introduction to the hymn suggests an analogy with his own role in making known the works of God (cf. the motif of God as giver of wisdom in Sir 43:33). Thus diction, characteristic forms of speech, and ways of representing God all contribute to the creation of the persona of the speaker.

In describing the representation of the speaker, the purpose of the speech has been broached. It is, as Wahl has observed, at the same time an act of instruction and an act of praise, a combination that serves as one of the most distinctive generic markers.[43] The hymnic qualities include the explicit summons to praise (Job 36:24; Sir 43:27–30), the *kî* clauses that substantiate the praise (Job 36:27; Sir 43:5, 11; etc.), and the various descriptions of God's power and works. There are, however, particular motifs that suggest a more fine-grained sense of generic style. In both, the praise, though an individual expression, is related to a collective, even universal act (Job 36:24; Sir 43:28, 30). Both exhibit toward the beginning of the hymn an epistemological modesty, expressed in the conundrum that though praise is essential, adequate knowledge of God's works and wonders is impossible (Job 36:24–26; Sir 42:16–17; 43:28–29).

Above all, however, what gives these two compositions the feel of a distinctive genre is the content itself and the way it is organized and developed. Both praise God by means of descriptions of cosmological or meteorological phenomena. In both, the account is tightly structured and systematically organized. In Ben Sira the order follows a "top to bottom" sequence, and the organization is developed in the style of the lists of phenomena that occur in other hymnic and didactic compositions. Though some suggest the list structure is also present in Elihu's hymn, he seems rather to organize his praise by means of a systematic and carefully observed description of one complex phenomenon: the winter thunderstorm. The main part of the description concerns the expanse of clouds, the lightning and thunder, the rain and snow, the cold wind and the consequent ice that forms.

In a way even more marked than in Ben Sira's poem, Elihu emphasizes the act of contemplative gazing that gives rise to praise: "Remember to magnify his work of which people sing. All people look upon it, humanity gazes from afar" (36:24–25). Unfortunately, the body of Elihu's hymn is obscured in several places by a questionable text. Nevertheless, enough of the poem remains accessible to get a sense of his imagery. Though his descriptions are not as visually detailed as those of Ben Sira, Elihu's contain their own exquisite observation. He begins with a reference to the cycle of evaporation and rain (36:27–28). Elihu notes not only the occurrence of lightning and thunder but also their temporal sequence (37:3–4). And in his description of the cold, he creates the complementary image of the animals retreating to their dens as the wind comes forth from its chambers (37:8–9). The phenomenon of lightning seems to engage Elihu particularly, as he refers to it at least three times, describing God's spreading it about himself and covering his hands with it (36:30a, 32a). God causes the lightning-bearing clouds to go round about, scattering lightning (37:11-12), reaching to the ends of the earth (37:3b), and covering (or uncovering?) the roots of the sea (36:30b). As in Sirach, Elihu's poem also comments upon the purposiveness of the divine acts in nature (governing the people and providing food, 36:31; expressing punishment, acceptance, or love, 37:12-13). Commentators who compare Elihu's speech only with the following divine speeches often conclude that Elihu is "moralizing" nature in a somewhat simplistic way. Though a real difference between the two speeches exists, this judgment overlooks the fact that Elihu is not simply reacting to the divine speeches but performing a type of speech with its own norms. In Elihu's hymn, as in Ben Sira's, such references to the purposiveness of nature alternate with an apparent pleasure in the act of vivid description itself. Elihu even makes use of a dramatic device— the injection of his own emotional response to the (imagined) sound of thunder (37:1), followed by an imperative to "listen!" (šimʿû šāmôaʿ), as though the sound were indeed now present. When viewed from the perspective of generic norms, references to the purposiveness of nature work together with close observation and the vivid description to create a sense of wonder.

These comparable features and others that might easily be teased out suffice to show that both Ben Sira and Elihu make use of a common genre, the sapiential hymn. Yet each develops the potential of the genre differently for different contexts. Since Elihu positions his hymn just before the answer of God to Job from the tempest, the subject of the thunderstorm is a natural focus, whereas a list or chain construction would not serve so well. The storm was also felt to be the phenomenon of nature most transparent to the presence of God (associated with both voice and purposive action) and most calculated to suggest the power of God. Thus, his focus on the storm lends itself well to the creation of a sense of awe that the divine speeches will also emphasize.

At the end of the hymn, after he has again admonished Job to "stand and contemplate the wonders of God," Elihu shifts to a different form of rhetoric. Continuing to use examples from the realm of meteorology (lightning, clouds, winds, the heavens themselves), Elihu addresses to Job aggressive rhetorical questions that anticipate those of the divine speeches (37:14-20). Though it appears that in some sense the hymn provides the background necessary for Job's proper response to the rhetorical questions, the difference in tonality between the two rhetorical forms is striking.

Both the tonality of the hymn and its function within Elihu's speech can perhaps be better appreciated if one looks back to what precedes it in chapter 36. Elihu opens his final speech, characteristically, with an appeal for a hearing and a recommendation of his own knowledge (36:1-4). His theme, which characterizes the entire final speech, is the power and generous character of God (36:5). He develops this theme initially in relation to how different sorts of people deal with affliction, arguments that recapitulate ideas advanced in his earlier speeches. Elihu recalls the work of God in instructing the arrogant concerning their behavior, attempting to turn them back from sin, so that they may live and not perish prematurely (36:6–12; cf. chap. 33). He also contrasts the failure of the godless to cry to God "when he binds them" with the deliverance that comes to the afflicted who become attentive to God through their affliction (36:13–16; cf. 35:9–13). Job's own obsession with seeing judgment meted out in a legal sense and his Promethean defiance (36:17–19; cf. 35:14–16) are themselves signs of the moral danger into which he has placed himself. Thus, ironically, the night of judgment that he seeks (36:20; cf. 34:21–30) may be the night of his own judgment. In concluding this section, Elihu warns Job not to turn to iniquity and declares that it is for this very tendency that he has in fact been afflicted (36:21). The following verses (36:22–23) return to his opening themes of the greatness of God and God's desire to instruct, as they also provide a segue to the sapiential hymn.

Elihu's diagnosis of Job's moral problem illumines his choice of the sapiential hymn as an appropriate therapy. Job's framing of issues and thus his understanding of the nature of God and world has proceeded by means of a tight focus on the presence or absence of a lawlike justice executed by God in the world. Elihu has been willing to argue with Job more or less on these terms, though he has rejected the forensic categories as adequate and has attempted to reframe the discussion of God's interaction with humans in the world in a broader context. Without question, Elihu is prepared to argue theodicy if Job so wishes. But the sudden introduction of the hymn ("Remember to extol his work") suggests an alternative strategy. As I suggested earlier, the sapiential hymn is a type of spiritual discipline, one in which the centrality of the human, his perspectives, and his needs, is temporarily displaced or bracketed. The human becomes the observer and recounter, present as eye and voice, but differently related to world and to creator than in other forms of discourse and reflection. Though the sapiential hymn is related to the project of theodicy in that it coordinates the beauty and wonder of the phenomenal world with its fundamental goodness and purposiveness, it is not an argumentative mode of discourse. Despite his confidence in the soundness of his own arguments and their persuasive force, in his reading of the book of Job the author of the Elihu speeches has understood that Job is finally moved from his apparent arrogance not by arguments but only by an encounter with the divine that displaces him from the center of value and judgment (42:2–6). Thus, if a human (and not God) is to persuasively address Job (32:13), it would have to be by means that attempt a similar change of perspective. Elihu knew that within his contemporary culture's repertoire of modes of discourse there existed just such a genre, alongside the more argumentative forms of speech. And so, at the end of his arguments he supplies what has perhaps most been lacking in the dialogue of the friends with

Job—a form of speech that does its work as much by aesthetics as by reason, one that shifts the forms of attention and thus the perspective and disposition of the speaker.

My attempt to represent sympathetically the nature of Elihu's final speech should not be taken for complete agreement or endorsement either of his particular speech or for the genre to which he appeals. There are several things that might give one pause. His fascination with the power and violence of the storm and with the austere and unyielding force of the icy cold is striking and perhaps disturbing. Though Elihu insists on the nurturing as well as the fierce aspects of the power of God as manifested in these phenomena, his description lacks the emotional and tonal range of Ben Sira's more varied depiction of the wondrous nature of creation. Perhaps one might simply say that Elihu more narrowly exploits the aesthetics of the sublime that is present but not so dominant in Sirach.

The more serious question, however, is whether the genre can be properly urged upon a person in pain or even whether it can properly be spoken by a person in pain. Is its displacement of everything else except the sense of wonder before the creative power of God an evasion, a looking away? As I suggested earlier, Ben Sira's repertoire of images at least avoids the assumption that everything about nature is benign. But the genre itself has no place for the voice of grief and misery. The human voice that speaks is not allowed to speak of its own fear or pain but only of the glory of God manifest in nature. That is, of course, a somewhat unfair judgment, for every genre, in having its own genius, has its limits. But it is not unfair to hold Elihu to account for the use he makes of the genre in the ensemble of his whole address to Job. And though I am sympathetic to his intuition about the necessity of a shift of perspective, neither the genre nor his instantiation of it are adequate to the moral demand posed by the presence of Job in his pain.

The divine speeches that follow will in their own way also employ the sublime as a means of displacing the egocentricity of pain, though that is not their primary purpose. Even if one prefers them to the sapiential hymn of Elihu, the question must remain whether or not that displacement evades the full moral demand of Job's situation. Could the biblical tradition have developed the resources to find a place for the voice of suffering within the context of contemplation of creation and the praise it gives rise to? Perhaps. The lament tradition knew how to combine lament and praise in an authentic fashion, but its modes of thinking about the divine were dominated by excessively personal models of God and an embedded trope of patronage relationships. But if one could envision a marriage of the emotional voice of the lament with the contemplative perspective of the sapiential hymn, then perhaps one would have the kind of speech that Job could not find for himself and that no one was able to offer to him. But that discussion, as Bakhtin would say, is a matter of drawing further dotted lines from within the book of Job and from other voice-ideas to a point of convergence that the book itself does not contain.

The embodied, perspectival character of human understanding and the historicity of the moral imagination makes the act of interruption a necessity of every serious act of reading a disturbing text about a fundamental human dilemma. The signal contribution of the Elihu speeches may not finally be in their content but in the way they model this process. Though modern readers may disagree with Elihu's perceptions and values, I have tried to make the case that he deserves to be respected as just such a serious reader who understood much about the challenges of the book and who engaged them in a significant manner. The highest form of respect one can pay, of course, is to interrupt his own speech and to continue to quarrel with him as he quarreled with Job and his friends.

9

The Voice from the Whirlwind

The Tragic Sublime and the Limits of Dialogue

"The object in the background of the tragic," says Max Scheler, "is always the world itself, thought of as a unity. . . ." The indifference of the course of events to human values, the *blind* character of necessity—of the sun that shines on the good and the bad—play the role of the Greek *moira*, which becomes a *kakos daimon*, as soon as value-relations and personal relations are confronted with relations of the causal order.

Paul Ricoeur, *The Symbolism of Evil*

When we have been abandoned by meaning, the artist has a professional duty to bear witness that *there is*, to respond to the order to be.

Jean-François Lyotard, *The Inhuman*

Throughout this book, I have drawn heuristically on the Bakhtinian notion that one might read Job as a polyphonic text in which a variety of different voice-ideas, embodied not only in characters but also in genres, engage one another without privilege. The divine speeches present a problem for this mode of reading, for here one does not simply have one voice-idea engaging others but rather an attempt to represent the voice of God. When God speaks, it tends to bring conversation to an end. So at least it appears here, with Job initially choosing silence (40:4–5), and when forced to speak, replying briefly and apparently casting his own words in relation to the "authoritative words of another" (42:2–6), as Bakhtin might say. In the first chapter, I considered the ways in which, despite the ostensible closure of dialogue, the book nevertheless finds ways to evade the finalizing effect of the divine speeches. Job, who does have the "last word," gives a famously enigmatic utterance[1] that serves as a kind of Bakhtinian "loophole," reserving the possibility of a word yet to be spoken. More abruptly, the didactic tale resumes its narrative, continuing as though it does not realize it has been interrupted. This juxtaposition generates a series of destabilizing ironies in which Job's words, just declared "words without knowledge" (38:2), are redescribed as "speaking rightly" (42:7), while the events of the story unfold almost as though they had been scripted by the friends (cf. 5:24–26, 8:5–7, and 11:13–19 with 42:11–17). Thus, what seemed settled by the intervention of God is disclosed as still subject to question, comment, and con-testation, even if obliquely.

To characterize the divine speeches simply as an attempt to finalize what has gone before, however, is seriously to underread them, for they have a much more ambiguous relationship to dialogue and its limits than that representation suggests. In their own way they also ensure that "the ultimate word of the world and about the world has not yet been spoken."[2] Almost all commentators draw attention to the ambiguity and obliqueness of the divine speeches. Pages upon pages have poured from critics who puzzle over how and in what way the divine speeches serve as a reply to Job. Thus, even if the power of the divine voice shuts down explicit dialogue within the book, its teasing resistance to under-standing serves to increase the flow of dialogue in the interpretive process. Considered from the perspective of a polyphonic reading, Job's own enigmatic reply in 42:1–6 seems almost complicit. He says he has understood something transformative in the divine speeches, yet he refuses to play the role of hermeneut for the audience, for he never makes clear exactly what he has understood. Consequently, we bystanders begin to argue among ourselves.

The Elusiveness of the Divine Rhetoric

What is it that makes the divine speeches so enigmatic? One might argue the contrary, of course. At one level they have a perfectly clear meaning, which can be traced through the introductory words of each speech and through the rhe-torical questions that follow. The challenge to Job is framed in terms of the difference in identity between God and Job ("Who is this . . . ?" 38:2), specifi-cally in relation to the power and wisdom required for the planning (38:2) and governance (40:8) of creation. God is God, and Job is not. So much is clear. But rarely does an interpreter wish to stop with that. A strong sense persists that much more is being said, if only one knows how to listen.

This perception of a surplus of meaning is generated in several ways. The disconnect between Job's framing of issues and God's reply is the most obvi-ous, as it seems to create a sort of hermeneutical synaptic space. One can also point to the uncertain tonality of the speeches. Should they be read in a tone of overpowering mastery? Of mockery? Of agonistic pedagogy? How one hears the "accents" of the utterance depends in part on how one recognizes and privileges one or more of the many discourses evoked by the divine speeches. If one takes the paradigm of the theophany of the divine warrior as the starting point, the speech sounds quite different than if one privileges the interrogative modes of wisdom instruction.[3] If the speech is an exercise in the rhetoric of honor,[4] it will have a different tone than if one reads it primarily in relation to the discourse of creation myths. The number of different discourses indexed by the speeches is so great (one might add legal discourse, royal discourse, etc.) and the possibilities for interanimation so numerous that quarreling over their meaning is guaranteed. Since the frames of reference, values, and images of God in these different discourses are not even wholly compatible with one another, interpretations often implicitly (and sometimes explicitly)[5] secure themselves by excluding those discursive elements inconvenient for the interpreter's thesis. But voices ignored have a way of becoming persistent undertones, so that what is repressed by one interpretation becomes the starting point for another, unraveling interpretive certainty. Though this is true for all texts, as deconstructive critics and radical hermeneuts have caused us to appreciate, the divine speeches seem to flaunt this aspect of textuality.

Equally important to the way in which the divine speeches invite quarrels over meaning is the fact that so much of what is said is carried by intensely visual images. Both in detail and in number these images seem excessive if considered merely as illustrative material for the surface argument of the speeches. That excess entices the mind to grasp the images and their patterning as cognitively significant. But even if they are carriers of a subtext, they are no code to be deciphered. The natural polyvalency of images, evocative and often saturated with emotional resonances, resists reduction to propositional summation. What this suggests is that the divine speeches are not merely invoking an elusiveness appropriate to the dignity of divine transcendence but that they also engage the reader's understanding in a way different from other modes of speech in the book. Whereas the prose tale asked of the reader a relatively passive acknowledgment and the wisdom dialogue highlighted the exercise of critical and comparative judgment, the divine speeches engage specifically aesthetic dimensions of understanding. Hermeneutically, to borrow Ricoeur's words, the symbol gives rise to thought.

There is something else, however, which points to the limits of both a Bakhtinian, idea-oriented dialogism and even to the limits of an aesthetically keyed hermeneutics. What both of these approaches have difficulty grasping is the rhetoric of the sublime. The notion of the sublime is so notoriously difficult to define that one almost shies away from introducing it. But without denying the genuine differences, discussions of the sublime from Longinus to Lyotard do reflect a sufficient family resemblance to yield a recognizable set of features.[6] Although one often speaks of a sublime object or text, properly speaking the sublime is not an object but rather an experience that emerges from an encounter with something. As a recent philosophical discussion of the sublime suggests, this experience is one of "being on the outer fringe of our existence." Its locus is "at the threshold from the human to that which transcends the human; which borders on the possible and the impossible; the knowable and the unknowable; the meaningful and the fortuitous; the finite and the infinite."[7] Consequently, the sublime is classically described in terms of a crisis of understanding. Crucial to the sublime is the perceiving subject's sense of being overwhelmed by something too immense, vast, or powerful to be grasped by the categories available to the mind. More than merely a cognitive crisis, it is a crisis of subjectivity itself. And yet what is in some respects a negative experience is paradoxically accompanied by a sense of "transport" or "elation," or a moment in which the self is "realized" in a new way. Not surprisingly, the divine speeches in Job have often served as parade examples of the sublime and figure prominently in Edmund Burke's classic account.[8]

Traditional interpretations of the sublime, however, have tended to focus almost exclusively on psychological or experiential dimensions and so represent something of an opposite problem for understanding the divine speeches than hermeneutical approaches. Indeed, those interpretations of the divine speeches that stress the sublime only (here one thinks of Otto's classic description)[9] tend to obscure the ideational content of the divine speeches. In more recent philosophical discussions of the sublime, however, a place is made for the cognitive. As Lap-chuen Tsang has argued, although the sublime is an experience and not a objective thing, it is an experience that must always be *construed* within a framework of meaning and value.[10] Especially where one is talking about the rhetorical sublime, the aesthetic image mediates both experience and idea. Thus, although the primary framework for my discussion of the divine speeches will continue to be their dialogic role in the book, both the hermeneutical significance of the images and their role in the creation of an experience of the sublime will be crucial to understanding them.

The Place of the Divine Speeches in the Dialogical Structure of the Book

How the divine speeches are to be understood dialogically depends in large part in how one construes their relation to other parts of the book. Those who read the book in a strongly unified fashion may draw attention to the relation between the divine speeches and the narrative framework. Since the adversary's challenge, the reader has been waiting to see if Job will indeed curse God to God's face. What had been a figure of speech now becomes a literal possibility. Those who see the wisdom dialogue as the intellectual center of the book may read the divine speeches as a refutation both of the friends (there is no retributive justice in the scheme of creation) and of Job (the world is a cosmos and not the mad chaos Job envisions in chap. 12). These and many other ways of relating the divine speeches to other voices are legitimate and fruitful. The particular analysis I argue for in this study, however, is one that takes the book of Job as a series of different but juxtaposed ways of exploring the potentialities of the Job tradition. The prose tale makes use of its own distinctive genius to illumine one set of issues, as the wisdom dialogue between a sufferer and his friends illumines an overlapping but different set. I take the two final speeches of Job and God in chapters 29–31 and 38:1–42:6 as yet a third major way of recasting potential matters of interest, in this case by means of a disputation between a person and his God.

Since the didactic tale and the wisdom dialogue allude to identifiable genres, I would like to be able to say that the disputation between a person and his God also can be situated in relation to a generic tradition. But I think this is not the case. In his study of the way in which the book of Job adapts and parodies various ancient Near Eastern wisdom genres and traditions, Zuckerman distinguishes between the Mesopotamian dialogue texts and those he calls the "Righteous Sufferer's appeal to the deity."[11] He understands both to be taken up and joined by the Job poet in creating a dialogue/appeal form. Yet the one thing that is almost completely missing in the Mesopotamian appeals by a sufferer is the dramatic representation of a direct reply by the deity. Marduk's response to Subshi-meshre-Shakkan in *Ludlul* is mediated by emissaries who appear to the sufferer in a dream. In AO 4462, the Dialogue of a Man with His God, there is a dramatization of the divine reply (strophes 8 and 9, lines 48–67), but in scope and content it bears virtually no resemblance to the book of Job. Moreover, Job's speech in chapters 29–31, as discussed in chapter 7 of this book, bears little resemblance to Mesopotamian appeal texts but rather seems to posit as its audience an assembly of elders, however much it may be implicitly addressed to the deity. It only becomes explicitly a part of a disputation with God when God surprisingly appears and addresses Job directly.

So far as one can tell, there is no literary precedent for a pair of speeches that set over against one another the voice of a sufferer and the response of his God. What the author of the book of Job has composed is something of a tour de force. Nevertheless, one is warranted in setting the speech of Job in chapters 29–31 and the speech of God in particular relation to one another. They are, if the Elihu speeches are rightly judged to be a later addition, intended to be immediately juxtaposed in the book. Dramatically, too, they are linked. Though Job does not primarily address God in chapters 29–31, his rhetorical challenge in 31:35–37 sets up the divine response. When Job replies to God in 40:1–5 and 42:1–6, he does so with words and images that allude back to his own speech in chapters 29–31. The gesture of placing one's hand on one's mouth and being silent is both how Job described deference paid to him (29:9–10) and how he describes that which he now pays to God (40:4–5). He interprets the gesture in terms drawn from the discourse of honor and shame (40:4a) that was so important in his own self-presentation. The climactic words in Job's final reply in 42:6b, "dust and ashes," are those he had previously used in 30:19b to describe God's treatment of him. Thus, the verbal profile of Job's speech and his characterization in these replies are linked to his representation in chapters 29–31, not to his characterization in the wisdom dialogue or the prose tale.[12]

What these details suggest is that the speech by Job and the speech by God stand over against each other somewhat like the facing panels in a diptych. Examined in this fashion, as contrasting but linked utterances, one can see better what they contribute to the complex conversation that is the book of Job. For one thing, they supply what was absent from the wisdom dialogue. The genius of the wisdom dialogue is its capacity to split and engage two human perspectives on the nature of suffering, the world, and the divine. By generic convention if not rhetorical necessity, though the dialogue raises questions about the divine mind, it conducts itself exclusively on a human plane, without the answering voice of the gods. But what if one wanted to set up a second type of disputation, one that set the poles as the human versus the divine? In that case, rather than splitting the human perspective, one would need some discourse that represents it without drawing attention to its possible internal fracturing. Job's utterance in chapters 29–31, as I argued in chapter 7 of this book, speaks with just such a self-confident and monologic voice. His speech, in which he attempts to claim affirmation for a moral life lived in a moral community and situated within a moral universe, brings together in a coherent articulation perspectives developed by both sides of the wisdom dialogue. It embodies not only the assumptions of retributive justice and the fundamental moral coherency of the world characteristic of the friends' position but also Job's conviction that in his situation there exists a wrong to be righted and that the divine can be held to moral, perhaps even legal, account.

Almost every commentator notes that the divine speeches refuse to engage Job's arguments on his terms—and for good reason. What is in dispute between them is the nature of reality itself and the forms of moral imagination by which it can be grasped. As discussed in chapter 5 in connection with the poems that deal with the fate of the wicked, a deliberative rhetoric of argument can only take place within a context in which one can take for granted the basic tropes upon which argument is founded. If the very grounds are to be questioned, then the rhetoric must shift to an epideictic rhetoric that evokes more than it argues, a rhetoric in which the vivid presentation of images and tropes is foregrounded.[13] Obviously one cannot push the distinction to the extreme. All attempts at persuasion mix both arguments and tropes in varying degrees, and that is certainly true of the divine speeches.

If one looks at the engagement between Job's speech and God's not simply as a misfired propositional argument but as a contest of tropes, then some of what is at stake between them becomes evident. One is the relation of the divine and the human in the rhetoric of the two speeches. As pointed out in the discussion of chapters 29–31, Job's rhetoric repeatedly inscribes God into his speech as warrant and model for his conduct and his moral world (31:2-4, 6, 14-15, 23, 28). Divine and human beings occupy the same familiar territory. By contrast, the rhetorical questions addressed to Job by God (Where were you? Can you? Do you know?) eliminate him from presence, participation, or knowledge of the foundation and maintenance of the cosmos even as they address him. The issue that lurks in the contrasting rhetorics is that of the fundamental continuity or alterity of the divine and the human, an issue that has an almost obsessive persistence in the different voice-ideas of the book of Job.

The second point of comparison is the way in which both speeches display a fundamentally spatial imagination. Job's moral reasoning was enabled by his conception of a world constructed of privileged spaces and defining shapes: the circle of children about the father, the transactional space of the ranking elder at the plaza with his peers and dependents gathered around but at a certain remove, and the clearly differentiated spaces that distinguished the moral world of the town from the savage and desolate world of the desert. The divine speeches are equally as spatial in their imagination, in particular in chapter 38. But rather than shapes of center and circumference, they direct the imagination to the remotest points of the cosmos: to the foundations of the earth, the doors of the primordial sea, the horizon of dawn, the recesses of the sea and the gates of death, the home from which light and darkness emerge, the storage places of snow, hail, rain, and wind. The patterns of meaning and value embedded in the divine geography will be explored in more detail below, but the contrast between the way space is imagined could not be more radical, and consequently the nature of moral argument that it might support is very different. The spaces that fund Job's moral imagination are thoroughly parochial ones, and for that very reason are rich with meaning and value. But how, if at all, could one map Job's "neighborhood" into this divine space? The one point at which their geographies overlap is in the reference to the "waste and desolate" land (30:3b; 38:25-27). Yet nothing underscores the incommensurate nature of their perceptions more than their construals of this common space. Job invokes it as the place of punishment, utterly "outside," where those whose humanity is itself questionable are driven out. Although he does not call it godforsaken, that is how he envisions it, since in expressing his own sense of godforsakenness, he invokes the images of himself as "brother to jackals, companion to ostriches" (30:29), the denizens of this landscape of desolation. God, by contrast, describes it as human-forsaken (*lōʾ-ʾîš, lōʾ ʾādām bô*, 38:26) and represents it in an image of beauty, caught in the brief moment when rains cause a sudden burst of vegetation to grow. Indeed, God's language borders on the parodic, since the watering of the desolate land is described in terms of canal building (*pillag laššeṭep tĕʿālāh*),[14] that quintessential human activity that claims waste land for its own support.

Thirdly, the language of mutual but asymmetrical social relationship, which is fundamental to Job's moral imagination, is contested by the images of God's speech, particularly in chapter 39. It is not just that God chooses not to speak of human beings. More significantly, the way in which God speaks of animals implicitly challenges the adequacy of Job's moral and religious language. Although Job did not refer to domestic animals, one would have no difficulty in inserting them into his moral landscape, for they are part of his culture of obligation and protection. To their owners they owe their labor and products; in return they receive food and care. Israelite legal tradition even dealt with them in terms of legal responsibilities (Exod 22:28) and rights (Deut 5:14; 25:4). Yet in the social map of the cosmos as God describes it, what is celebrated is the refusal of the social bond between wild animals and humans, most explicitly in the references to the wild ox and wild ass, which will not serve in farm or city (39:5–12), but perhaps even within the animal world itself in the weak kinship bonds among wild goats and ostriches (39:4, 14–16). Without ever raising the issue to propositional explicitness, the tension between Job's images and God's challenges the embedded metaphor by which Job organizes his understanding of reality. The confident moral realism that Job takes for granted finds little anchorage in the divine speeches.

Sublimity and Argument in the Divine Speeches

The Sublime

Before examining more closely the nature of the argument that is implicitly developed in the sequence of images, I wish to say more about the dimension of the sublime. One can easily see how the divine speeches have come to serve as the epitome of sublime rhetoric. The theophanic stormwind (38:1) presents the divine by means of a phenomenon of nature that is inhuman and overpowering. As a device that both manifests and conceals the divine presence (cf. Ezek 1:4), the storm is a figure of ambiguity and obscurity, features frequently associated with the sublime.[15] The rhetorical questions that punctuate the divine speeches ("Where were you . . . ? Do you know . . . ? Can you . . . ? Who . . . ?") explicitly lift up the theme of human incapacity in the face of an overwhelming divine supercapacity. All of these questions can be answered, of course, but the very answers they require underscore that what is *apprehended* in the divine speeches cannot be *comprehended*.[16] The incessant repetition of the questions and the seemingly endless succession of highly vivid tableaus of inaccessible reality manifest the exorbitance of the sublime and its assault on the imagination.

More subtle is the use of spatial imagery in the divine speeches. It is not merely a matter of evoking the vastness of the cosmos, though the areas described span the distance from the abysses of the sea and underworld to the high heavens, and from the foundations of the earth to the homes of light and darkness beyond its uttermost edges. More significantly, the imagery is often cast in terms of limits and boundaries. The things to which Job's attention are directed are things at the edges of creation: the place where the very bases of the earth are sunk, the boundary between the sea and land, the place of dawn at the edge of the earth, the springs of the abyssal sea, the gates of the underworld, the paths that terminate at the houses of light and darkness at the edge of the cosmos. These mark the boundary between formlessness and structure, order and disorder, life and death, the darkness that harbors violence and the light that dispels it. The very oppositions that simultaneously make life possible and threaten it are thus manifested even as they are declared to be unknowable and uncontrollable by human understanding and will. Analogously, even as Job is refused access—Job was not there, does not know, was not the one to do such things—the very descriptions create a virtual experience. This play of presence and absence is crucial to the functioning of the sublime. Psychologically, it is the mechanism by which Burke understands the sublime to be generated by pain and its negation. More significantly, presence and absence is the key to Thomas Weiskel's semiotic theory of the sublime in the collapse of the ordinary relationship of signifier and signified.[17] That is similar to what happens here in the simultaneous withholding and offering of knowledge of the ultimately unknowable.

Toward the end of chapter 38, as the meteorological phenomena are introduced, the imagery takes a centripetal turn to focus on what is within the range of ordinary human experience. No easy familiarity is offered. Instead, the world is viewed through a lens of wondrous estrangement. In part the ordinary is made sublime by shifting attention from the presence of the phenomenon to its absent source—the storehouses from which snow and hail are dispensed, the unknowable point of origin for the lightning and the east wind. The everyday realia of rain, dew, frost, and ice are estranged by pressing the question of their generation, their mysterious way of being absent one day and suddenly present the next. The familiar scene of wadis rushing with water after a rainstorm is rendered uncanny by describing it in terms used for the human activity of canal building and the watering of cropland. Nature's parody of human purposive behavior is, as Kant would put it, experienced as bafflingly "counterpurposive."[18]

Chapter 38 is largely concerned with what Kant would call the "mathematical sublime," which engenders sublimity by overwhelming the mind with what it cannot comprehend in the categories available to it. Although that aspect continues in the description of the five pairs of animals, whose habits and abilities are mysterious to humans, chapters 39–41 are more concerned with the "dynamically sublime," which evokes fear through a dynamic of terror.[19] The term "terror," though a standard part of the vocabulary of the sublime, may be somewhat misleading. What is at issue is not so much stark terror as a kind of anxious dread. Burke's own analysis of the animal imagery in Job in relation to the sublime is particularly subtle, for he shows that not only are the images of violent animals capable of engendering sublime terror but also that those animals whose control eludes human capacity create the anxiety of human power-lessness.[20] The perplexity of many nineteenth and twentieth-century critics as to the function of the Behemoth and Leviathan speeches, a perplexity that often resulted in declaring them spurious, lay in their forgetfulness of what Burke and Lowth had analyzed so acutely. It lay in their failure to understand the divine speeches under the category of the sublime. The Behemoth and Leviathan pericopes, far from being alien to the divine speeches, are simply the crescendo of the sublime terror developed throughout chapters 38–41.

Tropes and Their Cognitive Claims

Although one may appreciate the sublime for its psychological and experiential function in the drama of the book, it is part of a rhetoric that also makes cognitive claims by means of the very images that generate a sense of the sublime. To grasp those claims, one must investigate the tropes and images more closely, both in themselves and in their patterning and sequencing. These cognitive claims, as many critics have noted, have to do with the relation of order and chaos in the world.

To understand the cognitive claims of the speeches, however, one must attend particularly to the progression of images.[21] The first divine speech begins with images of the firm and secure structures of an orderly creation. Even as they create an experience of sublime fear for the human who contemplates them, they also assert the stability of the cosmos. Notably, the leading image is that of the foundation of the earth itself, represented in architectural terms as the construction of a great temple (38:4–7). But in the second half of the speech (38:39–39:30) the imagery of the wild animals shifts the balance, moving beyond the boundary that separates the sown from the unsown, to the places and creatures that represent a hostile and alien other for the human. The final image of the second speech is the terrifying Leviathan (40:25–41:26), a legendary creature with mythic overtones, associated with primeval chaos. The divine speeches are thus structured to take Job, imaginatively, from places of secure boundaries to places where boundaries are put at risk. Although they invoke many of the images of creation accounts, they run counter to the narrative sequence of creation myths in which the creator god defeats the chaos monster and then proceeds to create a secure and stable world in which culture can flourish (cf. *Enuma Elish*; Ps 74:12–17; Isa 51:9–11). Here, although no narrative structure is used, the sequence enacts something of an "uncreation," as the divine speeches lead Job progressively closer to a sustained and intimate encounter with the primary symbol of the chaotic.

Chapter 38: The Cosmos   The key interpretive question for understanding the significance of the divine speeches has to do with the nature of the relationship established in these images between God and the symbols of the chaotic. In chapter 38 one seems to be on familiar ground. The repetition of terms for boundary, path, way, and place contributes to the sense of the security of a well-ordered cosmos, a mood already established by the initial imagery of architectural stability. Even when the forces that threaten order are introduced—the sea, night and its violence, the deep, death—they are described in terms of the limits imposed upon them ("bars and doors," "gates," the daily "shaking out" of the bedbugs of criminality). Yet even here there are intimations of a divine orientation at odds with what one finds in other representations of creation. Most strikingly, this occurs in the imagery for the sea in 38:8–11. In keeping with traditional imagery the sea is represented as violent and aggressive, "bursting out" and threatening to exceed its place until confined within the limits of "doors and bars." The description of the sea's waves as "proud" anticipates a theme that becomes prominent in the second divine speech. This pericope radically departs from traditional imagery, however, in that it does not cast the sea as God's opponent in battle (cf. Ps 74:13–14; 89:10–14; Isa 51:9–10; *Enuma Elish* IV) but instead represents God as the midwife who births the sea and wraps it in the swaddling bands of darkness and cloud. Whether this imagery represents an innovation of the Job poet or the use of an otherwise unknown tradition cannot be determined.

What can be investigated are the dynamics of the metaphor of birthing as it engages and transforms the traditional topos. In birth a force that will not be denied breaks through containment and transgresses a boundary. Quite literally, the breaking through of the birth waters of the womb marks the onset of the process. Wrapping a baby in swaddling bands serves to restrain its arms and legs from moving about and so to calm the child. Through this imagery both the traditional aggressiveness of the sea and the restraints placed upon it are taken up. But the image of the baby in place of the battle foe transforms the emotional register and introduces novel implications. The metaphorical filter diminishes the sense of the sea as a hostile, alien power and associates it rather with the vigor of new life. Moreover, the restraints placed upon it are cast in terms of nurture and protection. The traditional resonance of the sea is not wholly overturned, of course, but rather reaccented. Here the chaotic waters of the sea are represented not only as the object of divine limitation but also of divine care.

Chapter 39: The Wild Animals   The sense of inverted values evoked by the description of the sea, and perhaps also by the transformation of the wilderness where there is emphatically no human presence, remain relatively mild. With the introduction of the five pairs of animals, however, the sense of dislocation intensifies. Here, again, themes of nurture are presented through images of birth, food, and freedom. But the unsettling thing, still sometimes overlooked in interpretations of the divine speeches, is the fact that the animals selected for presentation almost all belong to the hostile and alien realm of the desert wilderness. Although commentators had long noted the fact that the animals celebrated in God's speech are nondomesticated, the crucial context for establishing their proper interpretation was presented in Othmar Keel's *Jahwehs Entgegnung an Ijob*. Keel observed the difficulty modern western interpreters have in properly understanding the symbolic significance of these animals and what is said about them. The modern, humanly created threat to the existence of wilderness has made its creatures seem both precious and fragile. In antiquity, however, the wild served as the Other against which human culture defined itself.[22] A common image of divine punishment was the transformation of a city (a place of order and human values) into a desert waste (a chaotic place hostile to human culture; Ps 107:33–38; Isa 34:8–15; Hos 2:5b, 14), occupied by its characteristically eerie and uncanny animals (Isa 13:19–21; 34:8–15; Jer 50:39–40; Zeph 2:13–15), several of which also occur in the divine speeches (the lion, the raven, the wild ass, and the ostrich).

The basic perception embodied in these biblical passages is reflected also in two motifs from ancient Near Eastern art: the royal hunt and the depiction of the "Lord of the animals." Near Eastern kings are often represented as hunting many of the animals depicted in the divine speeches.[23] As a symbolic act, the royal hunt represented the king's role in protecting the integrity of the land against hostile forces. In the Mesopotamian iconic motif of the "Lord of the animals," a divine figure is flanked by wild animals, which he grasps in each hand in an evident enactment of control. Like the chaotic sea, the animals represent an anarchic force that is part of the world but limited by divine power (cf. Jer 27:5–7). The motif of nurture of the animals is also a part of this ancient Near Eastern background. In Mesopotamian art the "world tree" motif is sometimes combined with that of the "Lord of the animals," such that animals turn their heads to eat from the tree even as they are grasped and restrained by the deity.[24]

It is possible, as Psalm 104 attests, to create out of this material a vision of the world as a harmonious place in which the spheres of the human and the animal coexist as complementary creations of God. But that is not what the divine speeches are about.[25] Here the suppression of descriptions of human activity, the explicit opposition between the animals and human purposes, and repeated references to God's provision for these creatures (38:39–41; 39:5–8, 26–30) destabilizes the customary binary oppositions of order and the chaotic, culture and nature, blessed and godforsaken. More disturbingly, it seems to associate God in a positive fashion with these creatures of the fearful beyond. Since these images play such an important role in the development of the significance of the divine speeches, they deserve close attention.

The series begins, fittingly, with the lion, the predatory wild animal par excellence in the ancient world (Gen 49:9; Num 23:24; Ps 17:12; Isa 5:29; Amos 3:4; Nah 2:12).[26] The rhetorical question addressed to Job implies that what he cannot do, God does—namely, to hunt prey for the lion (cf. Ps 104:21), including presumably, the sheep kept by humans (1 Sam 17:34–37; Jer 25:36–38; Mic 5:7; cf. the metaphor in Job 29:17). Thus, in hunting on behalf of the lions, God appears to nurture an element of creation hostile to humans.

The choice of the lion to begin the series may also be a pointed retort to another form of moral discourse. In the Babylonian Theodicy the lion and the wild ass are specifically mentioned in a passage in which the sufferer invokes their flourishing as evidence of the moral disorder of the world. "The on[ager], the wild ass, that had its fill of [wild grass?], / Did it carefully ca[rry out?] a god's intentions? / The savage lion that devoured the choicest meat, / Did it bring its offerings to appease a goddess' anger? / The parvenu who multiplies his wealth, / Did he weigh out precious gold to the mother goddess for a family?" (lines 48–53).[27] Although there is little likelihood that the Job poet is consciously invoking the Babylonian Theodicy, it is plausible that these animals served as part of a conventional trope in the poetics of the wisdom dialogue tradition or more broadly in poetry that reflected on the moral order. Together with the human upstart they are represented as by definition godless and impious; consequently, their well-being is an offense. To single out the lion and the wild ass as objects of providential care, as the divine speeches do, is to issue a radical challenge to the fundamental images that informed moral thought in this tradition.

The following two pairs of animals in the sequence establish the important motif of the evasion of human purpose and control. This theme is explicit in the case of the wild ass and wild ox (39:5–12), as noted earlier, but it is also present in more subtle form with the mountain goats and wild deer (39:1–4). The wild ass, as evident in the Babylonian Theodicy, is often a symbol for the moral outlaw (cf. Gen 16:12; Job 24:5; 30:7; 39:7). Here, God's care for the wild ass is presented in terms of an inversion of the values of human culture. Its habitat, the desolate salt flats and nearly barren mountains (39:6, 8), is not only the opposite of the human "sown" land but also serves as an image of punishment for people (Ps 107:34; Jer 17:6). By contrast, the city, the quintessential place of human culture, is presented as a locus of noise and oppression (Job 39:7), a place of bondage from which God sets the wild ass free (39:5). Similarly, the wild ox is represented in such a way as to mock the logic of domestication. The defining feature of domestication is the exchange of food for service (Isa 1:3), an arrangement patently absurd in relation to the wild ox (Job 39:9), as are the psychological relationships of domestication—domination (39:10) and trust (39:11).

Though the mountain goats and wild deer are not fearsome or traditionally despised animals, they are the counterimage to domesticated sheep and goats. The essential knowledge of the animals' reproduction that a shepherd needs to increase his flocks cannot be known for mountain goats and wild deer (39:1–

3). Moreover, instead of forming ever increasing herds, as useful domesticated animals do, their young disperse (39:4).

The ostrich had been invoked by Job in 30:29 as his companion, a figure meant to stress his isolation from human society and perhaps to suggest his mournfulness (30:31), since the ostrich's cry was associated with mourning (Mic 1:8). Here, in contrast, the ostrich is an image of pure heedless joy. In its heedlessness the ostrich represents the absence of "wisdom" and "understanding," terms closely associated with the rationality of creation (e.g., Prov 3:19–20; 8:22–31), which humans seek to know in order to live securely (Prov 3:21–26; 8:32–36). What the ostrich possesses instead is anarchic joy. The term by which she is named in Job 39:13 is not the usual one (*ya'ānāh*), but *rĕnānîm*, literally, "cries of joy." Similarly, the verb that describes the movement of its wings (*'ālas*) literally means "to be glad." That the ostrich laughs at the pursuit of horse and rider is of particular significance, since it evokes the scene of the hunt, that symbolic enactment of the opposition between culture and nature and the defense of human order against the chaotic.[28] Though the deliberately elusive style of the divine speeches draws no explicit conclusion, God's celebration of the ostrich's evasion seems unnervingly to place God in considerable sympathy with the emblems of the chaotic.

The same effect, achieved by different means, occurs in the description of the war horse. What is celebrated in the war horse is its ecstatic delight in battle, a characteristic that is no product of domestication but comes from its own unfathomable nature. Like the ostrich, the horse "laughs at fear, afraid of nothing" (39:22a). This is not a form of courage, the overcoming of fear such as humans know, but something more elemental. By describing the horse as snorting when he scents battle from afar, the poet suggests that the desire for battle—with all its violence, noise, and confusion—is a kind of lust, as a stallion would scent a mare in heat. But this pericope is not just about horses. As has been noted,[29] the initial description of the horse is composed largely in terms elsewhere used to describe the appearance of God in glory: "might" (12:13), "thunder" (40:9), "majesty" (37:22) and "terror" (9:34; 13:21). The poet's touch is exquisitely subtle. Nothing is stated, yet much is evoked.

This unnerving coincidence of beauty and horror, so characteristic of the sublime, is more disturbingly present in the concluding pericope. The passage begins with a traditional image of mystery and beauty, the flight of the hawk (cf. Prov 30:18–19). The poet then shifts from the imagery of the vast distances of the hawk's flight to the vertical height of the vulture's nest, high on a rocky crag. The nest suggests the bird's provision of food for its nestlings (cf. the raven's young who cry to God for food, 38:41). But the poet delays that description, commenting first on the bird's extraordinary power of sight (39:29). The final verse follows the bird's line of vision and its flight—to the corpses of those killed in battle (*ḥalālîm*). Here is the food that God provides, the blood that the young will drink. With this sublimely horrific image of human beings as the foodstuff of young vultures, God concludes the speech.

Chapters 40–41: Behemoth and Leviathan   The second divine speech says nothing new. Since Job appears to be hard of hearing, God simply repeats the message, louder and more slowly. Though animals are again the vehicle, the rhetorical strategy is different. Whereas the first divine speech created a panorama of the cosmos through a flashing series of vivid but brief images, the second divine speech engages Job in a tightly focused exercise of close and rigorous contemplation. If the first speech employed the sublime mode of repetitive excess, the second employs that of exorbitance. But no more than in the first speech will these images be translated into conceptual discourse. Only primary images can evoke the necessary recognition and emotional response.

The introduction to the second speech presents it in relation to Job's criticism of God's *mišpāṭ* ("governance," 40:8). One anticipates that the speeches will defend God's governance and also define it in some way other than Job's forensic understanding. As in the preceding speech, God makes the case by means of images that both invoke and overturn conventional assumptions. From the point of view of Job or of any human, there is little question what Behemoth and Leviathan represent. Although they are unquestionably creatures of God (40:15; 41:25–26; cf. Ps 104:26), they partake of the primordial (Behemoth, 40:15) and the mythic (Leviathan, 41:10–17). These are liminal beings who belong to the boundaries of the symbolic world. More emphatically than the wild animals of chapters 38–39, they manifest the alien Other, with the terror of the chaotic present in their very being. The hermeneutically crucial question, however, is how the relationship between God and these creatures is represented in this second divine speech. The temptation is to read these speeches according to the script of the divine warrior creation myth, that is, along the lines of Psalms 74 and 89 and Isaiah 51, in which God defeats the manifestations of chaos in order to establish the world that he continues to rule. But although this speech may draw on materials from those traditions, it does not "say" the same thing.

More developed than its counterpart in chapter 38, the introduction to this speech cultivates vocabulary and imagery of power and pride. God asks Job if his power is as great as God's and if he can therefore bring low the proud. If he can, then God will praise Job's great victory (40:9–14). As the rhetoric of the rest of the speech makes evident, Behemoth and Leviathan serve as examples of proud creatures whom neither Job nor any other human could possibly bring low. One can see why many commentators are inclined to read the speeches simply as affirming that what Job cannot do, God can. That reading would deliver the comforting and deeply traditional view of the world as one organized and defended by a god who continually defeats the forces of chaos, even if he does not guarantee strict legal justice. It would allow Job to resume his proper place within that well-regulated world. But things are not so simple. The discourse concerning pride in this speech, as it figures God's relation to the great creatures and thus sheds light on God's governance, is both difficult and disturbing.

In Hebrew discourse, the vocabulary of pride often makes use of metaphors of height. Thus, the sea's waves in 38:11 are literally "high" (*gā'ôn*), metaphorically "proud." Here, as God describes the godlike qualities Job would need, the terms often rendered as "majesty" and "dignity" are derived from words for height (*gā'ôn* and *gōbāh*, v. 10), as is the word that negatively describes the "proud" (*gē'eh*) who are the objects of divine wrath in verses 11–12. The discourse of pride as height is complex. As a divine quality, it is always positive. When applied to creatures, it is for that reason ambivalent. The allegories of the tree in Ezekiel 31 and Daniel 4 illustrate. There the proud majesty of the king, figured by the height of the tree, is initially a sign of the positive quality that enables the tree-king to nurture other creatures. But excessive height represents arrogance that must be checked. Following the logic of the images the tree is cut down, an image of the proud "abased" and "brought low" (Job 40:11–12). Thus, *gā'ôn* is neither good nor bad in itself but a matter of appropriateness. The symbolic imagination that forms itself around a discourse of height-pride is one of regulation and containment. As a way of figuring the world and its governance, this discourse organizes itself in a way very different from the legal imagination. Nor does it map easily onto Job's honor-based moral imagination in chapters 29–31, despite some similarities.

All would be simple enough if the following descriptions of Behemoth and Leviathan functioned simply as images of proud creatures that Job cannot bring low but God can and does. The problem is that, although God's ability to overcome them is taken for granted, there is little or no reference to enmity or hostility between God and these creatures. Instead, God describes them with evident admiration. They are magnificent beings whose pride is appropriate to their place in creation. What is being said by means of these descriptions about divine governance is more difficult to grasp.

A closer look at Behemoth and Leviathan is required. Whether Behemoth is based on the water buffalo and the bull monsters of Semitic mythology or on the hippopotamus and Egyptian mythology of Horus and Seth matters less than what is said in the passage at hand, although an allusion to the Horus and Seth traditions might create an expectation of divine enmity toward the creature comparable to what is typical of Leviathan traditions. Such expectations, however, are not fulfilled by what is actually said about Behemoth. Here the stress is on Behemoth as a creature of God, one described with evident pride for his size and strength. The account of Behemoth's physical appearance is framed by two references to his creation: "whom I made along with you" (40:15b), and "he is the first/chief of the acts of God" (40:19a). The first comment associates Job and

Behemoth as fellow creatures. The second gives Behemoth a status exceeding Job's. Although the word *rē'šît* may be taken in a temporal sense, to suggest Behemoth's primordial antiquity (cf. the same word used to describe wisdom in Prov 8:22), it seems more likely here to be used in a qualitative sense. Like Behemoth, Leviathan will also be described as a creature "without equal," a king over all the proud (41:25–26).

If there is any anchor in the text for a suggestion of conflict between Behemoth and God, it depends on the grammatically anomalous and syntactically ambiguous verse 19b. As pointed, the clause reads "his maker brings near his sword." If "his sword" refers to God's sword, the claim would be that God (alone) is capable of confronting the power of this creature, thus forming a contrast with verse 24, which implies that no human can. Though plausible, it is not the only possible reading. Given the ambiguity of the pronouns, the words might also be taken to mean that it is God who has given Behemoth his great power (Behemoth's "sword") as a token of his lordship over other animals as the chief of the works of God. But the word translated "his maker" (*hā'ōśô*) is grammatically anomalous, being doubly determined. The Hebrew consonants suggest that the word should be pointed he *'āśû*, "made," the same word used to describe Leviathan as "made without fear" (41:25). A modest emendation in 40:19b (from *yaggēš* to *nôgēš*) yields "made to dominate his companions," a claim more in keeping with the context.[30] The following description is not at all evocative of violence but describes the peaceful, even stolid pleasures of Behemoth, whose food comes to him as he lies shaded in the water, unmoved even as the river's torrents rush against him.

However the interpretive issue of verse 19b is resolved, in this pair of monstrous creatures, Behemoth plays "immovable object" to Leviathan's "irresistible force." As placid strength was the hallmark of Behemoth, so fearsome violence is the characteristic of Leviathan. This depiction builds on the well-known traditions of Leviathan as the sea monster with which Yahweh in Israelite mythology and Baal and Anat in Ugaritic mythology do battle (Ps 74:13–14; Isa 27:1; cf. Job 3:8; KTU 1.5.I.1 = CTA 5.I.1; KTU 1.3.III.40–42 = CTA 3.III.D.37–39). In some texts, however, Leviathan and the typologically related *tannînîm* are featured simply as creatures of God (Gen 1:21; Pss 104:26; 148:7), without reference to any hostility. Both traditions appear to inform the description of Leviathan in Job 40–41.

The significance of the Leviathan pericope can scarcely be overstated. It is both the climax and the epitome of what God has to say to Job. But both the intensely visual, descriptive style and some unfortunately obscure verses make interpretation anything but easy. The inability of any human to capture or dominate Leviathan (40:25–32) is simply an amplification of the theme already addressed in relation to the wild ox and wild ass. What comes next, however, is more critical for understanding what specifically is at issue here, for it deals with the relation of God and Leviathan. Unfortunately, textual obscurities in 41:2–4 lead to very different translations and interpretations.

The perplexing, but for this very reason perhaps revealing, problem is the alternation between third person and first person pronouns. Having described the terror inspired by Leviathan (41:1) and declared that no one is fierce enough to rouse him up (41:2a), God then says either, "Who then can stand against him?" or "Who then can stand against me?" The manuscript tradition is divided. The following verse is clearly first person speech: "Whoever confronts me, I will repay! Under all the heavens, he is mine!" It can certainly be argued that the rhetoric is that of lesser to greater. Just as no one can stand against Leviathan, how much more can one not stand against God (cf. 40:7, 9). It is, however, rather abrupt in a passage that is otherwise dedicated to the description of Leviathan and his effect on lesser beings, so much so that some have suggested that the first person pronouns were inserted by scribes who were shocked by the godlike prowess attributed to Leviathan.[31] Perhaps that suggestion is correct, but no positive evidence exists for it. Yet even as the text stands, there is a curious level of identification between God and Leviathan. God represents himself as being in the image of Leviathan, only more so. Indeed, as has often been pointed out, the physical description of Leviathan is uncannily evocative of the theophanic descriptions of God.[32]

Interpreters divide most sharply, however, over the translation and interpretation of verse 4. Both syntax and semantics are ambiguous. The argument turns on the word *baddîm* (either "parts," "limbs," or "boasting"), and the phrases *dĕbar-gĕbûrôt* (either "the matter of strength" or "the powerful word"), and the phrase *ḥîn 'erkô* (either "graceful form" or "persuasive argument"). The verb *lō'-'aḥārîš* may be rendered either "I will not keep silent" or "I will silence," which can be taken as an implied question—"Did I not silence?" As so often with ambiguous phrases, the understanding of the larger context directs the resolution of the ambiguity. Those who wish to see in the passage a reflex of the *Chaoskampf* theme read something like, "Did I not silence his boastings, his mighty word, and his persuasive case?"[33] Those who see the emphasis in the passage as on the majesty of Leviathan read something like, "I will not keep silence concerning his limbs, his power, and his exquisite form."[34] My own frame of interpretation inclines me to the latter understanding, but not without good exegetical reason. There is no known tradition of Leviathan's boasting silenced by God.[35] Moreover, the continuation of the passage in fact does begin a detailed description of the physical appearance of Leviathan. And if there is any boast, it is one that God himself makes on behalf of Leviathan at the end of the speech: "On earth there is none who can dominate him, made as he is without fear. He looks down upon all that is haughty; he is king over all that are proud." The shock of this passage is that it runs counter to the expectations of those who think of Leviathan in terms of the *Chaoskampf*. Far from recounting a confrontation with Leviathan that results in its defeat, humiliation, and abasement, the passage celebrates its *rightful* pride, based upon its terrifying strength and violence.

The Tragic Sublime

The question remains: What is one to make of the divine speeches? There are many things that are obvious in them, including the power of God and the comparative impotence of humans, or the cosmos as a place of structure and order, within which the chaotic forces have their rightful place. But deeper recognition of what is being said emerges from the cumulative force of subtle suggestion. With what tonality does God speak of the things described? What does God delight in and nurture in the world? With what creatures does God identify? From the striking metaphor of the sea as swaddled infant, to the celebration of the wildness of those creatures who mock and spurn human control, to the ecstatic description of Leviathan, the uncomfortable sense grows that God's identification with the chaotic is as strong as with the symbols of order.

At the end of the divine speeches three characters dominate the scene: Job, God, and Leviathan. The crucial hermeneutical task posed by the images is to discern the relationships among them. Job, as was clear from chapters 29–31, laid claim to an essential continuity between himself and God. Knowing himself as embodiment and upholder of the order of moral values, he knows God. Although God says nothing that would encourage such an identification, the divine speeches need not be construed as an absolute rebuttal of such continuity (though such an interpretation could also be seriously argued). Here modern readers have to be wary of anachronistic projections. The distinction between the moral order and the physical order comes naturally to us as an inheritance of the Enlightenment, but it would have been a deeply alien notion in the ancient Near East.[36] Since God's speeches begin with such attention to the order of the cosmos, I would not be inclined to see the speeches as a rejection of God's role as source of moral order in the social realm. But the deity in these speeches takes pains to establish another relationship of congruence, that between God and Leviathan. Here the nonmoral and nonrational aspects of deity are highlighted. Knowing Leviathan, one knows something of the monstrous that is its own reflection of the numinous, wholly otherness of God.[37]

In this way of reading the divine speeches, Job and Leviathan emerge as paired opposites, both "perfected" embodiments of aspects of the divine, but neither representing a full image. Significantly, in this drama, it is not Leviathan's pride that is brought low and abased, but Job's. In what, though, does Job's pride consist? His pride, the characteristic human pride, I would argue, is precisely his "blessed rage for order." As Job's speech in chapters 29–31 illustrated, the human imperative is the creation of orders of value and meaning within which to make sense of experience. Being, as Geertz described us, "incomplete animals," who cannot rely on the hard-wiring of instinct for the structuring of our worlds, we use our symbolic capacity to construct what is lacking.[38] And we typically insist that our moral orders are not simply made up but are grounded in the structures of reality itself.[39] Consequently, it is very difficult for human ideologies to acknowledge the reality of that which resists rational organization into structures of meaning and human purpose.

The human passion for moral order is also a passion for security, for discerning a way of living that can keep the world whole and children safe: "And Job would rise early in the morning and would offer whole offerings according to the number of them all, for, Job said, 'Perhaps my children have sinned and cursed God'" (1:5). It is a passion to deny the tragic in existence. This is what underlies the baffled astonishment of the one who weeps for the unfortunate, grieves for the needy and yet finds evil and darkness instead of good and light (31:25–26). The face of Leviathan exposes the hubris and the self-deception of the human rage for order. But what makes for tragedy is not simply the nature of the cosmos in itself but rather the inevitable clash of two necessities. It is not possible that human beings could cease to be makers of moral worlds that shelter and protect what Ricoeur calls value-relations and personal relations.[40] Neither is it possible that the intrinsic and unmasterable violence of existence, its indifference to human values, will cease to "make the depths boil like a cauldron," with all the pain, loss, and moral shock that this image implies.

In response to what he has heard, Job briefly replies and then falls silent. Tragic knowledge gestures to the limits of dialogue, for there is nothing left to say. In an essay on tragedy and philosophy, in which he explores the challenges of tragedy to a discipline that embodies the human passion for rendering the world rationally transparent, William Desmond describes tragic insight as a kind of dying: "Thus we might liken [it] to a process of being drowned: the air of everyday instrumentalities is withdrawn, we cannot breathe, we are being asphyxiated by a knowing that we cannot process, cannot digest. We are brought under, going under, undergoing, in shock from a lightning-bolt out of the Once and the Never."[41] Though he does not invoke the category, he describes the tragic in terms of the sublime. The excess and exorbitance of what is recognized overwhelm the categories one had at hand. The rest, as Hamlet says, is silence.

Yet the sublime, including the tragic sublime, is not merely a sense of "going under," for it also includes that paradoxical and elusive sense sometimes described as "transport" or "elation." Those who experience the divine speeches as sublime—and not all do[42]—have at least an inchoate sense of what is meant by this "transport." One must be careful, however, for the sublime is not a mechanism for evading the tragic. It is emphatically not, as Gordis once suggested, that "the beauty of the world becomes an anodyne to man's suffering."[43] Exploring the paradox of sublimity does allow, however, for a more nuanced understanding of the human situation in a tragically structured world. It also facilitates a deconstruction of the overly neat opposition between Job and Leviathan offered earlier.

There is not, and indeed could not be, a single account of the paradoxical nature of sublime experience. Some are more suggestive for the experience of the divine speeches than others, however. Given the strong evocation of terror in the Leviathan speech, one might think first of Burke's analysis of sublime elation as the joy of experiencing oneself in the presence of danger and yet preserved. Transposed into more modern categories, Burke's analysis might suggest a kind of existential therapy, an exercise for the confrontation and mastery of the fear of the chaotic that threatens death. Though I will return to Burke's insights later, it is rather with Longinus that one can helpfully explore the *rhetorical* sublime of the divine speeches and its possible effect on the one who experiences it. Longinus describes the effects of sublime speech in terms of its two-stage effect on subjectivity. The first stage is the overwhelming force that scatters the self-presence of the hearer. The effect of sublime writing

> is not to persuade the audience but rather to transport them out of themselves. Invariably what inspires wonder casts a spell upon us and is always superior to what is merely convincing and pleasing. For our convictions are usually under our own control, while such passages exercise an irresistible power of mastery and get the upper hand. . . . A well-timed flash of sublimity scatters everything before it like a bolt of lightning.[44]

Even many of those who dislike what they hear in the divine speeches nevertheless recognize in them the power to displace the hearer from her self-possession.

But why is this experience so regularly associated with a sense of exhilaration? Longinus gropes somewhat for an explanation for the quality of pleasure that occurs within this sense of displacement. Ultimately, he suggests that the effect of "uplift" or "transport" that occurs in the presence of sublime objects or words is created by a kind of identification, the second stage of sublime experience. Here the distinction between speaker and hearer is blurred: "For the true sublime, by some virtue of its nature, elevates us: uplifted with a sense of proud possession, we are filled with joyful pride, as if we had ourselves produced the very thing we heard."[45]

Susanne Guerlac has suggested that Longinus's statement on the relation between sublime speech and the one who experiences it be understood in light of Heidegger's reflections on the reception of a work of art. For Heidegger this reception or "preserving" is also a second moment of creation. It is both a repetition and an appropriation (*Ereignis*), an owning of the experience. Thus, the experience of the sublime is not a matter of substantive identification with the sublime object or rhetor, but an act of re-enunciation, a heightened form of "citation."[46] The suggestiveness of this analysis of sublime transport for the book of Job is evident in the fact that Job's response to the divine speeches does in fact take, at least in part, the form of a citation (42:3a//38:2; 42:4b//38:3b; 40:7b).[47] However Job's enigmatic final words are understood (42:6), they point to a subjectivity that has been scattered and reformed by the divine speeches.

This way of thinking of sublime transport as a kind of re-enunciation opens up a manner of understanding Job's response that provides an important supplement to Bakhtin's categories. When Bakhtin talks about citation, he distinguishes between "the authoritative words of another" and "innerly persuasive discourse."[48] Authoritative words demand our acknowledgment with a binding force, independently of persuasive power. They permit no play, no contextualizing, no stylizing. Innerly persuasive words, by contrast, are those that, though still recognizably belonging to another, are appropriated and adapted for one's own understanding. On those terms one can merely debate whether Job submits without being persuaded or whether Job is in fact persuaded to a new understanding. Or, if one sees his reply as a Bakhtinian word with a loophole, one can say that he neither submits nor is persuaded. Although these are legitimate ways to think about Job's reply, what concerns me is that they move too entirely in the realm of the ideological. They cannot address the nonrational aspect of response that is characteristic of the sublime. What is helpful about the logic of the sublime is that it permits one to grasp a way in which the words of the divine speeches become Job's "own" words whether or not they effect an ideological persuasion, the way in which, despite their tragic dimension, they create a positive good.

The "ex-static" dynamic of sublime transport exalts insofar as the hearer momentarily experiences herself as though she were the source of the creative power of the enunciation. Under any circumstances this is a thrilling experience. In religious language it is one of the primary means of identification with the divine creative power and thus one of the primary modes of worship. Given the content of the divine speeches that Job has heard and now experiences "as though he had created what he heard," sublimity has a crucial role to play.

What Job has just heard in the divine speeches, however, is a devastating undermining of his understanding of the unproblematic moral continuity between himself, the world, and God. It is a profound loss of unity, a recognition of the deeply fractured nature of reality. The experience of sublime transport resolves nothing substantively. It does, however, provide a means by which the loss of unity is itself experientially displaced, as Job feels the words of the divine speech as though he himself were speaking them. As Guerlac says, the moment of *hypsous* serves "as a kind of 'antidote' to division and defeat."[49]

Job has, as it were, not only spoken his own words (chaps. 29–31) but also, through the displacement of the sublime, has spoken the words of God regarding the realities of the world. Job is thus not simply the unknowing opposite of Leviathan in the dynamic economy of creation but one who grasps in the sublime experience the nature of a tragically structured world and his place in it. Job has not necessarily endorsed but has owned the place of Leviathan in the world. The transport of tragic sublimity is what assists Job, in Ricoeur's words "to identify his freedom with inimical necessity . . . [to be] ready to convert freedom and necessity into fate."[50]

But why is this not merely sad? When Desmond spoke of tragic insight as a kind of dying, he also suggested that the aftermath of that recognition was the generation of a "posthumous mind," a way of grasping one's situation in life "as if from beyond death."[51] The very recognition of tragic loss can make possible the recognition of "the sheer 'once there is' of being at all."[52] Just as the acknowledgment of the tragic structure of existence points to the limits of human self-sufficiency, so conversely does it point to the preciousness of being—but this time in the mode of gift.

Once again, the analyses of the tragic and the sublime converge suggestively. As Lyotard muses over the ancient puzzle of how the sublime creates the sense of delight, he turns back to Burke's insight that terror arises from all those things that figure death. The dimension of fear in the sublime, Lyotard suggests, is that everything that is human ("the gaze, the other, language or life"[53]) may be extinguished. It is the bleakness of abandonment in the face of the inhuman— for Job, the face of Leviathan. But rather than reading Burke as existential therapy, as the mastery of one's fear, Lyotard locates the paradoxical sublime delight in "the feeling that something will happen, despite everything, within this threatening void, that something will take 'place' and will announce that everything is not over."[54] Thus, the play of death and life at the boundary between the human and the inhuman generates this "almost neurotic" pleasure. This is the consolation of the tragic sublime. "The only 'response' to the question of the abandoned that has ever been heard," says Lyotard, "is not *Know why*, but *Be*."[55]

The Divine Speeches and the Dialogue with the Prose Tale

Reading the divine speeches as a mode of the tragic sublime has the consequence of rendering the dialogic relationship between them and the conclusion of the prose tale more complex than I previously indicated. It is not enough to say that the prose tale serves to prevent closure by the divine speeches. The relations of power, contest, and subversion run in both directions, as the divine speeches and Job's reply pose their own challenge to the prose tale's configuration of issues. As I suggested in chapter 2, the prose tale taken by itself embodies a resolutely nontragic perspective. Terrible and unaccountable suffering can and does happen in human lives, but a stance of radical acceptance refuses to admit to a tragic rupture. The fabric of existence is whole and complete, and in that recognition lies strength and tranquility. Its aesthetic is not the sublime but the beautiful. The dialogue between Job and God in chapters 29–31 and 38:1–42:6, however, argues the opposite. Tragic rupture is the figure at the heart of human existence. One could actually imagine the Job of 42:1– 6 continuing his speech by uttering the words of the prose tale: "Naked I came from my mother's womb and naked I shall return there; YHWH has given and YHWH has taken." "We receive good from God, and do we not also receive trouble?" One could even imagine him, having experienced the sublimity of God, saying, "Blessed be the name of YHWH." But the same words, uttered by a person in a different context, never mean the same thing.

The deficiency in the moral imagination of the prose tale, from the perspective of Job's and God's exchange at the end of the book, is not in its depiction of piety but in its underestimation of what it takes to utter those words. The desire not to see the rent at the heart of the world allowed the Adversary's implicit definition of the nature of true piety to go unchallenged in the prose tale's airy dismissal of the significance of moral reciprocity (or the lack thereof) in divine-human relations. The wisdom dialogue in its various voices reasserted the human hunger for justice. But Job's attempt in chapters 29–31 to make a place for such moral reciprocity within an unbroken world collapses before the self-representation of God in chapters 38–41. Piety need not exclude a passion for justice, but if it would cling to such, it must situate that passion in a tragically structured existence. Thus, the prose conclusion's attempt to subvert divine finalization, by having God repudiate the friends' words and endorse Job's, may just as easily have the currents of irony reversed. Words spoken "without knowledge" (38:2) may nevertheless be correct (*nĕkônāh*, 42:8). The prose tale's attempted tweaking of God also facilitates the renewal of serious engagement between the divine speeches and the wisdom dialogue. Job's own fractured and contradictory imagining of God and God's relation both to violence and to justice is perhaps closer to the truth than even Job realized.

But what about the prose tale's happy ending? When the prose tale was taken on its own, the renewal it depicted was a triumphant expression of its confidence in the possibility of a moral and material wholeness in life. By being interrupted, however, and reappearing after the divine speeches, the end of the prose tale loses the monologic quality it possessed simply as the conclusion to its own nontragic story. The divine speeches invite a dialogic double reading of it. Without displacing the role of 42:7–17 as conclusion to the nontragic prose tale proper, the divine speeches encourage another reading of it as a posttragic epilogue to the whole book, one in which the goodness of life in all its fragility is embraced.

In such a reading the interest is on the character of Job, who emerges in some ways oddly like the ostrich described by God in the speeches from the whirlwind. Like the ostrich, Job, too, brings his children into a dangerous world, where they may well be crushed and trampled. Unlike the ostrich, however, which forgets the dangers to its offspring, it is unlikely that Job can be said to forget their vulnerability. But what of the ostrich's laughter? Not only the ostrich but several of the animals are said to laugh. As the ostrich laughs at her pursuers, so the wild ass laughs at the tumult of the city, and the stallion and Leviathan at the weapons of war. Theirs is a defiant laughter, heedless of danger. They lack the capacity for tragedy. Their limits in the world are not tragic ones. But can the tragic Job be said to laugh? That depends on how one construes the enigmatic information—strangely gratuitous information—about Job's naming of his daughters with the names of nature's beauty ("dove"), of sensuous beauty ("cinnamon") and of erotic beauty ("horn of eye shadow") and endowing them with his own substance as an inheritance. Such playful names are a form of laughter—not heedless or anarchic laughter—but human and therefore tragic laughter. Read in dialogic relation, the sublimity of the divine speeches and the beauty of the prose epilogue gestures toward the human incorporation of tragedy into the powerful imperatives of desire: to live and to love.

Yet, because the prose conclusion does not "belong" to the dialogue between Job and God in chapters 29–31, and 38:1–42:6 but to its own version of the Job tale, its voice will not merge without remainder into what has preceded. It remains another consciousness, perceiving from another perspective. That irreducible resistance means that there can be no end to the book, no end to its dialogue, and no end to the dialogue it provokes.

Conclusion

Onto a semidarkened stage the actors walk. They are dressed in abstract costumes that evoke a vaguely medieval quality, as though they had arrived to play the drama of Everyman. The narrator takes his place to stage left, while Job occupies the center. As the narrator begins the story of Job—"A man there was in the land of Uz . . ."—Job and his children begin to mime the parts they are given. As they move into their tableaux, the scene of the council in heaven unfolds its role to stage right. Thus, the players enact the prose tale of Job. As they complete the drama of the prose tale's chapters 1–2, Job's three friends gather about him, sitting in silence.

Suddenly a light picks up an echoing group of four actors, situated toward the front left of the stage. They are clearly in the same postures of Job and his three friends, but they are costumed very differently, in the rich robes one might associate with a nineteenth-century Shakespearean performance. Job begins to speak, in accents and diction sharply different from the Job character of the morality play: "Damn the day I was born. . . ." Over the course of two hours, the friends and Job debate the issues of the wisdom dialogue: the experience of turmoil, the plausibility of the moral order of the world, the nature of God, and the possibility of justice. As their passionate and vigorous debate begins to falter, the audience is aware that all the time they have been speaking, the characters of the morality play have been continuing their drama. And yet, though the audience can see that the actors in the background are engaging one another, the microphones do not pick up what they have been saying.

At this same moment, at the end of the speeches of the wisdom dialogue, the characters enacting it freeze in their stance, with Job hostilely confronting his fellows. After several seconds of silence, a disembodied voice comes over the sound system: "There is a mine for silver. . . . But where can wisdom be found?" As this voice finishes its haunting poetic speech, the character of Job from the group of actors playing the wisdom dialogue gets up from that tableau vivant and moves across to the center front of the stage. No longer talking to the actors who play the friends, he speaks directly to the audience with passionate sincerity: "O that I were as in months gone by. . . ."

As Job concludes his extraordinary oath to an audience that reacts with profound but not entirely unembarrassed silence, that silence is broken by a member of the audience who stands up and announces himself: Elihu Barachel. To the astonishment of the rest of the audience, this person refuses to sit down until he has finished a long and passionate, if not entirely comprehensible, response. The audience wonders:—Was he scripted? Or was this a genuine bit of audience reaction? In either case, his evocation of a divine theophany provides the transition to the play's climactic moment—God's speech from the whirlwind.

Depending on the theater's technical capacity, this is either an extraordinary tour de force or a bit of cheesy theatrics. But soon the audience is caught up in the verbal extravagance of the words themselves. The incredible, powerful speech seems to fill the entire theater, pausing only once, when Job speaks softly to refuse a reply. The divine voice resumes again with a crescendo of extraordinary poetry, concluding with the words describing Leviathan as "king over all proud beasts." Job's words of response come quietly, echoing the divine speech, weaving those words into his own. But just as Job says his final words, his voice becomes so quiet that the audience, leaning in to catch every word, realizes that it cannot quite hear what he has said.

Their intensity of focus is disrupted as the microphones, which have muted the dialogue of the actors in the morality play, now increase the volume so that everyone hears the narrator again. "After the Lord had spoken these words to Job . . ."And so, with the end of the narrator's final description of Job's restoration, old age, and death, the play of Job comes to an end. The lights come up and the audience departs, moving off to restaurants and wine bars, where they will debate what they have just experienced.

This imaginary theater production of the story of Job is merely a vivid way of envisioning what I have attempted to suggest about reading the book of Job as a polyphonic text. On the one hand, one has no difficulty in grasping the play described above as a unified work of art, even one created by a single author. On the other hand, it is constructed in such a fashion that it consists of several discrete components, all of which develop different claims about the meaning and significance of Job and his situation. The polyphonic construction ensures that these component elements retain their unmerged voices and are not subordinated to a single controlling perspective that represents the author's own voice. At the same time, the presence of so many perspectives in close proximity, yet not always directly engaging one another, shifts to the audience much of the work of teasing out the implicit quarrels among the disparate voices.

Ever since the historical critics of the late nineteenth century turned their attention to Job, readers have had to struggle with the implications of their insights for reading the book of Job. What assumptions about the composition of the book or what models for reading it would do justice to the existence of the book as a whole and to its bewildering alternation of genres, styles, and perspectives? Diachronic redactional theories, final-form literary analyses, and deconstructive readings have all provided alternative solutions to this perplexing problem. Like a latter day Elihu I have been anxious to enter the conversation, armed with Bakhtin's notions of dialogism and polyphonic composition. While I do think these ideas offer signal advantages for addressing the issues of unity and diversity in the book of Job, the sobering example of Elihu's own reception suggests that a large measure of humility is in order. I do not offer this model as a claim about how the book of Job actually came to be or what the intentions of its author were. The hypothetical Judean author I referred to in chapter 1 is as imaginary as the play described above. Nor do I think that this approach necessarily supersedes other ones. The persuasiveness of a polyphonic reading, however, if it is to be accepted, must satisfy several criteria. It must, of course, be answerable to the text itself. In addition, it should be able to deal with some of the problems generated or left unresolved by other approaches; however, it also needs to respond to something distinctive in the sensibilities of its own postmodern culture.

As I have attempted to show in this book, a polyphonic reading attends with particular care to issues of genre and verbal texture, as well as to the multiple ideological claims of the text. In addition it offers a means of conceptualizing the book as an unified composition without sacrificing the hermeneutical significance of the many genres that comprise the book. In many previous approaches to reading the book, the only voices taken seriously were those of Job and God. The others were mere foils. Not only do such approaches seem unnecessarily reductive, but they also flout the hermeneutical assumptions of the wisdom dialogue itself. Reading the book as a polyphonic text provides a model of reading that allows all of the voices to "mean directly" and so to be taken seriously in the play of ideas.

Perhaps the strongest motivation for invoking a Bakhtinian dialogic and polyphonic reading, however, is the desire to read Job as a book of our own age. This is a frankly and unashamedly "allegorical" interpretation, in Bruns's sense of the term. In the postmodern, multicultural world, one cannot escape the reality of the multiplicity of differently situated consciousnesses that continually engage one another over questions of meaning and value. There is no culture, no tradition, no society—indeed, no person—that is not itself composed of multiple voices, dialogically situated. This recognition is reflected also in postmodern aesthetics and forms of attention, from literary pastiche to the split screen to acoustic sampling. A polyphonic approach to the book of Job is a recognition of an evocative and productive correspondence between the structure of the book and the sensibilities of the present age. The interpretive insight does not flow in only one direction, however. The book's own moral seriousness, coupled with its generosity toward a variety of perspectives, serves as a critique of those forms of postmodern intellectual display that embody pastiche without purpose. Nor, I think, can a Bakhtinian reading of Job rightly be criticized for "mere relativism," as are some forms of postmodern fascination with the play of differences. As Bakhtin rightly insisted, in a polyphonic composition the author (and one might add, the reader) does not give up holding passionately to claims of truth. But such positions are held in humility, as one engages in the discipline of seeing how one's position appears from the perspective of another, listening to the objections that one must answer, seeing what one's own position hides from itself, and being open to the possibility of modification in light of dialogical engagement.

Although Bakhtinian perspectives on dialogism and polyphony have provided the necessary starting place for my enquiry, they are not of themselves sufficient. What I have tried to do in this study is to bring to articulation the variety of forms of moral imagination that contend with one another in the book of Job. Moral imaginations are more than ideas, even the complex, socially situated ideas that Bakhtin describes. Moral imaginations are the fundamental aesthetic and cognitive means by which persons and cultures construct meaning, value, and significance. No one can grasp a situation or frame a response without drawing, consciously or unconsciously, upon the resources of narrative, metaphor, image, verbal style, and many other such devices. In the central chapters of this work, I have attempted to tease out what seem to me some of the most characteristic of these formative tropes in each of the distinctive voices of the text. The moral imagination that represents Job's situation by telling a certain kind of story, for example, is strikingly different from that which represents it by means of a clash of unmediated opposing voices. Each invites its readers into a differently structured world of values and commitments. Similarly, the friends' moral imagination, articulated, for instance, in Bildad's generative metaphor of good and evil as well-watered and dry plants not only frames the world in a particular way but also entails patterns of response to misfortune that are incontrovertible, so long as one moves within the logic of the metaphor. Appropriate action is very differently configured, however, if the generative metaphor is that of legal injury, as Job eventually comes to claim. Although each of the voices represented in the text articulates propositional claims, what makes those claims seem so persuasive to the speaker (and often so impossible to others) are the foundational beliefs already inscribed in the genres and images and figures with which he speaks. No wonder the characters speak past one another. No wonder the book seems like "oil and water" to its readers, for it is not just ideas that are dialogically engaged here but also sensibilities, that is, entire moral imaginations.

What emerges from all of this? Bakhtin himself warned about the danger of trying to summarize a conversation. Such an attempt turns a dialogical form of speech into a monologic one. It substitutes for a dynamic unity of event the logical unity of the proposition. This observation is even more to be heeded where what is at issue is not just what someone says but how she says it. When I began this book, I had naively imagined that in the conclusion I would at least be able to map the way in which the prose tale's idea about the basis of piety and virtue comes to be dialogically engaged. Bakhtin had spoken of how an idea "loses its monologic, abstractly theoretical finalized quality, a quality sufficient to a *single* consciousness . . . [and] acquires the contradictory complexity and living multi-facedness of an idea-force, being born, living and acting in the great dialogue of the epoch and calling back and forth to kindred ideas of other epochs. Before us rises up an *image of the idea.*"[1] So I had thought that it would be possible to take *haśśātān*'s airy dismissal of the notion of moral reciprocity in the human/divine relationship and to show how that idea comes to engage many others in a variety of ways that complicate what is at issue. All of this happens in Job, but in such a way that it is utterly beyond simple description. This complexity is in part due to the difference between the literary form of a Dostoevsky novel and the book of Job. Arguments over ideas in Dostoevsky are often explicit and relatively linear. In Job much of what is at issue is implicit or embedded in the figures of speech used by the characters, thus requiring the reader to draw out the quarrel beneath the quarrel.

Nevertheless, even at the cost of being reductive, some acknowledgment should be given of the extraordinary range of issues, questions, and topics that seem to explode out of the dialogue initiated by *haśśātān*'s question. By practical necessity these are my "allegorical" formulations of the issues, but among the many questions raised and engaged in the course of the book are the following: Does acute suffering reveal human existence to be characterized as essentially turmoil or, despite dissonance, can its underlying structures be represented in meaning-giving narratives? If one attempts to speak of human experience in narrative form, what is the appropriate governing figure of the plot or plots? What kinds of stories are adequate? How is temporality to be figured? Is the past, present, or future the critical moment for grasping the meaningfulness of a situation? Situations, of course, are understood in light of broader sets of beliefs, and these, too, are drawn into the discussion. Are there deep structures to the world and human experience of it? If so, what is the foundation? The vitality of good? Wisdom? Justice? What the twentieth century has called "the absurd"? What is the difference between seeking justice and seeking wisdom? How does one go about it? Is evil something to be "managed"? Or is the anarchy of the world an expression of a malign divine intentionality? Is a person who would deny that reality has a moral order himself evil, or at least a danger to social order? Theological questions are essential to the discussion, too. What is the nature of the human-divine relationship? Is it one of fundamental continuity or radical alterity? What is the operative image of God? Even if God is "like us," what specific social model structures the relationship? In the face of disaster, does one pray or litigate? Is justice built into the nature of things, or is it a contingent possibility only? If the latter, how does one evoke justice? But if God is radically other and the cosmos is not knowable by analogy with human society, what are the implications? Is human existence finally tragic or nontragic?

Not all of the questions raised by the voices in the book of Job have to do with substantive matters, however. Their argument also involves the forms by which one knows truth. Is it best grasped by means of a narrative that models what it teaches? By a contest of equally matched minds? By an urbane and ironic commentary on the inadequacy of all such attempts? By a rhetoric of sublimity? By the privilege of a transcendental belatedness?

Other readers might well quarrel both with the selection and formulation of these questions. But the list would not be improved by revision and supplementation. The poverty of such a bare inventory of issues is intrinsic, as it only serves to underscore the wisdom of Bakhtin's warning. Listing topics suggests that there is a logical entailment of issues that might have been as appropriately developed in a nuanced essay as in a complexly dialogic work. But what Bakhtin understood about dialogue, and what the book of Job models so effectively, is that the true "image of an idea" is produced by the lively and often surprising interaction of persons speaking from noninterchangeable positions and with differently formed moral imaginations. The only conclusion to a study of the dialogic structure of Job can be the advice to go and reread the book in the company of others who will contest your reading.

Notes

1. The Book of Job as Polyphonic Text

1. *NPNF*[2] 6:490–91.
2. Simon, *Critical History of the Old Testament*, bk. 1, ch. iv, 34.
3. Budde, *Das Buch Hiob*, xii–xiv; Duhm, *Das Buch Hiob*, vii–viii.
4. Macdonald, "Original Form," 63–71.
5. For the classic articulation of the hypothesis see Volz, *Hiob und Weisheit*, 1–2.
6. See Müller, *Das Hiobproblem*, 49–72.
7. Dhorme, *Commentary on the Book of Job*, lxv.
8. Ibid.
9. Kautzsch, *Das sogenannte Volksbuch*, 80.
10. Ibid., 85.
11. Dhorme, *Commentary on the Book of Job*, lxiv.
12. Kautzsch, *Das sogenannte Volksbuch*, 86–87 (my trans.).
13. For a convenient summary of the development of the discussion and the variations of opinion see Müller, *Das Hiobproblem*, 23–48.
14. Pope, *Job*, xxx.
15. Westermann, *Structure of the Book of Job*, 7.
16. Zuckerman, *Job the Silent*, 14 (order of sentences reversed).
17. Ibid., 175–79. Penchansky, *Betrayal of God*, similarly retains a historical-critical analysis of the composition of the book, but deals with its dissonance by means of an ideological criticism indebted to the work of Fredric Jameson and Pierre Macherey.
18. Andersen, *Job*, 55.
19. Cf. the introductions to such standard commentaries as those of De Wilde, *Das Buch Hiob*, and Hartley, *Book of Job*, with the literary-exegetical commentary of Clines, *Job 1–20*, and with the theological commentary of Janzen, *Job*. Although she assumes a complex redactional history for the book, Köhlmoos (*Das Auge Gottes*) discusses the book's text-strategies from the perspective of its developed, if not final, form. Her approach is based on the theories of Umberto Eco.
20. Two exceptions merit note. Westermann (*Structure of the Book of Job*) attempts to interpret the poetic sections of the book as a dramatized lament. Similarly, Richter (*Studien zu Hiob*) argues that the structure of the poetic material is that of a lawsuit. Neither deals in a substantive way with the relation of the prose tale to the poetic materials. Moreover, in my opinion, al-

though both studies make important contributions to identifying critical discourses in the book of Job, they are not persuasive as accounts of the genre of the poetic portions of the book.

21. Habel, *Book of Job*, 25.

22. Ibid., 26.

23. Ibid., (emphasis added).

24. Clines, "Deconstructing the Book of Job," 123.

25. Good, *In Turns of Tempest*, 181.

26. Ibid., 8–9, 290.

27. Ibid., 179–81.

28. Derrida, "Law of Genre," 203.

29. Good, *In Turns of Tempest*, 9–11, 189–90, 208–9.

30. Clines, "Deconstructing the Book of Job," 107.

31. Ibid., 115–16.

32. Ibid., 120.

33. An important exception to the neglect of genre in recent studies of Job is Cheney's *Dust, Wind, and Agony*. In my opinion, however, his work is limited by an underdeveloped theory of genre.

34. Fowler, *Kinds of Literature*, 37. The literature on genre is vast. An excellent sampling of recent perspectives can be found in Duff, *Modern Genre Theory*.

35. Fowler, *Kinds of Literature*, 20–24. See also Culler, *Structuralist Poetics*, 135–39, 145–48.

36. Fowler, *Kinds of Literature*, 60–73.

37. Culler, *Structuralist Poetics*, 139.

38. Guillén, *Comparative Literature*, 114.

39. Ibid., 114.

40. Bakhtin and Medvedev, *Formal Method*, 133.

41. Ibid., 134–35.

42. Guillén, *Comparative Literature*, 138.

43. Fowler, *Kinds of Literature*, 51.

44. See Guillén's discussion of "Literary Relations: Internationality," chap. 15 in *Comparative Literature*.

45. Rosmarin, *Power of Genre*, 29.

46. Fowler, *Kinds of Literature*, 50.

47. See Müller, "Die weisheitliche Lehrerzählung."

48. The arguments for this understanding of chaps. 32–37 will be given in chap. 8 of this book.

49. Ezekiel 14:14, 20 implies that Job, by means of his righteousness, managed to save his sons and daughters from some danger rather than losing them in an inexplicable catastrophe. See Zuckerman, *Job the Silent*, 29–31. Wahl ("Noah, Daniel, und Hiob," 542–53) argues that Ezekiel refers to the actual text of the book of Job, which he would therefore date earlier, but this remains a minority view.

50. Zuckerman, *Job the Silent*, 97, suggests that these speeches be read in relation to ancient Near Eastern texts of appeal to a god with divine response, but it is not clear that such texts reflect a sufficiently conventionalized type of speech to be recognizable as a genre. In my opinion, attempts to characterize the speeches individually with respect to genre have also not been persuasive.

51. For an introduction to Bakhtin and biblical studies, see Green, *Mikhail Bakhtin and Biblical Scholarship*.

52. Bakhtin develops his ideas in *Problems of Dostoevsky's Poetics*. The best systematic study of Bakhtin's notoriously unsystematic thought is that of Morson and Emerson, *Mikhail Bakhtin*.

53. The distinction is between two senses of truth. What interests Bakhtin is not how one distinguishes truth from falsity but the contrasting ways in which claims about any matter are articulated. The dialogic sense of truth is more adequate than the monologic, in Bakhtin's view, because it discloses the dynamic and multicentered nature of ideas in ways that the monologic sense of truth cannot.

54. Janzen, *Job*, 23.

55. Andersen, *Job*, 55.

56. Bakhtin, *Problems of Dostoevsky's Poetics*, 81.

57. Ibid., 93.

58. Ibid., 93.

59. Ibid., 166.

60. Morson and Emerson, *Mikhail Bakhtin*, 253. See Bakhtin, *Problems of Dostoevsky's Poetics*, 91.

61. Guillén, *Comparative Literature*, 138.

62. Bakhtin, *Problems of Dostoevsky's Poetics*, 110.

63. Ibid., 110.

64. Ibid., 271.

65. Buccellati, "Wisdom and Not," 39.

66. Bakhtin, *Problems of Dostoevsky's Poetics*, 183–84.

67. Bakhtin, *Dialogic Imagination*, 342–43.

68. See Patrick, "Translation of Job 42.6"; Morrow, "Consolation, Rejection, and Repentance"; Wolde, "Job 42, 1–6."

69. Similarly, Habel, *Book of Job*, 575. Cf. Scheindlin, *Book of Job*, 155: "I retract. I even take comfort for dust and ashes."

70. Similarly, Janzen, *Job*, 251, 257.

71. Similarly, Good, *In Turns of Tempest*, 171, 378.

72. Bakhtin, *Problems of Dostoevsky's Poetics*, 233.

73. Ibid., 280.

74. See Fogel, *Coercion to Speak*, 219–20.

75. Cf. Neher's discussion of Job in *Exile of the Word*, 192–98.

2. The Impregnable Word

1. See, for example, Dorothee Soelle's sharp and scathing comparison of the structure of the prose tale to the fairy tale tradition of the despotic king who sets impossible tests for the hero (*Suffering*, 109–12).

2. As in Clines, "False Naivety."

3. See, e.g., Johnson, *Moral Imagination*; Turner, *Literary Mind*.

4. See, e.g., Coles, *Call of Stories*; Alasdair MacIntyre, *After Virtue*; Ricoeur, *Oneself as Another*; Taylor, *Sources of the Self*.

5. MacIntyre, *After Virtue*, 144.

6. Ibid., 216.

7. See Carr, "The Self and the Coherence of Life," pp. 73–99 in *Time, Narrative, and History*. Both Turner, *Literary Mind*, and Carr argue that narrative construction of experience is fundamental to human existence and hence universal. When one moves to more complex ways in which identity is constituted narratively, perhaps one should restrict this claim to certain cultures. Anthropologists concerned with the relation of narrative and social construction have cautioned that in some cultures non-Aristotelian forms of narrative and story-telling practices exist (i.e., without emplotment of the beginning-middle-end structure or at least with inhibitions

on telling what westerners would call "the whole story"). See, e.g., Robbins, "Secrecy and the Sense of an Ending." How and whether such narrative practices are implicated in the formation of selves and societies has not been fully explored.

8. See Johnson, *Moral Imagination*; Lakoff and Johnson, *Metaphors We Live By*.

9. See Schön, "Generative Metaphor."

10. Johnson, *Moral Imagination*, 35–52.

11. Goodman, *Ways of Worldmaking*, 23–40.

12. Nussbaum, *Love's Knowledge*, 168–94.

13. Ibid., 3.

14. White, *When Words Lose Their Meaning*, 14–20, 54–55.

15. Ibid., 17.

16. Booth, *Company We Keep*, 239.

17. Ibid., 201.

18. Newton, *Narrative Ethics*, 308 n. 58, suggests that "two clarifying frames for Booth's idea [of the trope of friendship] can be found in Aristotle's chapters on friendship in Nichomachean Ethics and Eudemian Ethics (which, curiously, Booth does not invoke) and in Jacques Derrida's 'The Politics of Friendship,' *Journal of Philosophy*, 35, no. 11 (1988) 632–644."

19. Nussbaum, *Love's Knowledge*, 171.

20. Newton draws particularly on Bakhtin, *Art and Answerability*; Levinas, *Totality and Infinity*; and *Otherwise Than Being*.

21. One can see this dynamic in the comments of Cheyne, *Jewish Religious Life*, 160–61, who is confident that he knows the content of what should be there, but cannot quite compose something that fits stylistically.

> The chief value of the Epilogue is, that it enables us to reconstruct the main outlines of the omitted portion of the story. Thanks to it we are able, in some sense, to "call up him who left half told" (or whose editors have transmitted to us half told, or told amiss) the story of the most patient of men. The result of an inquiry would probably be that in lieu of Job iii.- xlii.,7, there stood originally something like this, only in a style of flowing, natural eloquence:
>
> And these three men, moved at the sight of Job's grief, broke out into lamentations, and withheld not passionate complaints of the injustice of God. They said: Is there knowledge in the Most High? And does God judge righteous judgment? But Job was sore displeased, and reproved them, saying, Bitter is the pain which racks me, but more bitter still are the words which ye speak. Blessed be the Most High for that which He gave, and now that I am empty, blessed still be His name. I will call unto Him and say, Shew me wherein I have erred; let me not depart under the weight of Thine anger. For God is good to all those who call upon Him, and will not suffer the righteous to fall for ever. And Job reasoned ofttimes with his friends, and bade them repent, lest God should deal with them as with transgressors. And at the end of a season, God came to Eliphaz in a dream and said, My wrath is kindled against thee and thy two friends, because ye have not spoken of Me that which is right, as My servant Job has.

22. Gordis, *Book of Job*, 573–75. Alt, "Zur Vorgeschichte des Buches Hiob," 265, made a similar suggestion concerning the relationship of chap. 1 and 42:11–17, though his proposal also included a hypothesis about the secondary nature of chap. 2.

23. For an introduction to the categories of folklore and its relation to biblical studies, see Niditch, *Folklore and the Hebrew Bible* and Kirkpatrick, *Old Testament and Folklore Study*.

24. Toorn, *Sin and Sanction*, 58–61.

25. Even the cogency of this comparison has been questioned. Weinfeld, "Job and Its Mesopotamian Parallels," argues that the Sumerian and Akkadian compositions are not so much comparable with the book of Job as with biblical psalms of thanksgiving.

26. See the seminal study of Spiegel, "Noah, Danel, and Job."

27. See Macdonald, "Some External Evidence." Clines, "In Search of an Indian Job," demonstrates that the alleged Indian parallels are not in fact substantiated by the primary sources themselves.

28. Zuckerman, *Job the Silent*,14, argues that James's reference "you have *heard* of the patient endurance of Job" indicates that the story was an oral one.

29. Niditch, *Folklore and the Hebrew Bible*, 9.

30. Niditch's example is the account of Rebekah and Jacob's theft of Esau's blessing from Isaac in Genesis 27.

31. In this regard one might compare the stylistically similar eighth-century Assyrian composition The Poor Man of Nippur. It, too, uses schematically opposed characters, as well as closely parallel narrative and verbal repetition. The character type of the clever "nobody" who bests his social betters and the humorous and class-conscious revenge plot makes this composition a better candidate than Job for the status of folktale. See Gurney, "Tale of the Poor Man." Here, too, however, one may be dealing with a literary perfecting of folk style. So Finet, "Les trois vengeances."

32. See the report of Isho'dad of Merv, the ninth-century C.E. author who summarizes Bishop Theodore's views, cited in Zaharopoulos, *Theodore of Mopsuestia*, 45–48.

33. See, e.g., Clines, "False Naivety."

34. See Müller, "Die weisheitliche Lehrerzählung." See also his "Die Hiobrahmenerzählung." Though I find Müller's studies highly insightful, I do not find the adjective "sapiential" particularly helpful in clarifying the genre. I prefer simply "didactic tale."

35. Müller refers to it as "the briefest and most precise example" of the genre ("Die weisheitliche Lehrerzählung," 77).

36. Müller recognizes that the Joseph story, the Aramaic Ahiqar, Daniel 2, 4, and 5, and Esther are also to be related to what he calls *Marchen*, whereas Tobit and Daniel 3 and 6 also have characteristics of *Legende*.

37. Wolfgang Iser, *Act of Reading*, 77–78, for instance, refers to the late medieval romances of Chretien in which knights who embodied certain courtly values left the court for quests, during the course of which the values they represented were tested and confirmed. At the end of the quest the knights returned to the court. Both the motifs of testing and proving and of isolation and reincorporation served to stabilize values that were being challenged by changing social conditions.

38. Suleiman, *Authoritarian Fiction*, 54.

39. Ibid., 10.

40. Ibid., 10, 54, 240.

41. Eco, *Role of the Reader*, 8. See Köhlmoos, *Das Auge Gottes*, for a reading of Job in light of other aspects of Eco's work.

42. Suleiman, *Authoritarian Fiction*, 72.

43. Ibid., 71.

44. Ibid., 185.

45. Ibid., 55.

46. Ibid., 159–70.

47. Ibid., 202.

48. Ibid., 142.

49. Ibid., 10.

50. See, e.g., Kilpatrick et al., *Books That Build Character*; Guroian, *Tending the Heart of Virtue*.

51. See, e.g., Coles, *Call of Stories*.

52. Suleiman, *Authoritarian Fiction*, 10–11.

53. In addition to Clines, "False Naivety," see the brilliant study of Cooper, "Reading and Misreading."

54. Müller, "Die weisheitliche Lehrerzählung," 87, counts wisdom as one of the character virtues (Joseph, Daniel). One might question whether it functions more as a gift from God than as a virtue, although the very distinction raises an interesting question about the borderlines between modern western moral language and that of the Hebrew Bible.

55. Cited in Kilpatrick et al., *Books That Build Character*, 29.

56. So, similarly, Müller, "Die Hiobrahmenerzählung," 27, 35.

57. One could question whether Nebuchadnezzar is in fact a secondary character. (See the analysis of Fewell on the centrality of the kings in *Circle of Sovereignty*.) Perhaps it would be more apt to say that in Daniel 1-4 the framework of a series of didactic tales in which Daniel and his friends are the ostensible heroes has been adapted to a more complex type of moral literature.

58. Cf. the analysis of comic resolution by NorthropFrye, *Anatomy of Criticism*, 163-86.

59. See Müller, "Die Hiobrahmenerzählung," 31.

60. Fewell's attempt to read Daniel as such a character is one I find unconvincing (*Circle of Sovereignty*, 35-36, 70). Although her reading is a "good" reading in Eco's sense of the term (in that it bases itself scrupulously on details in the text), it ignores generic codes and conventions in construing character.

61. Nussbaum, *Love's Knowledge*, 171.

62. Booth, *Company We Keep*, 177.

63. If one includes the episode with the three friends as part of the prose tale, then the structure is slightly more complex but still marked by extensive features of symmetry and balance. I am persuaded by Gordis (*Book of Job*, 573-75), however, that the brief prose sections introducing and disposing of the friends in 2:10-13 and 42:7-9 are better understood as the "hinges" that serve to join the dialogue to the prose tale.

64. Soelle, *Suffering*, 107-8.

65. See Brenner, "Job the Pious?" 43-44. Her evaluation of the significance of the phenomenon differs from that suggested here.

66. Linafelt, "Undecidability of *BRK*."

67. Pope, *Job*, 9-10. For an analysis of all the biblical references to the *haśśātān*, see Day, *Adversary in Heaven*.

68. Gordis, *Book of Job*, 14.

69. Good, *In Turns of Tempest*, 52, 198.

70. The oddity of *haśśātān*'s question should be noted. Most biblical and other ancient Near Eastern texts would probably take it for granted that a person does not serve a deity *ḥinnām*, "for nothing." The social models that underlie images of divine-human relationships are characteristically those that embody relationships of mutual obligation and benefit, for example, patron/client, king/subject, husband/wife, or parent/child. Though these are non-symmetrical relationships, the inferior party has a legitimate expectation of certain benefits. Haśśātān's question, does not, so far as we know, reflect a widespread discussion about the nature and status of piety vis-à-vis blessing. Yet here it is, presented in a way that takes for granted that the audience will see it as a question of significance that must be answered. Perhaps the issue emerges out of the generic concerns of the didactic narratives of character to establish the absolute claims of virtue. How the issues of the prose tale relate to a larger cultural conversation within wisdom traditions will be discussed at the end of this section.

71. Gordis, *Book of Job*, 18.

72. Burke, *Grammar of Motives*, 77: "When 'defining by location,' one may place the object of one's definition in contexts of varying scope. . . . The choice of circumference for the scene in

terms of which a given act is to be located will have a corresponding effect upon the interpretation of the act itself."

73. The perspective is comparable to that of Ps 104:27–29: "All of them look to you to give them their food in its proper time. You give it to them, they gather it. You open your hand, they are satisfied with goodness. You hide your face, they are terrified. You take away their breath, they perish and to the dust they return. You send forth your breath, they are created and you renew the face of the earth."

74. Her significance is quite different in the polyphonic book as a whole, of course. Job's rebuke of her in the prose tale is the last word he speaks until the outburst that introduces the wisdom dialogue in chap. 3. When he speaks there, his wife's iconoclastic perspective has become his own. He curses, if not God, then the creation that made his birth possible. Though he does not die, he speaks longingly of death. The juxtaposition of the two genres has produced a revaluation of her words that opens them up for serious consideration by the reader.

75. Driver and Gray, Book of Job, 25–26.

76. Soelle, Suffering, 88.

77. Ibid., 107.

78. Ibid., 108.

79. Hartley, Book of Job, 84, for instance, argues that the line affirms Job's complete piety.

The lips express a person's deepest thoughts (cf. Prov. 18:4). Consequently when one strives for moral purity they are the hardest member to bring under control. They are obstinate to discipline. That is why the Wisdom tradition taught that the one who controls his speech has his whole life in focus (Prov. 13:3; 21:23; cf. Jas. 3:2). Therefore to say that Job did not sin with his lips is to state unequivocally that Job did not commit the slightest error. Whereas God had declared prior to this testing that Job was without sin, this statement asserts that Job had come thus far through his trial unscathed by any wrongdoing.

80. Brinker, "Theme and Interpretation," 26.

81. Bakhtin, Dialogic Imagination, 276–77.

82. Nussbaum, Love's Knowledge, 171.

83. Newton, Narrative Ethics, 3–8. Levinas develops these terms in Otherwise Than Being. For another appropriation of the significance of Levinas for criticism of literature, see Eaglestone, Ethical Criticism.

84. Newton, Narrative Ethics, 11.

85. Dadlez, What's Hecuba to Him? 41.

86. Ibid., 43, 112. Ricoeur's subtle analysis of mimesis (Time and Narrative, 1:46; cf. 52–87) also examines its centrality to the relationship between literature and ethics: "But that the praxis belongs at the same time to the real domain, covered by ethics, and the imaginary one, covered by poetics, suggests that mimesis functions not just as a break but also as a connection, one which establishes precisely the status of the 'metaphorical' transposition of the practical field by the muthos."

87. Dadlez, What's Hecuba to Him? 108–9; Nussbaum, Love's Knowledge, 41. See also Nussbaum's essay "Narrative Emotions: Beckett's Genealogy of Love," pp. 286–334 in Love's Knowledge.

88. Newton, Narrative Ethics, 5–7.

89. Ibid., 74: "In the act of narrating, storytellers lay their hands on those they address, possibly to minister to them, possibly to do them violence (if only verbal). And those addressed, in the ways they construe or respond, perform answering actions in turn."

90. Not of course in the sense with which Levinas uses the term.

91. Bakhtin, Problems of Dostoevsky's Poetics, 59–60.

92. One should not be too smugly condescending toward the character of God. Deciding whether to live without knowledge of the basis upon which a relationship is based presents one of the most difficult moral dilemmas. Yet to force such knowledge oftentimes would destroy the relationship itself.

93. Levinas, *Otherwise Than Being*, 46.

3. Critical Curiosity

1. Culler, *Structuralist Poetics*, 139.

2. Müller, "Keilschriftliche Parallelen," 137–39.

3. So Weinfeld, "Job and Its Mesopotamian Parallels." Similarly, Soden, *TUAT* III.1, 146. Cheney, *Dust, Wind, and Agony*, 33–41, is interested in the formal features of the frame tale in relation to Job and so analyzes the pattern of similarities between Job and the ancient Near Eastern parallels somewhat differently.

4. Foster, "Self-Reference of an Akkadian Poet," examines the various forms of self-reference and their rhetorical force. Sitzler, *Vorwurf gegen Gott*, proposes a different grouping of Egyptian and Mesopotamian texts based on the thematization of a lapse by the deity and the address of a reproach to the god or to a third person. Of the Mesopotamian texts she includes only the Sumerian Job, AO 4462, *Ludlul bēl nēmeqi*, and the Babylonian Theodicy.

5. Toorn, *Sin and Sanction*, 58.

6. Mattingly, "Pious Sufferer."

7. Soden, ("Das Fragen nach der Gerechtigkeit," 46–47), argues that AO 4462 does contain an accusation against the god for ill-treatment, but the complaint is mild and politely indirect.

8. The copy is from the 14th or 13th century B.C.E., though the original may be about a century older, according to Soden, *TUAT* III.1, 141.

9. Unless otherwise noted, all quotations of Mesopotamian texts are taken from Foster, *Before the Muses*.

10. For a recent discussion of the form of *Ludlul*, see Moran, "Notes on the Hymn to Marduk." Toorn, *Sin and Sanction*, 58–67, discusses the similarities and differences between penitential and thanksgiving songs and the sapiential poems.

11. Lambert, *Babylonian Wisdom Literature*, 25–26. The popularity of *Ludlul* in the Neo-Assyrian and Neo-Babylonian periods is attested in the number of copies found at Nineveh, Babylon, and Sippar, dating from the eighth century and later.

12. Scholars disagree about the sequencing of the fragments of tablet 4. This summary follows the arrangement of Soden, *TUAT* III.1, 131–35.

13. Moran, "Notes on the Hymn to Marduk," 258.

14. Kramer, "Man and His God," 170.

15. See the survey of opinions and citations in Mattingly, "Pious Sufferer," 310.

16. Klein, "'Personal God' and Individual Prayer," 298.

17. Trans. Kramer, *ANET*, 589.

18. Mattingly, "Pious Sufferer," 329–36.

19. Soden, *TUAT* III.1, 136. The composition dates from the 17th century B.C.E.

20. So the original editor, Nougayrol, "Juste Souffrant," 243: "L'homme, pour (son) ami, implore son dieu." Similarly, Soden, *TUAT* III.1, 136.

21. So Lambert, "Further Attempt," 189, and Foster, *Before the Muses*, 75.

22. Müller, "Keilschriftliche Parallelen," 146–47, attempts to argue that the role of a comforting friend is a conventional topos in exemplary sufferer texts. But the argument seems strained. In the Sumerian Man and His God, the references to friends are to their betrayal of the sufferer. That is, they are part of the description of suffering. So, too, in *Ludlul*. The family described in

RS 25.460 makes funeral preparations, so reference to them is also part of the description of suffering. These references do not seem sufficient to underwrite Müller's case.

23. Cf. Lambert's slightly different translation in "Further Attempt," 193: "you who in future days will not forget [your] god, Your creator, and that you are well favored" (lines 56–57).

24. Gese, *Lehre und Wirklichkeit*, 63–66.

25. Zuckerman, *Job the Silent*, 97.

26. Toorn, "Ancient Near Eastern Literary Dialogue."

27. Buccellati, "Wisdom and Not," 43.

28. Toorn, "Ancient Near Eastern Literary Dialogue," 69.

29. Zuckerman, *Job the Silent*, 97.

30. Müller, "Keilschriftliche Parallelen," 148 n. 65, treats chaps. 4–27 as the segment of Job comparable to the Babylonian Theodicy, taking chaps. 3 and 29–31 as framing chapters. However, it appears to be characteristic of the genre to begin with the complaint of the sufferer. Hence, chap. 3 properly belongs to the dialogue, though in the overall structure of the book it serves several purposes.

31. Lambert, *Babylonian Wisdom Literature*, 66. Buccellati, "Tre saggi sulla sapienza mesopotamica," 166–67. See also Denning-Bolle, *Wisdom in Akkadian Literature*, 136–40.

32. Contra Skehan, "Strophic Patterns."

33. Denning-Bolle, *Wisdom in Akkadian Literature*, 141; Habel, *Book of Job*, 46–47.

34. Lambert, *Babylonian Wisdom Literature*, 63. Soden, TUAT III.1, 143–44.

35. Zuckerman, *Job the Silent*, 95.

36. Lambert, *Babylonian Wisdom Literature*, 90–91, suggests that a highly fragmentary Assyrian text might be a similar type of composition, but too little is preserved for certainty.

37. Gray, "Book of Job," 262.

38. Buccellati, "Wisdom and Not," 39.

39. Fowler, *Kinds of Literature*, 66.

40. Buccellati, "Wisdom and Not," 43.

41. Ibid.

42. Ibid.

43. Toorn, "Ancient Near Eastern Literary Dialogue," 69.

44. Ibid.

45. Ibid.

46. Ibid.

47. Ibid.

48. Gray, "Book of Job," 258.

49. Denning-Bolle, *Wisdom in Akkadian Literature*, 70.

50. Zuckerman, *Job the Silent*, 249 n. 279.

51. Bakhtin, *Problems of Dostoevsky's Poetics*, 110.

52. Ibid.

53. Ibid., 93.

54. Buccellati, "Wisdom and Not," 43.

55. Vanstiphout, "Sumerian Disputations," 30.

4. *"Consolations of God"*

1. See, e.g., Mattingly, "Pious Sufferer."

2. Bruns, *Hermeneutics Ancient and Modern*, 180.

3. The double role chap. 3 plays in the book as a whole and in the component genre of the wisdom dialogue is signaled by the double introduction in vv. 1–2. Verse 1 continues the nar-

rative style of the prose tale and relates Job's speech after seven days and nights of silence to the dramatic plot, in which everything hangs on whether or not Job will curse God. Verse 2 introduces Job's words with the stylized heading that will structure the dialogue between Job and his friends. The double heading is not a crude editorial seam but an acknowledgment of how the book is composed of genres dialogically related to one another.

4. The beginning of the Egyptian *Lebensmüde* is missing.

5. Foster, *Before the Muses*, 2:806. All translations of Mesopotamian literature, unless otherwise noted, are from Foster.

6. Lambert, *Babylonian Wisdom Literature*, 71.

7. See the commentaries of Clines, Habel, and Fohrer in particular, as well as Fuchs, "Die Klage des Propheten"; Jacobsen and Nielsen, "Cursing the Day"; Fishbane, "Jeremiah IV 23–26 and Job III 3–13."

8. Zuckerman, *Job the Silent*, 125–26.

9. If one reads the verb with MT as *yiḥad*. Alternatively, in view of the word "enter" in the next line, one might construe the verb as *yēḥad*, "join with." In either case, the image is a social one.

10. Good, *In Turns of Tempest*, 56.

11. Nemo, *Job and the Excess of Evil*, 17–41. See also Carr, *Time, Narrative, and History*, 87–88.

12. Carr, *Time, Narrative, and History*, 21–28.

13. Ibid., 33–34, 49.

14. Ibid., 73.

15. Ibid., 74.

16. Ibid., 87.

17. Ibid., 91.

18. Ibid.

19. "The many stuffs—matter, energy, waves, phenomena—that worlds are made of are made along with the worlds. But made from what? Not from nothing, after all, but *from other worlds*. Worldmaking as we know it always starts from worlds already on hand; the making is a remaking" (Goodman, *Ways of Worldmaking*, 19).

20. Turner, *Literary Mind*, 134.

21. Ibid., 5.

22. Ricoeur, *Time and Narrative*, 1:ix.

23. Ibid., 1:45.

24. Ibid., 1:45–46.

25. Ibid., 1:54.

26. Ibid., 1:59, 74.

27. Ibid., 1:64.

28. Ibid., 1:66.

29. Golden and Hardison, *Aristotle's Poetics*, 236, cited in Ricoeur, *Time and Narrative*, 1:239 n. 21.

30. Ricoeur, *Time and Narrative*, 1:81.

31. Turner, *Literary Mind*, 18, 133.

32. Turner, *Literary Mind*, 117–18.

33. Ricoeur, *Time and Narrative*, 1:74.

34. Turner, *Literary Mind*, 4–5.

35. I disagree with those who construe Eliphaz as slyly attempting to apply the story of the wicked to Job. The structure of the book as a whole does create a series of ironies, first at Eliphaz's expense (since neither of his paradigmatic stories is truly applicable to Job) and then at the expense of the reader (since eventually things turn out much as Eliphaz had predicted). In the

latter part of this chapter I examine in more detail the nature and function of the paradigmatic story of the "fate of the wicked."

36. Ricoeur, *Time and Narrative*, 1:66.

37. Clines, *Job 1–20*, 144.

38. Aristotle, *Poetics*, 7.4, 1450b.

39. Ricoeur, *Time and Narrative*, 1:44.

40. Ibid., 1:43.

41. I do not deal here with Eliphaz's account of his revelatory vision. This account belongs to a quite different moral imagination than do the stories of reversal of fortune that otherwise furnish his narrative repertoire. It is, however, of utmost importance in the overall development of the dialogue and will be dealt with in the context of the discussion of Job 9.

42. Gordis, *Book of Job*, 521. See also Habel, *Book of Job*, 170-73, 175-78.

43. Lakoff and Turner, *More Than Cool Reason*, 223.

44. See Janzen, *Job*, 85–86, for a discussion of the grammar.

45. Bourdieu, *Theory of Practice*, 164.

46. Quoted in Dreyfus and Rabinow, *Michel Foucault*, 187.

47. Bell, *Ritual Theory, Ritual Practice*, 109.

48. Bourdieu, *Theory of Practice*, 94.

49. Rappaport, *Ecology, Meaning, and Religion*, 199-200.

50. Bell, *Ritual Theory, Ritual Practice*, 215.

51. Ibid., 99.

52. Burridge, *New Heaven, New Earth*, 6-7.

53. See the summary in Miller, *They Cried to the Lord*, 7-8. Keel, *Symbolism of the Biblical World*, 308-23, includes many illustrations.

54. Keel, *Symbolism of the Biblical World*, 313.

55. Clines, *Job 1–20*, 269, takes Zophar's spatial imagery concerning sin as characteristic of wisdom discourse, citing Ps 1:1; Prov 1:10-15; 4:14, 24; 5:8; 30:8. By contrast, other discourses use imagery having to do with covering up, cleansing, or forgiving.

56. Ricoeur, *Time and Narrative*, 1:44.

57. Clines, *Job 1–20*, 269.

58. For an analysis of the grammar of this verse see Gordis, *Book of Job*, 252.

59. Bell, *Ritual Theory, Ritual Practice*, 141.

60. Ibid., 217-18.

61. Jost and Hyde, "Introduction," 12-20.

62. Demos, "On Persuasion," 229.

63. Tromp, *Primitive Conceptions of Death*, 74.

64. For the reading see Dahood, "Some Northwest-Semitic Words in Job"; Pope, *Job*, 136.

65. This sentiment, if not the exact formulation, is taken from Rorty, *Philosophy and the Mirror of Nature*, 315-56.

66. Janzen, *Job*, 130.

67. Girard, *Job*, 10-18.

68. Nemo, *Job and the Excess of Evil*, 44. Cf. the anaysis of *techne* and its artifacts in Kohák, *Embers and the Stars*, 13-18, 101-9.

69. Nemo, *Job and the Excess of Evil*, 62-63.

70. Ibid., 70, n. 16.

71. Ibid., 81, n. 1.

72. Ibid., 90.

73. Ibid., 91.

74. Ibid., 113.

5. Broken in Pieces by Words/Breaking Words in Pieces

1. See, e.g., Habel, *Book of Job*, 118–23. Forher gives an extended discussion of the evocation of various genres in "Form und Funktion in der Hiobdictung."

2. Bakhtin, *Problems of Dostoevsky's Poetics*, 189.

3. These and other examples are discussed by Dell, *Sceptical Literature*, 125–36.

4. Felman, "Education and Crisis," 26.

5. Ibid., 27.

6. Ibid., 30–31.

7. White, *When Words Lose Their Meaning*, 89.

8. In the sense that Turner, *Literary Mind*, 13, uses the term. Turner's broad claims concerning narrative as constitutive of the human mind are not entirely helpful when the task is that of distinguishing among various forms of expression in a given text or culture.

9. Cited in Dhorme, *Commentary on the Book of Job*, 101.

10. Ricoeur, *Time and Narrative*, 1:72.

11. Scarry, *Body in Pain*, 53.

12. For an extended discussion of the presence and transformation of psalmic lament motifs in Job's speeches see Westermann, *Structure of the Book of Job*, 31–66.

13. Habel, *Book of Job*, 155–56.

14. Levinas, *Totality and Infinity*, 191.

15. Ibid., 193.

16. Westermann, *Structure of the Book of Job*, 55, argues that Job creates the shocking images in chap. 16 largely by taking language otherwise used in laments to describe the speaker's human enemies and applying it to God. (See also Dell, *Sceptical Literature*, 130.) Yet he himself notes the close connection between the imagery of violence in Job 19:7–12 and Lamentations 3 (Westermann, *Structure of the Book of Job*, 56, 66). The verbal and imagistic connections are even closer between Lamentations 3 and Job 16.

17. Forensic language may begin to appear in Job's words with v. 17. See Habel, *Book of Job*, 265, and Scholnick, "Lawsuit Drama," 27 n. 37.

18. See Crenshaw, *Whirlpool of Torment*, 57–75.

19. Clines, *Job 1–20*, 111.

20. Ibid., 112; Fohrer, *Das Buch Hiob*, 131; cf. De Wilde, *Das Buch Hiob*, 108.

21. E.g., De Wilde, *Das Buch Hiob*, 108.

22. Trans. Kramer, *ANET*, 590.

23. Mattingly, "Pious Sufferer," 315.

24. Trans. Foster, *Before the Muses*, 2:813.

25. See, e.g., lines 7–22 of the hymn to Marduk (Foster, "Against Marduk's Anger," *Before the Muses*, 2:591):

> O great lord Marduk, merciful lord! Men, by whatever name,
> What can they understand of their own sin?
> Who has not been negligent, which one has committed no sin?
> Who can understand a god's behavior?
> I would fain be obedient and incur no sin,
> Yes, I would frequent the haunts of health!
> Men are commanded by the gods to act under curse,
> Divine affliction is for mankind to bear.
> I am surely responsible for some neglect of you,
> I have surely trespassed the limits set by the god.
> Forget what I did in my youth, whatever it was,
> Let your heart not well up against me!

Absolve my guilt, remit my punishment,
Clear me of confusion, free me of uncertainty,
Let no guilt of my father, my grandfather, my mother, my grandmother, my brother,
         my sister, my family, kith, or kin
Approach my own self, but let it be gone.

See, similarly, the prayers to the "Furious God" (Foster, 2:641) and "To Any God" (Foster, 2:685–87). The strategy of preemptive confession to a series of sins also occurs in "Who Has Not Sinned?" (Foster, 2:644–45). The religious context of these motifs has been recently examined by Sitzler, *Vorwurf gegen Gott*, 167–93.

26. Trans. Briggs, *ANET*, 597.

27. Moran, "Notes on the Hymn to Marduk," 258. Cf. the lines in "A Sufferer's Salvation," an Akkadian poem from Ugarit.

Praise, praise, do not be bashful, but praise!
[He it] is, Marduk, I entreat (?) him, I entreat (?) him,
[He it] was who smote me, then was merciful to me,
He scuttled (?) me, then moored me,
He dashed me down, then grabbed me (as I fell),
He scattered me wide, then garnered me,
He trust me away, then gathered me in,
He threw me down, then lifted me high (trans. Foster, *Before the Muses*, 1:326–27).

28. In Isa 41:14 the MT reads *mĕtê* ("men of" Israel) but is translated "maggot," based on Akkadian *mutu*, or emended, following the Syriac, to *rimmat* ("maggot of" Israel). See Elliger, *Jesaja II*, 146–47.

29. The exception is perhaps Ps 14:1–3 (= 52:2–4), where the acts of all humankind are described with similar vocabulary of corruption and loathsomeness. But that psalm presents itself as a critique of the language of the "fool" (*nābāl*) and so may be indebted to wisdom discourse.

30. My thanks to Jon Levenson (private communication) for insisting on the background of priestly purity conceptions in this language. Lévêque's attempt (*Job et son Dieu*, 263) to argue for the moral rather than the cultic resonance of *yithar* is unnecessary. Words bring with them a range of resonances, and in this instance the cultic and moral nuances of the word cannot readily be separated.

31. Berger, *Sacred Canopy*, 55.

32. Ibid., 55–56; see also 74.

33. See, e.g., Habel, *Book of Job*, 189; Clines, *Job 1–20*, 227.

34. Scarry, *Body in Pain*, 49.

35. The nuance and precise translation of this verse is debated, but, however translated, the line connotes a dissociation of self-awareness or self-care that is part of the normal, healthy self. See Clines, *Job 1–20*, 237.

36. Scarry, *Body in Pain*, 41.

37. Ricoeur, *Symbolism of Evil*, 25–46.

38. Habel, *Book of Job*, 196.

39. Volf, *Exclusion and Embrace*, 91.

40. Ibid., 74.

41. See the analysis of abjection in Kristeva, *Powers of Horror*, 1–4.

42. Levinas, *Totality and Infinity*, 203.

43. Ibid., 199.

44. Ibid., 198.

45. The issues are similar to the dynamics of knowledge, otherness, and violence in the prose tale discussed in chapter 2. On the issue of human opacity to God see Carasik, "Limits of Omniscience."

46. Nemo, Job and the Excess of Evil, 56–63.

47. Levinas, Totality and Infinity, 201.

48. Ibid., 200.

49. Levinas argues against the resolution of same and other in such a fashion, which he sees as the traditional response of philosophies of being.

50. See Richter, Studien zu Hiob; Gemser, "Rib- or Controversy-Pattern"; Roberts, "Job's Summons to Yahweh"; J. B. Frye, "Legal Language of the Book of Job"; Scholnick, "Lawsuit Drama"; Dick, "Job 31"; Habel, Book of Job.

51. Habel, Book of Job, 54.

52. Ibid., 178–81.

53. Bildad has also introduced the theme of God's righteousness. The "this" to which Job expresses agreement in 9:2a, however, is the statement of Eliphaz that he paraphrases in 9:2b.

54. Bakhtin, Dialogic Imagination, 295–96.

55. Ibid., 296.

56. E.g., Gordis, Book of Job, 522; Westerman, Structure of the Book of Job, 73–74; Janzen, Job, 90–91; Dell, Sceptical Literature, 148.

57. Bakhtin, Speech Genres, 163.

58. The language of legal contest between divine and human participants is most common in the Bible in the context of the relationship between God and the nation (Isa 3:13–14; Mic 6:1–2; cf. Isa 49:25b; Jer 50:34). In a few instances God is said to "enter into judgment" with an individual (Ps 143:2; Eccl 11:9) or to "argue the case" for a petitioner (Ps 119:154a). The only close parallel to Job's bold use of trial imagery is found in Jer 12:1: "You will win, O LORD, if I make claim against You, / Yet I shall present charges against You" (NJPS). In Jeremiah, however, the image remains isolated and does not fund a developed rhetoric.

59. Schön, "Generative Metaphor," 138.

60. Lakoff and Turner, More Than Cool Reason, 38–39.

61. Lakoff and Johnson, Metaphors We Live By, 91–96.

62. Jacobsen, Treasures of Darkness, 157–60.

63. In actual social practice both legal and patronage models might be in play. The narrative of Jeremiah's trial represents such impassioned but rational argument (Jer 26:7–19), yet his deliverance is also attributed to the intervention of his patron, Ahikam son of Shaphan (Jer 26:24).

64. Dick, "Job 31," 39–40.

65. Trans. Briggs, ANET, 601–2, 604.

66. Felman, "Education and Crisis," 6.

67. Ibid., 5.

68. The term "hermeneutics" has several frames of reference. Here I use it to refer to the process of understanding a situation rather than a text. See Iser, Range of Interpretation, 55–69.

69. Ricoeur, Time and Narrative, 1:43.

70. The most thorough review of scholarly attempts to deal with the perceived difficulties of the third cycle of speeches is Witte, Vom Leiden zur Lehre.

71. Gordis, Book of Job, 533; Janzen, Job, 171–74; Good, In Turns of Tempest, 9, 284–90.

72. Andersen, Job, 219; Wolfers, "Speech-Cycles in the Book of Job"; Witte, Vom Leiden zur Lehre, 19, notes the long line of interpreters from the sixteenth through the twentieth century who have offered some version of this integrative understanding of the tensions.

73. Reventlow, "Tradition und Redaktion in Hiob 27," has noted the similarity to the psalmic complaint but takes Job in the course of the third cycle of speeches to be recapitulating some-

thing of the spiritual movement that takes place in the psalm. I understand Job's evocation of the genre quite differently.

74. See the discussion in chapter 3 concerning the reiterative rather than the dialectical movement of the wisdom dialogue.

75. Seitz, "Job," 12-13, makes a similar observation: "Job moves to a position of defending the moral order, but this does not happen in such a way as to slacken his complaint. In fact, he is all the more resolute in defending his innocence and demanding a fair trial (27:1-6). What happens in Round 3 is that the ground is effectively cut out from under the friends. . . . [Job] defends the moral order—in support of his own position and against the friends. He emerges as the righteous sufferer after all, the one who asks God to vindicate him against evil-doers rising up against him." In my opinion, however, Seitz downplays the radical nature of Job's rhetoric and sees him too much in terms of the piety of the psalter (e.g., Ps 27:7).

76. E.g., Anderson, *Job*, 214, 219; Hartley, *Book of Job*, 352-53.

77. See Dhorme, *Commentary on the Book of Job*, 352; contra Pope, *Job*, 173; cf. Gordis, *Book of Job*, 263; Habel, *Book of Job*, 346.

78. Although the proper translation of 24:1 is disputed, the basic sense is clear. For a discussion of the grammatical issues see Gordis, *Book of Job*, 264. Wolfers, "Speech-Cycles in the Book of Job," 386 n. 6, disputes Gordis's interpretation.

79. Buber, *Prophetic Faith*, 191, 192.

80. Gordis, *Book of Job*, 263-64.

81. Good, *In Turns of Tempest*, 286.

82. Felman, "Education and Crisis," 25. The quotation refers to the poetry of Paul Celan.

6. Dialogics and Allegory

1. Budde, *Das Buch Hiob*, 158-59; 162-64; Janzen, *Job*, 187; Lugt, *Rhetorical Criticism*, 526-29.

2. As Good, *In Turns of Tempest*, 290, says, "I join [the majority of scholars] in doubting that the "Hymn to Wisdom" was here in the earlier stages of the book's composition. But here it is now, and it makes a contribution to the context."

3. See, e.g., Dhorme, *Commentary on the Book of Job*, xcvii, who ascribes to the poem the function of "providing a pause and moment of rest, after the poetic dialogue." Hartley, *Book of Job*, 26, notes that "it bridges the dialogue (chs. 4-27) with the final sets of speeches (29:1-42:6)." Similarly, Westermann, *Structure of the Book of Job*, 137, "an intermezzo."

4. Pope, *Job*, xxvii; Fohrer, *Das Buch Hiob*, 392. For a survey of earlier opinion see Rowley, "Book of Job," 166-68.

5. Perdue, *Wisdom in Revolt*, 84.

6. Ibid., 84.

7. See, e.g., Lévêque, *Job et son Dieu*, 595 n. 3, 606; Geller, "Where Is Wisdom?" 174.

8. So Andersen, *Job*, 53; Habel, *Book of Job*, 392; Hartley, *Book of Job*, 27; Geller, "Where Is Wisdom?" 176-77 n. 1.

9. Andersen, *Job*, 53.

10. Habel, *Book of Job*, 392. Similarly, Andersen, *Job*, 53.

11. Zuckerman, *Job the Silent*, 142.

12. Gordis, *Book of God and Man*, 102-3.

13. Zuckerman, *Job the Silent*, 143. Similarly, Lugt, *Rhetorical Criticism*, 324. Geller, "Where Is Wisdom?" 174, argues that "v. 27 makes a strong conclusion to the poem."

14. I discuss this in more detail later. Oorschot, "Hiob 28," 187, argues similarly.

15. Bakhtin, *Dialogic Imagination*, 262-63; Voloshinov, *Philosophy of Language*, 22-23.

16. Fox, *Proverbs 1–9*, 352. By "interludes" Fox refers to Prov 1:20–33; 3:13–20; 6:1–19; 8:1–36; 9:1–18.

17. Ibid., 32–34.

18. Newsom, "Woman and the Discourse," 144–49; Blenkinsopp, "Social Context," 472–73, argues that the context is the social self-definition of the Judean běnê haggôlāh in the early Achemenid period. The problem of identifying the social context may not be simply one of distance from the sources. As Jameson argues in *Political Unconscious*, 79, literature often negotiates cultural conflicts by symbolically transferring them to another realm of discourse, where they can be resolved in a way that they cannot be in real life.

19. Hengel, Judaism and *Hellenism*, 1:210–15.

20. See in particular Albertz, "Der sozialgeschichtliche Hintergrund,"; Zuckerman, *Job the Silent*; and Wolfers, *Deep Things*.

21. Zuckerman, *Job the Silent*, 144.

22. E.g., *Ludlul* II.33–38; Babylonian Theodicy, lines 82–84, 256–57.

23. Perdue, *Wisdom in Revolt*, 247.

24. Janzen, *Job*, 188.

25. Lévêque, *Job et son Dieu*, 614.

26. Oorschot, "Hiob 28," 197–98.

27. Bakhtin, *Problems of Dostoevsky's Poetics*, 93.

28. Morson and Emerson, *Mikhail Bakhtin*, 258. Cf. Bakhtin, *Problems of Dostoevsky's Poetics*, 118.

29. Bruns, *Hermeneutics Ancient and Modern*, 202.

30. Ibid., 203.

31. Ibid.

32. Bruns's observations are another way of recognizing Gadamer's dictum that we understand differently if we understand at all.

33. Habel, "In Defense of God the Sage," 32.

34. Oorschot, "Hiob 28," 197–98.

35. Ibid., 197.

36. Buccellati, "Wisdom and Not," 43.

37. Habel, "In Defense of God the Sage," 32. Cf. Geller, "Where Is Wisdom?" 166–67.

38. Similarly, Habel, *Book of Job*, 401.

7. A Working Rhetorical World

1. Dell, *Sceptical Literature*, 125–33. I disagree with her choice of an extremely broad definition of parody (148–50) and would limit it to those misuses of form or discourse that have the force of ridicule. Thus, I do not include Job 31 among the texts exhibiting parody, as she does.

2. See the discussion of these passages in chapter 5.

3. Although his understanding of the function of these chapters is different from mine, Holbert, "Rehabilitation of the Sinner," 231, similarly notes "the complete loss of irony" and a "remarkable 'deironization' technique" at work in these chapters.

4. See, e.g., Fohrer, "Righteous Man"; Dick, "Legal Metaphor" and "Job 31"; Lévêque, "Anamnèse et disculpation"; Holbert, "Rehabilitation of the Sinner"; Zuckerman, *Job the Silent*, 107; Westermann, *Structure of the Book of Job*, 38–42.

5. Habel, *Book of Job*, 404.

6. See, e.g., Good, *In Turns of Tempest*, 317: "Job has dropped back to the full retributionist position, has departed the depth of his despair about receiving a fair trial (chap. 23) and the savage redefinition of terms that in chap. 27 portrayed him as the god's moral superior. Now he trots out the standard terms of reward and punishment to which he so furiously objected when

the friends enunciated them." More substantively, there is a close similarity between the moral obligations Eliphaz claims Job has violated in 22:6–9 and those Job claims he has upheld in 29:12–17.

7. Holbert, "Rehabilitation of the Sinner," 229, n. 1, lists those who make this argument. See also Williams, "Theodicy in the Ancient Near East," 22. Though I disagree with Holbert on the question of authorship, his insight that the Job of chaps. 29–31 is a different character than that constructed in the dialogue is perceptive (237).

8. Concerning chap. 29, Good, "In Turns of Tempest," 299, describes it as "an arrogant man's testimony to the successful exercise of his arrogance." Even chap. 31 he calls "self-serving" (313).

9. As Habel, *Book of Job*, 404, puts it, "Chapters 29–31 are not a soliloquy in which Job reflects on his past and present situation, but a formal testimony (*māšāl*, 29:1) addressed to a public assembly." Similarly, Andersen, *Job*, 230.

10. Bakhtin, *Speech Genres*, 126 (emphasis added).

11. Morson and Emerson, *Mikhail Bakhtin*, 135.

12. One can tease out the social unconscious in the prose tale, of course. See, e.g., Clines, "Why Is There a Book of Job?" My interest here, however, is in the surface strategies of the text, not in what a hermeneutics of suspicion might uncover.

13. See Crüsemann, "Hiob und Kohelet,"; Albertz, "Der sozialgeschichtliche Hintergrund."

14. Wright, "Family," 762.

15. Lemche, "Kings and Clients," 119–25.

16. See Blenkinsopp, "Family in First Temple Israel."

17. Lemche, "Kings and Clients," 129–31. This is not to deny the possibility of differences between this and other social discourses or even ideological contradictions within the moral world of village patriarchy itself. The exposure and exploitation of contradictions does not, however, figure prominently in Job's rhetoric in chaps. 29–31.

18. The literature on honor and shame is vast, and the complexities of the use of these concepts in biblical studies is still under discussion. See, provisionally, the collection of essays in *Semeia* 68 and in particular the thoughtful response by Chance, "Anthropology of Honor and Shame." See also Bechtel, "Shame as a Sanction," and Olyan, "Honor, Shame, and Covenant Relations." In this study I am not attempting to make specific, direct claims about Israelite society. The social world constructed by Job 29–31 is a fictive world and not directly transparent to any social entity, but its images and values I take to be derived in some fashion from those recognizable to the original audience.

19. The translation of these verses is difficult. Cf. NRSV, "Through want and hard hunger they gnaw the dry and desolate ground, they pick mallow and the leaves of bushes, and to warm themselves the roots of broom." The major issues reflected in the differences between the NJPS and the NRSV are as follows. The verb *ʿāraq* means "to gnaw," but an Aramaic verb *ʿāraq* means "to flee," the meaning presupposed by the LXX. Some interpreters find the image of "gnawing the dry land" too bold and assume that Job here, as in other places, reflects an Aramaizing vocabulary. The word *ʾemeš*, "yesterday," makes no sense. NJPS apparently connects it with the gloom of night (see Pope, *Job*, 220); others emend to *ʾereṣ*, "land," or connect it with a Ugaritic root *ʾmt*, meaning "brushwood" (De Wilde, *Das Buch Hiob*, 292). In v. 4 the primary dispute, other than the identification of the plants in v. 4a, is whether to take *lḥmm* as the infinitive of *ḥāmam* ("to grow warm") or the noun *leḥem* plus the third plural masculine suffix ("their food"). Broom was ordinarily used as fuel, but as a foodstuff it was used only as camel fodder. If "their food" is read, the image is hyperbolic. However one resolves the philological issues, the resulting imagery is of wretched people, barely subsisting in a desolate place.

20. Girard, *Job*, 10–13, 124–37.

21. Albertz, "Der sozialgeschichtlicht Hintergrund," 358–66.

22. Following a suggestion of Gordis, *Book of Job*, 334, adopted by NJPS that *yĕšuʿāti* is related to the noun *šōaʿ*, "noble," and means "the station of a nobleman." The pair of nouns *nādib* and *šōaʿ* are parallel in Isa 32:5.

23. It is not possible to define the relationship of patronage in ancient Israel with the level of detail in which it can be studied in some other cultures (e.g., ancient Rome). Nevertheless, if used in a broad sense, "patronage" is a useful shorthand designation for certain asymmetrical social relations of mutual obligation between persons of different status in a society. Although other social models also influence specific psalmic terminology and imagery (family relationships, king-subject relationships, human-animal relationships), the patron-client relationship appears to be important to the construction of subject roles in the psalms. The king-subject relationship is itself a specific development of that broader social model. See Lemche, "Kings and Clients," and Hobbs, "Reflections on Honor, Shame, and Covenant Relations," for provisional assessments of the value of patron-client frameworks for Israelite society and literature.

24. So Pope, *Job*, 223. The LXX makes this a first person expression: "I did not strike." See Dhorme, *Commentary on the Book of Job*, 443–44. For other interpretations and emendations see De Wilde, *Das Buch Hiob*, 296, and Gordis, *Book of Job*, 336.

25. Fohrer, "Righteous Man," 87; Gordis, *Book of Job*, 542.

26. Dick, "Job 31," 31, refers to it as "a legal fiction."

27. Fohrer, *Das Buch Hiob*, 433, sees a series of ten expanded to twelve. Gordis, *Book of Job*, 543, identifies fourteen, a double heptad.

28. In the dialogues, of course, Job takes up both the position of accuser and wrongly accused. Here, however, the accusation against God is carefully muted.

8. The Dissatisfied Reader

1. Gibson, *Job*, 268–81. Mitchell, *Book of Job*, similarly excises the speeches from his translation, though he can claim a poet's license.

2. Rowley, *Job*, 216.

3. Habel, *Book of Job*, 443.

4. Janzen, *Job*, 217, observes that "several features of his presentation work to subvert his own claims to speak for God. In fact he serves the narrative progression in a manner analogous to the snake in the garden story and the many prophets *vis-à-vis* Micaiah in Kings."

5. These arguments have often been rehearsed. Dhorme's discussion (*Commentary on the Book of Job*, xcviii–cv) remains one of the most balanced. He finds persuasive the following arguments for the secondary nature of the Elihu material. (1) Elihu is mentioned neither in the prologue nor in the epilogue. (2) The prose introduction of Elihu in chap. 32 differs in tone and style from the introduction of the other characters, as does the extended genealogical information supplied for Elihu in 32:2. (3) The style of Elihu's refutation of Job differs sharply from that of the friends. He calls Job by name nine times and quotes from the preceding debate. (4) Although Dhorme is cautious about arguing from different authorship on the basis of style, he finds persuasive the evidence for a distinctive linguistic profile in the Elihu speeches, which includes numerous Aramaisms. For other arguments see Driver and Gray, *Book of Job*, xl–xlvii; Pope, *Job*, xxvii–xxviii. Counterarguments may be found in Habel, "Role of Elihu."

6. Andersen, *Job*, 50.

7. Zuckerman, *Job the Silent*, 153.

8. Burke, *Philosophy of Literary Form*, 111.

9. Bloom, *Agon*, 21.

10. Ibid., 43.

11. Hurvitz, "Date of the Prose Tale."

12. Zuckerman, *Job the Silent*, 156–57.

13. For example, Hölscher, *Das Buch Hiob*, 85, and more recently Wahl, *Der gerechte Schöpfer*, 183, are persuaded. Snaith, *Book of Job*, 104–12, is not.

14. Wahl, *Der gerechte Schöpfer*, 182–87.

15. Although a few commentators, notably Perdue, *Wisdom in Revolt*, 249, and Habel, *Book of Job*, 451, have argued that the "spirit" to which Elihu refers is not a special divine gift but simply the ordinary animating spirit in every human being, Elihu's argument seems to depend on the assumption that his knowledge is based on something more than ordinary human intelligence. The supposed parallel in 33:4 is part of the discourse of creation, not of inspiration, and so does not control the meaning here.

16. Fohrer, *Das Buch Hiob*, 451.

17. Haag, *Die Errettung Daniels*, 110, 117.

18. Trans. Steussy, *Gardens in Babylon*, 106.

19. Yes, according to Engel, *Die Susanna-Erzählung*, 142; no, according to Steussy, *Gardens in Babylon*, 136–43.

20. Habel, *Book of Job*, 452.

21. Ibid., 460–61.

22. For my views on the appeal and limitations of the position see Newsom, "Book of Job" (NIB), 571–72.

23. Ross, "Job 33:14–30," understands the angel's role and hence the sequence of events differently. If the decisive action takes place entirely between the angel and God, then the sinner's prayer is the consequence of God's acceptance and not its precondition. The "ransom" would presumably be the angel's own intervention.

24. Duhm, *Das Buch Hiob*, 159.

25. Plöger, *Das Buch Daniel*, 79.

26. Haag, *Die Errettung Daniels*, 108–9.

27. Ibid., 112; Fohrer, *Das Buch Hiob*, 460.

28. If vv. 31–32 also refer to the person of the ruler, then the possibility of recognition and repentance is also a part of the envisioned set of relationships.

29. Skehan and Di Lella, *Wisdom of Ben Sira*, 224.

30. Ibid.

31. Wahl, *Die gerechte Schöpfer*, 113–14.

32. Ibid., 113.

33. Ibid., 113–14 n. 94.

34. Ibid., 120.

35. Beentjes, *Ben Sira in Hebrew*, 169. Strugnell, "Notes and Queries," 116–17, reads *'dny ṣyṣ wḥẓwt mr'h*.

36. Prato, *Il problema*, 116–208.

37. Rad, "Job XXXVIII," 285.

38. Skehan and Di Lella, *Wisdom of Ben Sira*, 29.

39. So Prato, *Il problema*, 145–46.

40. Kohák, *Embers and the Stars*, 70–71.

41. Ibid., 83–84.

42. Ibid., 84.

43. Wahl, *Der gerechte Schöpfer*, 113–14 n. 94.

9. The Voice from the Whirlwind

1. Wolde, "Job 42, 1–6," 233–50, contains the best recent discussion and bibliography on Job 42:6.

2. Bakhtin, *Problems of Dostoevsky's Poetics*, 166.

3. See, e.g., Mettinger, "God of Job," on the one hand, and Rad, "Job XXXVIII," and Habel, "God the Sage," on the other.

4. So Rowold, "Yahweh's Challenge."

5. Wilcox, Bitterness of Job, 170.

6. The literature on theories of the sublime has burgeoned in recent years. The foundational texts are those of Longinus, Peri Hypsous (On Great Writing), Edmund Burke, Philosophical Enquiry (1757), and Immanuel Kant's "Analytic of the Sublime" in the Critique of the Power of Judgment (1790). Discussion of the sublime was revived in early modernism through Boileau's translation of Longinus in 1674, and during the eighteenth century the sublime became a major category of aesthetic and philosophical discourse. See the studies of Monk, Sublime, and Bolla, Discourse of the Sublime. Psychoanalytic and structural linguistic dimensions of the sublime are explored by Hertz, End of the Line, and Weiskel, Romantic Sublime. In the last two decades considerable interest in the sublime as a category for engaging the postmodern condition has developed. Though the literature is voluminous, Lyotard's close rereading of Kant (Lessons on the Analytic of the Sublime) is perhaps the most influential. For a critical but appreciative engagement of both the psychoanalytic and postmodern analyses of the sublime see Crowther, Critical Aesthetics and Postmodernism.

7. Tsang, Sublime, 3, 6.

8. Burke, Philosophical Enquiry, 65–67. Burke also cites Eliphaz's night vision in chap. 4 (63) and Job's majestic self-presentation in chap. 29 (67) as examples of the sublime. See also Lowth, Sacred Poetry, 176–77, 180.

9. Otto, Idea of the Holy, 74–84. Although he does not explicitly invoke the category of the sublime, Otto's discussion of the divine speeches in terms of their numinous character is in essence an analysis of their sublimity. For Otto and the sublime, see Poland, "Idea of the Holy."

10. Tsang, Sublime, 45–48.

11. Zuckerman, Job the Silent, 96.

12. Other verbal connections might also be noted (e.g., the contesting of the terms mišpāṭ and ṣedeq/ṣādaq, used by Job in 29:14 and by God in 40:8; the desert land described as šō'ah/šu'āh ûmēšō'āh in 30:3b and 38:27a).

13. Jost and Hyde, "Introduction," 19–24.

14. Keel, Jahwehs Entgegnung, 58 n. 209.

15. Burke, Philosophical Enquiry, 58–64.

16. Kant, Critique of the Power of Judgment, 135 (5:251–52).

17. Weiskel, Romantic Sublime, ix.

18. Kant, Critique of the Power of Judgment, 150–51 (5:267).

19. Ibid., 143–48 (5:260–64).

20. Burke, Philosophical Enquiry, 67–68. Significant differences exist between Burke's and Kant's analyses of the function of terror, but for present purposes it is not essential to distinguish them.

21. For the following discussion I draw heavily on the analysis developed in my commentary. See Newsom, "Book of Job" (NIB), 600–27.

22. Perhaps something of a hermeneutical equivalent might be established if, instead of wild animals, modern readers thought in terms of anthrax, staph bacilli, the Ebola virus, or the cancer cell. Our sense of the terrifying biological other now rests in the microscopically small rather than in the large and imposing.

23. Keel, Jahwehs Entgegnung, 71.

24. Ibid., 87. ANEP, pl. 464.

25. For the possibility that Psalm 104 is the intentional foil for the divine speeches see Newsom, "Book of Job," (NIB) 596–97.

26. For a comprehensive analysis of lion imagery in the Hebrew Bible see Strawn, "What Is Stronger Than a Lion?"

27. Foster, *Before the Muses*, 2: 808.

28. Keel, *Jahwehs Entgegnung*, 72, reproduces a depiction of Pharaoh Tutankhamen hunting ostriches.

29. Habel, *Book of Job*, 547.

30. So the commentaries of Duhm, Dhorme, Weiser, Hölscher, Fohrer, De Wilde, and many others.

31. See Gibson, "New Look," 136, who considers but rejects this possibility.

32. Habel, *Book of Job*, 572; Greenstein, "In Job's Face," 311.

33. Habel, *Book of Job*, 551, 555.

34. See, e.g., Gordis, *Book of Job*, 470, 483–84; Hartley, *Book of Job*, 527; NRSV (Eng. 41:12).

35. Gibson, "New Look," 134.

36. Similarly, Geller, "Where Is Wisdom?" 170. For a recent discussion see Assman et al., "Richten und Retten."

37. See Beal, *Religion and Its Monsters*, 50–54.

38. Geertz, *Interpretation of Cultures*, 49.

39. Since the Enlightenment this has been a more contested notion, but the energy with which it is contested suggests how important a stance of moral realism remains.

40. Ricoeur, *Symbolism of Evil*, 323.

41. Desmond, "Being at a Loss," 179.

42. Some, like Robertson, *Old Testament*, 48–49, read them as bathos.

43. Gordis, "Temptation of Job," 85.

44. Longinus, *On the Sublime*, 125.

45. Ibid., 139.

46. Guerlac, *Impersonal Sublime*, 3–4.

47. Wolde, "Job 42, 1–6," 231–32.

48. Bakhtin, *Dialogic Imagination*, 341–47.

49. Guerlac, "Longinus and the Subject of the Sublime," 286.

50. Ricoeur, *Symbolism of Evil*, 321.

51. Desmond, "Being at a Loss," 183.

52. Ibid.

53. Lyotard, *Inhuman*, 84.

54. Ibid., 84.

55. Ibid., 87.

Conclusion

1. Bakhtin, *Problems of Dostoevsky's Poetics*, 89.

Bibliography

Albertz, Ranier. "Der sozialgeschichtliche Hintergrund des Hiob-Buches und der 'Babylonischen Theodizee.'" In *Die Botschaft und die Boten: Festschrift für Hans Walter Wolff zum 70. Geburtstag*, edited by J. Jeremias and L. Perlitt, pages 349–72. Neukirchen-Vluyn: Neukirchener, 1981.

Alt, Albrecht. "Zur Vorgeschichte des Buches Hiob." *Zeitschrift für die alttestamentliche Wissenschaft* 55 (1937): 265–68.

Andersen, Francis I. *Job: An Introduction and Commentary*. Leicester, England: Inter-Varsity Press, 1976.

Aristotle. *The Poetics*. Translated by W. Hamilton Frye. Loeb Classical Library. Cambridge: Harvard University Press, 1982.

Assmann, Jan, Bernd Janowski, and Michael Welker. "Richten und Retten: Zur Aktualität der altorientalischen und biblischen Gerechtigkeitskonzeption." In *Gerechtigkeit*, edited by J. Assmann, B. Janowski, and M. Welker, pages 9–35. Munich: Wilhelm Fink, 1998.

Bakhtin, Mikhail. *The Dialogic Imagination: Four Essays*. Edited by M. Holquist. Translated by C. Emerson and M. Holquist. Austin: University of Texas Press, 1981.

——. *Problems of Dostoevsky's Poetics*. Edited and translated by C. Emerson. Theory and History of Literature 8. Minneapolis: University of Minnesota Press, 1984.

——. *Speech Genres and Other Late Essays*. Translated by W. M. McGee. University of Texas Press Slavic Series 8. Austin: University of Texas Press, 1986.

——. *Art and Answerability: Early Philosophical Essays*. Edited by M. Holquist and V. Liapunov. Translated by V. Liapunov and K. Bostrom. University of Texas Press Slavic Series 9. Austin: University of Texas Press, 1990.

Bakhtin, Mikhail, and Pavel Medvedev. *The Formal Method in Literary Scholarship: A Critical Introduction to Sociological Poetics*. Translated by A. Wehrle. Cambridge.: Harvard University Press, 1985.

Beal, Timothy K. *Religion and Its Monsters*. New York: Routledge, 2002.

Bechtel, Lyn M. "Shame as a Sanction of Social Control in Biblical Israel: Judicial, Political, and Social Shaming." *Journal for the Study of the Old Testament* 49 (1991): 47–76.

Beentjes, Pancratius C. *The Book of Ben Sira in Hebrew: A Text Edition of All Extant Hebrew Manuscripts and a Synopsis of All Parallel Hebrew Ben Sira Texts*. Supplements to Vetus Testamentum 68. Leiden: E. J. Brill, 1997.

Bell, Catherine. *Ritual Theory, Ritual Practice*. New York: Oxford University Press, 1992.

Bennett, William. *The Book of Virtues: A Treasury of Great Moral Stories*. New York: Simon & Schuster, 1993.

———. *The Moral Compass: Stories for a Life's Journey*. New York: Simon & Schuster, 1995.

Berger, Peter. *The Sacred Canopy*. Garden City, N.Y.: Doubleday, 1967.

Blenkinsopp, Joseph. "The Social Context of the 'Outsider Woman' in Proverbs 1-9." *Biblica* 72 (1991): 457-73.

———. "The Family in First Temple Israel." In *Families in Ancient Israel*, edited by L. Perdue, pages 85-92. Louisville, Ky: Westminster John Knox Press, 1997.

Bloom, Harold. *Agon: Towards a Theory of Revisionism*. Oxford: Oxford University Press, 1982.

Bolla, Peter de. *The Discourse of the Sublime: Readings in History, Aesthetics, and the Subject*. Oxford: Basil Blackwell, 1989.

Booth, Wayne. *The Company We Keep: An Ethics of Fiction*. Berkeley: University of California Press, 1988.

Bourdieu, Pierre. *Outline of a Theory of Practice*. Translated by R. Nice. Cambridge: Cambridge University Press, 1977.

Brenner, Athalya. "Job the Pious? The Characterization of Job in the Narrative Framework of the Book." *Journal for the Study of the Old Testament* 43 (1989): 37-52.

Brinker, Menachem. "Theme and Interpretation." In *The Return of Thematic Criticism*, edited by Werner Sollors, pages 21-37. Cambridge: Harvard University Press, 1993.

Bruns, Gerald L. *Hermeneutics Ancient and Modern*. New Haven, Conn.: Yale University Press, 1992.

Buber, Martin. *The Prophetic Faith*. New York: Harper & Row, 1949.

Buccellati, Giorgio. "Tre saggi sulla sapienza mesopotamica, III. La teodicea: condanna dell'abulia politica." *Oriens antiquus* 11 (1972): 161-78.

———. "Wisdom and Not: The Case of Mesopotamia." *Journal of the American Oriental Society* 101 (1981): 35-47.

Budde, Karl. *Das Buch Hiob übersetzt und erklärt*. 2nd ed. Göttingen: Vandenhoeck & Ruprecht, 1913.

Burke, Edmund. *A Philosophical Enquiry into the Origin of Our Ideas of the Sublime and Beautiful*. Edited by J. T. Boulton. London: Basil Blackwell, 1987.

Burke, Kenneth. *A Grammar of Motives*. Berkeley: University of California Press, 1969.

———. *The Philosophy of Literary Form: Studies in Symbolic Action*. 3rd ed. Berkeley: University of California Press, 1973.

Burridge, Kenelm. *New Heaven, New Earth: A Study of Millenarian Activity*. New York: Schocken, 1969.

Carasik, Michael. "The Limits of Omniscience." *Journal of Biblical Literature* 119 (2000): 221-32.

Carr, David. *Time, Narrative, and History*. Bloomington, Ind.: Indiana University Press, 1986.

Chance, John K. "The Anthropology of Honor and Shame: Culture, Values, and Practice." *Semeia* 68 (1994): 139-51.

Cheney, Michael. *Dust, Wind, and Agony: Character, Speech, and Genre in Job*. Coniectanea biblica: Old Testament Series 36. Stockholm: Almqvist & Wiksell International, 1994.

Cheyne, Thomas Kelly. *Jewish Religious Life after the Exile*. New York: G. P. Putnam's Sons, 1898.

Clines, David. "In Search of an Indian Job." *Vetus Testamentum* 33 (1983): 398-418.

———. "False Naivety in the Prologue to Job." *Hebrew Annual Review* 9 (1985): 127-36.

———. *Job 1-20*. Word Biblical Commentary 17. Dallas: Word Books, 1989.

———. "Deconstructing the Book of Job." In *What Does Eve Do to Help? And Other Readerly Questions to the Old Testament*, pages 106-23. Sheffield: JSOT Press, 1990.

———. "Why Is There a Book of Job, and What Does It Do to You if You Read It?" In *The Book of Job*, edited by W. A. M. Beuken, pages 1–20. Bibliotheca ephemeridum theologicarum lovaniensium 114. Leuven: Louvain University Press, 1994.

Coles, Robert. *The Call of Stories: Teaching and the Moral Imagination*. Boston: Houghton Mifflin, 1989.

Cooper, Alan. "Reading and Misreading the Prologue of Job." *Journal for the Study of the Old Testament* 46 (1990): 67–79.

Crenshaw, James L. *A Whirlpool of Torment: Israelite Traditions of God as an Oppressive Presence*. Philadelphia: Fortress, 1984.

Crowther, Paul. *Critical Aesthetics and Postmodernism*. Oxford: Clarendon, 1993.

Crüsemann, Frank. "Hiob und Kohelet: Ein Beitrag zum Verständnis des Hiobbuches." In *Werden und Wirken des Alten Testaments: Festschrift für Claus Westermann zum 70. Geburtstag*, edited by R. Albertz, et al., pages 373–93. Göttingen: Vandenhoeck & Ruprecht, 1980.

Culler, Jonathan. *Structuralist Poetics: Structuralism, Linguistics, and the Study of Literature*. Ithaca, N.Y.: Cornell University Press, 1975.

Dadlez, Eva M. *What's Hecuba to Him? Fictional Events and Actual Emotions*. University Park, Pa.: Pennsylvania State University Press, 1997.

Dahood, Mitchell. "Some Northwest-Semitic Words in Job." *Biblica* 38 (1957): 312–14.

Danby, Herbert. *The Mishnah: Translated from the Hebrew with Introduction and Brief Explanatory Notes*. New York: Oxford University Press, 1983.

Day, Peggy L. *An Adversary in Heaven: Satan in the Hebrew Bible*. Harvard Semitic Monographs 43. Atlanta: Scholars Press, 1988.

De Wilde, A. *Das Buch Hiob*. Oudtestamentische Studiën 22. Leiden: E. J. Brill, 1981.

Dell, Katharine J. *The Book of Job as Sceptical Literature*. Beihefte zur Zeitschrift für die alttestamentliche Wissenschaft 197. Berlin: Walter de Gruyter, 1991.

Demos, Raphael. "On Persuasion." *Journal of Philosophy* 29 (1932): 225–32.

Denning-Bolle, Sara. *Wisdom in Akkadian Literature: Expression, Instruction, Dialogue*. Leiden: Ex Oriente Lux, 1992.

Derrida, Jacques. "The Law of Genre." *Glyph* 7 (1980): 202–13.

———. "The Politics of Friendship." *Journal of Philosophy* 35 (1988): 632–44.

Desmond, William. "Being at a Loss: Reflections on Philosophy and the Tragic." In *Tragedy and Philosophy*, edited by N. Georgopoulos, pages 154–86. New York: Macmillan, 1993.

Dhorme, Edouard. *A Commentary on the Book of Job*. Translated by H. Knight. London: Nelson, 1967.

Dick, Michael B. "The Legal Metaphor in Job 31." *Catholic Biblical Quarterly* 41 (1979): 37–50.

———. "Job 31, the Oath of Innocence, and the Sage." *Zeitschrift für die alttestamentliche Wissenschaft* 95 (1983): 31–53.

Dreyfus, Hubert L., and Paul Rabinow. *Michel Foucault: Beyond Structuralism and Hermeneutics*. 2nd ed. Chicago: University of Chicago Press, 1983.

Driver, Samuel R., and George B. Gray. *A Critical and Exegetical Commentary on the Book of Job*. Edinburgh: T. & T. Clark, 1921.

Duff, David, ed. *Modern Genre Theory*. Harlow, England: Pearson Education, 2000.

Duhm, Bernhard. *Das Buch Hiob*. Freiburg: J. C. B. Mohr (Paul Siebeck), 1897.

Eaglestone, Robert. *Ethical Criticism: Reading after Levinas*. Edinburgh: Edinburgh University Press, 1997.

Eco, Umberto. *The Role of the Reader: Explorations in the Semiotics of Texts*. Bloomington, Ind.: Indiana University Press, 1979.

Elliger, Karl. *Jesaja II*. Biblischer Kommentar Altes Testament 11. Neukirchen-Vluyn: Neukirchener, 1970.

Engel, Helmut. *Die Susanna-Erzählung: Einleitung, Übersetzung, und Kommentar zum Septuaginta-*

Text und zur Theodotion-Bearbeitung. Orbis Biblicus et Orientalis 61. Göttingen: Vandenhoeck & Ruprecht, 1984.

Felman, Shoshana. "Education and Crisis, or the Vicissitudes of Teaching." In *Testimony: Crises of Witnessing in Literature, Psychoanalysis, and History*, edited by S. Felman and D. Laub, pages 1–56. New York: Routledge, 1992.

Fewell, Danna. *Circle of Sovereignty: Plotting Politics in the Book of Daniel.* 2nd revised and extended ed. Nashville: Abingdon, 1991.

Finet, André. "Les trois vengeances du pauvre homme de Nippur. Conte Babylonian." In *L'atelier de L'orfevre*, edited by M. Broze and Ph. Talon, pages 87–106. Louvain: Peeters, 1992.

Fishbane, Michael. "Jeremiah IV 23–26 and Job III 3–13: A Recovered Use of the Creation Pattern." *Vetus Testamentum* 21 (1971): 151–67.

Fogel, Aaron. *Coercion to Speak: Conrad's Poetics of Dialogue.* Cambridge: Harvard University Press, 1985.

Fohrer, Georg. *Das Buch Hiob.* Kommentar zum Alten Testament 16. Gütersloh: Gütersloh Verlagshaus Gerd Mohn, 1963.

———. "Form und Funktion in der Hiobdictung." In *Studien zum Buche Hiob (1956–1979)*, pages 60–77. Berlin: Walter de Gruyter, 1983.

———. "The Righteous Man in Job 31." In *Studien zum Buche Hiob (1956–1979)*, pages 78–93. Berlin: Walter de Gruyter, 1983.

Foster, Benjamin R. "Self-Reference of an Akkadian Poet." *Journal of the American Oriental Society* 103 (1983): 123–30.

———. *Before the Muses: An Anthology of Akkadian Literature.* 2nd ed. 2 vols. Potomac, Md.: CDL Press, 1996.

Fowler, Alastair. *Kinds of Literature: An Introduction to the Theory of Genres and Modes.* Oxford: Oxford University Press, 1982.

Fox, Michael. *Proverbs 1–9: A New Translation with Introduction and Commentary.* Anchor Bible 18A. Garden City, N.Y.: Doubleday, 2000.

Frye, J. B. "The Legal Language of the Book of Job." Ph. D. diss., University of London, 1973.

Frye, Northrop. *The Anatomy of Criticism.* Princeton, N.J.: Princeton University Press, 1957.

Fuchs, Gisela. "Die Klage des Propheten: Beobachtungen zu den Konfessionen Jeremias in Vergleich mit den Klagen Hiobs." *Biblische Zeitschrift* 41 (1997): 212–28.

Geertz, Clifford. *The Interpretation of Cultures.* New York: Basic Books, 1973.

Geller, Stephen A. "'Where Is Wisdom?': A Literary Study of Job 28 in Its Settings." In *Judaic Perspectives on Ancient Israel*, edited by J. Neusner, B. Levine, and E. S. Frerichs, pages 155–88. Philadelphia: Fortress, 1987.

Gemser, Berend. "The *rib*- or Controversy-Pattern in Hebrew Mentality." In *Wisdom in Israel and in the Ancient Near East* (Rowley Festschrift), pages 120–37. Supplements to Vetus Testamentum 3. Leiden: E. J. Brill, 1955.

Gese, Hartmut. *Lehre und Wirklichkeit in der alten Weisheit: Studien zu den Sprüch Salomos und zu dem Buche Hiob.* Tübingen: J. C. B. Mohr (Paul Siebeck), 1958.

Gibson, John C. L. *Job.* Philadelphia: Westminster, 1985.

———. "A New Look at Job 41.1–4 (English 41.9–12)." In *Text as Pretext: Essays in Honour of Robert Davidson*, edited by R. Carroll, pages 129–39. Sheffield: JSOT Press, 1992.

Girard, René. *Job: The Victim of His People.* Translated by Y. Freccero. Stanford. Calif.: Stanford University Press, 1987.

Golden, L., and O. B. Hardison. *Aristotle's Poetics: A Translation and Commentary for Students of Literature.* Englewood Cliffs, N.J.: Prentice-Hall, 1968.

Good, Edwin M. *In Turns of Tempest: A Reading of Job with a Translation.* Stanford, Calif.: Stanford University Press, 1990.

Goodman, Nelson. *Languages of Art: An Approach to a Theory of Symbols.* Indianapolis: Hackett, 1976.

——. *Ways of Worldmaking.* Indianapolis: Hackett, 1978.

Gordis, Robert. *The Book of God and Man.* Chicago: University of Chicago Press, 1965.

——. "The Temptation of Job—Tradition versus Experience in Religion." In *The Dimensions of Job,* edited by N. Glatzer, pages 74–85. New York: Schocken, 1969.

——. *The Book of Job: Commentary, New Translation, and Special Studies.* New York: Jewish Theological Seminary, 5738/1978.

Gray, John. "The Book of Job in the Context of Near Eastern Literature." *Zeitschrift für die alttestamentliche Wissenschaft* 82 (1970): 251–69.

Green, Barbara. *Mikhail Bakhtin and Biblical Scholarship: An Introduction.* Atlanta: Society of Biblical Literature, 2000.

Greenstein, Edward L. "In Job's Face/Facing Job." In *The Labour of Reading: Desire, Alienation, and Biblical Interpretation,* edited by F. Black, R. Boer, and E. Runions, pages 301–17. Atlanta: Society of Biblical Literature, 1999.

Guerlac, Suzanne. "Longinus and the Subject of the Sublime." *New Literary History* 16 (1984–85): 275–89.

——. *The Impersonal Sublime: Hugo, Baudelaire, Lautréamont.* Stanford, Calif.: Stanford University Press, 1990.

Guillén, Claudio. *The Challenge of Comparative Literature.* Translated by C. Franzen. Cambridge: Harvard University Press, 1993.

Gurney, Oliver R. "The Tale of the Poor Man of Nippur and Its Folklore Parallels." *Anatolian Studies* 22 (1972): 149–58.

Guroian, Vigan. *Tending the Heart of Virtue: How Classic Stories Awaken a Child's Moral Imagination.* New York: Oxford University Press, 1998.

Haag, Ernst. *Die Errettung Daniels aus der Löengrube: Untersuchungen zum Ursprung der biblischen Danieltradition.* Stuttgarter Bibelstudien 110. Stuttgart: Katholisches Bibelwerk, 1983.

Habel, Norman C. "The Role of Elihu in the Design of the Book of Job." In *In the Shelter of Elyon: Essays on Ancient Palestinian Life and Literature in Honor of G. W. Ahlström,* edited by W. B. Barrick and J. R. Spencer, pages 81–88. Sheffield: JSOT Press, 1984.

——. *The Book of Job.* Old Testament Library. Philadelphia: Westminster, 1985.

——. "In Defense of God the Sage." In *The Voice from the Whirlwind: Interpreting the Book of Job,* edited by L. G. Perdue and W. C. Gilpin, pages 19–38. Nashville: Abingdon, 1992.

Hartley, John E. *The Book of Job.* New International Commentary on the Old Testament. Grand Rapids: Eerdmans, 1988.

Hengel, Martin. *Judaism and Hellenism.* Translated by John Bowden. 2 vols. Philadelphia: Fortress, 1974.

Hertz, Neil. *The End of the Line: Essays on Psychoanalysis and the Sublime.* New York: Columbia University Press, 1985.

Hobbs, T. R. "Reflections on Honor, Shame, and Covenant Relations." *Journal of Biblical Literature* 116 (1997): 501–3.

Holbert, John. "The Rehabilitation of the Sinner: The Function of Job 29–31." *Zeitschrift für die alttestamentliche Wissenschaft* 95 (1983): 229–37.

Hölscher, Gustav. *Das Buch Hiob.* 2nd ed. Handbuch zum Alten Testament 1. Tübingen: J. C. B. Mohr (Paul Siebeck), 1952.

Hurvitz, Avi. "The Date of the Prose Tale of Job Linguistically Reconsidered." *Harvard Theological Review* 67 (1974): 17–34.

Iser, Wolfgang. *The Act of Reading: A Theory of Aesthetic Response.* Baltimore: Johns Hopkins Press, 1978.

——. *The Range of Interpretation.* New York: Columbia University Press, 2000.

Jacobsen, Thorkild. *Treasures of Darkness: A History of Mesopotamian Religion.* New Haven, Conn.: Yale University Press, 1976.

Jacobsen, Thorkild, and Kirsten Nielsen. "Cursing the Day: Mesopotamian and Biblical Examples." *Scandinavian Journal of the Old Testament* 6 (1992): 187-204.

Jameson, Fredric. *The Political Unconscious: Narrative as a Socially Symbolic Act.* Ithaca, N.Y.: Cornell University Press, 1981.

Janzen, Gerald. *Job.* Interpretation. Atlanta: John Knox, 1985.

Johnson, Mark. *Moral Imagination: Implications of Cognitive Science for Ethics.* Chicago: University of Chicago Press, 1993.

Jost, Walter, and Michael J. Hyde. "Introduction: Rhetoric and Hermeneutics: Places along the Way." In *Rhetoric and Hermeneutics in Our Time: A Reader*, edited by W. Jost and M. Hyde, pages 1-42. New Haven, Conn.: Yale University Press, 1997.

Kant, Immanuel. *Critique of the Power of Judgment.* Edited by Paul Guyer. Translated by Paul Guyer and Eric Matthews. Cambridge: Cambridge University Press, 2000.

Kautzsch, Karl. *Das sogenannte Volksbuch von Hiob.* Tübingen: J. C. B. Mohr (Paul Siebeck), 1900.

Keel, Othmar. *Jahwehs Entgegnung an Ijob.* Forschungen zur Religion und Literatur des Alten und Neuen Testaments 121. Göttingen: Vandenhoeck & Ruprecht, 1978.

——. *The Symbolism of the Biblical World: Ancient Near Eastern Iconography and the Book of Psalms.* Translated by T. Hallett. Winona Lake, Ind.: Eisenbrauns, 1997.

Kilpatrick, William, Gregory Wolfe, and Suzanne M. Wolfe. *Books That Build Character: A Guide to Teaching Your Child Moral Values through Stories.* New York: Simon & Schuster, 1994.

Kirkpatrick, Patricia G. *The Old Testament and Folklore Study.* Journal for the Study of the Old Testament Supplement Series 62. Sheffield: JSOT Press, 1988.

Klein, J. "'Personal God' and Individual Prayer in Sumerian Religion." *Archiv für Orientforschung: Beiheft* 19 (1982): 295-306.

Kohák, Erazim V. *The Embers and the Stars: A Philosophical Inquiry into the Moral Sense of Nature.* Chicago: University of Chicago Press, 1984.

Köhlmoos, Melanie. *Das Auge Gottes.* Forschungen zum Alten Testament 25. Tübingen: J. C. B. Mohr (Paul Siebeck), 1999.

Kramer, Samuel Noah. "'Man and His God': A Sumerian Variation on the 'Job' Motif." In *Wisdom in Israel and in the Ancient Near East* (Rowley Festschrift), edited by M. Noth and D. W. Thomas, pages 170-82. Supplements to Vetus Testamentum 3, Leiden: E. J. Brill, 1955.

Kristeva, Julia. *Powers of Horror: An Essay on Abjection.* Translated by L. Roudiez. New York: Columbia University Press, 1982.

Lakoff, George, and Mark Johnson. *Metaphors We Live By.* Chicago: University of Chicago Press, 1980.

Lakoff, George, and Mark Turner. *More Than Cool Reason: A Field Guide to Poetic Metaphor.* Chicago: University of Chicago Press, 1989.

Lambert, W. G. *Babylonian Wisdom Literature.* Oxford: Clarendon, 1960.

——. "A Further Attempt at the Babylonian 'Man and His God.'" In *Language, Literature, and History: Philological and Historical Studies Presented to Erica Reiner*, edited by Francesca Rochberg-Halton, pages 187-202. New Haven, Conn.: American Oriental Society, 1987.

Lemche, Niels Peter. "Kings and Clients: On Loyalty between the Ruler and the Ruled in Ancient 'Israel.'" *Semeia* 66 (1995): 119-32.

Levinas, Emmanuel. *Totality and Infinity: An Essay on Exteriority.* Translated by A. Lingis. Pittsburgh: Duquesne University Press, 1969.

——. *Otherwise Than Being, or Beyond Essence.* Translated by A. Lingis. Pittsburgh: Duquesne University Press, 1981.

Lévêque, Jean. *Job et son Dieu.* 2 vols. Paris: Gabalda, 1970.

——. "Anamnèse et disculpation: La conscience du juste en Job, 29–31." In *La sagesse de L'ancien Testament,* rev. ed., edited by M. Gilbert, pages 231–48. Bibliotheca ephemeridum theologicarum lovaniensium 51. Louvain: Leuven University Press, 1990.

Linafelt, Tod. "The Undecidability of BRK in the Prologue to Job and Beyond." *Biblical Interpretation* 4 (1996): 154–72.

Longinus. *On the Sublime.* Translated by W. Hamilton Frye. Loeb Classical Library. Cambridge: Harvard University Press, 1982.

Lowth, Robert. *Lectures on the Sacred Poetry of the Hebrews.* Translated by G. Gregory. London: S. Chadwick, 1847.

Lugt, Pieter van der. *Rhetorical Criticism and the Book of Job.* Oudtestamentische Studiën 32. Leiden: E. J. Brill, 1995.

Lyotard, Jean-François. *The Inhuman: Reflections on Time.* Translated by G. Bennington and R. Bowlby. Stanford, Calif.: Stanford University Press, 1991.

——. *Lessons on the Analytic of the Sublime: Kant's Critique of Judgment.* Translated by E. Rottenberg. Stanford, Calif.: Stanford University Press, 1994.

Macdonald, D. B. "The Original Form of the Legend of Job." *Journal of Biblical Literature* 14 (1895): 63–71.

——. "Some External Evidence on the Original Form of the Legend of Job." *American Journal of Semitic Languages and Literature* 14 (1898): 137–64.

MacIntyre, Alasdair. *After Virtue: A Study in Moral Theory.* 2nd corr. ed. London: Duckworth, 1985.

Mattingly, Gerald L. "The Pious Sufferer: Mesopotamia's Traditional Theodicy and Job's Counselors." In *The Bible in the Light of Cuneiform Literature: Scripture in Context III,* edited by W. Hallo, B. Jones, and G. Mattingly, pages 305–48. Lewiston, Maine: Edwin Mellen, 1990.

Mettinger, Tryggve N. D. "The God of Job: Avenger, Tyrant, or Victor?" In *The Voice from the Whirlwind: Interpreting the Book of Job,* edited by L. G. Perdue and W. C. Gilpin, pages 39–49. Nashville: Abingdon, 1992.

Miller, Patrick D. *They Cried to the Lord: The Form and Theology of Biblical Prayer.* Minneapolis: Fortress, 1994.

Mitchell, Stephen. *The Book of Job.* San Francisco: HarperCollins, 1992.

Monk, Samuel H. *The Sublime: A Study of Critical Theories in XVIII-Century England.* Ann Arbor: University of Michigan Press, 1935.

Moran, William L. "Notes on the Hymn to Marduk in Ludlul Bēl Nēmeqi." *Journal of the American Oriental Society* 103 (1983): 255–60.

Morrow, William. "Consolation, Rejection, and Repentance in Job 42:6." *Journal of Biblical Literature* 105 (1986): 211–25.

Morson, Gary Saul, and Caryl Emerson. *Mikhail Bakhtin: Creation of a Prosaics.* Stanford, Calif.: Stanford University Press, 1990.

Müller, Hans-Peter. "Die weisheitliche Lehrerzählung im Alten Testament und seiner Umwelt." *Die Welt des Orients* 9 (1977): 77–98.

——. "Keilschriftliche Parallelen zum biblischen Hiobbuch: Möglichkeit und Grenze des Vergleichs." In *Mythos–Kerygma–Wahrheit: Gesammelte Aufsätze zum Alten Testament in seiner Umwelt und zur biblischen Theologie,* pages 136–51. Berlin: Walter de Gruyter, 1991.

——. "Die Hiobrahmenerzählung und ihre altorientalischen Parallelen als Paradigmen einer weisheitlichen Wirklichkeitswahrnahme." In *The Book of Job,* edited by W. A. M. Beuken, pages 21–39. Bibliotheca ephemeridum theologicarum lovaniensium 114. Louvain: Leuven University Press, 1994.

——. *Das Hiobproblem: Seine Stellung und Entstehung im Alten Orient und im Alten Testament.* 3rd enl. ed. Erträge der Forschung 84. Darmstadt: Wissenschaftliche Buchgesellschaft, 1995.

Neher, Andre. *The Exile of the Word: From the Silence of the Bible to the Silence of Auschwitz.* Translated by D. Maisel. Philadelphia: Jewish Publication Society of America, 1981.

Nemo, Philippe. *Job and the Excess of Evil.* Translated by M. Kigel. Pittsburgh: Duquesne University Press, 1998.

Newsom, Carol A. "Woman and the Discourse of Patriarchal Wisdom: A Study of Proverbs 1-9." In *Gender and Difference in Ancient Israel*, edited by Peggy L. Day, pages 142-60. Minneapolis: Fortress, 1989.

——. "Cultural Politics in the Reading of Job." *Biblical Interpretation* 2 (1993): 119-34.

——. "The Moral Sense of Nature: Ethics in the Light of God's Speech to Job." *Princeton Seminary Bulletin* 15 (1994): 9-27.

——. "Bakhtin, the Bible, and Diologic Truth." *Journal of Religion* 76 (1996): 290-306.

——. "The Book of Job: Introduction, Commentary, and Reflections." In *The New Interpreter's Bible*, vol. 4, pages 317-637. Nashville: Abingdon, 1996.

——. "Job and His Friends: A Conflict of Moral Imaginations." *Interpretation* 53 (1999): 239-53.

——. "The Book of Job as Polyphonic Text." *Journal for the Study of the Old Testament* 97 (2002): 87-108.

——. "Narrative Ethics, Character, and the Prose Tale of Job." In *Character and Scripture: Moral Formation, Community, and Biblical Interpretation*, edited by W. P. Brown, pages 136-49. Grand Rapids: Eerdmans, 2002.

Newton, Adam Zachary. *Narrative Ethics.* Cambridge: Harvard University Press, 1995.

Niditch, Susan. *Folklore and the Hebrew Bible.* Minneapolis: Augsburg Fortress, 1993.

Nougayrol, Jean. "Une version ancienne du 'Juste souffrant.'" *Revue Biblique* 59 (1952): 239-50.

Nussbaum, Martha. *Love's Knowledge: Essays on Philosophy and Literature.* New York: Oxford University Press, 1990.

Olyan, Saul M. "Honor, Shame, and Covenant Relations in Ancient Israel and Its Environment." *Journal of Biblical Literature* 115 (1996): 201-18.

Oorschot, Jürgen van. "Hiob 28: Die verborgene Weisheit und die Furcht Gottes als Überwindung einer generalisierten Chkmh." in *The Book of Job*, edited by W. A. M. Beuken, pages 183-201. Bibliotheca ephemeridum theologicarum lovaniensium 114. Louvain: Leuven University Press, 1994.

Otto, Rudolf. *The Idea of the Holy: An Inquiry into the Non-Rational Factor in the Idea of the Divine and Its Relation to the Rational.* Translated by J. Harvey. London: Oxford University Press, 1923.

Patrick, Dale. "The Translation of Job 42.6." *Vetus Testamentum* 26 (1976): 369-71.

Penchansky, David. *The Betrayal of God: Ideological Conflict in Job.* Louisville, Ky.: Westminster/John Knox, 1990.

Perdue, Leo. *Wisdom in Revolt: Metaphorical Theology in the Book of Job.* Journal for the Study of the Old Testament Supplement Series 112. Sheffield: Almond Press, 1991.

Plöger, Otto. *Das Buch Daniel.* Kommentar zum Alten Testament 18. Gütersloh: Gütersloher Verlagshaus Gerd Mohn, 1965.

Poland, Lynn. "The Idea of the Holy and the History of the Sublime." *Journal of Religion* 72 (1992): 175-97.

Pope, Marvin. *Job.* 3rd ed. Anchor Bible 15. Garden City, N.Y.: Doubleday, 1973.

Prato, Gian Luigi. *Il problema della teodicea in Ben Sira: composizione dei contrari e richiamo alle origini.* Rome: Biblical Institute Press, 1975.

Pritchard, James B., ed. *Ancient Near Eastern Texts relating to the Old Testament.* 3rd ed. Princeton, N.J.: Princeton University Press, 1969.

———, ed. *The Ancient Near East in Pictures relating to the Old Testament*. Princeton, N.J.: Princeton University Press, 1969.

Rad, Gerhard von. "Job XXXVIII and Ancient Egyptian Wisdom." In *The Problem of the Hexateuch and Other Essays*, pages 281–91. New York: McGraw-Hill, 1966.

Rappaport, Roy A. *Ecology, Meaning, and Religion*. Berkeley, Calif.: North Atlantic Books, 1979.

Reventlow, H. Graf. "Tradition und Redaktion in Hiob 27 im Rahmen der Hiobreden des Abschnittes Hi 24–27." *Zeitschrift für die alttestamentliche Wissenschaft* 94 (1982): 279–93.

Richter, Heinz. *Studien zu Hiob: Der Aufbau des Hiobbuches dargestellt an den Gattungen des Rechtslebens*. Berlin: Evangelische Verlangsanstalt, 1959.

Ricoeur, Paul. *The Symbolism of Evil*. Translated by E. Buchanan. Boston: Beacon, 1967.

———. *Time and Narrative*. Translated by K. McLaughlin and D. Pellauer. Vol. 1. Chicago: University of Chicago Press, 1984.

———. *Oneself as Another*. Translated by K. Blamey. Chicago: University of Chicago Press, 1992.

Robbins, Joel. "Secrecy and the Sense of an Ending: Narrative, Time, and Everyday Millenarianism in Papua New Guinea and in Christian Fundamentalism." *Comparative Studies in Society and History* 43 (2001): 525–51.

Roberts, J. J. M. "Job's Summons to Yahweh: The Exploitation of a Legal Metaphor." *Restoration Quarterly* 16 (1973): 159–65.

Robertson, David. *The Old Testament and the Literary Critic*. Philadelphia: Fortress, 1977.

Rorty, Richard. *Philosophy and the Mirror of Nature*. Princeton, N.J.: Princeton University Press, 1979.

Rosmarin, Adena. *The Power of Genre*. Minneapolis: University of Minnesota Press, 1985.

Ross, J. F. "Job 33:14–30: The Phenomenology of Lament." *Journal of Biblical Literature* 94 (1975): 38–46.

Rowley, H. H. "The Book of Job and Its Meaning." In *From Moses to Qumran: Studies in the Old Testament*, pages 141–83. New York: Association Press, 1963.

———. *Job*. Rev. ed. New Century Bible Commentary. Grand Rapids: Eerdmans, 1980.

Rowold, Henry. "Yahweh's Challenge to Rival: The Form and Function of the Yahweh-Speech in Job 38–39." *Catholic Biblical Quarterly* 47 (1985): 199–211.

Scarry, Elaine. *The Body in Pain: The Making and Unmaking of the World*. New York: Oxford University Press, 1985.

Scheindlin, Raymond P. *The Book of Job*. New York: W. W. Norton, 1998.

Schoff, Philip, and Henry Wace, eds. *Jerome: Letters and Select Works*. 2nd series ed. Nicene and Post-Nicene Fathers 6. Peabody, Mass.: Hendrickson, 1995.

Scholnick, Sylvia. "Lawsuit Drama in the Book of Job." Ph. D. diss., Brandeis University, 1975.

Schön, Donald A. "Generative Metaphor: A Perspective on Problem-Setting in Social Policy." In *Metaphor and Thought*, edited by A. Ortony, pages 137–63. Cambridge: Cambridge University Press, 1993.

Seitz, Christopher. "Job: Full-Structure, Movement, and Interpretation." *Interpretation* 43 (1989): 5–17.

Simon, Richard. *A Critical History of the Old Testament*. Translated by H. D. London: Jacob Tonson, [1678] 1682.

Sitzler, Dorothea. *Vorwurf gegen Gott: Ein religiöses Motiv im alten Orient (Ägypten und Mesopotamien)*. Studies in Oriental Religions 32. Wiesbaden: Harrassowitz, 1995.

Skehan, Patrick. "Strophic Patterns in the Book of Job." *Catholic Biblical Quarterly* 23 (1961): 125–42.

Skehan, Patrick, and Alexander Di Lella. *The Wisdom of Ben Sira*. Anchor Bible 39. New York: Doubleday, 1987.

Snaith, Norman H. *The Book of Job: Its Origin and Purpose*. Studies in Biblical Theology Second Series 11. London: SCM Press, 1968.

Soden, Wolfram von. "Das Fragen nach der Gerechtigkeit Gottes im alten Orient." *Mitteilungen der Deutschen Orient-Gesellschaft* 96 (1965): 41–59.

——. "'Weisheitstexte' in Akkadischer Sprache." In *Weisheitstexte I. Texte aus der Umwelt des Alten Testaments*, edited by W. H. Ph. Römer and W. von Soden, pages 110–88. Gütersloh: Gütersloher Verlagshause Gerd Mohn, 1982.

Soelle, Dorothee. *Suffering*. Translated by E. Kalin. Philadelphia: Fortress, 1975.

Spiegel, Shalom. "Noah, Danel, and Job: Touching on Canaanite Relics in the Legends of the Jews." In *Louis Ginsberg Jubilee Volume 1 (English Section)*, pages 305–56. New York: American Academy for Jewish Research, 1945.

Steussy, Marti J. *Gardens in Babylon: Narrative and Faith in the Greek Legends of Daniel*. Society of Biblical Literature Dissertation Series 141. Atlanta: Scholars Press, 1993.

Strawn, Brent. "What Is Stronger than a Lion? Leonine Image and Metaphor in the Hebrew Bible and the Ancient Near East." Ph. D. diss., Princeton Theological Seminary, 2001.

Strugnell, John. "Notes and Queries on 'the Ben Sira Scroll from Masada,'" *Eretz Israel* 9 (1969): 109–19.

Suleiman, Susan Rubin. *Authoritarian Fiction: The Ideological Novel as a Literary Genre*. 2nd ed. New York: Columbia University Press, 1992.

Taylor, Charles. *Sources of the Self: The Making of the Modern Identity*. Cambridge: Harvard University Press, 1989.

Toorn, Karel van der. *Sin and Sanction in Israel and Mesopotamia: A Comparative Study*. Studia semitica neerlandica 22. Assen and Maastricht: Van Gorcum, 1985.

——. "The Ancient Near Eastern Literary Dialogue as a Vehicle of Critical Reflection." In *Dispute Poems and Dialogues in the Ancient and Medieval Near East: Forms and Types of Literary Debates in Semitic and Related Literatures*, edited by G. J. Reinink and H. L. J. Vanstiphout, pages 59–75. Louvain: Uitgeverij Peeters, 1991.

Tromp, Nicholas. *Primitive Conceptions of Death and the Nether World in the Old Testament*. Biblica et Orientalia 21. Rome: Pontifical Biblical Institute, 1969.

Tsang, Lap-chuen. *The Sublime: Groundwork towards a Theory*. Rochester, N.Y.: University of Rochester Press, 1998.

Turner, Mark. *The Literary Mind*. New York: Oxford University Press, 1996.

Vanstiphout, Herman L. J. "Lore, Learning, and Levity in the Sumerian Disputations: A Matter of Form, or Substance?" In *Dispute Poems and Dialogues in the Ancient and Medieval Near East: Forms and Types of Literary Debates in Semitic and Related Literatures*, edited by G. J. Reinink and H. L. J. Vanstiphout, pages 23–46. Louvain: Uitgeverij Peeters, 1991.

Volf, Miroslav. *Exclusion and Embrace: A Theological Exploration of Identity, Otherness, and Reconciliation*. Nashville: Abingdon, 1996.

Voloshinov, V. N. *Marxism and the Philosophy of Language*. Translated by L. Matejka and I. R. Titunik. Cambridge: Harvard University Press, 1973.

Volz, Paul. *Hiob und Weisheit*. 2nd ed. Göttingen: Vandenhoeck & Ruprecht, 1921.

Wahl, Harald-Martin. "Noah, Daniel, und Hiob in Ezechiel XIV 12–20 (21–3): Anmerkungen zum traditionsgeschichtlichen Hintergrund." *Vetus Testamentum* 42 (1992): 542–53.

——. *Der gerechte Schöpfer: Eine redaktions- und theologiegeschichtliche Untersuchung der Elihureden—Hiob 32–37*. Beihefte zur Zeitschrift für die alttestamentliche Wissenschaft 207. Berlin: Walter de Gruyter, 1993.

Weinfeld, Moshe. "Job and Its Mesopotamian Parallels: A Typological Analysis." In *Text and Context: Old Testament and Semitic Studies for F. C. Fensham*, edited by W. Classen, pages 217–26. Sheffield: JSOT Press, 1988.

Weiskel, Thomas. *The Romantic Sublime: Studies in the Structure and Psychology of Transcendence.* Baltimore: Johns Hopkins University Press, 1976.

Westermann, Claus. *The Structure of the Book of Job: A Form-Critical Analysis.* Translated by C. Muenchow. Philadelphia: Fortress, 1981.

White, James Boyd. *When Words Lose Their Meaning: Constitutions and Reconstitutions of Language, Character, and Community.* Chicago: University of Chicago Press, 1984.

Wilcox, John T. *The Bitterness of Job.* Ann Arbor: University of Michigan Press, 1989.

Williams, Ronald J. "Theodicy in the Ancient Near East." *Canadian Journal of Theology* 2 (1956): 14-26.

Witte, Markus. *Vom Leiden zur Lehre: Der dritte Redegang (Hiob 21-27) und die Redaktionsgeschichte des Hiobbuches.* Beihefte zur Zeitschrift für die alttestamentliche Wissenschaft 230. Berlin: Walter de Gruyter, 1994.

Wolde, Ellen. J. van. "Job 42,1-6: The Reversal of Job." In *The Book of Job,* edited by W. A. M. Beuken, pages 223-50. Bibliotheca ephemeridum theologicarum lovaniensium 114. Louvain: Leuven University Press, 1994.

Wolfers, David. "The Speech-Cycles in the Book of Job." *Vetus Testamentum* 43 (1993): 385-402.

———. *Deep Things out of Darkness: The Book of Job, Essays and a New English Translation.* Grand Rapids: Eerdmans, 1995.

Wright, C. J. H. "Family." In *The Anchor Bible Dictionary,* edited by D. N. Freedman, vol. 2, pages 761-69. New York: Doubleday, 1992.

Zaharopoulos, Dimitri. *Theodore of Mopsuestia on the Bible: A Study of Old Testament Exegesis.* New York: Paulist Press, 1989.

Zuckerman, Bruce. *Job the Silent: A Study in Historical Counterpoint.* New York: Oxford University Press, 1991.

Index